S. CHAND'S SUCCESS GUIDES
(Question and Answers)

MEDIEVAL HISTORY OF INDIA

S. CHAND'S SUCCESS GUIDES
(Questions and Answers)

MEDIEVAL HISTORY OF INDIA

(For B.A. (Pass & Hons.) Students of History. Based on UGC Curriculum and also Modified Curriculum of Several Universities)

(Including Solved Long Answer Type, Short Answer Type, and Very Short Answer Type Questions)

J.C. AGGARWAL

Former Lecturer

Dayanand College, Hissar (Haryana)

S. CHAND
PUBLISHING

S Chand And Company Limited

(ISO 9001 Certified Company)

S Chand And Company Limited
(ISO 9001 Certified Company)
Head Office: Block B-1, House No. D-1, Ground Floor, Mohan Co-operative Industrial Estate, New Delhi – 110 044 | Phone: 011-66672000
Registered Office: A-27, 2nd Floor, Mohan Co-operative Industrial Estate, New Delhi – 110 044 | Phone: 011-49731800
www.**schandpublishing.com**; e-mail: **info@schandpublishing.com**

Branches

Chennai : Ph: 23632120; chennai@schandpublishing.com
Guwahati : Ph: 2738811, 2735640; guwahati@schandpublishing.com
Hyderabad : Ph: 40186018; hyderabad@schandpublishing.com
Jalandhar : Ph: 4645630; jalandhar@schandpublishing.com
Kolkata : Ph: 23357458, 23353914; kolkata@schandpublishing.com
Lucknow : Ph: 4003633; lucknow@schandpublishing.com
Mumbai : Ph: 25000297; mumbai@schandpublishing.com
Patna : Ph: 2260011; patna@schandpublishing.com

First Edition 1999
Revised Edition 2002
Reprints 2005, 2016, 2018 (Twice), 2020

Reprint 2022

ISBN : 978-81-219-1890-9 **Product Code** : H5MDQ41HIST40ENAB02R

PRINTED IN INDIA
By Vikas Publishing House Private Limited, Plot 20/4, Site-IV, Industrial Area Sahibabad, Ghaziabad – 201 010 and Published by S Chand And Company Limited, A-27, 2nd Floor, Mohan Co-operative Industrial Estate, New Delhi – 110 044.

PREFACE FOR THE REVISED EDITION

The book has been revised in the light of the latest UGC curriculum and also Modified Curriculum by Various Indian Universities.

It is hoped that the revised edition will prove all the more useful to the students.

J.C. AGGARWAL

CONTENTS

Introduction : Survey of Sources of Medieval Indian History

Q. 1. Give the main sources of history of Medieval India, with one example of each source. Explain the phases of the growth of histography and evaluate them.

Ans. *Sources of the History of Medieval India.*

Compared to the history of ancient India, a large member of reliable sources are available. They provide a good deal of insight and knowledge about the conditions of those times–art and architecture, history and literature, agriculture and industry, commerce and trade, culture and civilisation, philosophy and religion etc. In fact available sources cover almost all areas of socio-economic life.

These sources may be categorised as:

Categorisation of Chief Sources of Medieval Indian History

- (1) Historical Accounts of Scholars written on paper
- (2) Historical Accounts by Foreign Travellers
- (3) Literary Accounts
- (4) Archeological Sources

1. *Historical Accounts by scholars written on paper*

(*i*) *Tahquiq-Hind* (11th cent. A.D.) by Al-Beruni

(*ii*) *Tarikh-i-Subuktikin* (10th cent. A.D.) by Baihaki

(*iii*) *Tarikh-i-Firoze Shahi* (13th cent.) by Zia-ud-Barni

(*iv*) *Tuzak-i-Babri* (Memoirs of Babur) by Babur

(*v*) *Humayun Nama* (16th cent.) by Begum Gul Badan

(*vi*) *Ain-i-Akbari* (16th cent.) by Abul Fazal

(*vii*) *Akbar Nama* (16th cent.) by Abul Fazal

(*viii*) *Tuzki-Jahangiri* (17th cent.) by Jahangir

(*ix*) *Fatuhali-i-Aurangzeb* (17th cent.) by Muhammad Masum

2. *Historical Accounts by Foreign Travellers*

(*i*) *Tuhfat-un-Nuzzar fi Gharibi-il-Amsar* by Ibn Batuta

(*ii*) *Accounts of Marco Palo* (13th cent.)

(*iii*) *Accounts of Nicolo Conti* (16th cent.)

(*iv*) *Tarikh-i-Frishta* (16th cent.) by Firishta (translated by J.Briggs, titled *Rise of the Mohammedan Power in India*)

3. *Literary Accounts*

(*i*) *Shahnama* (10th cent.) by Firdausi

(*ii*) *Rajtarangini* (11th cent.) by Kalhan

(*iii*) *Prithvi Raj Raso* (12th cent.) by Chandbardai

(*iv*) *Padmavat* (14th cent.) by Jayasi

4. *Archaeological Sources*

A. *Medieval Temples*: (*i*) Khajuraho (*ii*) Konark (*iii*) Dilwara

B. *Medieval Mosques*: (*i*) Jama Masjid (*ii*) Moti Masjid (*iii*) Fatehpur Sikri Dargah

C. *Medieval Forts*: (*i*) Agra Fort (*ii*) Chittor Fort (*iii*) Gwalior Fort (*iv*) Red Fort

D. *Medieval Palaces*: (*i*) Jaipur Palace (*ii*) Jaisalmer Palace (*iii*) Jodhpur Palace

E. *Medieval Pillars*: (*i*) Qutab Minar (*ii*) Char Minar

F. *Ruins of Medieval Buildings* : (*i*) Hastinapur (*ii*) Firozabad (*iii*) Tughlaqabad.

G. *Coins of Emperors*: (*i*) Akbar's Louis (*ii*) Ala-ud-din's coins

Prominent Historians of Indian history of Medieval Period

In the 11th century, Alberuni, an Iranian scholar who accompanied Mahmud Ghazni during his invasions of India gave an account of the Indian society in his *Tahquiq Hind*. Chand Bardai in his epic narrated the exploits of Prithvi Raj Chauhan. Kalhan in that century wrote the history of Kashmir.

In the 13th century, Hasan Nizami, a migrant from Ghazni, gave information about Qutub-ud-din Aibak and Marco Polo provided an account of South India.

In the 14th century, Ibn Batuta, a Moorish traveller wrote about Muhammad Tughlaq, Khwaja Abu Malik described the history of Delhi Sultans, and Zia-ud-Barni covers the history from Balban to Firoz Tughlaq.

In the 15th century Abdul Razzaq described about the times of Vijayanagar kings.

In the 16th century Babur's *Babur Nama*, and Abul Fazal's *Ain-i-Akbari* and *Akbar Nama* provided detailed information about these two emperors. In the 17th century, Jahangir himself wrote *Tuzki - Jahangiri* throwing a lot of light on the period.

Note. For details see pages 26, 27, 61, 109, 110, 125, 144 and 188.

Phases of the Growth of Historiography

Historiography of medieval India *i.e.* the writing of history falls into the three phases as listed below :

1. Medieval Chroniclers—mostly contemporary
2. Colonial trend in historiography
3. Modern trend in historiography.

Medieval Chroniclers. These comprised court historians and the rulers themselves. Since by and large, histories were written by courtiers or rulers, it is very difficult to determine the extent of objectivity of the records. Histories were written in Persian and Turkish languages.

Colonial trends. In general it is observed that the "British historical writing on the period was intimately linked with the expansion of their rule in India." The perspectives of historians in general did not encompass developments in the economic and social fields.

Following are the important publications of the colonial trends.

1. *History of India as told by its own Historians*. This eight-volume history was published between 1867-1877. It was a compilation of extracts of over 160 medieval accounts. It formed the basis of early reconstruction of the medieval India.
2. *Medieval India under Muhammadan Rule*. by Lane Poole. (1903)
3. *Oxford History of India* by Vincent Smith, 1919.

Modern Trends. In the 20th century, historians broadened the scope of history to encompass administrative developments, economic policies and religious and social movements.

Regarding historiography following points may be kept in view :

1. Absolute historical truth is exclusive.
2. Absolute impartial historiography is rather impossible.
3. Every kind of prejudice—caste, faith, personal, political, racial, regional, religious, etc. of the historiographer exercises some influence in recording of events and facts.
4. Since quite a large number of history works during the medieval period were written either by rulers or their relatives and the scholars patronised by them, their contents must be sifted carefully and scientifically and collaborated with other works.

Significance of the Medieval Period of Indian History. The medieval period has certain distinct characteristics which lend importance to this period. First, the medieval period is closer to us than the ancient period. Second, we have several sources which provide almost correct and objective information about this period. Third, it was during this period that Indian beliefs and social customs were greatly influenced by the Turks, Afghans and the Mughals who came as invaders but made India their home. Fourth, many items of our food and dress can be traced back to this period. Fifth, a composite culture of India developed with the fusion of the Hindu and the Muslim cultural traits. This is reflected particularly in the field of art, architecture, literature, painting and music.

Q.2. Explain in brief historical sources of the Sultanate Period of History of India.

Ans. *Principal Sources of Sultanate Period.* Our principal sources of the Sultanate period are primarily in Persian and Arabic. These are divided into two categories : (1) Chronicles (2) Travels.

Chronicles

1. *'Chach-Nama'*. *Chach-Nama* was originally written in Arabic. It was translated into Persian by Muhammad Ali-bin-Abu Bakr Kufi during the period of Nasir-ud-din Qubachah. It provides an account of the history of the Arab conquest.

2. *'Kitab-ul-Yamini'*. It was written by Abu Nasr bin Muhammad al Jabbaral Utbi. It is the history of the reign of Subuktigin and Mahmud Ghazani. It is deficient in dates. It is more a work of literature than of history.

3. *Tarikh-ul-Hind*. It is written by Al Beruni who belonged to Khawarigm. A detailed account of the observations made by Al beruni is given separately. (pages 26 and 27).

4. *'Kamil-ut-Tawarikh'*. The author of this book Shaikh Abdul Husan, popularly, known as 'Ibn-ul-Asir' belonged to Mesopotamia. This work was completed in 1230. It provides some account of Muhammad of Ghur's conquest of India. Dates given in the book are correct, by and large but descriptions are believed to the based on hearsay.

5. *'Taj-ul-Maasir'*. Hasan Nizami is the author of this book and he covers the period from 1192 to 1228. It is considered as a reliable account on the career and reign of Qutub-ud-din Aibak and the early years of Iltutmish. Hasan Nizami was a contemporary of these two rulers.

6. *'Tabqat-i-Nasiri'*. Minhaj-u-e-din Abu Umar bin Siraj-udal-din Juzjani, popularly known as Minhaj-us-Siraj is the author of this book. It was completed in 1260. Minhaj-us-Siraj was a contemporary of the rulers whose events he has described. He held the office of the Chief *'Qazi'* at Delhi under Nasir-ud-din Mahmud. Minhaj is not usually considered as an impartial writer. He is biased in favour of Balban. Still his work is considered as an important authority on the early history of the Sultanate of Delhi.

7. *'The Khaza' in ul Fatuh'*. Amir Khusrao, the author of this book was pre-eminently a poet. He was a contemporary of all rulers of Delhi from Jalal-ud-din Khalji to Muhammad Bin Tughlaq. He has exaggerated the achievements of Ala-ud-din, his patron. Nevertheless this work is considered of great merit. It was written in Persian. (for details see page 61).

8. *'Tarikh-i-Firozshahil'*. Zia-ud-din Barani is the author of this book. Barani was the contemporary of Ghias-ud-din Tughlaq, Muhammad bin Tughlaq and Firoz Tughlaq. His work begins with the accession of Balban and comes down to the sixth year of the reign of Firoz Tughlaq. It was completed in 1359. It has ignored chronological arrangement. It is full of ancedotes. At times Barani is guilty of distortion of facts. Barani held an important post in the revenue department and he has described revenue matters in detail. Barani was a highly educated person.

9. *'Fatawah-i-Jahandari'*. This book is also written by Zia-ud-din Barani. In this work, Barani provides details of his views on government policies–religious and secular. Barani considered this political code as an ideal one for a Muslim ruler to follow.

10. *'Kitab-in-Rahlab'*. Ibn Battutah, a famous Moorish traveller is the author of this book. It is a book of travels which furnishes a lot of historical information. Ibn Battutah started on his travels in 1325 and visited Northern Africa, Arabia, Iran and Constantinople. Thereafter he came to India and reached Sindh in September 1333. He spent about 9 years in India. he was appointed '*Qazi*' of Delhi by Muhammad Bin Tughlaq. He occupied this post for about 8 years. He lost the favour of the emperor and was imprisoned. Sometimes after he was released, he was made an Ambassador to China in 1342. On account of a mishap on the ship, he returned to Delhi. Then he went to Maldive Islands. He was appointed as a judge there. He stayed in Maldive for one year.

During his stay in India, he was closely connected with the court and had a good opportunity to study the affairs in the country. His book written in Arabic is considered as an authority on the reign of Muhammad Tughlaq. It is observed by some historians that sometimes Ibn Battutah is inclined to gossips. Besides he was not acquainted with Parsian and any Indian language.

11. *'Futuhat-i-Firozeshahi'*. A small autobiography of Firoz Shah Tughlaq, it is considered as an authority on important events and policies of his reign.

12. *'Tarikh-i-Firozshahi'*. Written by Shams-i-Siraj, it is a history of the reign of Firoz Tughlaq. The author was a member of Firoz's Shah's court.

13. *'Tarikh-i-Salatin-i-Afghana'*. Ahmad Yadgar is the author of this book. It gives an account of the rise and fall of the Lodis and Suris. The book was written during Akbar's reign.

Important Travellers and the Travels

1. *Al-Beruni*. Already discussed.
2. *Ibn Battutah*. Already discussed.
3. *Macro Polo and his Travels* (Edited by Yule). This book describes the various aspects of people's life and other events of Southern India of the 13th Century.
4. *Abdur Razzaq*. Razzaq was a Persian who came to the court of the king of Vijayanagar as an envoy. He stayed there in 1442-1443. He has left a detailed account of the conditions–administrative, cultural, economic and political. Razzaq's description is considered of great historical value.
5. *Nicolo Conti*. Nicolo Conti was an Italian traveller who visited India in 1520. He gave an account of customs, manners and conditions of the people of this period.
6. *Domingos Paes*. Paes was a Portuguese traveller and has left a detailed account of Vijayanagar empire.
7. *Edoardo Barbosa*. Barbosa visited India in 1516 and gave an account of Southern India in general and Vijayanagar in particular.

Indian Publications during the Medieval Period

1. '*Prithviraja Raso*'. Chand Bardai described the events relating to Prithviraj.
2. *Hamira Mahakavya*. It gives the achievements of Hammira, the Chauhan ruler of Ranthambor. Hammira was a descendant of Prithviraja.
3. *Surjana Charita Kavya*. Written by Chandrasekhar, it is a valuable source of information of the Chauhan rulers.
4. *Rasamala*. The stories in Bengali verse provides history of Muslim rule in Bengal.

Q.3. Give in brief the sources of information about the Mughals in India.

Ans. *Introduction*. The Mughals ruled India for about two and a half centuries. They were the descendants of the two great warriors of Central Asia—Timur and Changez Khan. Babur was the founder of the empire in India after the First Battle of Panipat in 1526.

Sources of Information about the Mughal Period

1. '*Tuzuki-i-Baburi or Babur Nama*' (Babur's Memoirs). It is the first work of the period written by Babur himself. It was written in Turkish language and first translated in English in 1826. Babur had the invader's prejudices and his impressions about India should be taken with critical analysis. In the words of Beveridge. "It is one of those priceless records which are for all time". According to Elpinstone,

Babur's Memoirs were "almost the only piece of real history of Asia."

2. '*Tazkirat-ul-Waqiat*' written by Jahaur Aftabh Persian, it deals with the rule of Humayun.
3. '*Humayun-namah*' written in Persian by Gulbadan, a daughter of Babur, it primarily deals with the domestic relation of the first two. Mughal rulers with their wives and children and the state of affairs during Humayun's reign.
4. '*Akbarnamah*'. '*Akbarnama*' was written by Abul Fazal a great scholar of the court of Akbar. It describes in detail the history of the reign of Akbar, year by year and gives reasons for every important act of the ruler.
5. '*Tabaquat-i-Akbari*'. It was written by Nizamuddin Bakshi who held several important posts under Akbar. It covers the period upto the end of the 36th year of Akbar's reign.
6. '*Tuzauki Jahangiri*'. Written by emperor Jahangir himself it relates to the period from his accession to the 12th year of his reign. It is considered as the foremost authority on Jahangir's personality and the events of his reign.
7. '*Iqbal-nama-i-Jahangiri*'. It was written by Mutamid Khan who held an important post in Jahangir's reign. It is the second work in point of importance after Jahangir's autobiography. It has three parts and covers events of the reigns of Babur, Humayun, Akbar, Jahangir and Shah Jahan.
8. '*Padshah-Nama*'. Muhammad Amin Qazni wrote this book after the orders of emperor Shah Jahan. It covers the minute account of all events and happenings during the first ten years of Shah Jahan's reign.
9. '*Badshah-Nama*'. It was written by a famous historian. Abdul-Hamid. It is a detailed work covering the first 20 years of Shah Jahan's rule.
10. '*Alamgir-Nama*' written by Mirza Muhammad Kazim, it is the primary authority on the first 10 years of the reign of Aurangzeb.
11. '*Maasir-Alamgiri*'. Muhammad Saq Mustain Khan was the author of this book. It provides a good deal of account of the reign of Aurangzeb.

Q.4. Give in brief the main Indian works on Medieval Indian History which are considered important source books.

1. '*Mahmud of Ghazni*' by Mohammad Habib. This book written in 1927 points out the economic motives underlying the Sultan's invasions of India.

2. '*Life and Conditions of the People of Hindustan*' written by K.M. Ashraf. It stresses the point that there was no cultural strife in India during the medieval period.
3. '*The Administration of the Sultanate of Delhi*'. The author of this book I.H. Qureshi claims that the administration of the Sultanate was more efficient than that of contemporary native states.
4. *History of Aurangzeb* by Sir Jadu Nath Sarkar. This runs into five volumes.
5. '*The Fall of the Mughal Empire*' by Sir Jadu Nath Sarkar. It runs into four volumes.

Sir Jadunath Sarkar has been described as the 'father of modern historical research' on account of his fidelity to original documents and meticulous checking of details and testing of evidence.

Among other historians of the period, mention may be made of G.S. Sardesai, P. Saran, R.P. Tripathi, K.S. Lal, and Ishwari Prasad.

1

The Rajput States : Polity and Society (Administrative Structure and Institutions)

Q. 1. Describe in brief the political state of affairs in India before the Turkish invasions. Name the important Rajput states existing at the time and their importance.

Ans. *No Strong Central Authority During the Rajput Period.*

From Harsha's death to the twelfth century, the destiny of India was mostly in the hands of various Rajput dynasties which were in general constantly at war among themselves. A struggle for supremacy was at work. There was no strong central authority. Earlier in the ancient period there was the strong Magadha empire which frightened the soldiers of Alexander's army so much that they refused to move further and in fact forced Alexander to go back to Greece—their own country. But at the time of Turkish invasions India lacked such a strong central authority.

The Rajput rulers usually remained busy in utilising their energy in fighting among themselves :

There was little sense of national unity and the frontiers of India remained neglected.

The consequences of such a political state of affairs proved very harmful and costly to India.

Important Rajput States

The most important of the Rajput states in North India were the Chauhans of Ajmer and Delhi, the Gahadavallas or Rathors of Kanauj, the Chandellas of Bundelkhand, the Guhilas or Sisodiyas of Mewar, the Parmars of Malwa, the Tomars of Delhi, the Pratiharas or Gurjaras of Kanauj, and the Palas of Bengal. The Hindushahi kingdom and the kingdom of Kashmir were the two other important Hindu kingdoms of North India.

Two Muslim kingdoms were of Multan and Sindh.

The Rashtrakutas of Malkhid (Deccan), the Chalukya kingdom of Kalyani and the Chola kingdom of Tanjore were the important kingdoms of the South India.

Other Small Kingdoms

Besides the kingdoms mentioned above, there were many small kingdoms like Thaneshwar, Kangra, Gwalior etc. in other parts of India.

The Chauhans of Delhi and Ajmer. The Chauhans were the feudatories of the Pratiharas of Kanauj. Later on they declared their independence and established their kingdom first in Ajmer in the 11th century A.D. In the early part of the 12th century, they defeated the Parmars of Malwa and captured Ujjain. Thereafter they captured Delhi from the Tomars and shifted their capital to Delhi. Prithviraj Chauhan was the most famous ruler of this dynasty. Several legends revolve around his personality. His military exploits have been immortalised in the epic poem *'Prithviraj Raso'* composed by his court poet Chandbardai.

Prithviraj had strained relations with Jaichand, the ruler of Kanauj. A legend relates to the carrying away of Sanyokta, the daughter of Jai Chand, from her 'Swyamvara' function by Prithviraj. The bitter enmity between the two great Rajput rulers *i.e.* Prithviraj and Jaichand resulted in the destruction of both these kingdoms at the hands of Mohammad Ghori. In fact this rivalry led to the subordination of India to the foreign invaders in due course.

The Tomars of Delhi. The Tomars founded the city of Delhi in 736 A.D. They were the feudatory chiefs of the Pratiharas but later on they established their own kingdom at Delhi. In 1043, Mahipala Tomar captured Thaneswar, Hansi and Nagarkot. In the middle of the 12th century they came under the suzerainty of the Chauhans who captured Delhi from them.

The Pratiharas of Kanauj. According to legend Nagabhatta (725-40 A.D.) was the first famous Pratihara ruler who captured Kanauj after the death of King Harsha and he carried on a successful war against the Arab conquerors of Sindh and prevented them from extending their kingdom. The Pratihara rulers had several parts of India under their control. They had the best cavalry in India.

Mahmud of Ghazni gave a severe blow to the Pratiharas of Kanauj in 1019 A.D.

The Gahadavalas or Rathors of Kanauj. After the fall of the Pratiharas there was a lot of confusion. Ultimately, the Gahadavalas established themselves on the throne of Kanauj from 1090 to 1194 A.D. Jai Chand was the last great ruler of this dynasty. Usually very unkind words are said about him by some historians on account of his role in the struggle between Mohammad Ghori, and Prithviraj . He was killed in a battle in 1194 with Mohammad Ghori. Earlier he had sided with Mohammad Ghori against Prithviraj.

The Chandellas of Bundelkhand. Bundelkhand was a part of the Pratihara kingdom of Kanauj. It was established in the 9th century. Its capital was Mahoba and Kalinjar was its most important fort. The Chandellas built a number of beautiful temples at Khajuraho, the most famous temple being the Kandariya Mahadeva Temple (1050 A.D.)

The Guhilas or Sisodiyas of Mewar. Bapa Rawal was the founder of the Sisodia dynasty with his capital at Chittor. Rana Ratan Singh of Mewar was defeated by Ala-ud-ddin Khalji in 1307. Queen Padmini performed

'Johar'. Later on Rana Sanga and Maharana Pratap gave a tough fight to the Mughals.

The Parmars of Malwa. Once they were the feudatory chiefs of the Pratiharas. Taking advantage of the weakness of the Pratihvaras, they established their kingdom in the 10th Century A.D. Dhara in Madhya Bharat was their capital. Raja Bhoj (1018-1069) was the most famous ruler of this dynasty. He was a great scholar and writer of several books. He founded the famous Sanskrit college at Dhara. He constructed a beautiful lake near Bhopal. The last ruler of this dynasty was killed by one of the generals of Ala-ud-din in 1305.

The Palas of Bengal. The kingdom founded in the middle of the 8th century lasted for about four centuries. The dynasty had 17 rulers. The Pala kingdom during the zenith of its power in the 10th century included most parts of Bengal, Bihar, Orissa and Assam. The Pala reputation transcended the boundaries of India into Tibet and East Indies. The Palas heralded an era of cultural renaissance in Bengal.

The Vikramsila University founded in the 8th century became an international university :

The Palas revived Buddhism. Trade with Southeast Asia greatly added to the prosperity of the Pala kingdom.

The Rashtrakutas of Malkhid (Deccan). The Rashtrakutas remained in power for about three centuries i.e. 8th, 9th and 10th. During the middle of the 8th century, the Rashtrakutas were the master of Central and Southern Gujarat, the whole of Madhya Pradesh, Maharashtra, most parts of Bihar and Karnataka.

The rock-cut shrines of Ellora and Elephanta belong to this period. The Kailasha Temple at Ellora was unrivalled during the period.

The sculptured reliefs of Natraja at Elephanta are unique. The Trimurti or Maheshamurti representing god in Triple form corresponding to its three functions of Creation, the Preservation and Destruction of the universe has also unique sculptured reliefs.

Conclusion. The disintegration of India into small territories as a result of mutual conflicts gave a great blow to the political unity of India. Indian rulers failed to realise the gravity of the situation posed by the foreign invaders who had constantly set their eyes upon India. With the weakening of their powers, the defence of India was threatened. The result was it became easy for foreigners like Mahmud Ghazni to invade any part of India he wanted and looted its wealth.

Q 2. Discuss the nature of polity of the Rajputs. How far was it responsible for their defeat against the Turks?

(Delhi University, 1997)

Ans. *Nature of the Polity of the Rajputs.*

The Turkish invaders came to India from outside. They were very few in number. However, they defeated the brave Rajputs primarily on account of the defective structure of the Rajput polity. The Rajput polity had the following main features :

1. *Small kingdoms.* The period between 1000-1200 A.D. is usually referred to as the Rajput period of Indian history. During the period several independent states came to be established. There was no strong central authority in India that could weld together into a strong unit. Some of these kingdoms were quite extensive and powerful. Multan and Sindh constituted the two Arab (Muslim) states of India. In the north-west was the Hindushahi kingdom whose ruler at the time of Mahmud was Jayapala. Kashmir was also an independent state. Others were Rajput states. Among the important ones were the Chauhans of Ajmer and Delhi, the Gahadavallas or Rathors of Kanauj, the Chandellas of Bundelkhand, the Guhilas or Sisodiyas of Mewar, the Paramars of Malwa, the Pratiharas of Kanauj and the Palas of Bengal. The Rashtrakutas of Malkhid (Deccan), the Chalukyas of Kalyani and the Cholas of Tanjore ruled over several parts of South India.

2. *Mutual hostility and jealousy.* Mostly all the Rajput kingdoms indulged in warfare with their neighbours. Each powerful Rajput state was inspired by expansionist and imperial ambitions. Because of their internal conflicts none of them could utilise its entire resources nor they could unite themselves against Turkish invaders.

3. *Feudal organisation.* The political organisation of the Rajputs was based on the feudal system. The king allotted land to the Jagirdars who were the feudal lords or nobles. They paid the king fixed annual revenue and rendered military service in the time of need or any crisis or war. The Jagirdars or nobles usually belonged to the family of the ruler. They had their own ambitions also. They further allotted some portion of the land to sub-jagirdars. This system proved to be defective. It all depended on the ruler how he exercised his control over the jagirdars and infused in them a sense of loyalty to him. If there was a weak ruler on the throne, these feudal nobles would tend to declare their independence or would quarrel among themselves due to mutual jealousies. No doubt the Rajputs were brave, courageous, chivalours, loyal and patriotic but they lacked political insight and were too proud to join hands to save a frontier kingdom under the fatal grip of a foreign invader. Their insensitivity and personal animosity blocked their mind though they were quick to show their generosity and mercy to an unarmed enemy or one who sought their shelter.

Since the army of a Rajput ruler was constituted by collecting the armies of his feudal chiefs, it lacked cohesion, unity of command and military skill and strategy.

Rajput Polity Responsible for their Failure

According to Dr. Ishwari Prasad, "There was no dearth of military talent or fighting skill in the country, for the Rajputs were the finest soldiers scarcely inferior in the qualities of courage, valour and endurance to men of any other country. But they lacked unity and organisation. Pride and prejudice alike forbade obedience to a common leader and in critical moments when concentrated action was essential for a victory, they renewed their individual plans and thus neutralised the advantages they possessed over the enemies."

There were mutual fights among the Pratiharas of Kanauj, the Palas of Bengal and Rashtrakutas of the Deccan. Constant wars had crippled their strength and resources. They had grown very weak. Prithviraj Chauhan and Jaichand were great enemies. There may be some exaggeration in the remarks made by Chandbardai "Ninety out of a hundred of Prithviraj's *'Sumantas'* chiefs or generals fell in his conflicts with Jaichand on account of his carrying away Samyuka" but the moral of this episode is very clear. All these factors weakened the defence of India. The Rajput rulers failed to present a united front against an enemy that had made India as a target. Had the Rajput rulers forgotten their differences against the common danger and combined together, the history of India would have been written altogether in a different manner !

Q 3. Describe the political, social and economic conditions of India on the eve of Turkish invasions. (Delhi University, 1997)

Ans. *Political Unstability in India*

The period on the eve of the Turkish invasion on India is usually called the Rajput period in the history of India. There were several big and small Rajput states in different parts of India. Almost all these states vied each other for supremacy. The result was that there emerged no central authority to face any foreign invasion.

Political Condition

Following were the chief features of the political condition of India that were primarily responsible for the political unstability of India.

(1) Political disunity.

(2) Mutual distrust and acrimony.

(3) Auto-cratic and self-willed rulers.

(4) Feudal system.

(5) Absence of border defence policy.

(6) Old military organisation.

(7) Old military strategy.

(8) Traditional high ethical norms in fighting *i.e.* protection to refugees and vanquished enemies, not attacking the unarmed enemies; adhering to lofty moral conventions inspite of being harmed several times.

(9) False sense of pride.

Social Condition

General conditions of the people. Feudalism was the dominating feature of the society. There was a great disparity in the standard of living of the people. The ministers, officials, feudal chiefs, and those having the opportunity to accumulate wealth lived in luxury and splendour. They adorned their bodies with costly clothes, Chinese silk, jewels and ornaments of gold and silver. They lived in imposing houses of several storeys competing with the grandeur of palaces. A train of servants attended to their needs and comforts and a large number of women in their household glorified their super status. The ordinary people had to remain contended with rice and wild vegetables that they could procure.

The peasants were burdened with the land revenue and other taxes levied at the whims of the feudal lords. Besides they had to render forced labour.

Caste system. During this period the disabilities which the lower castes suffered increased. Most of the workers like weavers, fishermen, barbers, etc. as well as tribals were treated very harshly. Rajputs as a new caste had appeared on the scene. In course of time all ruling families belonging to various castes were classified as Rajputs.

Condition of women. Women suffered from several handicaps although their honour was very dear to the Rajputs. They continued to be denied the right to study the Vedas. However families of higher families received higher education. They followed higher ideals. They gladly immolated themselves along with the dead bodies of their husbands. This practice later degenerated and *'Satipratha'* emerged; earlier there was the *'Johar'* ceremony. The womenfolk immolated themselves *'en-masse'* on a burning pyre. There was no 'purdah' system. *'Swayamvar'* type of marriage was in vogue in several royal families. Infanticide and early marriage of girls came into practice.

Specific characteristics of the Rajputs. Rajputs were great fighters. Fighting was their *'Dharma'*. They valued specific qualities and ideals. They were large-hearted and generous. They took pride in their descent. They were brave and self respecting. They gave shelter to the refugees and their vanquished foes. They were very loyal. They were somewhat haughty and emotional.

Absorption minimised. Earlier the Hindu society had an enormous capacity to absorb into its fold several foreign races like the Greeks, the Shakas and the Huns etc. But now the Rajput society, by and large, did not possess this capacity to absorb foreign elements. Perhaps it was also on account of the fact that the Muslims had some distinctive elements in their religion.

Education and science. Education was confined to a small section—Brahmans and some sections of upper classes. Nalanda in Bihar was the famous centre of higher learning. Other important centres were Vikramasila and Uddandapura. Several Saiva centres of learning flourished in Kashmir. Religion and philosophy were the popular subjects for study and discussion. On the whole, growth of the knowledge of science slowed down. Since society became increasingly rigid, thinking was mostly confined to traditional philosophy and India developed an insular attitude cut off from the main currents of scientific thought outside India. Science did not get proper scope or opportunity to develop.

Religious conditions. Hinduism remained the dominant religion in India. It was patronised by most of the rulers. The prevalent forms of Hinduism were either Vaishnavism or Saivaism. Buddhism had lost its popularity. It had a great patronage under the Palas of Bengal. Jainism was patronised by the Chalukyan rulers of Karnataka.

Art and architecture. The Rajputs were great patron of art and architecture. They built several canals, dams, forts, palaces, temples and towers. The palaces of Jaipur and Udaipur and forts of Chittor, Mandu, Jodhpur and Gwalior are the fine specimens of palace and fort architecture.

The Lingaraj Temple at Bhubaneswar and Surya (Sun) Temple at Konark exhibit the excellence of temple architecture.

Khajuraho has several famous temples including the Kandariya Mahadeva Temple.

Among the many Jain temples, two at Dilwara at Mount Abu are exemplary.

Literature. Several Rajput rulers patronised scholars and their literary works. Among the historical works, Kalhana's *'Rajtarangini'* a history of Kashmir and Chandbardoi's *'Prithviraj Raso'* dealing with the exploits of his patron Prithviraj Chauhan may be mentioned.

Economic Condition

Agriculture as the main occupation. Agriculture was the mainstay of the people. The Rajput rulers dug out canals and tanks and collected rain water in artificial lakes for purpose of irrigation. Dams were also raised. Irrigation facilities improved agriculture and the economic condition of the cultivators though they sometimes had to suffer at the hands of some autocratic feudal chiefs.

Taxes. Land revenue was the chief source of income and it was determined under a set formula depending upon the fertility of the soil, irrigation facilities etc. Land revenue was paid mainly in farm produce and a part in cash. Gifts, fines, minerals, forests and leased-out lands were additional sources of income.

Industry. Although there were several types of industries, on the whole, the state of industry declined during the period.

Important industries were : (*i*) cotton cloth making, (*ii*) woollen cloth, (*iii*) weapon industry, (*iv*) manufacture of salt (*v*) carving high quality artistic pieces, (*vi*) statues making from 'Ashtadhatus' (eight metals), (*vii*) pottery making, (*viii*) Ornament making, (*ix*) other industries were : 'gur' making, sugar, oil and liquor etc.

Trade and commerce. Internal as well as external trade declined. The balance of trade did not remain so much favourable to India.

Along with seaborne trade, India also had foreign trade through land.

On account of the decline of the Roman empire, seaborn trade of India suffered.

India imported several condiments from south-east Asian countries probably to meet the demand of the Eastern countries. From Central Asia and Western countries India imported horses of high breed and high quality wine, Chinese silk, grapes from Cambodia and some other articles.

India's exports consisted of sandalwood, camphor, cloves, indigo, ivory, coconut, herbs of many types, black pepper, cardamoms, hides, 'tusar', and woollen clothes.

2

Turkish Invaders : Mahmud Ghaznavi and Muhammad Ghori : (Causes of the Success of Turks)

Q 1. Who were Turks? Why did Mahmud invade India? Describe his important invasions and their effects on India.

Ans. *Origin of Turks.*

The Turks were originally the inhabitants of Central Asia. After their conversion to Islam, they became its strong adherents. They were also great fighters. Many among them rose to the ranks of commanders and generals. With the declining power of the Khalifas, some Turks established their independent kingdoms and in time covered parts of Persia, Afghanistan and Khorasan. Ghazni was the capital of a large Turkish kingdom. Aptigin, a Turkish slave rose to become the ruler of Ghazni. After his death in 963, his slave and son-in-law Subaktigin seized power and conquered many regions around Ghazni. After his death in 997 his son *Mahmud* ascended the throne. His swift and decisive conquests of Khorasan, Sistan and Ghur made him the most formidable power in that region. He now turned his attention on India. He is usually associated with 17 invasions in 25 years. His first invasion directed against the frontier towns was in the years 1000 and his last and most important was at Somnath Temple in 1025.

Usually four reasons are assigned to Mahmud's invasions.

(1) He wanted to establish the glory of Islam by destroying the images of the Hindu gods and spreading Islam. (2) He wanted to loot the wealth of India for he loved wealth. (3) He wanted wealth also to meet the cost of the army and warfare for he wanted the expansion of his empire. (4) He wanted to satisfy his ego as one of the greatest conquerors of the world.

Important Invasions of Mahmud

First invasion : Capture of frontier forts (1000 A.D.). During his first invasion, Mahmud captured a few forts and towns of Khyber. He appointed his own governors and went back.

Second invasion.Victory over Jaipal of Hindushahi kingdom (1001) A fierce battle near Peshawar was fought in which the invaders became victorious. Mahmud got 2,50,000 'dinars' and 50 elephants. Lanepoole states, "Jaipal refused to survive his disgrace. Preferring death to dishonour, he cast himself upon a funeral pyre."

Third invasion : attack at Bhera (1005). The ruler Bijai Rai offered stiff resistance but was defeated. Finding himself helpless, the ruler committed suicide. Mahmud looted the kingdom and killed people mercilessly.

Fourth invasion at Multan (1006). Mahmud invaded Multan which was under an Arab ruler and after seven days he conquered it.

Fifth invasion at Multan (1007 A.D.). A grandson of Jaipal who had embraced Islam had been appointed the governor of Multan with a Muslim name. He renounced Islam and declared himself as an independent ruler. Mahmud invaded and defeated him.

Sixth invasion : Defeat of Anand Pal and his allies (1008-1009 A.D.). Anand Pal was able to organise a confederacy of the rulers of Ujjain, Gwalior, Kalinjar, Ajmer etc. According to contemporary historians, "Hindu women sold their jewels and sent the money from distant parts to be used against the invaders." Regarding the fate of the war Lane-poole states, "Anand Pal's elephant took fright, the rumour ran that the *'raja'* was flying from the field, vague suspicion and distrust spread about, and a general stampede ensued. Mahmud found himself pursuing a panic stricken crowd. For two days, invaders slew, captured and despoiled to their hearts' content".

Seventh invasion : Conquest of Nagarkot—Kangra (1009 A.D.). After his victory, Mahmud returned to Ghazni with such a vast collection of riches and jewels which "far exceeded the treasures of the mightiest king of the world."

Mahmud's invasion at Mathura (1018). The city of Mathura was a beautiful city and a sacred place of the Hindus having about 1,000 temples. Mahmud wrote about this city. "If anyone should undertake to build a fabric like this, he would spend thereon one lakh packets of a thousand *'dinar'* and would not complete in 200 years and with the assistance of the most ingenious architects".

As usual, Mahmud looted and broke down all the idols and destroyed temples.

Mahmud's invasion at Somnath temple (1025). Expedition of the Somnath temple made Mahmud a great hero of Islam. According to Lanepoole, "The attack of Somnath has made Mahmud of Ghazni, a champion of the faith in the eyes of Muslims for nearly two centuries, and the feat, has been embellished with fantastic legends."

The temple's importance and wealth can be gauzed from the fact that lakhs of visitors offered prayers and made huge offerings daily and also the temple had a permanent income from the revenue of ten thousand villages attached to it.

The loot of the temple was worth 20 lakh *dinars'*. The idol of Shiva was broken into pieces.

Effects of Mahmud's Invasions

Important effects of Mahmud's invasion were as under :

1. Punjab became a part of the empire of Ghazni.
2. Weakness of the Rajputs was exposed.
3. Mahmud's conquests paved the way for the Muslim conquest of India.
4. India's enormous wealth was plundered and taken away to Ghazni.
5. The invasions gave a severe blow to the art of India as several important temples were destroyed by the invaders.
6. Mahmud's invasion played an important role in the spread of Islam in India.
7. The frequent invasions further weakened the political stability.
8. In every invasion India lost thousands of soldiers.

Q 2. Examine critically the nature of Mahmud's invasions on India. Mention some of his important invasions and their consequences.

Ans. *Nature of Mahmud's Invasion.*

Mahmud was the third important Turkish ruler who is said to have invaded India seventeen times—the first being in 1000 A.D. on the frontier towns of India and the last being the most important invasion at Somnath Temple in 1025 A.D.

Historians have given divergent views regarding the nature and objects of Mahmud's invasion.

Greed for wealth. Mahmud was very greedy as is corraborated by his behaviour towards the famous poet Firdausi whom he refused to pay the promised amount for writing the epic *'Shahnama'*. It is said that Mahmud asked Firdausi to write the epic for which he promised to pay Firdausi a gold 'mohar' for every couplet but later on went back on his word and wanted to pay him 60,000 silver coins. No historian has contradicted this view. Havell has rightly remarked, "Mahmud would have sacked Baghdad (an important place of Muslims) with a little compunction as he plundered Somnath if the undertaking had seemed as profitable."

Nizamuddin and Ferishta tell us about the state of Mahmud's mind when he was about to die in these words, "Mahmud not only ordered all his wealth to be placed under his eyes but also grieved his separation from it and sighed bitterly but did not give the smallest thing to anybody."

Prof. Habib is of the view that getting wealth of India was the real motive and other motives were subsidiary. According to him, it was not unusual that like the Catholic Church of Europe, the Hindu temples attacked powerful invaders to loot the wealth contained therein.

Religious objective. Some historians like Utabi, a contemporary of Mahmud are of the view that his chief objective was to spread Islam in India and to break the idols of non-believers. Mahmud's invasions have been termed as 'Jihad'–crusade to spread Islam in India. According to

Mahmud's contemporary historians, he had vowed at the beginning of his reign that he would carry out an annual invasion on India to propagate Islam. Several modern historians also share their views and hold that because of this motive, he carried out seventeen invasions on India; important invasions being on important temples. They argue that had wealth been the only objective, Mahmud would not have broken idols. He forced non-Muslims to embrace Islam.

Historians like Habib, Khalik Ahmad Nizami and Zaffar vehemently disapprove of this objective. They argue that there is no principle of Islamic law which supports the acts of temple destruction or encourages them. Prof. Habib points out," Islam sanctions neither vandalism nor plundering motives of the invader." Mahmud destroyed temples of Hindus not because he wanted to crush idolatory. It was because these temples were storehouses of wealth. Again whatever conversions took place in India, they were incidental and not deliberate. According to Dr. Nazimi, "It was due to the invader's fury that some people left their religion and embraced Islam." Again he emphasises that it should be remembered that if "he harassed the Hindu rajas of India, he did not spare the Muslim sovereigns of Iran and Trans Oxians." Similar views have been expressed by S.M. Jaffar when he observes "To say that he invaded India time and again for the spread of his religion is historically incorrect and psychologically untrue."

Dr. Ishwari Prasad is very emphatic that "wealth and not territory, extirpation of idolatory and not conquest were the objects of his raids."

Taking into account several factors, the views of Utbi, the court historian of Mahmud carry more weight. Keeping in view the situation of that age and the religious zeal of the Turks who were new converts to Islam, it is quite possible that Mahmud invaded India for the spread of his religion. Rational thinking is hardly a match against fanatical zeal.

Political motive. It is also argued by some historians that Mahmud's objective was to conquer India. But this view does not hold ground when it is seen in the context of his seventeen successful victories. The question arises; what prevented Mahmud from annexing the conquered territories to his empire? However, he did annex the Punjab. According to Lanepoole, "Mahmud did not aim at permanent conquest. Time had not yet come when Turks could think seriously living in India."

Fame motive. It is said that like all ambitious rulers, Mahmud wanted to have name and fame by his conquests.

Acquisition of artisans. Some scholars are of the opinion that one object of Mahmud was acquisition of skilled artisans from India as he was very fond of constructing beautiful buildings. He carried with him several skilled artisans.

To sum up, it may be said that there were several reasons for Mahmud's invasion over India. All historians agree that wealth was certainly an important reasons. Regarding his religious motive, opinions differ.

Effects of Mahmud's Invasions

In the words of Al-Beruni, "Mahmud utterly ruined the prosperity of the country and performed those wonderful deeds by which the Hindus became like atoms of dust, scattered in all directions". Prof. Habib observes, "The worst enemies of Islam had been its own fanatical followers of which Mahmud was one. He showed to the philosophical Hindus the darker and the more tyrannical side of Islam and the Hindus, who would naturally judge a creed from the character of its followers, began to hate Islam for all times to come."

Sir Woolsely Haig has observed, "He was the first to carry the banner of Islam into the heart of India and to tread the path which so many followed him."

Following were the important effects of Mahmud's invasions on India :

1. Mahmud's victories exposed the weakness of the Rajput rulers. It is an irony and sad commentary on the helpless political conditions of India that Mahmud roamed about in India without facing any serious resistance. "He took from India whatever he could and destroyed the rest."
2. Mahmud's invasion exposed the military weakness of India.
3. Mahmud carried huge wealth out of India and thereby weakened the economic condition of India.
4. Mahmud, by destroying idols., temples and beautiful places, gave a great setback to Indian art and sculpture.
5. Mahmud paved the way for foreign invaders to invade India.
6. Mahmud provided a foot-hold in India for the promotion of Islam in India.
7. Mahmud's invasions which were mainly directed upon Hindu temples cracked a feeling of ill-will among the Hindus towards the Muslims.
8. Along with Mahmud came several Muslim saints who preached lofty ideals of life. These Muslim saints called the 'Sufis' started the process of interaction between the Hindus and the Muslims.
9. Mahmud was accompanied by a famous historian Alberuni whose accounts serve as a very useful source of information about the various aspects of life in India.
10. A new chapter in the history of India began. Earlier all the invaders like the Sakas, Kushans and Huns were absorbed in the main-stream of India's life and lost their separate identities but the new Muslim invaders paved the way for establishing their separate identity.

Q 3. Why did Muhammad Ghori attack India. After mentioning his invasions, describe his encounters with Prithviraj Chauhan. What was the effect of his invasions on the history of India?

Ans. *Muhammad Ghori or Muhammad Ghor or Shihab-Ud-Din Ghori.*

After a lapse of about 150 years of Mahmud's invasions, Muhammad Ghori, an other Turk invader invaded India and laid the foundations of Muslim rule in India. Some historians describe Ghori as an Afghan but it is usually accepted that he was a Turk.

Muhammad Ghori was the ruler of Ghazni. He was very enterprising and he had an eye over the wealth of India. He had also a great desire to spread Islam. First of all he conquered Multan. Thereafter he invaded Gujarat but was defeated and was lucky to escape with his beaten army. However he was determined to conquer India. He diverted his attention to Punjab. In 1179 A.D., he attacked and captured Peshawar which came under the ruler of the Punjab. Again in 1185 and 1186 AD, he attacked the Punjab and captured it. After conquering Punjab, Multan and Sindh, he thought of penetrating into the interior of India. He advanced towards Delhi with his bid to carve out an empire in India. He fought two battles at Tarain, one in 1991 when he was defeated and in 1992 when he defeated Prithviraj. Thereafter he conquered Kanauj, Gujarat, Bundelkhand, Bengal and Bihar. After conquering several parts of India, he turned westward to conquer central Asian Turks but had to suffer defeat. Encouraged by the news of his defeat, a warrior tribe Khokar in the Punjab rose in revolt. He himself marched to crush the revolt. He was successful in putting down the revolt but was killed in his own camp on March 15, 1206 by his Khokhar enemies. The body of Ghori was carried to Ghazni.

Ghori's Encounters with Prithviraj Chauhan

Ghori and Prithviraj fought two battles at Tarain. (now in Haryana)

The first battle at Tarain (1191). Prithviraj was the ruler of Delhi and Ajmer when Ghori was marching towards Delhi after conquering several parts of Punjab. Prithviraj was able to unite some Rajput states to present a united front against the common enemy. However Jai Chand, the ruler of Kanauj did not join the confederation of some Rajput states headed by Prithviraj, on account of his personal animosity. A fierce battle between Ghori and Prithviraj took place at Tarain. Ghori was wounded and defeated. He was carried away from the battle-field by a Khalji soldier. His army fled. True to Indian traditions, the Rajputs did not follow the fleeing enemy—a blunder which India had to repent for centuries.

The second battle of Tarain (1192). Muhammad Ghori was determined to establish his authority over India. He was not disheartened over his defeat. He wanted to avenge his humiliation. He reorganised and strengthened his army. With a large cavalry of unrivalled marks-men, he again descended the plains of Tarain in 1192. Prithviraj again formed a confederation of the north Indian Kings. Nevertheless, Jai Chand of Kanauj, not only kept himself aloof from the battle but is also said to have helped Muhammad Ghori in order to wreck his vengeance on Prithviraj. Conflicting accounts of the defeat and ultimate fate of Prithviraj as well as Muhammad Ghori are given.

The numerical strength of the Rajput forces was far greater than Ghori's army which, however, was better organised. The fighting quality of the Turkish cavalry decided the issue. A large number of Indian soldiers lost their lives. Prithviraj was captured and slain. Chandbardai, the court poet of Prithviraj has another version to tell. According to him Prithviraj was taken to Ghori as a prisoner. In a show of exhibiting his skill as an archer, the blind Prithviraj shot a sound-guided arrow at Muhammad Ghori killing him instantly. Prithviraj later committed suicide. Col-Todd, the well known historian of the Rajput period, does not attach credence to this version of Chandbardai.

Results of the Second Battle of Tarain

The crux of the defeat of Prithviraj is that the sovereignty of a considerable part of India passed into the hands of the foreigners. The sovereignty of the Rajputs ended to a great extent. In the words of V.S. Smith, "The second battle of Tarain in 1192, may be regarded as the decisive contest which ensured the ultimate success of the Mohammadan attack on Hindustan."

The victory of Ghori settled the future course of Indian history and as Dr. D.C. Ganguly writes, "The defeat of Prithviraj in the second battle of Tarain not only destroyed the imperial power of the Chauhans, but also brought disaster on the whole of Hindustan."

S. Lanepoole has said, "The result of this victory was the annexation of Ajmer, Hansi and Sirsuti, ruthless slaughter and a general destruction of temples and idols and building of mosques."

Q 4. Who in your opinion was the founder of Muslim rule in India, Mahmud Ghaznavi or Mohammad Ghori? State reasons.

Ans. *Mohammad Ghori as the Founder of Muslim Rule in India.*

Ghori as a conqueror of territory. Undoubtedly as a military commander, Mahmud was far ahead of Ghori. In the words of S.M. Jaffar, "Mahmud was verily endowed with a genius of war. He was a scientific general, skilful in planning and thorough in execution." In the words of Dr. R.C. Majumdar, "Sultan Mahmud was undoubtedly one of the greatest military leaders, the world has ever seen. It is true that he never faced any defeat. It is, however, equally true that he never tried to consolidate his position. He came like "a wind and went back like a whirl wind." Unlike Mahmud, Ghori was not a great general and had to suffer humiliating defeats several times. He was defeated by Mularaja II, the ruler of Gujarat;

by Prithviraj Chauhan in the first battle of Tarain and by Khwarizam Shah, the ruler of Persia. In fact, he was killed in his own camp by his Khokar enemies. But the greatness of Ghori was that none of these defeats could weaken his spirits or check his ambitions. He took his every failure as a valuable experience. He improved upon his weaknesses, removed them and ultimately got success.

The conquests of Ghori brought about more permanent results than the conquests of Mahmud.

Mahmud was contented to plunder the wealth of India and did not think of establishing his empire.

Mahmud kept himself busy in invading and looting but Ghori attempted to build up an empire which lasted for centuries. As Dr. Iswari Prasad has observed, "Wealth, not territory, extirpation of idolatory and not conquest, were the objects of Mahmud's raids, and when these were accomplished, he cared nothing for the myriad people of India." According to Sir W.W. Hunter, "He (Muhammad Ghori) was no religious knight-errant of Islam like Mahmud of Ghazni but a practical conqueror. The objects of his distant expeditions were not temples but provinces."

Ghori as a practical statesman. Dr. Habibullah regards Ghori as a practical statesman who took the fullest advantage of the rotten political structure of India.

Ghori gave proof of his statesmanship while dealing with different Rajput rulers.

After his victory over Prithviraj, instead of annexing Delhi and Ajmer to his territories, he handed over the administration of Delhi and Ajmer to the relatives of Prithviraj.

Ghori did not change the status of those Hindu chiefs who accepted his suzerainty and did not interfere in their administration. Of course, he established forts in these territories.

Political realism of Ghori. Prof. K.A. Nizami puts stress on two qualities of Ghori *i.e.* his digged tenacity of purpose and his grim political realism. He wrote, "This Hero of three stupendous defeats at Andh-khud, Tarain and Anhilwara had to his credit the establishment of one of the greatest empires of the middle ages and in this he definitely rises above Mahmud of Ghazni."

According to Stanley Lane-poole, Ghori's conquests in India were wider and far more permanent than Mahmud's. He wrote, "of the two tides of Mohammedan invasion that surged into India, Mahmud's had left little trace. It had been but a series of triumphant raids."

Great ability to select officers. Ghori had the art of selecting the best men for his services. He trained generals and administrators like Qutab-ud-din Aibak, who proved quite competent to maintain his empire.

Appointment of governors. Ghori appointed governors of the provinces he conquered. These governors consolidated the position of Turks and they suppressed rebellions. After the death of Ghori, Qutub-ud-din Aibak, his most able military commander founded the Slave Dynasty that ruled India for about one hundred years.

Summing up

Thus from the above details it becomes quite clear that though Mahmud was a great military commander and always a victor but he did not try to establish his kingdom in India. There is no doubt that he paved the way for the establishment of Turkish empire. Ghori also accumulated vast wealth without any scruples but his main objective always remained the founding of an empire and he was successful in that aim.

Q 5. "As compared with Mahmud Ghaznavi, Muhammad Ghori is an obscure figure." ***S. Lane-poole. Discuss.***

Or

Compare Mahmud Ghaznavi and Muhammad Ghori.

Ans. *Comparison between Mahmud and Ghori*

Before we discuss the statement of Lane-poole regarding Mahmud and Ghori, it would be pertinent to have a brief comparison between their similarities and dissimilarities and that would help us to find in what respects Ghori is an obscure as compared with Mahmud.

Similarities

1. Both came from Ghazni.
2. Both were Turkish invaders.
3. Both were brave, hardworking and great conquerors.
4. Both plundered the wealth of India.
5. Both inflicted atrocities on non-Muslims.
6. Both used archers and cavalry in their army.
7. Both took recourse to any means—fair or foul–to win a war.
8. Both, by and large, gave the slogan of *'Jihad'* (Holy war) to acquire military success.

Dissimilarities

Mahmud was a great conqueror and he never faced any defeat in his 17 invasions of India. On the other hand, Ghori had to face a number of defeats. Not only this he lost his life at the hands of his enemy in India and did not reach his kingdom of Ghazni. Even in Central Asia, Mahmud was more successful and Ghori had to face defeat.

Mahmud did not try to establish his empire in India. He was more interested in plundering the wealth of India.

Mahmud was more of a fanatic who wanted to spread Islam in India. He destroyed temples and idols of Hindu gods. His attacks were mostly directed on the religious places of the Hindus. Ghori on the other hand directed his attacks on important towns and forts.

Estimate of Both

When we compare the military qualities of Mahmud and Ghori, we can certainly say that Ghori is an obscure figure and he stands no comparison with Mahmud.

Similarly in the matter of spreading Islam, Mahmud was more aggressive and he destroyed several places of worship of the Hindus, broke their idols and converted them to Islam. So as a fanatic Muslim, Mahmud outshines Ghori. Mahmud's objective in invading India, according to the contemporary historian Utabi was to spread Islam. He was given the title of 'Idol Breaker'. Though such claims are disputed by several modern historians, yet to his contemporary Muslim historians, "Mahmud was undoubtedly a great Ghazi and the greatest monarch of his age." For ages he has been considered the 'worst plunderer of temples' by the Hindus in general.

Mahmud was a great patron of art and literature while Ghori was a mere military commander and a politician. Ghazni under Mahmud was a great cultural centre. Famous architects, artists, poets and scholars flocked to his court. As observed by Lane-poole, "Napoleon imported the choicest work of art from the countries he subdued to adorn his palace, Mahmud did better, he brought the artists and poets themselves to illuminate his court." Among the most important scholars of his court mention may be made of two historians, Alberuni and Utbi, poets and scholars like Firdausi, Unsari and Baihaqi.

Mahmud founded a University at Ghazni with a vast collection of valuable books of various languages.

Mahmud set up a museum at Ghazni . He awarded scholarships to scholars. Mahmud built a number of *'madaras'* (institutions of higher learning) and mosques.

The most famous of his monuments is the 'Celestial Bride', the great Jama Masjid of Ghazni. It was verily 'a wonder of the East' and attracted people from far and wide for a visit.

On the contrary, Ghori showed very little interest in art and literature.

Thus from the point of view as a conqueror, as a patron of art and literature and as a promoter of Islam we can certainly share the views of Lane-poole, "compared with Mahmud, the name of Muhammad Ghori has remained obscure. He was no patron of letters and no poet or historian vied one another to praise his magnificence and power."

On the other hand if we make a comparion on the basis of an empire builder, the name of Mahmud would remain obscure. Lane-poole himself has stated, "Of the two tides of Muhammedon invasion that surged into India, Mahmud's had left little trace'. He has further observed, "Mahmud was no constructive or far-seeing statesman. We hear no laws or institutions or methods of government that sprang from his initiative."

Q 6. Discuss the causes of the success of the Turks against the Rajputs.

Or

Explain the causes of the failure of the Rajputs against Mahmud Ghaznavi and Muhammad Ghori.

Ans. *Causes of the success of the Turk Invaders and Failure of the Rajputs.*

It is an irony of fate that the Rajputs who were a paragon of rare bravery, chivalry, courage and valour lost to the Turk invaders who came from barren, destitute and distant lands. Several reasons are assigned to this phenomenon. These reasons may be grouped under the following seven heads :

I. Political causes.
II. Military causes.
III. Religious causes.
IV. Social causes
V. Geographical causes.
VI. Administrative causes.
VII. Economic causes.

I. Political Causes

(1) *Lack of a powerful central authority.* There was no powerful central authority in India that could have offered strong resistance to the invaders as did the Magadha empire at the time of Alexander's invasion.

India at that time was divided into a number of independent Rajput states.

(2) *Disunity among the Rajput rulers.* As stated by Dr. Iswari Prasad, "State fought against state for leadership and there was no paramount power which could effectively hold them together by any principle of unity or cohesion."

There were tough mutual fights among Rajputs states, particularly among the Chauhans and the Rathors, the Chandelas and the Chalukyas and the Pratiharas, Palas and the Rashtrakutas. According to Chandbardai, "Ninety out of a hundred of Prithviraj's *'Samantas'* (chiefs) fell in his conflicts with Jai Chand on account of his carrying away Samyukta."

(3) *Lack of political insight.* Even a series of Muslim invasions did not produce a single Rajput ruler with political insight to visualize as to what would happen to all of them, one by one, if the foreign inroads were not faced and checked unitedly.

(4) *Neglect of the frontiers.* The Rajput rulers failed to evolve any frontier policy and could not forget their internal feuds and rise above personal prejudices to save the frontier states being crushed under the foreign soldiers.

(5) *Feudalism:* The army of a Rajput ruler was constituted by collecting

the armies of the feudal chiefs. The soldiers demonstrated more loyalty to their feudal chief than to the ruler. Feudal system led to the weakening of the power of the king.

II. Military Causes

1. *Interior war art.* In the words of Dr. V.A. Smith, "Hindu Kings though fully equal to their assailants in courage and contempt of death, were distinctly inferior in the art of war and for that reason lost their independence."

2. *Lack of appropriate military strategy.* The Rajput army advanced with all the wings together—the right, the centre and the left. The Turks used a special strategy with their two units—one advanced guard and other the reserve. The advance guard was meant to test their strength and to find out the weak areas. The reserve was thrown into the battlefray after the Rajputs had exhausted their resources.

3. *Lack of offensive.* The Rajputs mostly fought defensive battles with the foreign invaders and this was not the appropriate way of winning a battle.

4. *Outdated weapons and war strategies.* The Rajputs did not try to find out the latest techniques and weapons used in foreign lands.

5. *Swordsmen versus archers.* The Turkish archers shooting arrows from their horses were more than a match for the Rajput soldiers with their swords which could become effective only if they could reach close to the enemy.

6. *Elephants versus horses.* The Rajputs depended to a considerable extent upon the elephants. The elephants were easily struck with fear with the swiftness of the horses' movements and the war cries. They ran helter-skelter spreading fear and disorder in their own camp. The strength of the Turks lay in their efficient cavalry.

7. *Lack of military leadership.* Military leadership is quite different from bravery and chivalry. The Rajput rulers and their commanders did not have the requisite capacity to infuse zeal in their armies. On the other hands, the Turk invaders could easily arouse the battle cry 'to do or die'.

8. *Overdependence on the ruler.* Usually the soldiers of the Rajput rulers had the impression that after the death or disappearance of the Raja, they could not face the enemy. The disappearance of the Raja even for a short while created panic in the army. The disappanee of Anand Pal for a while when his elephant was hit by an arrow caused panic in his army and his army lost heart and consequently battle against Mahmud of Ghazni. Lane-poole has described the fate of the war as, "Anand Pal's elephant took fright, the rumour ran that the Raja was fleeing from the field, vague suspicions and distrust spread about, and a general stampede ensued. Instead of retreating before a vivacious army, in an instant Mahmud found himself pursuing a panic stricken crowd."

9. *Only Rajputs in the army.* Only Rajputs had the duty to fight. Other classes were indifferent. Thus too much dependence on the Rajputs was one of the weaknesses of the military organisation.

III. Religious Causes

1. *Ghazi spirit of the Muslim army:* A Ghazi is one who gives his life in defence of Islam. According to Lane-poole, "The very bigotry of their creed (Muslims) was an instrument of self preservation." For the Muslim soldiers, the fight against the Rajputs i.e. the Hindus, was a *'Jihad'* (Holy war)—a crusade to protect as well as to spread their religion. The soldiers were thoroughly convinced that if they died for their religion they would go to paradise. If they won, they would get all the pleasures of the world, besides being the protectors of their religion.

2. *No unitary ideology of the Hindus.* Hinduism had no unified ideology to bind them together to the extent the Muslims had.

3. *Impact of Buddhist religion.* The Buddhist concept of Ahimsa did a great harm to the martial spirit of the Hindus. It made the Hindus timid and peace-loving.

IV. Social Causes

(1) *Decaying society.* The caste system had divided the Hindu society and injected the venom of hatred, humiliation, inequality, prejudices and untouchability. On the contrary, Islam had infused a spirit of brotherhood. It has been observed, "The fellowship of equal brotherhood in Islam surpassed in unity and strength in the world."

(2) *Superstition of the Hindus.* In the words of V.C. Vaiya, "Superstition acted like a double-edged sword towards the fall of Hindu India, While the Muslims believed that victory was bound to come to them, the Hindus believed that they were bound, to be conquered by the Muslims in *'Kaliyug'*, such a superstition demoralised and discouraged the Hindus."

(3) *Slave system of the Muslim rulers.* The slaves maintained by the Muslim rulers were very faithful to their masters. They were provided adequate opportunities to hold high offices according to their ability. They were always ready to die for their masters.

V. Administrative Factors

The Rajput rulers did not set up an efficient spy system to be adequately acquainted themselves with the overall position of their adversaries.

It is also very unfortunate that sometimes Rajput officials proved treacherous as they let out some of the military secrets to the enemy.

VI. Geographical Factors

Some historians have suggested that the hot climate of India sapped the strength and vigour of the Indian soldiers. The Muslim soldiers came from cold regions and were habitually hardy and sturdy. They were not bothered by the Indian heat as they were used to face climatic harshness. 'Heat or cold,' they thought they were their to conquer and that was the only thing that mattered to them.

The Muslim rulers had excellent recruiting grounds in lands beyond the Afghan hills. From there they could constantly bring new recruits to fight against the Hindus.

VII. Economic Factors

Large number of soldiers of the Turk invaders were attracted by the wealth of India. They, therefore, fought with full zeal. As already stated, religious fantacism was also there. Thus the two factors combined together to infuse vigour in them.

The wealth of the temples had a great attraction for the Muslim invaders. These temples however, were not properly protected. It, therefore, became easy for the invaders to plunder these places and this demoralised the people.

Summing up

We may close the discussion with the observations made by some prominent historians. According to Dr. Iswari Prasad, "There was no dearth of military talent or fighting skill in the country, for the Rajputs were the finest soldiers scarcely inferior in the qualities of courage, valour and endurance to men of any other country. But they lacked unity and organisation. Pride and prejudice alike forbade obedience to a common leader and in critical moments when concentrated action was essential for a victory they renewed their individual plans and thus neutralised the advantages they possessed over the enemies."

Sir Jadunath Sarkar is of the view that complete equality and social solidarity, fatalism that sprang from an absolute reliance on god and freedom from drunkenness of Muslim soldiers were primarily responsible for the success of the Turks.

According to Prof. K.A. Nizami, "The real cause of the defeat of the Indians lay in their social system and the invidious caste distinctions, which rendered the whole military organization rickety and weak."

R.C. Datt has emphasised that the Hindus had reached the last stage of their political, religious and social decline at that time and therefore, became an easy prey to the invading Turks.

Dr. A.L. Srivastva observes that the absence of political unity, social divisions and moral degeneration of the Hindus and the superiority of the Turks in military organisation, skill and resources were responsible for the success of the Turks.

Dr. K.S. Lal lists these reasons for the defeat of the Rajputs : Social division and rivalry between different groups, the absence of an efficient spy system and defective and out-dated military skill. He has further observed that it was very much easy for the Muslims to get traitors from a society which was so unjustly divided. This was one of the reasons why all important cities of North India were lost to the invader within fifteen years.

Sardar K.M. Panikkar assigns the responsibility of the defeat of the Hindus on their lack of contact with the outside world and their declined culture.

Prof. A.B.M. Habibullah writes, "Rajput recklessness has an element of romance in it but is of little practical wisdom."

Dr. U.N. Ghoshal thinks that want of leaders with sufficient skill was the primary reason of the failure of the Rajputs.

Q 7. Discuss the impact of Turkish conquest on political, social and economic life of North India. (Delhi University, 1997)

Ans. *Impact of Turkish Conquest on North India.*

Several walks of Indian life were greatly affected by the Turks conquest. Following significant changes took place in the political, social and economic life of India.

I. Political Changes or Effects.

1. *Establishment of the Muslim rule in North India.* The Arab invasion had led to the establishment of two independent Muslim Kingdoms of Sindh and Multan. But the Turk invasion led to the establishment of the Muslim rule over a large part of North India.

2. *Political importance of Delhi.* Iltutmish made Delhi the capital of the Sultanate in India. Earlier it was Lahore. Thus the political importance of Lahore declined and of Delhi increased.

3. *Supremacy of the Caliph of Bagdad.* Though the Turkish Sultans of Delhi were independent rulers yet they took the help of Caliph to give stability to their rule and they considered themselves a part of the Islamic world. In other words foreign religious elements were introduced in Indian political life.

4. *Law of succession.* Islamic law enjoins the election of a ruler but in practice any of the issues of the Sultan could be chosen as the successor of the throne. Likewise it was essential that the Sultan should be a male. However there were deviations also. These practices affected the political situation in India.

5. *Turkish monopoly of high offices.* Indians, whether Hindus or Muslims were by and large deprived of high offices in administration.

6. *'Iqta' System. 'Iqta'* literally means an area. Empire was divided into Iqtas or provinces. The Turkish rule put an end to the independent small kingdoms and these were replaced by Iqtas. Every Iqta was placed under the charge of a chief military commander. The head of each Iqta was

designated as Iqtadar. These Iqtadars were not the independent rulers of these areas. Their appointments, tenures and transfers depended on the will of the ruler. The Iqtadar met the expenditure of the army stationed under him, out of the income of the Iqta and thereafter sent the balance to the ruler. The Iqtadar had to perform two important duties *i.e.* the collection of revenue and maintenance of law and order. The Iqta system was designed to put an end to the feudal system of the Rajputs. The Iqta system brought distant areas of the empire in contact with the Central Government.

7. *Changes in military organisation.* Recruitment in the army was now no longer the monopoly of one particular class *i.e.* the Rajputs/Kshatriyas and it was opened to all classes.

Another important change took place in the army organisation. The Sultans organised their permanent standing armies in place of the feudal armies i.e. the armies supplied by the feudal chiefs whenever asked for.

The third change was that cavalry men and archers began to be recruited in large numbers as against the infantrymen.

Fourthly, elephants gave place to trained horses.

Fifthly, more importance began to be given to the training of the army.

Sixthly, suitable arrangements were made for the security of the frontiers.

Lastly, Rajput ideals of warfare were completely abandoned.

II. Social Changes

1. *Condemnation of caste system.* The Turkish conquest reduced the importance of the caste system. Turkish society had a firm belief in social equality.

2. *Check on the privileged class in villages.* The Iqtadars who were mostly urban people put a check on the privileged feudatories in the villages.

3. *Changes in urban areas.* Prof. Habib has observed that the doors of the ancient 'noble cities' of the Rajputs were now opened for the different sections of society *i.e.* the artisans as well as the labourers, the Hindus and the Muslims and the Brahmins and the so-called Chandals, without any consideration of high and low.

III. Economic Changes

(*a*) *Encouragement to trade.* According to Sir Jadurnath Sarkar, trade contacts which had broken in the 8th century with the countries of Asia and Africa were revived towards the close of the 12th century. Indian traders started trading on a large scale with Ghazni and China.

Several new trading centres like Multan, Lahore, Delhi and Lakhnauti came to be established.

Changes in the taxation system. The Turk rulers followed the taxation system as prescribed in Islamic scriptures. They primarily imposed four taxes *i.e.* 'Zakat', 'Khams', 'Jijya' and 'Khiraj'.

'Zakat' was levied on the Muslims. It was obligatory for every Muslim to give about 2½ per cent of his income as tax.

'Kham' was war booty as a source of state income.

'Jijya' was levied on non-Muslims.

'Khiraj or land tax was fixed generally at 50 per cent of the produce by the Mamluck or slave Sultans.

With the exception of the land tax, the other three were introduced by the Turks.

Besides these four taxes, some old taxes were also continued.

Growth of medieval economy. Historians like Habib and Nizami in their work have observed that the Turkish conquest led to the growth of the medieval economy which was characterised by the uniformity of the taxation system, growth of currency, growth of handicrafts, cities and trade. It was an economy in which agricultural surplus could be utilised for building the various sectors of economic life. The slave system of the Turks proved very helpful in this regard.

IV. Cultural Effects

Importance of Persian. Persian became the language of administration and in this respect a new era of cultural development came into being.

Development of Hindvi. The contact between the Hindus and the Muslims led to the development of a new language called Hindvi used by Amir Khusru.

Architecture. The Turks constructed mosques, minarets, forts and other buildings in the Persian style. New materials with lime mixture came to be used increasingly. This was very useful in making buildings strong.

Establishment of educational institutions. With the popularisation of Persian, a new class of scholars emerged.

V. Religious Changes

Divergent views are found on the issue whether the Turks forced the Hindus to embrace Islam.

It appears the Hindus continued to celebrate their religious and social festivals.

The influence of Sufi saints was visible on the religious outlook of the people.

VI. Administrative Uniformity of the people

The use of Persian as the language of administration greatly helped in bringing about administrative uniformity, The Rajput rulers used different dialects.

Q 8. Write Notes on (*i*) Alberuni (*ii*) Firdausi

Alberuni (977 A.D. to 1084 A.D.)

Abu Rehn Alberuni whose real name was Mohammad Bin Ahmad was a famous historian, mathematician, philosopher, poet and scholar of the court of Mahmud Ghaznavi. He spent several years in India. His book *'Tahquiq-e-Hind'* is a very valuable source of information of economic, political, religious and social conditions prevailing in contemporary India. He studied Sanskrit with a view to read the philosophical and religious books of the Hindus. He also rendered the Puranas and the Bhagwadgita into Persian. On astronomy, he wrote a scholarly book entitled *'Alqanuwal-Masudi'*. His books have now been translated in almost all the major languages of the world.

Alberuni's Account of India

(*i*) *Social conditions.* Indian society was cast-ridden. Several evil practices like child marriage, prohibition of widow marriage, *'Sati'* and *'Jauhar'* existed in the Hindu society. Only the Brahmans had the right to attain salvation. People had a very narrow outlook.

(*ii*) *Religious conditions.* Idol worship was prevalent. Brahamans had the sole privilege of reading the Hindu scriptures.

(*iii*) *Political conditions.* Alberuni informs as that the feeling of nationalism among the Indians was almost absent. The country was fragmented into a number of independent states. These states were jealous of each other and constantly engaged in fights against one another.

(*iv*) *Legal system.* According to Alberuni, criminal law was very mild in India. The Brahmanas were exempted from death punishment. The limbs of serious offenders were amputated.

(*v*) *Economic conditions.* King was not the owner of the land. He took land tax from the peasents at the rate of one-sixth of the produce.

(*vi*) *Philosophical conditions.* Albe.. ni has unreservedly praised Indian philosophy. He was particularly impressed by the Upanishadas and the Bhagvadgita.

(*vii*) *Little historical sense.* Alberuni found that the Indians did not evince much interest in writing chronological history.

Firdausi

Firdausi was the most important court poet of Mahmud Ghaznavi. On account of his excellence poetry in Persian, he is sometimes called the 'Homer of Asia'. He had composed the epic poetic work entitled *'Shahnama'.* As the legend goes, this work was composed at the behest of Mahmud Ghaznavi. Mahmud is said to have promised to pay Firdausi one gold *'mohar'* for each verse of the *'Shahnama'* Firdausi composed 60,000 verses in praise of Persian rulers and Mahmud in particular. When the monumental book was presented to Mahmud, he offered 60,000 silver coins for it. At this Firdausi's self-respect was hurt. Annoyed at this, Firdausi left for his home town. In anger, he appended some verses to his *'Shahnama'* which were defamatory to the conduct of Mahmud. When Mahmud learnt about this, he realised his mistake and sent 60,000 gold '*mohars*' to Firdausi. But now it was too late. The amount reached Firdausi's house when he was no more and his dead body taken to the grave.

'Shahnama' is considered a valuable source of contemporary history. It contains the events of some of the important kings of Persia including Mahmud. Of course facts have to be sifted from fiction.

3

Foundation & Consolidation of the Delhi Sultanate : The Slave Dynasty

Q 1. Evaluate the achievements of Iltutmish as a ruler.

(Delhi University, 1997)

Or

Would you consider Iltutmish as the real founder of the Delhi Sultanate? Give reasons. (Delhi University, 1997. Alterative Paper)

Or

The history of Muslim soverignty in India begins properly speaking with Iltutmish" Discuss.

Or

Give your assessment of Aibak and Iltutmish as rulers. Whom do you consider the real founder of the Delhi Sultanate out of the two?

Or

"Aibak laid the outlines of the Delhi Sultanate and its royal office but undoubtedly Iltutmish was its first Sultan" Discuss the above statement in the context of the state reorganisation of Iltutmish.

Ans. *Founder/Real founder of the Delhi Sultanate.*

Achievements of Aibak (1206 to 1210). It appears that quite a large number of historians have been very generous to Iltutmish in their praise and rather unfair to Aibak. It is usually forgotten that had there been no Aibak there would not have been any Sultan by the name of Iltutmish. There is no doubt that Qutab-ud-din Aibak founded the Mameluk of Slave Dynasty which had elveven rulers who ruled over Delhi from 1206 to 1290. *Mameluk* means a slave born of free parents. Iltutmish strengthened the Sultanate founded by his predecessor. Main achievements of Aibak are as under :

1. It was Aibak who rendered a very useful service to Mohammad Ghori in the battle of Tarain. It was an important event which changed the course of Indian history.

2. Again it was Aibak who conquered the area of Hansi, Delhi and Ranthambore in the absence of Mohammad Ghori.

3. It was Aibak who helped Ghori to defeat Jaichand of Kanauj.

4. Not only this he defeated Bhimdeva II of Anhilwara who on one occasion had defeated Ghori. Aibak thus avenged the defeat of his master.

5. After Ghori's death, Aibak had declared himself the ruler of his Indian possessions and he protected and extended' the Delhi Sultanate.

6. By marriage diplomacy Aibak was able to overpower the difficulties that he faced in founding the empire. He entered into marriage alliances with three of the most important Turk nobles i.e. Qubacha, Yilduz and Iltutmish.

7. Aibak subdued several Rajput rulers.

In the words of Prof. S.R. Sharma, "Among these (rulers) Aibak must rank with Balban as pioneer founder of a great dynasty of rulers. Some of his successors might have added more glory to the empire as a whole. But the groundwork and examples were Aibak's"

Dr. Iwwari Prasad ranks Aibak "among the great pioneers of Muslim conquert in India."

Iltutmish (1211-1235) as the Consolidator of the Delhi-Sultanate

Iltutmish, a "slave of a slave" is regarded by several historians as the real founder and consolidator of the slave Dynasty and the Delhi Sultanate. According to them, Aibak was the ruler for four years only. There was so much anarchy after his death that the Sultanate of Delhi seemed slipping and a powerful ruler was needed to control the situation and Iltutmish rose equal to the occasion. When we peruse the history we find that Mohammad-bin-Qasim was the first Muslim invader who came to India but he conquered only Sindh and Multan. In the words of Lane-poole "it was a mere episode in the history of India". Mahmud Ghaznavi was the second great Muslim invader but his seventeen successful expeditions were primarily meant for plunder. His invasions did not lead to the establishment of any Muslim Kingdom in India. For about 150 years there was no attempt to found any Muslim empire in India. Mohammad Ghori conquered the bulk of Hindustan but most of his time was spent in Ghazni-out of India. He himself did not rule over India but left to his viceroy Aibak. Aibak extended his kingdom and formed an independent Muslim state in India. Since his rule was very short-lived, he could not consolidate the Sultanate. But the credit of founding the Sultanate must go to him. Of course, Iltutmish strengthened the foundation and saved the infant Muslim empire from collapsing.

On account of Iltutmish's achievements in bringing about political consolidation out of turmoil, Dr. R.P. Tripathi has observed, "Qutub-ud-din cannot be regarded ever as sovereign ruler of Muslim India because no coins of his name are available and his name is conspicuous by its absence in the list of kings prepared by Ibn Batuta and in that prepared by Firoz-Shah Tughlaq for Khutba." He has further observed, "The history of Muslim sovereignty in India begins properly speaking with Iltutmish."

In the words of Dr. A.L. Srivastva, "Iltutmish was a brave but cautious soldier. He was also a successful general. He laid the foundation of a military monarchy that was to serve later as the instrument of a military imperialism under the Khaljis".

In the opinion of Lane-poole, "Iltutmish is the true founder of the Dynasty of the Slaves, Kingdom."

"It was he," writes Prof. K.A. Nizami "who gave the country a capital (Delhi), an independent state, a monarchial form of government and a governing class."

Prof. A.B.M. Habibullah states, "Aibak outlined the Delhi Sultanate and its sovereign status, Iltutmish was unquestionably its first king."

Sir Wolseley wrote, "Iltutmish was the greatest of all the slave kings."

Minhaj-us Siraj, a contemporary historian of Iltutmish wrote, "Never has a sovereign so virtuous, kind hearted and revered towards the learned and the divine sat upon the throne."

Dr. Iswari Prasad regards Iltutmish "undoubtedly the real founder of the Slave Dynasty."

According to Dr. R.C. Majumdar, "Iltutmish may justly be regarded as the greatest ruler of the early Turkish Sultanate of Delhi which lasted till 1290 A.D."

Difficulties of Iltutmish

With a view to appreciate the role of Iltutmish, it is very necessary to know the difficult circumstances under which he acceded to the throne. The newly Muslim empire was threatened with disintegration. Important difficulties facing Iltutmish are mentioned here in brief.

1. Iltutmish had no hereditary claim to the throne.

2. Iltutmish was slave of a slave (Aibak) and according to Muslim law no slave could ever occupy the throne.

3. There was several equally powerful nobles who would not tolerate the rise of an equal to the position of a Sultan.

4. Nasir-ud-din Qubachah, the governor of Sindh and Multan and Taj-ud-din Yalduz, the ruler of Ghazni refused to recognise Iltutmish as the rightful successor to the throne of Delhi.

5. Some of the Muslim generals asserted their independence taking advantage of the confusion.

6. Rajput rulers of Jalaun, Kalinjar, Ranthambhore and Gwalior declared their independence.

7. The Mongol invasion posed a great threat to the Sultan.

Solving Difficulties by Iltutmish

Iltutmish exhibited remarkable emergy and patience in solving the difficulties. Some of his achievements were as under :

1. He quelled the nobles who opposed him in becoming the Sultan. He defeated Aram Shah, the son of Qutub-ud-din who had declared himself as the Sultan.

2. He defeated Yalduz, made him prisoner and executed him.

3. Qubachah was defeated and he lost his life while crossing the river Indus.

4. Iltutmish suppressed the revolt in Bengal.

5. Iltutmish conquered the Rajput states of Gwalior, Malwa, Ujjain and Ranthambore.

6. Iltutmish got recognition as the Muslim Sultan of India by the Khalifa of Baghdad, Iltutmish, thereafter assumed the title of 'Amir-ul-Mommin or 'Commander of the Faithfuls' and had the name of Khalifa inscribed on his coins. As a result of recognition by Khalifa, Iltutmish's power and status were enhanced. According to Prof. S.R. Sharma, "It is for this reason that Iltutmish has been considered as the real founder of the Muslim Kingdom of Delhi, though it is too much an exaggeration to call him the greatest of all slave kings."

7. Iltutmish with great diplomatic skill prevented the Mongols from invading India. He very politely put off the king of Khwarizm who sought refuge in India from the Mongols.

8. One of the momentous measures of Iltutmish was that he changed his capital from Lahore to Delhi, and it for the first time became the capital of Hindustan.

9. With the help of Fakh-ud-din Ismani, an experienced Wazir of Baghdad, Iltutmish organised his administrative set up and provided a benign and sound administration to the hitherto, disorganised and dismembered empire.

10. According to Thomas, "Iltutmish instituted the veritable commencement of the silver coinage of the Delhi Sultanate."

11. Iltutmish created a 'Corps of Forty' slaves who were very loyal to him and kept a watch on the activities of nobles.

From the above account it is clear that Iltutmish was undoubtedly a successful ruler. His greatness lay not only in saving the infant Muslim empire in India but also in organising the scattered conquered territories of Ghori and Aibak into a well-organised and well-administered empire. Besides being a conqueror, he was a good administrator. He provided a systematic administrative set-up. By dint of his dauntless bravery and wisdom he transformed a weak and vulnerable kingdom into a stable empire in India. He freed the Delhi Sultanate from the claim of suzerainty by the rulers of Ghazni. On account of these features, Iltutmish is often called the real founder of the Muslim empire in India.

Q.2. Write notes on (*i*) Sultana Razia. (*ii*) Nasir-ud-din Mahmud Ans.

Sultana Razia (1236-1240)

Accession to the throne. Raziyyat-ud-din commonly known as Razia Begum or Sultana Razia was the first and the last woman among the Muslims as well as the Hindus to occupy the throne of Delhi. Her rule according to contemporary historian Minhaj, lasted for three years six months and six days. Iltutmish had been succeeded by his son Ruskum-ud-din. who proved to be an incompetent ruler and therefore was deposed by the nobility. His sister Razia was chosen to be the ruler.

Qualities of Razia. To give a befitting reply to a section of people that being a woman, Razia was unfit for royal office, she took the following measures.

1. She gave up her `Purdah' and started appearing in the court in male attire wearing a 'Kuva' (Coat) and a 'Kulah' (Cap).

2. She started horse riding, hunting and commanding the army etc.

3. She took a keen interest in all the administrative activities of the state.

4. She herself appointed several Iqtadars, commanders, and other officers.

5. She conducted the affairs of the state in an open 'durbar'.

Razia's failure. Minhaj-us-siraj, a contemporary historian has aptly described the causes of her failure in these words, "She was endowed with all qualities befitting a king-beneficent, the patron of the learned, a dispenser of justice etc. But she was not born of right sex and so in the estimation of men all these virtues were useless." Thus being a woman was an important cause of her failure.

Secondly, Razia's becoming Sultana was against the traditions of Islam. This made many Turkish Chiefs against her as they considered it a great humiliation to work under a woman. Perhaps it was the first case in the Islamic history under a monarchical form of government. Lane-poole states that nothing would convince the Turkish chiefs that they should be led by a woman. In fact this practice was far ahead of the times.

Thirdly in place of winning favour of her opponent chiefs, she adopted retaliatory measures which annoyed them all the more.

Fourthly, Razia began to shower several favours to an Abyssinian slave Yakut. This provided a good deal of ammunition to the Turkish chiefs who were already against her.

Fifthly, Razia's brothers considered her usurper of the throne. So they were able to gather round them several disgruntled elements.

Sixthly, the situation was further worsened by the orthodox Muslim clergies.

Revolts. Several governors revolted against Razia. However, the most serious was that of Altunia, the governor of Bhatinda. Razia accompanied by Yakut marched against Altunia. On the way, Yakut was murdered by Turk soldiers and Razia was imprisoned. Razia, finding no way of her rescue, married Altunia. Razia and Altunia marched towards Delhi. In the meanwhile, Razia's brother Bahram had been raised to the throne. The fate turned against Razia. Razia and her husband Altunia were defeated and murdered near Kaithal. Thus ended the four-year rule of Razia—the only woman to occupy the throne of Delhi.

Nasir-ud-din Mahmud (1246-66)

Nasir-ud-din Mahmud's accession to the throne after Razia's death and as a matter of fact while she was away from Delhi in connection with checking revolts, the 'Corps of forty' had made Bahram Shah, (1240-1242) the son of Iltutmish as the Sultan of Delhi. The 'Corps of Forty' pressurised the Sultan to work according to their dictates. The Sultan, however, tried to exert himself which cost him his life.

After Bahram Shah, the 'Corps of Forty' managed to make Masood Shah (1242-46) the Sultan of Delhi. The Sultan was forced to delegate all his power to the 'Corps of Forty'. A conspiracy was hatched against the Sultan and he was murdered.

After the deposition of Masood, the 'Corps of Forty' made Nasir-ud-din the youngest son of Iltutmish, as the Sultan of Delhi. Balban one of the 'Corps of Forty' became so powerful that he assumed all the real powers of the Sultan. Nasir-ud-din remained the Sultan in name only. The new Sultan knew the power of the Turkish nobles and was aware of the fact that his two predecssors who had dared to challenge the authority of the nobles were murdered. Balban was the 'Naib' or the Deputy to the Sultan and enjoyed vast powers. He married his daughter to the Sultan.

An estimate of Nasir-ud-din

Some historians hold the view that Nasir-ud-Din was a religious minded man. He had no wordly desires or ambitions.

Several anecdotes became popular about him. It is said that he earned his living by copying the 'Quran' and selling it.

Again it is stated that his wife prepared his meals. One day, her fingers were burnt and she requested the Sultan to keep a maid-servant. But the Sultan refused to do so on the plea that he was simply a trustee of the state and therefore, could not utilise public money for his personal convenience. It may also be remembered that his wife was the daughter of Balban, his 'Naib'-holding the most important post.

It is stated by several historians that such claims are exaggerated. According to P. Saran, the Sultan was very much afraid of the Turkish nobles and therefore kept himself aloof from active politics. It is accepted that he possessed the virtues of continence, frugality and practical piety and simplicity but more than that the circumstances had forced him to behave like that. He knew the power of the Turkish nobility. Therefore, as Prof. K.A. Nizami writes, "The surrender was absolute" the Sultan did nothing which could provoke the displeasure of 'forty.' According to historian Islami," He expressed no opinion without their prior permission, he did not move his hands or feet except at their order. He would never drink nor go to sleep except with their knowledge. "In the words of Thomas, "Mahmud (Nasir-ud-Din) seems, like the sons of Iltutmish to have been but little fitted to dominate over his own turbulent nobles or to coerce imperfectly conquered native, races, nominally subject to his "sway."

Q 3. Explain Balban's theory of Kingship and its impact on his administration

Or

"Balban's theory of Kingship was instrumental in the consolidation of Delhi Sultanate." Discuss. (Delhi University, 1997)

Ans. *Policy of Blood and Iron;*

Theory of Kingship

The stern, harsh and violent policy adopted by Balban to suppress the internal revolts and meeting with the challenges posed by foreign invaders of Mongols is known an the policy of blood and iron.

The theory of kingship propounded by Balban led to the adoption of the policy of blood and iron . Balban was convinced that the only way to face the internal and external dangers was to increase the power and prestige of the Sultan (King).

'Sword' was the chief weapon of Balban to achieve his objectives. He used this weapon with a great vengeance against his rivals, rebels, robbers, thieves and the invaders. By following this policy, he wanted to create terror in the minds of the people that whosoever dared to challenge the authority of the Sultan, he would not be spared. On account of this policy he was able to remain at the helm of affairs for about 40 years i.e. 20 years as the Naib/Prime Minister of Nasir-ud-din Mohmud and then after as the Sultan of Delhi. He executed his policy of blood and iron very successfully and raised the prestige and power of the Sultan in the eyes of the nobles and his subjects.

Main principles of Balban 's theory of Kingship

Main principles of the theory of Kingship were as under:

1. *Divine right of Kings:* Balban said that the king was the representative of God on the earth and Kingship was a divine institution. He declared this to make the nobles believe that he got the crown or the Kingship not through their mercy but by the mercy of God.

2. *Royal descent.* Balban realised that people at that time believed that it was only the prerogative of the ancient royal families to rule and exercise power, he therefore declared that he was the descendant of the legendary Turkish warrior Afrasiyab and that circumstances only had made him a slave.

3. *King as a despot.* He said to his son Bughra Khan that " Kingship is the embodiment of despotism". He believed that it is the "King's superhuman awe and status which can ensure people's obedience.

4. *Word of difference between descendants of noble lineage and commoners.* Historian Zia-ud-Din Barni has gone to the extent of remarking that whenever Balban saw a man of low birth, his eyes started burning with rage and anger and his hands reached his sword to murder him. This view

seems to be on the extreme side. However this much is believable that because of this outlook of Balban, he dismissed all officials not born of noble families, from all important posts.

5. *Recognition of tripartite relationship.* Balban emphasised the relationship between God and the Sultan, Sultan and the people and the God and the people. He considered himself the representative of God on the earth to look after the welfare of the people—people created by God. Accordingly he emphasised that treasury should be used for the benefit of his subjects. Likewise the king should be impartial in dispensing justice.

Practical measures to translate the theory of Kingship into operation

1. *Decorum and grandeur of the court :* Balban enforced strict discipline in the court. No one was allowed to indulge in humour or loose talk. He maintained considerable distance from the courtiers. He prescribed the court dress.

2. *Adoption of several ceremonies :* Balban introduced the practice of `Sijada' in which the people were required to kneel and touch the ground with their forehead in salutation to the king.

3. *Appointment of guards :* Balban appointed fearsome and tall guards who were to stand round the king's person with naked swords in their hands. Whenever he used to go outside the palace, his bodyguards marched with him with naked swords and shouting 'Bismillah-Bismillah.'

4. *Following Persian traditions :* Balban was convinced that the glory of Kingship was possible only by following the Persian traditions and he very carefully followed these traditions in his personal and public life. He named his grandsons on the pattern of Persian kings. He introduced several Persian etiquettes in his court.

5. *Always reserved :* Balban never expressed unusual joy or sorrow in public. It is said that even when the news of the death of his eldest son, Mohammad was conveyed to him, he remained unmoved and carried on the administrative work though in his private apartment, he wept bitterly.

6. *Strong army :* These is no doubt that a strong army is needed for the sustenance of a powerful monarch. Balban, therefore, strengthened his army.

7. *Policy of blood and iron :* A strong and absolute monarch is expected to follow a strict policy in dealing with his enemies. Balban accordingly adopted this policy.

8. *Protection from foreign invaders :* The strength of a despotic ruler is also measured by his ability to protect his subjects from external danger. Balban in this regard took effective steps.

Impact/Achievements of Balban

Balban's theory of Kingship coupled with his policy of blood and iron paid him good dividends. He enhanced the prestige of the Sultan. He crushed the powers of his opponents. He brought about peace and order. He saved the country from the invasions of the Mongols.

Q.4. Explain the policy of 'blood and iron' followed by Balban.

Or

Assess the achievements of Balban as a ruler.

Or

"But for Balban's vigour and energy, the Kingdom of Delhi would have hardly survived the shocks of revolts and external invasions" Discuss.

Ans. *Balban's policy of Blood and Iron.*

It is not without significance that out of about 84 year's rule of the Slave Dynasty, Balban's rule lasted for about 40 years i.e. 20 years as 'Naib' or Prime Minister but virtually the Sultan and 20 years as the Sultan of Delhi. Other 10 Slave rulers ruled for 44 years i.e. just 4 years more than the rule of a single Sultan i.e. Balban. It became possible to achieve this distinction by Balban on account of the successful execution of his policy of blood and iron. Balban displayed great vigour and energy to follow this policy and saved the Delhi. Sultanate from the shocks of internal revolts and external invasions. He enhanced the prestige of the king. His rise from the low position of a water carrier to the rank of the Sultan speaks of his extraordinary qualities.

Meaning of the policy of blood and iron

This policy implied being ruthless to the enemies, use of sword, harshness and strictness and shedding blood. It allowed use of all sorts of methods of terrorising the enemies and inflicting violence upon them. Even before becoming the Sultan of Delhi, Balban had tried these measures to some extent to rise to high posts. He had betrayed Razia and engineered revolts against her. He was responsible for the dethronement of Bahram Shah and instalment of Masud as a King. Later he conspired and removed Masud and enthroned Nasir-ud-Din Mahmud and usurped all the powers of the Sultan by becoming his Prime Minister. By all means Nasir-ud-Din was a sort of captive of Balban. Thus even before assuming the reigns of administration, Balban had gained sufficient experience to make use of the power of the sword against his enemies.

A few example of Balban's policy of blood and iron

1. Prof. S.R. Sharma states that when Amir Khan, one of his generals who was defeated by a rebel came back with this news, "the infuriated Sultan in his paroxysm of rage ordered the defeated generals to be hanged over the gates of Ayodhya."

2. After killing a rebel Tughril Khan, the Sultan ordered the killing of all his friends and rebels. The situation has been described by Lane-poole as, "Even a beggar to whom the usurper had been kind was not spared."

3. According to Barani, "Such punishment as was inflicted on Lakhnauti had never been heard of in Delhi nor could anyone remember such a thing in all Hindustan."

4. Several members of the 'Corps of Forty' were poisoned to death secretly.

5. Dr.V.S. Smith states, "By royal command many of the rebels were cast under the feet of elephants... Skinned from head to feet... some of them were hung over every gate of Delhi... One never heard such a tale of terror.

Following were the backgrounders which necessitated the policy of blood and iron :—

Theory of Kingship. Balban realised that problems arose on account of the weak position of the king. He therefore put forward the concept of Divine Right of Kings i.e. the king was the representative of God on earth. None could challenge him. The king was there to rule and the nobles and others were there to obey him. The powers of the king were absolute and he was a despot.

Loose administration. The administration needed a strong ruler to bring about order out of chaos.

Corps of Forty. Balban himself belonged to they 'Corps of Forty' an institution or the group created by Iltutmish for strengthening his position. Iltutmish used this group to get all sort of information about his nobles.

Balban was fully aware of the destructive activities of these. In due course, these slaves became so powerful that the rulers became captives in their hands. Balban realised that they were responsible for the chaotic and unstable condition of the state. Balban considered them as trouble shooters and realised the necessity of getting rid of them through stern measures.

Revolts. There was the danger of revolts of some sections of Muslim chiefs and Rajput rulers.

Mongol invasions. The Mongols posed a serious threat to the empire.

Policy of blood and iron at work : Achievements of Balban

1. *Strengthening the position of the Sultan.* Balban took the following steps in this regard :

(*i*) He glorified the position of the Sultan. He declared that it was the duty of all to submit to him.

(*ii*) He enforced strict discipline in the court ; No one was allowed to indulge in humour or loose talk.

(*iii*) He himself set ideal examples. He gave up drinking. He never came to the court without proper dress.

(*iv*) He prescribed several practices for the nobles of his court. Court dress was fixed.

(*v*) He appointed fearsome and tall guards who were to stand round king's person with naked swords.

All the above mentioned measures created an environment of terror and fear.

2. *Efficient spy system* : Balban kept a close watch on the activities of the governors, nobles, military and civil officers and even on his own sons. Every spy had direct access to the Sultan. The spy system proved very helpful in checking conspiracies.

3. *Liquidation of the Corps of Forty* : Balban very skilfully and sternly eliminated the group of forty slaves. They were humiliated publicly and punished severely. A cup of poison and the dagger of an assassin were equally good for him.

4. *Strengthening administrative structure* : The administration of Balban was partly military and partly civil. All his officers were required to perform both types of duties. He himself kept control over the entire administration. He abolished the post of the 'Naib' (Prime Minister) or Deputy to the Sultan. Balban himself supervised the appointments of all officers. Only people of noble birth were appointed to higher posts.

5. *Providing justice* : Balban succeeded in providing justice to his subjects. Prof. Habibullah has highly praised the sense of justice of Balban. He has quoted instances of punishment of highly placed noble as examples of upholding justice by Balban.

6. *Confiscation of 'fiefs'* (Jagirs) Balban ordered an enquiry regarding the status of the 'Jagirdars'. It was revealed that most of the occupants of Jagirs were not the real owners. So he confiscated such jagirs. This had a salutary effect on feudal lords and they exhibited their loyalty to the Sultan.

7. *Liquidation of thieves and robbers*. Balban very ruthlessly uprooted the menace of thieves and robbers by clearing out their hide outs in the forests.

8. *Massacre of the Mewati Rajputs* : The Mewati Rajputs had become a terror for the people of Delhi. They used to loot, kill and abduct women. Balban crushed the Mewatis with an iron hand. Their hide-outs were besieged and every Mewati caught was immediately killed.

9. *Strengthening army*. Balban realised that to make his despotism effective, to safeguard the empire from the invasion of the Mongols and to suppress rebellion he needed a strong army. He therefore increased the number of officers and soldiers of his army, paid them good salaries and took personal interest in their training. He personally planned every military campaign and kept it secret till the operation day.

10. *Suppression of revolts* Balban suppressed rebellions in the Doab, crushed the revolts of the Hindus of Rohelkhand and mercilessly quelled the revolt of Tughril Khan of Bengal. Balban's reign of terror is described by Barani in these words "On either side of the principal bazar, in a street more than two miles in length, a row of stakes was set up and the followers of Tughril were impaled (put to death) upon them. None of the beholders

(eye-witnesses) had ever a spectacle so terrible, and many swooned with terror and disgust."

11. *Providing effective defence against Mongol invasions*. The Sultans of Delhi had to face the Mongol invasions from the north west. Balban too was not free. He accordingly prepared an effective defence policy which included the following steps :

(*i*) He constructed strong forts in the frontier.

(*ii*) He repaired the old forts.

(*iii*) He kept well-equipped forces therein.

(*iv*) He divided the North-West Frontier into two parts for the purpose of defence.

(*v*) Provinces of Multan, Sindh and Lahore were placed under the charge of prince Mohammad Khan.

The Mongols made their biggest invasion in 1285 in which Balban's son was killed but in the end, the Mongols lost and had to retreat.

Summing up

Dr. Habibullah points out, "By consolidating the conquered areas and destroying the forces of anarchy, he fulfilled a historical need namely, preparing the Sultanate for further expansion."

According to Lane-poole, Balban, the slave, the water carrier, huntsman, general, statesmen and Sultan is one of the most striking figures among notable men in the long line of kings of Delhi."

From Barani's account it is revealed that Balban was greatly loved by his subjects and nobles although he followed the policy of blood and iron. "The *'maliks'* (noble) in grief at Balban's death tore their garments and threw dust on their heads as they followed bare feet, the king's bier to the burial ground at *'Darul Aman'*. For forty days they mourned his death and slept on the bare floor."

In the words of Dr. Ishwari Prasad, "Balban, a great warrior, ruler and statesman, who saved the infant Muslim state from extinction at a critical time, will ever remain a great figure in the Medieval History of India."

About Balban, Elphinston writes, "He had no regard for human life, and no scruples about shedding blood. He was indeed a ruthless king. Fear and awe of him took possession of all men's hearts."

4

Khalji/Khilji Dynasty (1290 to 1320) : Conquests, Administrative and Economic Reforms

Q. 1. Who were Khaljis? Give an estimate of Jalal-ud-Din Khalji, the founder of this dynasty.

Ans. *Khalji Dynasty and Its Founding*

The Khaljis have been mentioned variously—sometimes Turks, sometimes Afghans and sometimes as Indian Muslims.

Achievements of Balban were of a personal nature. The Turkish Sultanate depended upon the personality of the Sultan. Balban, though, himself a successful ruler did not establish a well-organised administrative machinery. All powers were centralised in him. He did not provide adequate opportunity to his sons in the art of government. No wonder, therefore, that the moment his controlling hand disappeared there occurred a scramble to snatch power. After the death of Balban, power game started. Jalal-ud-Din Khalji, the leader of the Khalji group, who was holding the position of the commander of the army under Kaiquhad, the grandson of Balban, took the best advantage of the situation. Kaiqubad had lost all his physical ability because of excessive luxury. The Turkish chiefs made Kaiqubad's son as the Sultan. Jalal-ud-Din proved himself cleverer. He himself sat on the throne of Delhi by murdering Kaiqubad as well as his son and assumed the title of Jalal-ud-Din Firoz Shah. Jalal-ud-Din was 70 years old when he ascended the throne of Delhi. His rule lasted for about 6 years (1290 to 1296).

Policies and Temperament of Jalal-ud-Din

In the words of Prof. S.R. Sharma, "He was too lenient to be a king in an age when blood and iron alone would matter. He was soon overtaken by a whirlwind of troubles that ended, not only by removing the crown from his head but also the head from his shoulders."

Although Jalal-ud-Din had become the Sultan of Delhi after shedding a lot of blood, but after becoming the Sultan, he followed a policy of peace—peace with the robbers, peace with the nobles, peace with the Mongols and peace with all others excepting one of Siddi Maula as described in the later part of this answer. His policy of peace led to his downfall. By following the principle of peace, he sacrificed even the routine principles of governing a state. His policy of 'pardon' in the name of peace proved disastrous to him.

Main Events of the Reign of Jalal-ud-Din

1. *Appointment policy.* His policy of appointments to higher posts had two main features. (*i*) He allowed most of the Turkish nobles to hold their previous posts (*ii*) He assigned high ranks to his own sons and loyal officers to keep control over the administration.

2. *Revolt of Malik Chajju.* Malik Chajju, Balban's nephew and feudal lord of Kara in the district of Allahabad revolted. Arkali Khan, the eldest son of Jalal-ud-Din defeated him near Badaun, arrested him and presented him before the Sultan/ King. The king treated him well. His supporters were released. When his son and the nobles protested against the behaviour of the King, they were silenced by him saying that he was not prepared to shed the blood of the Muslims for the sake of throne. What a contrast in his attitude! He himself had ascended the throne by shedding the blood of several Muslims.

3. *Generosity to the 'thugs' and robbers.* Several thugs and robbers operating around Delhi were captured and presented before the King. However, in place of punishing them, the King let them off with a mild warning and sent them to far off places including Bengal.

4. *Attack on Ranthambhor.* The Rajputs offered a stiff resistance when attacked by the King. He returned without capturing it because he thought the conquest would cause huge bloodshed. He did not think the conquest "worth the hair of even one Musalman." So he ordered his soldiers to retreat.

5. *Generosity to erring nobles.* When Sultan has been campaigning against Ranthambhor, some nobles in a state of drunkenness at a party spoke that they would kill the Sultan. This news reached the ears of the Sultan. He called them to a private audience and instead of punishing them, challenged them for a duel. But when pacified he became satisfied just by turning them out of the court for one year.

6. *Kindness to the Mongols.* The Mongols launched a large scale attack on India during the reign of Jalal-ud-Din. There are two versions regarding the invasion. According to one version, the Sultan himself went to fight against them in Punjab and defeated them. They were pardoned and some of them were allowed to settle near Delhi. The Mongols became Muslims and came to be known as *'Neo Muslims'*.

According to another version, the Sultan succeeded in defeating the advance guard of the Mongols and captured many of them. But, afraid to face the main force of the Mongols, he made peace with them. The Mongols withdrew and some of them were allowed to settle in the suburbs of Delhi.

7. *Execution of Siddi Maula.* The Sultan came to know that some rebellious chiefs had gone to a *'faqir'* Siddi Maula to seek his blessings. It is also said that he suspected that they wanted to declare Siddi Maula as the King. It is not clear whether Siddi Maula was innocent or not or that

he was a party to the conspiracy against the Sultan. Nevertheless the Sultan got him trampled under the feet of an elephant. Other conspirators were either exiled or their property was confiscated. After becoming the Sultan of Delhi, this perhaps was the only case where the Sultan acted so sternly.

8. *Expeditions.* Two bold expeditions were undertaken by Ala-ud-Din, the nephew and son-in-law of the Sultan. One expedition was to Bhilsa undertaken after seeking permission of the Sultan. Ala-ud-Din plundered Bhilsa and sent a past of the booty to the Sultan.

The second expedition to Devagiri was undertaken by Ala-ud-Din without the permission of the Sultan. From this expedition, Ala-ud-Din got huge indemnity, horses and elephants etc. There is no doubt that Ala-ud-Din got enormous wealth from this expedition.

9. *Treachery of Ala-ud-Din and murder of Jalal-ul-Din.* Ala-ud-Din, after having defeated the ruler of Devagiri, returned with fabulous wealth. Jalal-ul-Din was besides with joy. However some of his close nobles suspected some foul play but the Sultan paid no heed to them and went to Kara to receive Ala-ud-Din. Ala-ud-Din had hatched a conspiracy and assassinated his uncle-cum-father-in-law treacherously and declared himself the king of Delhi. In this regard Dr. V.A. Smith has observed, "In fact, his attentions were potent to every body except his doting uncle and father-in-law, who closed his ears against all warnings and behaved like a person infatuated." Lane-poole has observed that Jalal-ud-Din's murder was the "most spiteful event" of the Indian history.

Q.2. Give an assessment of the rule of Ala-ud-Din Khalji. What is his place among the rulers in India?

Ans. *Assessment of Ala-ud-Din's Rule.*

For having an objective assessment of the rule of Ala-ud-Din, we may consider the following aspects :

1. Objectives of Ala-ud-Din.
2. Ala-ud-Din's Theory of Kingship.
3. Conquests of Ala-ud-Din
4. Suppression of Revolts : Administrative Reforms.
5. Economic Policy. Revenue Reforms, Market Control.
6. Military Reforms.
7. Religious Matters.
8. Development of Arts.

I. Objectives of Ala-ud-Din.

Ala-ud-Din was very ambitious. Two great ambitions in his mind were:

(*a*) Firstly, he began to dream of founding a new religion like Mohammad the Prophet.

(*b*) Secondly, he wished to be a world conqueror like Alexander.

The account of the means to achieve these ambitions and aims is given in his own words, "God had given Mohammad four friends with whose help Islam was founded, and by laying the foundation of Islam Muhammad immortalised his name until Doom's Day. Likewise, God has given me also four friends, Ulugh Khan, Zafar Khan, Nusrat Khan, and Alap Khan. (four commanders). If I wish I too can with the help of these four friends lay the foundation of a new religion. My friends swords and mine own can compelmankind to profess the new religion, my name and those of my friends will exist till Doom's Day. I possess treasure, elephants and a countless army. I wish to make over the charge of Delhi kingdom to a Viceroy and launch myself a course of conquests with this army like Alexander till I conquer the whole world."

However, on the advice of Qazi Ala-ul-Malik, the uncle of the famous historian Barani, Ala-ud-Din modified his plans.

In respect of his first aim the Qazi told Ala-ud-Din, "Religion and Law originate from God alone and they are never planned by man. Laying the foundation or religion has been the work of prophets since Adam to this day. The prophet's performance (work) is quite different from that of a king. No king can ever do the work of a prophet properly and adequately. Hence, it is my advice to you that you should ever avoid thinking about such matters."

With regard to Ala-ud-Din's second aim, the sagacious Qazi said to him, "To plan the world-conquest like Alexander is too impracticable (impossible) because the times are different from that of Alexander in the first place. Besides this, you do not have any adviser like Aristotle who planned Alexander's course of conquests. Hence, it is but proper for you to conquer far-lying parts of India and bring them under your domination. Moreover, it is imperative for you to defend the country from the Mongol invasions by ensuring the safety of the roads in the North-West Frontier of the country."

Now Ala-ud-Din aimed at the following:

1. Promotion of Islam but not according to the plans of the *Ulemas*, (Priestly Muslim Class)
2. Conquest of India.
3. Defending the country from Mongol invasions.

II. Ala-ud-Din's Theory of Kingship

Ala-ud-Din believed in the Divine Right of the King i.e. the King was God's representative on earth and was there to rule. Others were there to obey him. He used to say, "I do not know whether this is lawful or unlawful, Whatever I think to be for the good of the state or suitable for the emergency, I do". He did not allow anyone to interfere in his work. He was an autocrat, despot, expansionist and an imperialist.

III. Conquests of Ala-ud-Din

Ala-ud-Din's conquests may be categorised under the following two heads :

A. Conquests of North India.

B. Conquests of South India.

A. Conquests of North India

1. *Conquest of Gujarat* (*1299*). Chief cities of Gujarat namely, Anhilwara and Somnath were plundered and sacked. An enormous booty was collected. The Sultan's army also captured a promising Hindu youngman who later on came to be known as Malik Kafur. Malik Kafur played an important role in extending the Kingdom of Ala-ud-Din.

2. *Conquest of Ranthambhor* (*1299-1301*). The Sultan had to wage a fierce and prolonged battle to capture the strong fort of Ranthambhor.

3. *Conquest of Chittor* (*1303*). The popular episode of Rani Padmini, the beautiful queen of Raja Ratan Singh, saving from the captivity of Ala-ud-Din through not adequately authenticated by historical records is often cited in the conquest of Chittor. The Rajputs offered stiff resistance but were finally defeated. Padmini with other Rajput women performed *'Johar'* (Immolation of Rajput women to preserve their purity and to protect themselves from captivity or pollution by the enemy.)

4. *Conquest of Malwa* (*1305*). Ala-ud-Din conquered all the territories of Malwa, including Ujjain, Dhar, Chanderi and Mandu.

5. *Other conquests in North India.* Ala-ud-Din conquered Siwana, Jalor, Bundi, Mandor, Tonk and probably Jodhpur. Thus the whole of Rajasthan came under his domination.

B. Conquests of Deccan and South India

There were two important objectives of the conquests of the Deccan and South India:

1. To possess the wealth of the prosperous southern states whom Ala-ud-Din regarded as milch cow for gold. (2) To get the credit of conquering southern kingdoms.

It is important to remember that he did not annex these states. He accepted the kingdoms as tributary states. He felt contended when they accepted his suzerainty, agreed to pay annual tributes and to act in all manners as his subordinates.

The credit for making these states subordinate to Ala-ud-Din goes to Malik Kafur who attacked south four times and brought with him enormous wealth which included about 300 elephants, 20,000 horses, 2,700 pounds of gold/equal in value to 10 crores of Tankas—rupee), and chests of jewels. It is said, "No such booty had ever before been brought to Delhi."

IV. Suppression of Revolts : Administrative Reforms

On analysis of revolts of the nobles, Ala-ud-Din found the following causes :

(*i*) Ineffective Spy System

(*ii*) Drinking parties among the nobles.

(*iii*) Intermarriages among the nobles.

(*iv*) Social intercourse among the nobles.

(*v*) Excess of wealth with the nobles which gave them both leisure and power for indulging in devilish thoughts and rebellions.

Having analysed the causes, the Sultan took the following measures to curb the power of the nobles :—

(*a*) Organisation of an efficient Spy System to acquaint himself with the activities of the officers, governors and nobles etc.

(*b*) Restriction on social gatherings.

(*c*) Prohibition policy which prohibited the sale and use of wine.

(*d*) Setting an example by the Sultan himself to refrain from his wine and breaking down all his wine vessels in public.

(*e*) Confiscation of property and stoppage of grants on various pretexts.

V. Economic Policy : Revenue Reforms and Market Control

The economic policy of Ala-ud-Din was primarily guided by the huge expenditure to be incurred on the maintenance of a strong army and making the nobles poor by extracting wealth from them. The Sultan's main concern was to enable the soldiers to live on their pay and to have necessities of life i.e.. goods at a price within their reach. To this he evolved the system of controlling prices of daily use and ensured that these were easily made available.

(For details see the next question.)

VI. Military Reforms

Ala-ud-Din based his Kingship on military power. He, therefore, maintained a strong army for crushing internal revolts, for expanding his Kingdom and for checking the Mongol invasions. He provided the army with several types of new weapons and reasonable salaries.

(For details see the next question.)

VII. Religious Matters

Historians have expressed divergent opinions regarding the religious policy of Ala-ud-Din. Prof. S.R. Sharma, Dr. S. Roy and Sir Woolseley Haig are of the view that Ala-ud-Din policy towards the Hindus was actuated by communal and religious considerations. On the other hand, Dr. U.N. Dey, Dr. K.S. Lal and Dr. R.P. Tripathi are of the view that economic measures which Ala-ud-Din took to take away wealth did affect the Hindus adversely and were truly oppressive but these were adopted not on religious considerations but on economic and political considerations. The Hindus had to pay several taxes. One half of the gross produce of the land was extracted from them.

According to Eliot, "The Hindus were reduced to a state of abject misery to such an extent that the wives of '*Khuts*' and '*Muqaddams*' (Hindu officers of various ranks) went and served for hire in the house of *Musalmans*"

In the words of Dr. V.S. Smith," He required his advisers to draw up rules and regulations for grinding down the Hindus, and for depriving them of that wealth and prosperity which fosters disaffection and rebellion."

Dr. U.N. Dey has observed," The *'Khuts'* and *'Muqaddams'* at no stage of Indian history ever reached that stage of poverty as is told about his reign."

Sir Woolseley Haig writes, "Hindus, throughout the Kingdom were reduced to one dead level of poverty and misery."

To sum up, Ala-ud-Din's policy towards the Hindus was motivated by economic, political as well as religious considerations. Of course, in his policy he was not dictated by the Muslim Ulemas.

VIII. Development of Arts

Though Ala-ud-Din was illiterate yet he was a patron of art and literature. His court was adorned with great poets and scholars like Amir Khusro, Amir Hasan and Qazi Ala-ul-Malik. During his reign Delhi became the rival of Cairo. Ala-ud-Din also constructed several good buildings including the Siri Fort, Palace of One Thousand Pillars called *'Hazar Situn'*, many mosques, tanks including the famous Shamsi Tank and 'Sarais'. His *Alai Darwaza,* an extension of Qutbi Mosque in Delhi, is regarded as one of the best specimens of early Turkish architecture.

General Assessment of Ala-ud-Din by Historians

(a) Appreciation of Ala-ud-Din.

Dr. A.L. Srivastva concludes, "A balanced view of Ala-ud-Din's work and achievement must give him a high place among the rulers of Delhi during the medieval age."

Eliphinstone felt, "The rule of Ala-ud-Din was glorious and he was a successful monarch who exhibited a just exercise of his power."

Ferishta praises his law and order as, "The traveller slept secure on the highways and the merchant carried his commodities in safety from the Sea of Bengal to the mountains of Kabul and from Tellingana to Kashmir."

Lane-poole writes, "Though he might be wronged-headed and disdainful of the law, Ala-ud-Din was a man of determination."

Dr. K.S. Lal states, "From nothingness he rose to be one of the greatest rulers of medieval India."

Dr. S.R. Sharma writes, "Ala-ud-Din was the first Muslim Emperor of India. During his reign, for the first time, the present (Muslim flag) dominated over the whole country from the Himalayas to Cape Commorin and from Sea to sea."

Dr. S. Roy writes, "Ala-ud-Din was the Muslim administrator of India, The History of Muslim empire and administration in India really begins with him."

(b) Criticism of Ala-ud-Din

According to Dr. S. Roy, "As a king he was ruthless and as a man treacherous and ungrateful."

Prof. S.R. Sharma is very critical of Ala-ud-Din's policy towards the Hindus, "The choice forced by Ala-ud-Din to the Hindus was to be hewers of wood and drawers of water."

Dr. V.S. Smith writes, "Ala-ud-Din was a particularly savage tyrant with very little regard for justice. His reign was exceedingly disgraceful in many respects."

Sir Woolseley Haig's opinion is, "Hindus throughout the Kingdom were reduced to one dead level of poverty and misery."

Q. 3. Examine the administrative and military reforms introduced by Ala-ud-Din.

Ans. *Ala-ud-Din as a great Administrator.*

Main features of his Administrative Reforms

1. *Centralised administration.* Ala-ud-Din attempted to translate his theory of Kingship that the king was the representative of God on earth and that he was there to rule, through the administrative practices. His word was law. He was an absolute despot. He possessed unlimited powers. He was the head i.e. Commander in Chief of the army, head of the executive, head of the judiciary and the sole authority in enforcing religious matters. All powers of affairs of the state were centralised in him. He used to say, "I do not know whether this is lawful or unlawful, Whatever I think to be for the good of the state or suitable for the emergency that I decree." In the words of Ashraf, "the Sultan of Delhi was in theory an unlimited despot, bound by no law, subject to no material check and guided by no will except his own." The prevailing circumstances needed such a strong monarch to run the affairs of the state effectively and without any kind of interference.

2. *Administration free from the influence of the ulemas.* In the words of Dr. Ishwari Parsad, "Ala-ud-Din was opposed to the interference of the Ulemas in matters of state and in this respect he departed from the tradition of the previous Sultans of Delhi. The law was to depend upon the will of the monarch and had nothing to do with the law of the Prophet. This was the guiding maxim of the new monarch."

Dr. R.P. Tripathi has observed, "Kingship could exist without any special religious support and that the outlook of a King was very different from that of the clergy. This was the greatest contribution of Ala-ud-Din."

3. *Role of Ministers.* The Sultan appointed trusted ministers to assist him in the running of administration. Their advice was in no way binding on the Sultan. There were 10 ministers to assist him.

Next to Sultan was the 'Wazir', who was both a civil and military officer. Among the ministers, mention may be made of the *'Amir-Kohi'* incharge of agriculture and *'Shahana-i-Mandi'* and *'Dewan-i-Riyat*-looking after markets.

4. *Provincial administration.* The entire country was divided into 11 provinces. Each province was under a governor who enjoyed his position at the pleasure of the Sultan.

5. *Judicial administration.* According to Prof. K.S. Lal, the Sultan was as relentless and unflinching in administering justice as Balban. The Sultan was the fountain of justice. He was the final court of appeal . Next to him was 'Qazi-ul-Qazat or Lord Chief justice. Then were other junior judicial officers.

The punishments inflicted upon the accused persons were very severe. Mutilation of limbs and torture were very common.

6. *Efficient system of espionage.* The system of espionage organised by Ala-ud-Din was very systematic and effective. According to Zia-ud-Din Barani, "No one could stir without his (Ala-ud-Din's) knowledge and whatever happened in the houses of the Maliks and Amirs, officers and greatmen was communicated to the Sultan. Day and night did they tremble in their own houses an account of the activity of the patrol. Nor did they do anything nor utter a single word which would subject them to reproof or punishment." A similar account of the espionage is given by Moreland, "He (Ala-ud-Din) organised so effective a system of espionage that no body dared to whisper a seditious word. The jovial atmosphere of the capital turned into suspicious gloom but conspiracy for the time being was at its end."

7. ***Administrative measures to check the power of the nobles. and their tendency to revolt.*** After having wide-range consultations, Ala-ud-Din came to the conclusion that following were the causes of revolts :

(*i*) Inefficiency of the spy system resulting in the ignorance of the Sultan regarding the state of affairs in the country.

(*ii*) Existence of huge wealth with the nobles resulting in leisure time leading to conspiracies.

(*iii*) Drinking parties among nobles bringing them close to each other and encouraging them to conspire.

(*iv*) Social intercourse and inter-marriages among the families of nobles making them a compact body dangerous to the state and also forming antagonistic groups among themselves, leading to rivalry.

For exercising control over the activities of the nobles, the king took the following measures :

(1) Organisation of an efficient spy system.

(2) Confiscation of jagirs given to nobles, on one pretext or the other.

(3) Prohibition of the sale and use of wine and other intoxicating drugs.

(4) Restrictions on social gatherings and inter-marriages among the nobles.

8. *Administrative measures for the market control.* (Discussed separately).

9. *Organisation of the postal system.* Ala-ud-Din established a proper postal system for establishing a regular contact with various parts of the empire. In his book *"Medieval Routes in India,"* Dr. H.C. Varma writes that Sultan Ala-ud-Din posted several horsemen and clerks in the news posts. From the accounts of Ibn Batutah and Barani, it appears that postal system was in good condition during Ala-ud-Din's reign.

Military Reforms

Army as the basis of strength. Ala-ud-Din's position was threatened on the one hand by the revolts of the nobles and Rajputs and on the other hand by the Mongols who occasionally invaded the frontier of India in the north-west. Moreover, he desired to extend his empire. All these needed a well-equipped army. As observed by Dr. P. Saran, "The problem of maintaining the huge army in a good state of equipment and efficiency with limited resources of the kingdom was the sole motive which prompted control of prices of all necessities of life so as to make them cheap enough for the soldiery to maintain themselves on the low salaries which they were to be paid according to the decision of the Sultan."

It may be remembered that Ala-ud-Din based his kingship on his military power. He was fully aware that he had usurped power by force and the same could be maintained only by force and this force was his military force.

Ala-ud-Din owed everything to his efficient military.

Strength of the army. It is not possible to give the exact strength of his army. Ferishta informs us that Ala-ud-Din maintained 4,75,000 cavalry men. (Horse riders). The strength of the infantry must have exceeded the cavalry. War elephants also constituted an important part of the army.

Among other weapons like swords, bows and arrows, stone-throwing machines were also used in battles.

Main features of the reforms in the army

1. For the first time army was paid in cash.

2. Three grades of soldiers, were fixed. A foot soldier was paid 156 *'tankas'* (silver rupees) a year. The soldier with one horse was paid, 234 *'tankas'* and with two horses 312 *'tankas'* i.e. 78 *'tankas'* more. In this salary, the soldier had to look after his horse/horses and other things. It is

observed that the amount paid to a soldier was not a small sum for the first decade of the 14th century. During the reign of Sher Shah it was 230 *'tankas'* i.e. 4 *'tankas'* less. During Akbar's time in the 16th century, it was 240 *'tankas'* i.e. more by four *'tankas'* only.

3. The *'Ariz-i-Mamlik'* (Army Minister) himself recruited the soldiers of the army.

4. Ala-ud-Din was the first Sultan to keep a standing army at the centre. He did not depend upon the feudal chiefs for the supply of the soldiers.

5. Ala-ud-Din, instituted the practice of recording the *'hulia'* (description) of individual soldier and *'dagging'* (branding of horses). This helped to stop corrupt practices like giving inflated figures of the soldiers and horses.

7. Army was given suitable training.

7. Army was properly equipped.

8. A periodical inspection was made and horses and arms of the soldiers were thoroughly examined.

9. Old forts were repaired and new forts were constructed.

10. Soldiers were permanently kept in these forts and suitable arrangements were made for the regular supply of arms to them.

11. Grains and fodder always remained stored in the forts.

12. Well-trained and loyal commanders were appointed in the army organisation.

13. Ala-ud-Din kept spies in every unit of the army. They submitted regular reports to him about the movements of the military officers.

14. Ala-ud-Din controlled the price of the essential commodities which enabled the soldiers to make a good living within their salaries.

Q. 4. Critically examine the economic reforms of Ala-ud-Din Khalji.
(Delhi University, 1997 and Rajasthan University 1994)

Or

Discuss the revenue and financial policy of Ala-ud-Din.

Or

Examine the economic policy followed by Ala-ud-Din.

Ans. *Chief considerations in the formulation of the Economic Policy.*

Ala-ud-Din's economic policy was guided by the following considerations :

1. To raise as much finance as possible so as to maintain a well-equipped strong and large army.

2. To reduce the wealth of the nobles and other sections of the society as Ala-ud-Din believed that too much of wealth with them was the most importance cause of the revolts.

3. To provide essential commodities of daily use so that the soldiers could enjoy a reasonable standard of living in their pay.

4. To fix up price of the essential commodities and for this to control the market through a well-regulated system and machinery.

In the words of Dr. P. Saran, "The problem of maintaining the huge army in a good state of equipment and efficiency with limited resources of the kingdom was the sole motive which prompted control of all necessities of life so as to make them cheap enough for the soldiery to maintain themselves on the low salaries which they were to be paid."

Important Economic Measures

1. *Collection of wealth from the nobles.* All lands which were held by the people as gifts, pensions, endownments etc. from the state were confiscated. The officers were instructed to extort money from the people by every possible means so that no body remained rich.

2. *Reducing the wealth of the Hindus.* Although there is no unanimity among the historians regarding impoverishment of the Hindus by the Sultan, yet in general it is stated that his policy was guided by religious, political as well as economic considerations. According to Dr. K.S. Lal, Ala-ud-Din was convinced that the Hindus would not stop revolting unless their wealth was snatched away from them.

3. *Land revenue policy.* Ala-ud-Din raised the land revenue to one-half of the gross produce of the land. The land revenue was to be assessed by the method of measurement on the basis of standard yield. Land revenue could be paid in cash and kind but the king preferred payment in cash as he had introduced the practice of paying salaries to the soldiers in cash.

4. *Taxes other than land revenue.* Several kinds of taxes were in vogue. Grazing tax on milch cattle was the new tax imposed. House tax was another new tax. Other important taxes were : irrigation tax, *'Jizya'* tax and import and export duties on several articles.

Muslim merchants paid 5 per cent of their merchandise as tax and the Hindu merchants had to pay 10 per cent.

5. *Creation of the revenue department.* A new department known as *'Diwan-i-Mustakharaj'* was established to collect revenue systematically. This was also designed to have an effective check on the revenue officials so as to deter them from adopting corrupt practices. A close watch was kept on the 'Amils' and Patwaris. Their accounts were audited and the guilty were punished very severely. Ala-ud-Din also raised the salaries of the revenue officers so that they might not be tempted to bribery. The policy yielded good results.

6. *Market control.* Ala-ud-Din was the first monarch who fixed the prices of commodities like wheat, barley, gram, rice, urad, sugar, ghee, cloth, horses, milch animals and even of slaves.

7. *Grain markets.* The government set up grain markets and state granaries from where the people could buy grains at controlled prices.

8. *Rationing system.* During natural calamities, every family was given a fixed quantity of grain. In a way, this system was like the modern system of rationing.

9. *Control of weights and measures.* He introduced the system of fixed weights and measures. If any trader weighed less than the actual weight he was punished very severely.

The system of land revenue was confined to Delhi and nearby territories. According to Dr. R.S. Tripathi, this system was not introduced in lower Doab, Awadh, Bihar, Bengal, Malwa, West Punjab, Gujarat and Sindh.

Assessment of the Economic Policy of Ala-ud-Din

In general it is admitted by most of the historians that Ala-ud-Din succeeded in fulfilling his objectives by his economic policy. His primary objects were to increase the income of the state for the maintenance of the army and rooting out the possibilities of revolts. He achieved both.

However opinions differ regarding the impact of his policy on the peasantry and the common man.

The revenue policy of Ala-ud-Din imposed a heavy burden on the peasantry. Probably, in some cases, the peasants had to pay 75 per cent to 80 per cent of their income to the state as taxes.

In the words of Dr. Tara Chand, "The policy was suicidal for it killed the goose that laid the golden egg. It left no incentive for increasing the produce or improving the method of cultivation."

Dr. U.N. Dey has commended favourably. He states, "The peasants do not seem to have materially affected much." Dr. Ifran Habib has stated, "Ala-ud-Din consciously utilised the conflict between the two rural 'classes' by standing forth as the protector of the 'weak' against "strong' in these villages and was perfectly reasonable."

Dr. R.S. Tripathi justifies Ala-ud-Din's policy of confiscating land grants, "He took up this measure to assert the right of the monarch to deal with all classes of lands, cancelled all such grants which he did not approve and bestowed others on his own terms."

Merits of Ala-ud-Din's Economic Policy

1. With the abolition of land grants, the state treasury's revenue increased.

2. By reducing the wealth of the nobles, the chances of internal revolts were minimised.

3. Stern measures adopted to check the malpractices of the revenue officials provided some relief to the peasants and at the same time provided more revenue to the government.

4. Control over price of essential commodities enabled the soldiers to lead reasonable standard of life.

5. The system of rationing enabled the people to get relief from natural calamities.

6. Fixing of weights and measures proved very helpful to consumers.

7. By collecting sufficient revenue it became possible for Ala-ud-Din to maintain a strong army.

Demerits of the Economic policy of Ala-ud-Din

1. The peasants had to pay high taxes which sometimes were as high as 80 per cent of the produce of their land. This had an adverse affect on them.

2. The profit margin of the traders was reduced on account of market control. This reduced their incentive.

3. Economic policy had an adverse affect on agricultural production. The peasants were required to sell their produce at a fixed price which was not quite remunerative to them, Their motivation for increased production received some setback.

Q. 5. What is the meaning of market control? State the main characteristics of the market control policy of Ala-ud-Din? Why did he introduce this policy? What were its effects?

Or

Give an outline of the main characteristics of market system of Ala-ud-Din. Do you think that the market regulations were wholly superficial and impractical?

(Punjab University April 1997, April 1998)

Or

Critically examine the market control regulations of Ala-ud-Din.

Ans. *Meaning of Market Control.*

Market control implies the state interference in the supply and sale of commodities. In the open market buyers and sellers are free to enter into transactions. There is no check on the supply and sale price of the commodities. Government control in the supply and price of commodities is the minimum. There is free competition among buyers and sellers. Market control does not allow the free operation of the forces of demand and supply.

Market control is exercised through a number of regulations imposed by the government.

Market control may be limited or unlimited. It depends upon the objectives of the government.

Main Features of the Market Control

1. *Fixation of prices.* Prices were fixed not only of varieties of grains, pulses, cloth, cattle and horses but also of articles like meat, fish, dry fruits, sugarcane, vegetables, betal-leaves etc.—all articles of daily use. Even prices of slaves were also fixed.

A comparative study of prices would be quite interesting.

(*a*) *Prices of essential commodities*

(*i*)	Wheat-price	per *'maund'* (28/Lbs)	7.5 jitals
(*ii*)	Barley	price per *'maund'* (28 Pounds)	4 jitals
(*iii*)	Rice in bush	price per *'maund'*	5 jitals
(*iv*)	Mash	price per *'maund'*	5 jitals
(*v*)	Pulse	price per *'maund'*	2 jitals
(*vi*)	Sugar	price per *'seer'*	1.1 jitals
(*vii*)	Butter	price per *'seer*	1 jitals
(*viii*)	Salt	price per *'maund'*	2 jitals

(*b*) *Others*

(*i*) A maid servant 5-12 *'tankas'*

(*ii*) A slave labourer 10-15 *'tankas'*

Note : one *'tanka'* was equal to about one rupee, one *'jital'* was equal to 3 paisa.

Pay of the Soldiers

(*a*) A foot Soldier	156 *'tankas'*
(*b*) A soldier with one horse	234 *'tankas'*
(*c*) A soldier with 2 horses	312 *'tankas'*

Soldiers could lead a reasonable standard of living with this salary.

2. *Grain market.* Ala-ud-Din opened government stores of grains to sell them from where everybody could buy. The peasants brought their surplus grain in the market. The government officials made purchases of grain from them, stored it in their stores and sold it to the people.

3. *Cloth market.* The cost of cloth was comparatively higher than the food articles. The cloth market sold a variety of cloth. Cloth merchants were given advances to purchase cloth from outside and sell it in Delhi at fixed prices.

4. *Slave market.* In the slave market, slaves were bought and sold like any other commodity.

5. *Rationing system.* During the time of famine or other natural calamity, the king introduced rationing system for the people of Delhi. Under this system, half a maund of grain was given to every family in distress.

6. *Government granaries.* The Government had established godowns for storing grain in reserve to be released in time of scarcity. In every *'mohalla'*, there were two or three royal stores filled with food stuffs.

7. *Appointment of officials.* A special officer known as *'Diwan-i-Riyast'* was appointed to look after the working of the system. *The Shahana-i-Mandir* was the Superintendent of the grain market. Marketing officers were appointed to fix price, to ensure that the fixed prices were charged. The officials were required to ensure that the traders complied with the instructions issued to them by the Sultan.

Quality control officials were appointed to check the quality of the articles supplied by the traders to the consumers.

8. *Determination of weights and measures.* The government prescribed weights and measures and no body dared to sell any commodity underweights as the same amount of flesh was cut off from his body.

9. *Registration of traders.* A person desiring of entering into trade was required to get himself registered.

10. *Ban on hoarding.* No producer or trader could indulge in hoarding. Severe punishments were inflicted upon the law breakers.

11. *Information of market through children.* The king used to send small children to test the honesty of the traders. Those who cheated children were given severe punishment.

12. *Spy system.* Ala-ud-Din's spy system was very elaborate and trustworthy. The king kept himself well-informed of the working of the control system of the market through the spies.

13. *Control of supplies.* Ala-ud-Din realised that mere fixation of prices was not enough and it had to be enforced with the regular supply of commodities. He, therefore, established government stores of different commodities.

14. *Control of transport.* Traders and *'banjaras'* who carried goods from one place to another were registered. Every possible facility was provided to them in the transportation of goods.

Were market regulation enforced only in Delhi?

There is no unanimity among the historians whether the market control was in force in various parts of the country or in Delhi alone. Dr. S.K. Lal is of the view that the system was in force in Delhi only. He gives the following arguments in this regard :

(1) Barani has mentioned the officers namely Diwan-i-Riyasat and Shahana-Mandi only in the context of Delhi. No reference to these officers is found in respect of other cities.

(2) Registration of traders was compulsory only in Delhi.

(3) Only one cloth market is mentioned and that too at Sarai Adl in Delhi.

Reasons for the introduction of market control system

Military considerations. According to Dr. K.S. Lal, the system of market control was introduced on military considerations. Ala-ud-Din's army expenses were enormous. He therefore reduced the salary of the soldiers. However, for enabling them to have a reasonable standard of living, he fixed the price of the commodities in such a way as the soldiers could afford them. He writes, "It was simple arithmetical calculation and simple economic principle; since he had decided to reduce and fix the salary of soldiers, he also decided to reduce and fix the price of common use."

Checking price-rise. Dr. U.N. Dey does not agree with the views of Dr. K.S. Lal. According to him Ala-ud-Din did not pay a low salary to the soldiers when we compare their salary paid to soldiers by Sher Shah and Akbar. He has concluded, "Ala-ud-Din's motive was to check the rising prices which was due to manipulation of the business community and not to reduce the prices to a lower level than the normal."

Humanitarian considerations. According to Shaikh Nasir-ud-Din Chirag, the author of *'Khairul Majalis'*, the police of market control introduced by Ala-ud-Din was on humanitarian grounds. Ala-ud-din according to him was greatly concerned with public welfare.

Reducing wealth to check rebellions. Prof. Habib and Nizami do not agree with the views of Shaikh Nasir-ud-Din. They are of the view that Ala-ud-Din's clear motive was to make the people poor so that the word rebellion should go out of their mind.

Administrative necessity. Ala-ud-Din wanted to reduce administrative expenditure which meant reduced salaries but availability of essential commodities at low prices. Hence price regulation was an administrative necessity.

After perusing the arguments of various scholars, it may be concluded that no single reason can be subscribed. Ala-ud-Din's policy of market control was the outcome of several considerations.

Was the systems of market control artificial or effective?

Merits of the system. The system served the purpose for which it was introduced. Ala-ud-Din was able to maintain a 'well-armed' 'well equipped', 'well-mounted' and 'well trained' army for the system proved helpful in fixing the salaries of the soldiers in such a manner that they could get the necessities of daily use at reasonable prices.

With the introduction of rationing, people were relieved of the fear of drought and famine.

Common people were able to get essential commodities at reasonable rates.

Demerits. The merchants and the shopkeepers were not happy with the system. The fear of severe punishment deprived them of their peace of mind. In this regard Dr. Ishwari Prasad writes, "The Sultan used to send his slaves to the market to bring such things as bread, meat, etc. and when they came back, the articles which they brought were weighed. If they weighed less, an equal quantity of flesh was cut off from the hunches of the shopkeepers concerned to make up the deficiency in weight."

The nobles accustomed to a life of abundance did not cherish this system. The farmers condition was worsened.

According to Barani, "So long Ala-ud-Din ruled, prices of commodities never rose or fell but even remained fixed."

Lane-poole calls Ala-ud-Din "a great political economist."

Dr. S. Roy writes, "The capital was fed, while the country at large was bled."

Dr. K.S. Lal states, "The motive of the Sultan may not have been to crush the poor peasants against whom he possibly could have no grudge, but the exigencies of the state required him to take such steps under which the interests of commerce and cultivation were sacrificed to those of the army."

Dr. P. Saran has concluded, "A full consideration of their circumstances (traders) under the price control system leads as to the irresitible conclusion that they were the hardest hit."

Irrational and superficial policy. In the words of Dr. P. Saran, "The whole account of the new deal of Ala-ud-Din points to one conclusion and one alone that it was a thoroughly irrational, ill-conceived and artificial system being in flagrant violation of all economic laws, extended primarily for the benefit of the Government and it resulted in incalculable misery, poverty and humiliation of the people"

According to Eliot, "The Hindus were reduced to a state of abject misery to such an extent that the wives of *'Khuts'* and *'magadams'* (Hindu revenue officials) went and served for hire in the houses of Musalmans."

Dr. V.A. Smith's opinion about the economic reforms and market control policy of Ala-ud-Din is as, "His measures succeeded in preserving artificial cheapness in the markets of capital (Delhi) even during the years of drought but at the cost of infinite oppression. All his fantastic regulations died with him."

One of the wonders of the age. Even though Dr. K.S. Lal has pointed out several defects of the price control system, he appreciates this policy as "What is of real importance in Ala-ud-Din's reign is not so much the cheapness of prices, as the establishment of a fixed price in the market which was considered one of wonders of the age."

Q. 6. Discuss the principles of Ala-ud-Din's theory of kingship and their practical implications.

Ans. *Ala-ud-Din's theory of kingship.*

Ala-ud-Din maintained that the Sultan was God's representative on earth.

Ala-ud-Din's theory of kingship may be explained in the words of historian, Ashraf, "The Sultan of Delhi was in theory an unlimited despot, bound by no law, subject to no material check, and guided by no will except his own."

The Sultan used to say, "I do not know whether this is lawful or unlawful, whatever I think to be for the good of the state or suitable for the emergency, that I decree and as for what may happen to me on the approaching Day of Judgement that I know not."

Principles of Ala-ud-Din's theory of kingship

1. Kingship was the creation of God.
2. The king was God's representative on earth.
3. The king was there to rule.
4. The king's authority could not be challenged.
5. The king's word was law.
6. The king was not bound by the advice of anyone.
7. The king was supreme in matters of religion. He was not to be guided by the power of the Ulemas.
8. The king should expand his territories.
9. The king should devote himself to the good of the people.

Practical Implications of the Theory of Kingship

All powers in one individual. Ala-ud-Din combined in himself all powers. He was the Commander-in-Chief, the Supreme Administrator, the Chief Justice and the Temporal Head.

Desire for world conquest. Ala-ud-Din's desire to conquer the world was derived from his theory of Kingship. Ala-ud-Din wanted to be the ruler of the entire world. Of course, on the advice of the kotwal of Delhi, he gave up this idea but decided to bring the whole of India under his sway.

Desire for founding a new religion. Ala-ud-Din wanted to set up a new religion. However, again on the advice of Qazi Ala-ul-Mulk who was also the Kotwal of Delhi, he gave up this idea. Nevertheless he decided to work independently in matters of religion and freed himself from the religious scholars (Ulemas).

Vast conquests. Ala-ud-Din believed that a king should constantly extend his empire by conquests so that his name might become immortal. He, therefore, made all possible efforts to bring the whole of India under his influence.

Autocratic rule. He believed that an autocratic rule was necessary for the stability and consolidation of royalty. Accordingly, he took various severe measures to check the powers of the nobles, He confiscated the property of several nobles. He established an efficient spy system to keep himself well informed of the affairs of the state.

Issue of regulations. To prove that he was also a temporal head, he issued some regulations regarding inflicting punishments which were not in accordance with the Muslim law. Dr. Ishwari Prasad in this regard has observed, "Ala-ud-Din was opposed to the interference of the *'Ulemas'* in matters of state and in this respect he departed from the previous position of the Sultans of Delhi. The law was to depend upon the will of the monarch and had nothing to do with the law of the Prophet. This was the guiding maxim of the monarch."

As Dr. R.P. Tripathi observes, "Kingship could exist without any special religious support and that the outlook of a king was different from that of the clergy. This was the greatest contribution of Ala-ud-Din.

Ministers' advice. The king was the head of the administration. In the discharge of his kingly duties, Ala-ud-Din had certain ministers to assist him but their advice was not binding on him.

Public welfare. Though Ala-ud-Din believed in assuming all powers in accordance with his theory of kingship, yet he was not averse to public welfare. In his despotism where was no lack of concern for public welfare.

Dispenser of justice. His theory of justice derived its inspiration from the theory of kingship which proclaims that a king must do justice. He dispensed justice in the open court.

According to Dr. Ishwari Prasad, "The reign of Ala-ud-Din represents the high watermark of despotism."

Lane-poole calls Ala-ud-Din "a bloody and unscrupulous tyrant."

In the words of Dr. V.A. Smith, "He was particularly a savage tyrant—exceedingly disgraceful in many respects."

Lane-poole has summed up the personality and rule of Ala-ud-Din in these words, "Though he might be wrong-headed and disdainful of the low, he was a man of determination, who knew his own mind, saw the necessity of the situation, met it by his own methods, and carried out those methods, with persistence."

Q. 7. Write notes on

(*i*) Ala-ud-Din and Mongol Invasions.

(*ii*) Malik Kafur

(*iii*) Amir Khusro.

Ans. *(i)* Ala-ud-Din and Mongol Invasions.

The eyes of Mongols—a great power in Central Asia—were set on the fabulous wealth of India. They had threatened the security of the north-west of India during the time of Balban also. Balban proved to be a powerful king and he repulsed their invasions. During the reign of Ala-ud-Din, their attacks became more fierce as compared to previous ones. Now they had a different object. Earlier, they had invaded India to gain booty and to extend their sphere of influence but now they attacked India to avenge their earlier defeats and also to extend their empire. At times, dissatisficed nobles in the court of the Sultans of Delhi also used to help them.

During the reign of Ala-ud-Din, seven fierce invasions of the Mongols took place but Ala-ud-Din succeeded in defeating Mongols all the times.

Ala-ud-Din formulated a strong and a systematic frontier policy. He also planned to fight offensively instead of defensively.

The aggressive policy of Ala-ud-Din made the Mongols fearful of the Indian army. The terror created by Zafar Khan, one of the prominent generals of the Sultan in the minds of the Mongol soldiers was so great that "whenever their horses would not lower their mouths to drink water, the Mongol soldiers would mockingly shout at them whether they had seen Zafar Khan that they feared to stake their thirst."

Ala-ud-Din followed the measures mentioned below to check the Mongol invasions :

1. Old forts were repaired and experienced troops under the charge of capable officers were posted.

2. New forts were built and put under the charge of seasoned officers and well-trained soldiers.

3. Armament factories were set up and skilled engineers and technicians appointed.

4. A permanent and separate army was prepared for the defence of the North-West Frontier.

5. A special governor was appointed for the North-West Frontier.

6. In the frontier areas of Dipalpur, Samana and Multan, separate armies were stationed.

7. Army was reorganised and its striking power enhanced.

8. Experienced generals like Zafar Khan, Ghazi Malik and Malik Kafur were entrusted the responsibility of defending the border.

Ala-ud-Din's frontier policy proved very successful. According to Barani and Feristha, not only did the Mongols cease their agressions during the later years of Ala-ud-Din's reign, but also now they had to defend themselves against the troops of Ala-ud-Din. They have further stated that the governor of the North-West Frontier attacked Kabul, Ghazni and Kandhar and plundered the territories of the Mongols.

(*ii*) Malik Kafur

Malik Kafur, a Hindu enunch and once a slave became one of the most trustworthy generals of Ala-ud-Din. He was purchased for 1,000 Dinars by Nusrat Khan, a general of Ala-ud-Din when he invaded Gujarat.

The greatest achievement of Malik Kafur was that he conquered several kingdoms of the South. He brought huge wealth from the South during his expeditions from 1306 to 1312 A.D.

Malik Kafur also repulsed several of Mongol invasions during Ala-ud-Din's reign and became terror to them.

Kafur exercised a great influence on Ala-ud-Din. In several important matters, he assisted the Sultan.

Kafur's influence became so strong on Ala-ud-Din, that he believed his wife was conspiring against him. On Kafur's constantly poisoning the Sultan's ears, he imprisoned his own wife and sons.

The policy adopted by Malik Kafur after the death of Ala-ud-Din, led to a lot of dissatisfaction against him among the ardent supporters of the

Khalji dynasty. Several nobles combined against Kafur and got him killed in 1316.

(*iii*) Amir Khusro

Amir Khusro is regarded as one of the greatest Persian poets of his age and is said to have written four lakhs of couplets. He made use of Hindi words in his poems which was a novelty. He was also a great singer and enjoyed the title of *'Tuti-i-Hind'* or 'Parrot of India'. He lived in the court of Prince Mohammad, son of Balban. Mohammad patronised him liberally and on his death he wrote on 'Elegy on Mohammad'.

Amir Khusro also flourished during the reign of Ala-ud-Din and wrote *'Tarikh-i-Alai'* in which he described the conquests of Ala-ud-Din.

Amir Khusro wrote a romantic work *'Ashiqa'* in which he described the love affairs of the queen Debal Devi and prince Khizar Khan.

In *'Tughlak-Nama'*, Amir Khusro described the achievements of Ghias-ud-Din Tughlaq, the founder of the Tughlaq dynasty.

5

The Tughlaq Dynasty (1320-1414)

Q. 1. "The plans of Muhammad Tughlaq were well conceived but improperly executed and dangerously abandoned." Analyse this statement."

What were Mohammad Tughlaq's schemes of shift of capital and token money? Write about the causes of their failure.

(Rajasthan University 1997)

Or

Critically examine the experiments of Muhammad Tughlaq.

(Delhi University 1997, Punjab University April 1997)

Or

Review the schemes of Muhammad Tughlaq. How did they affect the Delhi Sultanate?

Or

Describe the various reforms of Muhammad Tughlaq. Why did these reform fail?

Or

Do you agree with the view that Muhammad Tughlaq was an ill starred idealist and a grossly mis-understood sovereign?

Or

"With the best intentions, excellent ideas but no balance or patience, no sense of proportions, Muhammad Tughlaq was a transcendent failure." Discuss this statement in the light of his reforms.

Ans. *Muhammad-Bin-Tughlaq* (*1325-1351*)

After the death of Ghias-ud-Din Tughlaq (1320-25) who was the founder of the Tughlaq dynasty, his eldest son Juna Khan ascended the throne of Delhi. It is generally held that Juna Khan was responsible for the murder of his father. After ascending the throne, he assumed the name of Muhammad Tughlaq. His rule lasted for about 26 years (1325-1351).

A much maligned ruler. On account of his utopian schemes and their failures, Muhammad Tughlaq has been often given bad epithets like 'blood thirsty', a 'visionary', a 'lunatic' and a 'tyrant'. He has been called a 'mixture of opposites' and a 'complex person.'

Visionary Schemes

Most of the plans of Muhammad Bin Tughlaq failed because these were ill-timed, ill-planned and badly executed.

Important schemes were as under :

1. Heavy taxation in the Doab
2. Transfer of the capital
3. Issue of token currency
4. Bribing to Mongols
5. Plan to conquer Khurasan and Iraq
6. The Quarajal expedition
7. The Deccan Policy.

1. *Heavy taxation in the Doab.* In the beginning of his reign, the Sultan increased the rate of taxes in the Doab—a very fertile area located between the Ganga and Yamuna rivers. The taxes were increased on account of the following reasons :

(1) The Sultan wanted to raise a strong army for conquests.

(2) The people of Doab were rich and were in a position to pay the increased taxes.

Mistakes made by the Sultan. There was nothing wrong in increasing the tax on land i.e. land revenue. But the time of the increase in the land revenue was not appropriate. The rains had failed and there were near-famine conditions. The government officials acted ruthlessly and persisted on the payment of the tax. The farmers suffered heavily. They left their lands. Riots broke out. Rebellions became common. When the Sultan came to know about the real situation, he withdrew his order and arranged help for the farmers. But it was too late. Damage had already been caused. This made the Sultan unpopular among the farmers and the common people. Even the normal revenue could not be collected from the Doab. The State Treasury suffered heavily.

2. *Transfer of the Capital.* The plan of the transfer of capital from Delhi to Devagiri which was renamed as Daultabad misfired. Following reasons are assigned to this transfer.

(*i*) Devagiri was made the capital according to Barani as the new place was centrally located.

The new capital had equal distance from Delhi, Gujarat, Lakhnauti, Tellanga, Dwarasamudra etc.

(*ii*) Ibn Batuta is of the view that the people of Delhi wrote abusive letters to Muhammad Tughlaq. The Sultan, therefore, wanted to teach them a lesson by depriving them of the capital.

The above view is also supported by Isami.

(*iii*) Gardner Brown ascribes the reason of the transfer of capital as the constant danger of the Mongol's attack at Delhi.

(*iv*) There was a revolt of a great magnitude in the South and accordingly the Sultan desired to strengthen his position there.

(*v*) It is stated by some historians that poets like Khusro had created a great fascination in the mind of the Sultan for the beauty of Devagiri.

(*vi*) The Sultan wanted to create an other major administrative centre so that Muslim population could be increased in the Deccan.

Mistakes committed by the Sultan while transferring capital. The most important error the Sultan made was that the entire population of Delhi was asked to move and cover a distance of about 700 miles. According to Barani, 'So complete was the ruin that not a cat or a dog was left in the buildings of the city." Ibn Batuta writes, "In the night the Sultan mounted the roof of his palace and looked around Delhi. When neither a light not even a smoke or lamp came into sight he remarked, "Now my heart is pleased and my soul is at rest." He further wrote, "A search was made and a blind man and a cripple man were found. The cripple man was put to death while the blind man was dragged to Daultabad where his only one leg reached."

Isami also wrote, "Muhammad Tughlaq ordered that the city (Delhi) should be set on fire and all the populace should be turned out of it."

The Sultan arranged all possible facilities for the people's forty days' journey from Delhi to Daultabad. However the scheme flopped. A large number of people died on the way.

Criticism of the Scheme. The Sultan committed a great blunder when he asked the people or even the elite of Delhi to go to Daultabad. He ought to have shifted his court. Some sections of the population must have followed voluntarily.

Secondly Daultabad was no good choice to be the capital of the empire. From this place it was not possible to check effectively the Mongol invasions.

Thus, the Sultan's choice of the new capital was not judicious. At the same time he did not use the appropriate methods in shifting the capital. Even assuming that the statements of some historians were exaggerated, it is concluded that this action of the Sultan was not a rational one.

3. *Use of token currency.* The Sultan needed more money on account of various reasons. He wanted to raise a huge army as he is said to have thought of conquering the whole world. He had also distributed a lot of money among nobles to please them when he ascended the throne after the death of his father which had occurred on account of his participation in a conspiracy.

Muhammad Tughlaq issued token currency because there was a shortage of gold coins and the Sultan on the other hand needed money.

Mistakes made by the Sultan. The Sultan issued copper coins and kept their value at par with the gold and silver coins. The Sultan did not exercise a strict check to ensure that the people did not make their own coins which we call *'jali'* or fake. The citizens began to melt coins in their homes and paid their taxes in fake coins. People also began to hoard silver and gold coins in their houses. The token currency remained in circulation for about three years. The Sultan realised the failure of the scheme and withdrew the entire new currency. People were asked to return the token coins and in exchange were paid back gold and silver coins by royal treasury. This put a heavy loss to the treasury. The people who minted fake coins were not punished.

Now-a-days all governments in the world use token currency that has a face value only and not any real value. The currency notes we use have a value printed on them but by themselves they are worth nothing. Similarly is the case with the coins that we use. During the days of Muhammad Tughlaq only gold coins were used and they had the face value almost equal to the real value. Use of token coins can be successful when the government alone makes them and takes people into confidence. At the same time strict checks are exercised to ensure that fake coins are not circulated by private parties. Mughammad Tughlaq failed to do so.

The token currency had an adverse effect on the foreign trade also. The foreign merchants stopped bringing their merchandise in India.

According to some scholars Muhammad Tughlaq wanted to follow the footsteps of the Emperor of China who had issued paper currency in China in the 13th century and also the Persian emperor who had made a similar experiment.

4. *Bribing the Mongols. The* Mongols were encouraged to attack Delhi, when the capital was shifted from Delhi to Daultabad. The Mongol general Tarmashirin is said to have trampled the entire region from Lahore to Delhi without facing any stiff resistance. Obviously Muhammad Tughlaq had neglected the frontier. Mohammad Tughlaq gave him five hundred dinars as bribes and persuaded him to return. This showed the weakness of the Sultan.

Some historians however, do not accept this version of bribe. But the fact remains that the Mongols did reach the vicinity of Delhi as on this issue there is little difference among historians. After the return of the Mongols the Sultan took preventive measures to safeguard his North-West Frontier province.

5. *Plan to conquer Khurasan and Iraq.* The unstable political conditions in Central Asia encouraged the Sultan to undertake the expedition of conquering these territories. The Sultan raised a large army of about 4 lakh soldiers for this purpose and payed it one year's salary in advance. In the meantime situation changed and the Sultan realised the futility of the scheme and disbanded the army.

Criticism of the Scheme. In the first place Muhammad Tughlaq should have considered all the pros and cons of the situation very carefully. Secondly the army should not have been given one year's salary in advance.

6. *Expedition to Qarajal.* The state was located at the foot of the Himalayas, probably in the region now called Kumaon. According to Ferishta, the primary objective of the Sultan was not the conquest of this state but that of China through this state. The army consisted of a hundred thousand horsemen besides a large infantry. The turbulent Qarajal came to terms and agreed to pay tribute to the Sultan. But almost the entire army

perished owing to the rigour of the cold climate and so difficult the climbing. It is said that only ten horsemen returned to blurt out the tragic tale.

7. *The Deccan policy.* Ala-ud-Din had conquered the Deccan but had not annexed it. He remained satisfied by plundering the wealth of the territory and making the rulers of the various states of Deccan accept his overlordship. Muhammad Tughlaq on the other hand was an annexcationist and his policy was to replace Hindu rule by direct Muslim government. His rule in the Deccan was very oppressive. The destruction of Dorasamudra, the capital of the Hoyasala Kings seriously outraged the Hindu population. In fact Muhammad Tughlaq found the Deccan revolts running sores which ultimately ruined him.

Summing up

In the words of Dr. R.C. Majumdar, "The Sultan lacked practical judgement and commonsense and rather obsessed with theoretical knowledge, indulged in lofty theories and visionary projects."

According to Dr. V.A. Smith. "He occupied the throne for twenty six years of tyranny as atrocious as any on record in the sad annals of human devilry and then died in his bed."

Elphinstone has observed, "His whole life was spent in pursuing visionary schemes, by means equally irrational and with a total disregard of the suffering which they occasioned to his subjects, and its results were more calamitous than those of any other Indian ruler."

According to Lane-poole, "He was a man with ideas far beyond his age."

Badauni commented on his death, "The king was freed from the people and they from their king."

Q. 2. "Muhammad Tughlaq's character was a mixture of opposite traits but his ideas were original." Explain.

Or

Why is Muhammad Tughlaq called a mixture of opposites?

Or

"Muhammad Tughlaq is often described as a visionary instead of a fool." Do you agree with the view? Explain.

Or

"Muhammad Tughlaq was the most controversial monarch of medieval India." Explain.

Or

Explain the strong and weak points in the character of Muhammad Bin Tughlaq and their impact on the empire.

Or

Form an estimate of the character and personality of Muhammad Tughlaq. What are the causes of his failure?

Ans. *An Estimate of Muhammad Tughlaq.*

Before arriving at an estimate of Muhammad Tughlaq, we may have some idea of his strong points as well as weak points.

Bright side of the character of Muhammad Tughlaq

Muhammad Tughlaq was very gifted in certain respects. He was an accomplished scholar, an expert caligraphist and his eloquence was magical. He was genuinely interested in mathematics, medicine, science, astronomy and philosophy etc. He was a devout Musalman. In an age of drunkenness and debauchary, he was singularly free from these vices. He was known for his generosity.

He was a patron of learned scholars. He was a man of great initiative. He was a dashing experimentor who would revert back if he got convinced that the experiments so launched were not productive.

Dark Side of the character of Muhammad Tughlaq

(1) Muhammad was very selfish and felt no hesitation in killing his father through conspiracy.

(2) He was a visionary and he wanted to conquer the whole world.

(3) He was over-ambitious. He desired to found a new religion.

(4) He was a poor plan executor. His plan of token currency emptied the state treasury. His plan of increasing state revenue through increase in taxation brought ruin to the farmers. His project of change of capital from Delhi to Daultabad brought immense hardship to the people and did not materialise. He collected a huge army for making conquests in Central Asia, paid the soldiers one year's salary in advance but afterwards gave up the plan. His plan to conquer Quarajal brought disaster to the army.

(5) He was a coward ruler. He bought peace by bribing the Mongols.

(6) He was blood-thirsty. He ordered the killing of hundreds of people even on minor matters.

(7) He was short-tempered. He flew into rage wherever his views were opposed.

(8) He was very stubborn and vindictive. He adopted stringent measures on the people of Doab when they refused to pay the taxes.

A complex personality. Historians have used various epithets while estimating Muhammad Tughlaq.

Barani and Ibn Batuta, his contemporaries found him a 'complex person', a 'mixture of opposites.' He had virtues and vices of extreme intensity. While he was generous, humble and kind, he was very narrow-minded, stubborn and most cruel. He gave gifts to all those whom he liked, he put to death who opposed him.

Dr. Ishwari Prasad, Dr. V.A. Smith and Dr. K.A. Nizami do not accept the view that Muhammad Tughlaq was a mixture of opposites. They are inclined to hold the view that contemporary historians of Mughammad Tughlaq have put things in an exaggerated manner.

Was he mad? Eliphinstone is of the view that Muhammad Tughlaq suffered from some degree of insanity. This view has been supported by Havell and S.R. Sharma. However historians like Brown and Ishwari Prasad do not accept this view. Brown has observed, "That he was mad is a view of which contemporaries give no hint; that he was a visionary, his many sided practical and vigorous character forbids us to believe; to call him a despot may be true but not other form of government was conceivable in the middle age."

Likewise Dr. Ishwari Prasad has stated, "Muhammad Tughlaq was unquestionably the ablest man among the crowned heads of the middle ages; some historians lay the charge of madness on him but neither in the pages of Ibn Batuta nor in the history of Barani...Edward Thomas and Havell have taken their clue from Badauni who was bitterly prejudiced against the Sultan and they have uncritically accepted most of his statements."

Welfare works of Muhammad Tughlaq. The Sultan did a lot for the peasants. He set up a separate department of agriculture. The primary object of this department was to bring uncultivated land under plough. *'Taccavi'* loans to peasants were given on bad times i.e. natural calamities like floods.

Administration of Justice. Ibn Batuta praises his love for justice, "Of all men he most loved justice." He did not even let the Qazis escape justice.

Causes of his failure

Causes of his failure may be listed under two heads (*i*) Causes for which he himself was responsible (*ii*) Causes for which he himself was not responsible.

Causes for which Muhammad Tughlaq himself was responsible

1. Visionary projects of Muhammad Tughlaq

These include (*i*) Taxation in the Doab (*ii*) Transfer of capital from Delhi to Daultabad (*iii*) Use of token currency. (*iv*) Military expeditions to Central Asia and other places (*v*) The Deccan policy.

2. Generosity of the Sultan
3. Alienation of the Ulemas
4. Brutal punishments.

Causes of failure for which Muhammad Tughlaq was not responsible

I Conservative nature of the people
II Lack of capable advisers—ministers and generals
III Natural calamities
IV Vast extent of empire
V Disloyalty of provincial governors.

VI Liberal grants to the scholars and the poor, thus putting heavy strain on state revenue.

Lane-poole has described the reasons of his failure in these words, "To him (Muhammad Tughlaq) what seems good must be done at once, and when it proved impossible or unsuccessful his disappointment reached the verge of frenzy and he wreaked his wrath indiscriminately upon the unhappy offenders who could not keep pace with his imagination. Hence with the best of intentions, excellent ideas but no balance or patience, no sense of proportion, Muhammad Tughlaq was a transcendent failure."

A balanced view of the personality and work of Muhammad Tughlaq

Elphinstone has given a balanced view of Muhammad Tughlaq in these words, "It is admitted on all hands that he was the most eloquent and accomplished prince of his age. His letters, both in Arabic and Persian were admired for their elegance long after he had ceased to reign. His memory was extraordinary, and besides a thorough knowledge of logic and the philosophy of the Greek, he was much attached to mathematics and to physical sciences, and used himself to attend sick persons for watching the symptoms of any extraordinary disease. He was regular in his devotions, abstained from wine, and conformed in his private like to all the moral precepts of his religion. In war he was distinguished for his gallantry and personal activity, so that his contemporaries were justified in esteeming him as one of the wonders of the age.

Yet on the whole as if these splendid talents and accomplishments were given to him in vain, they were accompanied by a perversion of judgement which, after every allowance for the intoxication of absolute power, leaves us in no doubt whether he was not affected by some degree of insanity. His whole life was spent in pursuing visionary schemes by means equally irrational and with a total disregard of the sufferings which they occasioned to his subjects; and its results were more calamitious than those of any other Indian ruler."

Q. 3. Critically examine the achievements of Firoz Shah Tughlaq.

Or

"The policy of Firoz Shah Tughlaq was a strange mixture of good and evil." Express your opinion about this statement.

Or

Analyse the administrative, military, religious and social reforms of Firoz Shah Tughlaq.

Or

It is said that Firoz Shah Tughlaq did more for the welfare of the people than any other Delhi Sultan. Do you agree with this and state if Firoz is entitled to be regarded as a great reformer and ruler? Give reasons.

Or

It is correct to say that Firoz Shah Tughlaq was neither a capable general nor an efficient administrator? Discuss.

Or

Give an account of administrative and economic policies of Firoz Tughlaq and their effects.

(Punjab University April 1996 and April 1998)

Ans. Bright and Dark-sides of the Rule of Firoz Shah Tughlaq.

Firoz Tughlaq a cousin brother of Muhammad Tughlaq ascended the throne after the death of Muhammad Tughlaq who was issueless and loved Firoz Tughlaq very much. His reign lasted for about 37 years from 1351 to 1388 A.D. During his rule, Firoz Tughlaq adopted measures like revenue reforms, irrigation works, charitable programmes and public works etc. which won praise from various quarters. At the same time, his military expeditions, slave system, feudal practice and religious policy etc. brought discredit to him. Accordingly his reign was a 'mixture of good and evil' as observed by Dr. Ishwari Prasad.

Bright side of Firoz Tughlaq's reign

1. *Assessment of the revenue.* Firoz Tughlaq appointed a special officer namely Khawja Hisan-ud-Din to prepare an estimate of the public revenue of the kingdom. It took 6 years to complete this work. The Khawja toured the entire kingdom and prepared proper records. Thereafter he fixed the revenue of the *'Khalsa'* land (Government land) in the kingdom at six crores and eightyfive lakhs of *'Tankas'* (silver coins). It was a rough estimate. The revenue which was fixed remained unchanged during the reign of Firoz Tughlaq. The chief merit of this system was that the income of the state was fixed and the expenditure of the state could be adjusted according to the income which was known before hand.

2. *New system of taxation.* In accordance with the Islamic law, he imposed the following four taxes.

(*i*) *'Kharaj'*. It was the land tax which was equal to one-tenth of the produce of the land.

(*ii*) *'Zakat'*. It was two-and-half per cent tax on property realised from the Muslims and utilised for specific religious purposes only.

(*iii*) *'Kham'*. It was one-fifth of the booty captured and the four-fifth was left for the soldiers.

(*iv*) *'Jijya'*. It was levied on the Non-Muslim subjects, particularly the Hindus. Women and children were, however exempted from the taxes.

3. *Levy of other taxes.* The irrigation tax, garden tax, octroi tax and the sales tax were the other important taxes.

4. *Irrigation works.* With a view to encourage irrigation, the Sultan paid a lot of attention to irrigation works. Following four canals were constructed :

(*i*) The first and the most important and the longest canal was one which carried the waters of the river Jamuna to the city of Hissar. It was 150 miles long.

(*ii*) The second canal was drawn from river Sutlej to Ghaghra. It was about 100 miles long.

(*iii*) The third canal was from Mandvi and Sirmur hills to Hansi.

(*iv*) The fourth canal ran from Ghaghra to the newly established town of Firozabad.

Irrigation tax was charged at the rate of one-tenth of the produce of the irrigated land.

5. *Laying out gardens.* The Sultan laid out about 1200 gardens in and around Delhi. These gardens produced so much fruit that they brought to the treasury an annual income of one lakh and eighty thousand *tankas'*.

6. *Welfare of the peasants.* The Sultan waived off the loans that were given to them by Muhammad Tughlaq at the time of drought. He issued strict instructions to the officers not to harass the peasants.

7. *Benevolent works.* These included the following :

(*i*) *'Diwan-i-Kherat'*. It performed two main functions. The marriage bureau gave grants to the poor parents for the marriage of their daughters. It also provided financial help to the destitutes.

(*ii*) *'Dar-ul-Shafa'*. Hospitals were set up in important towns where medicines were given free of charge. Poor people were also supplied food.

(*iii*) *'Sarais'*. About 200 ' *'sarais'* (rest houses) were built by the Sultan for the benefits of merchants and other travellers.

(*iv*) *Grants to sufferers.* The Sultan gave liberal grants to all those persons or their heirs who had suffered bodily or executed during the reign of Muhammad Tughlaq.

8. *Public works department.* The Sultan got constructed four canals, ten public baths, four mosques, thirty palaces, two hundred, *'Sarais'*, one hundred tombs, 30 towns and one hundred bridges. Firoz Shah had a passion for public works. About his building activities, Sultan himself observed, "Among the gifts which God has bestowed upon me, His humble servant, had a desire to erect public buildings. So I built many mosques and monasteries that the learned and the devout and the holy, might worship God in these edifices and aid the kind builder with their prayers."

Four important towns founded by him were of Firozabad, Fatehabad, Jaunpur and Hissar Firoza.

Two pillars of Ashoka were brought to Delhi—one from Meerut and the other from Topra, Ambala district—and erected in Delhi. In this regard Dr. V.A. Smith has observed, "Asiatic kings as a rule show no interest in buildings erected by their predecessors, which usually are allowed to decay uncared for. Firoz Shah was particular in devoting much attention to the repair and rebuilding of the structures of former kings and ancient nobles."

9. *Promotion of education and literature. Firoz* Tughlaq was a great patron of historians, poets and scholars. He himself was a man of learning and wrote his biography entitled *'Fatuhat-i-Firozshah'*. He established thirty educational institutions including three colleges. Teachers were liberally paid and stipends were granted to the students.

Zia-ud-Din Barani wrote *'Fatwah-i-Jahandari'* and Afif wrote his *'Tarikh-i-Firuzshah'*.

Maulana Jalal-ud-Din Rumi, the famous theologian also flourished in his court.

10. *Judicial reforms.* Firoz Tughlaq was opposed to severe punishments. He ended punishments like cutting of the limbs, extracting the eyes, putting melted glass in the throat, burning alive etc. He established courts at all important places of his empire and appointed Qazis etc. to administer justice.

11. *Reforms in the currency system.* The Sultan introduced several types of new coins and small coins and ensured that no false coins came into circulation.

Dark Side of Firoz Tughlaq's Reign

1. *Failure as a conqueror.* Firoz Tughlaq was not an able general. No significant conquests were made by him. Main military events are given below :

(*i*) *Bengal.* Firoz Tughlaq made two attempts to conquer Bengal but failed.

(*ii*) *Orissa.* While returning from Bengal, he attacked Orissa. The ruler agreed to pay tribute to the Sultan.

(*iii*) *Nagarkot* (Kangra). It took about six months to subjugate the Raja who acknowledged the Sultan's suzerainty.

(*iv*) *Sindh.* In the initial attacks by the Sultan himself, about three-fourth of his army was destroyed. Later the Sindh ruler accepted the suzerainty of the Sultan.

2. *Army organisation.* The Sultan introduced several reforms in the army which produced negative results.. (*i*) He did not maintain a standing army. (*ii*) Military service was made hereditary. (*iii*) The principle of merit was ignored, (*iv*) The Sultan introduced the system of paying salary by grant of land. This meant that a soldier had to go to his village for collecting his land revenue in lieu of salary.

3. *Evils of Jagirdari system.* Firoz Tughlaq introduced the system of granting jagirs (lands) to his officials in place of cash payment. In due course, jagirdars became very powerful and created difficulties for the rulers.

4. *Hereditary nobles.* **Firoz Tughlaq decreed that whenever a noble died, his son should be allowed to succeed to his position. This reduced the chances of competent persons being appointed at responsible posts.**

5. *Slave system.* It is said that Firoz Tughlaq had maintained about one lakh, eighty thousand slaves. It put great economic burden on the state. This slave system proved very harmful and became one of the contributory factors of the downfall of the Tughlaq empire.

6. *Fanatically intolerant religious policy towards the Hindus.* Firoz encouraged the Hindus for conversion to Islam. In his autobiography, he wrote, "I encouraged my infidel subjects (Hindus) to embrace the religion of the Prophet (Islam religion), and I proclaimed that everyone who left his creed and became a Mussalman should be exempted from *'jizya'*. He further wrote, "I also ordered that the infidel books, the idols and the vessels used in their worship (Hindus) should all be publicly burnt."

7. *Habit of drinking.* Firoz was so addicted to drinking that whenever he set out on a military expedition, he would remain in a state of drunkenness for several days. This was followed by his nobles and forces as well.

An estimate of Firoz Tughlaq

(*a*) *Appreciation by historians.* "The welfare of the people", says Dr. Ishwari Prasad, "was the watchword of his administration. Therefore, Firoz is considered by Barani as an ideal Muslim King."

In the words of Havell Firozj's reign "is a welcome breath in the long chain of tyranny, cruelty and debauchery which make up the gloomy annals of the Turkish dynasties."

Afif, a contemporary of Firoz writes, "Their (peasants) homes were replete with grain, everyone had plenty of gold and silver. "No women was without ornaments."

About the previous penal code and the changes brought about by Firoz, S.R. Sharma states, "it was left to his less appreciated successor (Firoz) to mitigate its ferocity."

About the judicial system, V.A. Smith has said, "One reform the abolition of mutilation and torture, deserves unqualified commendation."

About his love for buildings, Sir Woolseley Haigh has remarked, "He indulged in a passion for building which equalled if it did not surpass that of Roman emperor Augutus."

(*b*) *Criticism by historians.* About his lack of military skill, V.A. Smith states, "The campaign (Bengal) had no result except the wanton slaughter thus evidenced. No territory was annexed and the practical independence of the eastern empire continued unimpaired." He further observes, "It seems to be plain that Firoz Shah possessed no military capacity. His early campaigns in the east and the west were absolutely futile, and during the greater part of his long reign he abstained from war."

Likewise regarding Firoz's expedition to Sindh, Dr. Ishwari Prasad wrote, "The expedition was a singular instance of the Sultan's felinity and lack of strategic skill."

Regarding his religious intolerance, S.R. Sharma states, "It is a pity that such a Sultan should have besmirched his fair name by acts of religious intolerance."

In the same manner Dr. R.C. Majumdar writes, "Firoz was the greatest bigot of his age."

Professor B.P. Saxena also states, "...But in the last fifteen years of his reign Firoz was an incurable and degenerate fanatic."

Concluding Statement

We may conclude the discussion with the views of Dr. V.A. Smith, "Firoz Shah, whatever may have been his defects or weaknesses deserves much credit for having mitigated in some respects the horrible practices of his predecessors, and for having introduced some tincture of humane feelings into the administration."

Q. 4. Analyse the causes of the downfall of the Tughlaq dynasty. How far were Muhammad Tughlaq and Firoz Tughlaq responsible for it?

Ans. *Downfall of the Tughlaq Dynasty.*

The Tughlaq dynasty founded by Ghias-ud-Din Tughlaq in 1320 came to an end in 1412 with the death of its last ruler Mahmud Shah. During the 92 years of rule of this dynasty, 8 rulers ruled.

Causes of the Disintegration of the Tughlaq Dynasty

Broadly speaking disintegration of the Tughlaq dynasty took place on account of the following causes.

I. Policies of Muhammad Tughlaq
II. Policies of Firoz Tughlaq
III. Miscellaneous causes
IV. Timur's invasion.

I. Policies of Muhammad Tughlaq

These can be categorised as under :

1. *Five failed plans of Muhammad Tughlaq* namely (*a*) Change of capital (*b*) Taxation of the Doab. (*c*) Issue of token currency. (*d*) Khurasan expedition (*e*) Bribing the Mongols.

All these wild projects resulted in the loss of men and money and led to discontent against the Sultan. Several revolts took place during his reign which weakened the power and prestige of the Sultan.

2. *Complex personality of Muhammad Tughlaq.* Muhammad Tughlaq has been called a mixture of opposites, an unbalanced personality and the wisest fool. He is accused of some measure of insanity. All these traits of his personality had an adverse affect on the functioning of the government.

3. *Deccan policy of Muhammad Bin Tughlaq.* Unlike Ala-ud-Din Khalji, Muhammad Bin Tughlaq aimed at the annexation of the Kingdoms of Deccan. It is true that he shifted his capital from Delhi to Daultabad to exercise his control in the south but the scheme misfired and he was forced to change his decision. The Deccan policy of Muhammad Tughlaq led to the creation of the Hindu kingdom of Vijayanagar.

II. Firoz Tughlaq's responsibility for the disintegration of the Tughlaq dynasty

Following were the Chief factors :

4. *Religious intolerance of Firoz Tughlaq.* On this, Dr. Ishwari Prasad has commented, "The reforms of Firoz...failed to gain confidence of Hindus whose feelings were embittered by his religious intolerance. Altogether they produced a reaction which proved fatal to the interest of the dynasty which was by no means an unworthy representative."

5. *'Ulemas influence on administration.* Dr. U.N. Dey has observed on this as, "His supplication to the *'Ulemas'* only encouraged a group of unscrupulous selfish people to behave arrogantly and pose themselves as the custodians of Muslim conscience. All these combined to create a situation in which disintegration became inevitable."

6. *System of decentralisation.* Firoz gave extensive powers to his nobles and officials which ultimately went against the larger interests of the state.

According to Sir Woolesely Haig, "His system of decentralisation accelerated the downfall of his dynasty."

7. *Failure as a conqueror*
8. *Defective army organisation*
9. *Evils of Jagirdari system*
10. *Hereditary nobles*
11. *Slave system*
12. *Loose administration and prevailing corruption*
13. *Sultan's habit of drinking.*

(For details see the previous question-serial Numbers 7 to 12).

Dr. R.C. Majumdar has correctly remarked, "On the whole, inspite of peace, prosperity and contentment that prevailed during the long reign of Firoz Shah, no one can possibly doubt that his policy and administrative measures contributed to a large extent to the downfall of the Delhi Sultanate, and accelerated the process of decline that had already set in during his predecessor's reign."

III. Miscellaneous causes

14. *No definite law of succession.* There were several claimants of the throne after the death of the Sultan. This led to serious conflicts which adversely affected the stability of the empire.

15. *Autocratic rulers.* The Tughlaq rulers were all dictators by and large.

16. *No efforts to win over the Hindus.* The vast majority of the subjects of the Tughlaq rulers were the Hindus. The Sultans made little serious attempts to get their support.

17. *Unwieldy empire.* M.S. Ayyangar, in this context has observed, "The unwieldiness and the difficulty of communications between the various parts of the empire led to the rise of provincial governors into independence."

18. *Poor financial position.* The foolish and visionary schemes of Muhammad Tughlaq and the occasional droughts made the royal treasury quite empty.

19. *Paucity of able and faithful commanders and advisers.* The Tughlaq rulers did not follow the correct policy of selecting their advisers and commanders. They also could not win their whole hearted loyalty.

20. *Selfishness of the Amirs.* After Firoz's death, the selfishness of the Amirs went on increasing. They began to intrigue for acquiring larger jagirs and more power.

21. *Decadent army.* The stability of the state depended upon a strong and well disciplined army. Among other factors, the habit of drinking even during war operations led to loss of dexterity and courage among the soldiers.

22. *Weak successors of Firoz.* The successors of Firoz Tughlaq proved very incapable and failed to exercise their control. After Firoz Shah, five Sultans could rule just for twenty six years. The provincial governors became independent.

IV Timur's Invasion

23. *Death-blow to the Tughlaq empire.* Plundering and looting on the way, Amir Timur of Samarquand reached Delhi. The Tughlaq Sultan of Delhi fled away from Delhi. For fifteen days, Timur looted the capital.

Q. 5. Describe Timur's invasion on India. What were its effects?

Ans. *Timur's Conquests.*

Timur (1336-1405 A.D.) was a great military commander and conqueror of Central Asia. He conquered one kingdom after another. In course of a fight, his one leg was wounded and he limped for the rest of his life. Thereafter he came to be known as Timur-the Lame. The Persians called him *'Timur-i-Lang'*

Timur succeeded in establishing a vast empire which included Transoxiana, a part of Turkistan, Afghanistan, Persia, Syria, Qurdistan, Baghdad, Georgia and the major part of Asia Minor. He successfully looted southern Russia and several parts of India. Delhi was perhaps the worst sufferer.

It is said of Timur's invasions, "Wherever he went he brought about destruction, massacres, burning, looting and dishonour to women".

Timur's Invasion of India (1398-1399) : causes of Timur's invasion

Following were the chief motives of Timur's invasion on India :

1. *Timur's ambition.* Like other great conquerors, Timur was also very ambitious. He wanted to bring under his sway more and more lands.

2. *Eye on India's wealth.* Dr. A.L. Srivastava has described this motive in these words, "The huge wealth of Hindustan had attracted his attention. Delhi Sultanate was tottering and this gave an opportunity to the Turkish conqueror to fulfil his ambition." According to Dr. Srivastava, Timur had no intention of conquering Hindustan or ruling over it.

3. *Spread of Islam.* In his autobiography, Timur has stated, "My object in the invasion of Hindustan is to lead an expedition against the infidels, to convert them to the true faith of Islam and purify the land itself from the filth, infidelity and polytheism." Spreading Islam, he wanted to acquire the title of *'Gazi'*.

4. *Unstable political condition of India.* Timur wanted to make the best use of the political chaos of India.

5. *Fulfilling the task of Changez Khan.* It is said by some historians that Timur wanted to realise the dream of Changez Khan which he had seen at the time of Iltutmish.

Timur's attack of Delhi. Timur started his expedition from Kabul in August 1398 and reached Delhi in December 1398. On his way to Delhi, he captured and looted all the towns. Sultan Mahmud Shah, the last Sultan of the Tughlaq dynasty and his *Vazir'* (Prime Minister) fled from Delhi. Timur ordered a general massacre and plunder which continued for 15 days. According to Sharaf-ud-Din and Mir Khud, about one lakh people were put to death in Delhi by Timur. The three towns of Delhi namely Sri, Old Delhi and Jahan Panah were laid desolute by Timur.

According to Lane-poole, "The victory was complete and Timur, pitching his camp by the tomb of Firoz Shah gave thanks to God with tears of joy in his eyes for three days." About the fate of Delhi, he further wrote, "Unhappy city was turned into a place of bloodshed, ruin and destruction." Regarding looting and plundering he observed, "There were immense spoils of rubies, diamonds, pearls, gold and silver ornaments and vessels."

Lane-poole described the fanaticism of Timur as "Only the followers of Muslim religion escaped the general sack."

Timur started his back journey from Delhi in January 1399. On his way he plundered Meerut, Hardwar, Kangra and Jammu. Before leaving India, he appointed Khizr Khan as governor of Multan, Lahore and Dialpur.

Effects of Timur's Invasion

Effects of Timur's invasion may be studied under the following heads :

1. Cultural effects
2. Economic effects
3. Political effects
4. Religious effects
5. Social effects

1. Cultural effects.

(*a*) *Destruction of Indian art.* Timur destroyed a large number of beautiful buildings and temples.

(*b*) *Indian art in Central Asia.* Dr. V.A. Smith in this context has observed, "Timur was careful to bring away all the skilled artisans (for India) he could find to be employed for the buildings at his capital" (in Samarkand). These artisans designed and constructed several buildings in Central Asia.

2. Economic effects

(*a*) Carrying away enormous wealth of India to Central Asia.

(*b*) Destruction of standing crops and ravaging grain stores.

(*c*) Breaking out of diseases and famine.

3. Political effects

(*a*) Death blow to the already tottering power of the Tughlaq dynasty.

(*b*) Disintegration of the Delhi Sultanate.

(*c*) Exposure of India's military weakness and paving way for Babur's invasion.

4. Religious effects

(*a*) By perpetrating cruelties upon the Hindus, Timur's invasion increased the hostilities between the Hindus and the Muslims.

(*b*) Destruction of several Hindu temples annoyed the Hindus.

5. Social effects

(*a*) Timur had struck so much terror that the Indian women started dreading their children by the mention of Timur's name.

(*b*) The practice of child marriage among the Hindus was encouraged as they started marrying away their daughters and sisters at an early age to save them from being snatched away by the Muslims.

(*c*) On account of the massacre of the male population in general by Timur, many Hindu families were left without a single male member. This had an adverse effect on the social life.

6

The Sayeed Dynasty and the Lodi Dynasty

Q. 1. Describe in brief the rise and the fall of the Sayyed Dynasty.

Ans. *The Sayeed Dynasty* (1414-1451 A.D.)

The Sayeed Dynasty ruled for about 37 years. There were four rulers. Neither politically nor culturally, the Sayeed dynasty made any worthwhile contribution to the medieval history of India.

Khizr Khan (1414-1421)

Khizr Khan, the founder of this dynasty was once the governor of Multan appointed by Firoz Tughlaq. He sided Timur when the latter attacked India. Before leaving India, Timur appointed him the governor of Multan, Lahore and Dipalpur. After Timur's return, there was no strong power in Delhi for about 14 years. Taking advantage of the chaotic conditions, he occupied the throne of Delhi in 1414. He claimed to be the descendant of the Prophet. The seven years of his reign were spent in suppressing revolts in various parts of India. He was successful in protecting the Delhi Sultanate from the rulers of Gujarat, Malwa and Jaunpur who aspired to conquer Delhi.

Khizr Khan's personality and his rule have won praise from Fersihta in these words, "Khizr Khan was a great and a wise King and was always true to his word. His subjects loved him with so much a graceful affection that great and small, master and the servant sat and mourned for him in black garments, till the third day, when they laid aside their mourning garments and raised his son, Mubarak Shah, to the throne."

Mubarak Shah (1421-1434)

Yahya Bin Sirhindi, a famous historian of his time, in his book *'Tarikh-i-Mubarak Shah'* has written about his reign as, "The reign of Mubarak Shah was a period of disquiet and rebellions, so his entire reign was spent in suppressing these." One feature of his reign is remarkable. In the history of Sultanate, for the first time we learn that there were two Hindu Amirs in his reign."

Mubarak Shah built a city on the banks of river Jamuna and named it Mubarkabad.

He was assassinated in a plot.

Muhammad Shah (1434-45)

Muhammad Shah was a very weak ruler. The real authority of the Sultan extended merely 40 miles around Delhi. During his reign, disorder and mismanagement prevailed. The ruler of Malwa attacked Delhi during his reign. However with the timely help of Bahlol Lodi, the governor of Lahore and Sirhind, the Sultan was able to face the challenge successfully. Later on during the reign of Muhammad Shah, Bahlol Lodi tried to capture Delhi but he failed.

About the state of affairs during the reign of Muhammad Shah, the historian Nizam-ud-Din wrote, "The affairs of the state grew day by day more and more confused."

Ala-ud-Din Alam Shah (1445-1451)

Alam Shah was a pleasure-loving, incompetent and weak king. He used to reside at Badaun. According to some historians, he transferred his capital from Delhi to Badaun on account of the fear of Bahlol Lodi, governor of Lahore and Sirhind. Taking advantage of his absence from Delhi, Bahlol Lodi, supported by Sultan's *'Vazir'* occupied Delhi in 1451. Alam Shah continued to live at Badaun till his death in 1478.

Q. 2. Analyse the Chief events of the reign of Bahlol Lodi.

Ans. *Bahlol Lodi* (1451-1489).

Founder of the Lodi dynasty (1451-1526). The Lodi dynasty founded by Bahlol Lodi lasted for about 76 years. The dynasty derives its name from an Afghan tribe known as Lodi. There were three rulers of this dynasty. Bahlol Lodi founded the dynasty, Sikandar Lodi enhanced its prestige and power. The last ruler Ibrahim Lodi tried to increase its prestige and strength, but Babur a Mughal attacked India, defeated him and laid the foundation of the Mughal dynasty.

Achievements of Bahlol Lodi as a ruler

End justifies the means. Bahlol Lodi was a courageous soldier, successful general, a great diplomat and a realist. He believed in the principle that the end justifies the means. He understood his limitations and circumstances.

Pragmatic dealing with Afghan nobles. Bahlol won the confidence, cooperation and respect of the Afghan nobles with his very amiable behaviour. He gave them jagirs and high offices. He treated them as friends and considered himself as one of them. In a crisis, he would not hesitate to take off his turban from his head and solicit forgiveness from his Amirs saying, "If you think me unworthy of the situation I occupy, choose someone else and bestow on me some other office." This paid him dividends. This enabled him to consolidate and utilise the strength of the Afghans in the interest of the state.

It is said about him that he personally attended on the sick nobles.

The Sultan avoided showing his superior status. In the words of S.R. Sharma, "In social meetings he never sat on the throne and would not allow his nobles to stand; and even during public audiences he did not occupy the throne, but seated himself on a carpet."

Conquests of Bahlol Lodi. When he ascended the throne, the territory of his kingdom extended upto Palam and a few miles around Delhi. But the time he died at the age of eighty, his empire extended from Panipat to the frontiers of Bihar and included many important towns and cities. A part of Rajasthan was also under him.

Bahlol's most important conquest was that of the state of Jaunpur. This proved his military talents. It added to his resources and raised his prestige among nobles and other rulers.

A devout Muslim. He was liberal in his general as well as religious outlook. He offered Namaz regularly. He kept the company of the Ulemas, studied Quran carefully but he was not a fanatic. He gave several important offices to the Hindus.

Bahlol could be very generous to the defeated enemy. He captured twice the wife of his enemy ruler Hussain Shah but sent her back to her husband honourably both times. Dr. K.S. Lal's comment on this are, "For a victorious Muslim Sultan in medieval India, this treatment was unique."

Q. 3. Why is Sikandar Lodi considered the ablest of the Lodi Sultans?

Or

Whom do you consider the most successful amongst the Lodi Sultans and why?

Ans. *Lodi Sultans.*

Of the three Lodi Sultans namely Bahlol Lodi (1451 to 1489), Sikandar Lodi (1489 to 1517) and Ibraham Lodi (1517 to 1526), Sikandar Lodi is regarded as the ablest, the greatest and the most successful Sultan.

Most of the time of Bahlol Lodi was spent in checking revolts and consolidating his position. There was very little left at his disposal for bringing about administrative reforms. Ibram Lodi led to the downfall of the Lodi dynasty. As compared with these two Sultans, Sikandar Lodi gave ample evidence of his qualities as a general, as an administrator, a consolidator of the empire and a man of letters.

Sikandar Lodi (1489-1517)

Greatest Lodi Sultan. Sikandar Lodi has been accepted as the greatest Lodi Sultan. He established law and order. He was a brave and dauntless general. He encouraged agriculture and trade which resulted in economic prosperity. He enhanced the glory and power of the king. He was known for impartial justice. He asked all governors and officers to submit proper accounts of their income. He himself was a great scholar and patronised men of learning.

Sikandar Lodi's main achievements are discussed below.

1. *Conquests.* First of all Sikandar Lodi defeated his elder brother and seized Jaunpur and brought it under his direct control. He afterwards led his attack on Bihar, defeated its ruler and annexed it. He conquered the states of Dholpur, Bidar, Gwalior, Chanderi and other nearby kingdoms He entered into a friendship treaty with the ruler of Bengal.

Sikandar's empire extended from the Punjab to the borders of Bengal and included the territories between Sutlej and Bundelkhand.

2. *Control over nobles.* His control over his noble was so tight that he could boast, "If I order one of my slaves to be seated in a palanquin, the entire body of nobility would carry him on their shoulders at my bidding." By his stern justice, code of conduct for the nobles and its strict adherence without any distinction, spy system and following a policy of happy blending of sternness and generosity, he succeeded in commanding the respect of his nobles.

Sikandar's sole motive was to restore the prestige of the Sultan and in that he succeeded.

Important measures that he adopted to strengthen his position were as under :

(*i*) He started sitting on the throne and compelled his nobles to show formal respect to him in the *'darbar'* (court) and outside.

(*ii*) He framed certain rules which were observed by all his nobles and governors.

(*iii*) The governors were ordered to receive Sultan's *'firmans'* (orders) six miles ahead of their capital.

(*iv*) He asked all his governors and officers to submit their accounts of their income and expenditure. The offenders were punished. The governor of Jaunpur was punished on this very account and compelled to pay the embezzled money.

(*v*) A very efficient espionage system was organised. He posted spies and informers at every important place including the houses of his nobles.

3. *Efficient administration.* Sikandar Shah was a well-meaning Sultan. He was very laborious. He attended to the smallest matter of administration. He worked hard from morning till night to supervise the administrative work.

4. *Occasional tours in disguise.* Very often the Sultan toured in disguise to have the first hand information about the condition of the people and the activities of the Amirs and the Ulemas.

5. *Efficient espionage system.* He was so well informed about every thing significant in the state through his spy system and his own tours that the people believed the Sultan had supernatural powers to assist him.

6. *Impartial justice.* He brought about several reforms in the judicial system. He himself was the highest appeal of justice. He dispensed impartial justice to his subjects.

7. *Economic welfare of the people.* He kept with him the rate-list of all articles of everyday use so that he could assess the economic condition of the people. An informal system of price control prevailed in the market which enabled people to get necessities of life at affordable price.

8. *Development of agriculture.* He abolished duty on grain and encouraged farmers to improve agriculture.

9. *Progress of trade.* The Sultan abolished all internal trade duties.

10. *Development of literature.* The Sultan was an accepted scholar. He was well-versed in Persian and composed poems in this language. He was a partron of learned men.

11. *Promotion of education.* The Sultan invited two eminent philosophers from outside India to improve the system of education in his empire.

He encouraged education particularly among children of Afghan nobles so as to make them cultured. He made mosques as centres of education.

He appointed one religious preacher, one teacher and one scavenger in each mosque at state expense. His court was a centre of learning and several scholars adorned it.

It is said that about seventy scholars discussed academic and religious problems every night by the side of his bed.

Several scholarly works were translated from Sanskrit into Persian.

12. *Promotion of music.* The Sultan took a great interest in music. He enjoyed *'sehnai'* very much. A reputed work on music titled 'Lahjat-i-Sikandar Shahi' was prepared during his reign.

13. *Promotion of architecture.* The Sultan built the city of Agra which became an important administrative and cultural centre of the Mughals. He built many mosques and also the tomb of his father Bahlol Lodi in Delhi.

14. *Public welfare activities.* The Sultan made suitable arrangements for the free distribution of ration to the poor from the royal treasury and opened free kitchen.

15. *Reforms in Islam.* Sikandar tried to check certain customs which he considered bad in Islam. He forbade the visit of Muslim women to the shrines of saints. He prohibited the procession of *'Tazias* at the festival of Moharram.

Dark side of Sikandar Lodi : A fanatic

In religious matters, the Sultan is described as a fanatic and intolerant towards the Hindus. As observed by Nizam-ud-Din Ahmed, "His

(Sikandar's) bigotry in Islam was as great that in this regard he was beyond the bounds of even access." He destroyed several important temples like that of Jwalamukhi (Nagarkot), Mathura, Mandrail, Narwar, Chanderi etc. He broke images in the temples and raised mosques at their places.

Concluding observations. The above mentioned description, not withstanding his fanaticism, shows that undoubtedly Sikandar was a successful ruler. In the words of Dr. K.S. Lal, "Sikandar Shah had ruled for twenty-nine years full of glory and distinction. He was the greatest ruler of the Lodi dynasty and outshone both his father Bahlol and his son Ibrahim."

Likewise Dr. A.L. Srivastava has observed, "Sikandar was the greatest king of Lodi dynasty. Medieval chroniclers bestow much praise on him and maintain that he was an extremely able, just, benevolent and God-fearing ruler, the prestige of the Sultanate as well as of the crown which had fallen during the later Tughlaqs was restored."

Q. 4. Give the chief events of the reign of Ibrahim Lodi. How far was he responsible for the downfall of the Lodi dynasty?

Ans. *Ibrahim Lodi* (1517 to 1526) : *Main Events of His Reign.*

1. *Partition of the Kingdom.* The Afghan nobles were divided into two groups. They wanted to divide the empire into two parts. Ibrahim accepted his proposal and accordingly Jalal Khan, his brother became the ruler of Jaunpur. However, Ibrahim changed his mind and it resulted in a serious conflict with his brother. Jalal Khan was defeated.

Ibrahim got his brother poisoned to death and ruthlessly punished the supporters of Jalal Khan. This act created suspicion and distrust among the Afghan nobles for Ibrahim.

2. *Conflict with the nobles.* Ibrahim Lodi wanted to treat Afghan nobles as his servants. This led to a fierce conflict between Ibrahim and a large number of nobles. The battle was unprecedented.

Describing the battle Niamatullah, the author of 'Tarikh-i-Khan-i-Jahani' states, "Dead bodies, heap upon heap, covered the field, and the number of heads lying upon the ground was beyond the reach of recollection."

Streams of blood ran over the plain. Brother against brother and father against son, urged by mutual rivalry and in born bravery, mixed in the conflict.

3. *Conquest of Gwalior.* The ruler of Gwalior—a Rajput had given shelter to Jalal Khan, brother of Ibrahim. Therefore, Ibrahim attacked and annexed Gwalior to his kingdom.

4. *Conflict with Rana Sangram Singh popularly known as Rana Sanga of Mewar.* Encouraged by his success against Gwalior, Ibrahim decided to conquer Mewar whose ruler was Rana Sanga—a great warrior. The armies of Delhi met with several reverses. Ibrahim lost his prestige and resources.

5. *Battle of Panipat* (1526). Several Afghan nobles particularly Daulat Khan Lodi, governor of Punjab and Alam Khan Lodi, uncle of Ibrahim Lodi invited Babur, the ruler of Kabul to invade Delhi. This was done to take revenge from Ibrahim Lodi. Babur had already set his eyes upon India. He attacked India with about 12,000 soldiers and a number of cannon (machine guns). Ibrahim faced Babur at Panipat on April 21, 1526 with a force of about 1,00,000 soldiers. Ibrahim offered stiff resistance but was defeated and killed in the battlefield. This was perhaps the first instance in the history of Sultanate of Delhi that a Sultan lost his life in the battlefield. Thus came the end of the rule of the Lodi dynasty and the beginning of the Mughal rule in India.

Causes of the Failure of Ibrahim

Among the most important factors of his failure were the character traits of Ibrahim, his theory of kingship, treatment with the nobles, conflict with Rana Sanga and Babur's invasion.

1. *Character of Ibrahim.* Ibrahim was impolite, obstinate and rash. He failed to understand the character and sentiments of his own race i.e. Afghan nobles.

2. *Disregard of the agreement.* In the beginning of his reign, the division of the empire between the two brothers was agreed upon by Ibrahim in the presence of his nobles. He refuted it very soon. It displeased all those nobles who were in favour of the agreement.

3. *Theory of kingship.* Ibrahim declared, "Kingship knows no kingship" and treated the nobles as his subordinates. Dr. R.P. Tripathi writes, "He openly confessed that kings have no relations nor clans and that all men and clans were his servants."

4. *Ill treatment of the Afghan Amirs.* On the one hand the Afghan nobles desired that the Sultan should consider them as his associates or colleagues and on the other hand, to prove himself more powerful, the Sultan made a regulation that all the Amirs (nobles) would remain standing with folded hands before him in the court. Mian Bhuva Lodi, a reputed Amir was imprisoned because he could not perform his duties on account of old age. His death took place in prison itself. There were several other instances of the dictatorial attitude of the Sultan. His vindictive temperament created a lot of resentment among the nobles as well as the general public. Ibrahim's actions provoked the rebellious nature of the Amirs who felt humiliated. He lost several opportunities to compromise with them due to his adamant nature. He failed to appreciate the mood of the Amirs and his own weaknesses. This led to several revolts.

Ibrahim could neither command the respect of the nobles nor could utilise their strength in order to strengthen the empire. On the other hand he invited their wrath.

5. *Humiliation of the Sultan at the hands of Rana Sanga.* Ibrahim was over ambitious. He overestimated his strength. In all the conflicts with Rana Sanga, Ibrahim faced defeat. This had a great set back to him. His prestige suffered in the eyes of the Amirs.

6. *Defeat in the battle of Panipat.* Babur, the Mongol ruler inflicted the fatal blow to the already tottering power of the Sultan. Ibrahim was killed in the battlefield.

Following are usually ascribed the main causes of the defeat of Ibrahim in spite of his having about 10 times force than Babur.

(1) Use of artillery by Babur.

(2) Babur's well-disciplined army.

(3) War tacticts of Babur.

(4) Ibrahim's unpopularity and lack of unity among Afghan nobles.

(5) Ibrahim's war elephants no match to the cavalry of Babur.

(6) Martyr's spirit of the soldiers of Babur and their unflinching loyalty to him.

(7) Mutual rivalry of Indian rulers.

The defeat and death of Ibrahim Lodi led to the opening of a new chapter in the history of India.

Ibrahim neither had the qualities of a great general nor that of a skilful diplomat. His personal temperament was also very rash. He failed to have a correct estimate of his limitations and strengths. All these led to the fall of the Lodi dynasty.

7

Polity : Kingship and Administration During the Sultanate Period (State, Political and Administrative Institutions)

Q. 1. Discuss the concept of Kingship under the Delhi Sultanate. What was its relation with the religion?

Or

Discuss the relationship between the Delhi Sultanate and the Caliph.

Or

Briefly discuss the nature of the state during the Sultanate period?

Or

Analyse whether the state during Sultanate period was a theocracy or a military state.

Or

How did the Ulemas influence the state during the Sultanate period?

Or

Critically evaluate the Turkish concept of Kingship.

(Delhi University 1997)

Ans. *Chief Characteristics of the nature of Polity and Administrative system of the Delhi Sultanate.*

1. The government or the state was expected to be a theocratic state.
2. The government of the Delhi Sultanate was expected to work in accordance with the Islamic principles of sovereignty.
3. The government should follow the Islamic jurisprudence or law in all administrative matters.
4. The Sultan of India took pride to call himself the Deputy of the Caliph.
5. **The Sultan usually tried to believe in the divine right of kings.**
6. The Sultanate state was a military state to a considerable extent.
7. The Sultanate state was a feudal state.
8. The Sultanate state was greatly influenced by the Ulemas in general.
9. The state revenue was levied in accordance with Islamic law.
10. The Amirs or the nobles tried to exercise their influence over the appointment of the Sultan as well as his survival.
11. There was no clear-cut law of succession to the throne.

Theocratic as well as Military state

Before we discuss the issue whether the Delhi Sultanate was a theocratic state or a military state, it would be proper to say a few words about the nature of a theocratic state and military state.

A theocratic state is one whose entire functioning is based on the tenets of a religion and a military state is one which depends on the military strength for its survival.

The Sultanate state was a theocratic as well as a military state. It combined religious elements as well as military elements.

The Delhi Sultanate like that of all other Muslim states of the time was a theocracy. This meant that its political and administrative institutions were, in theory, derived from the Islamic Law (*Shariat*) based upon the precepts of Quaran. Islamic theocracy, in a larger sense, also meant that the entire Islamic world was united under the religious and political authority of the Caliph, the representative of the Prophet. Every Muslim State was look upon as the Caliph's dependency and its ruler had to pay allegiance to the Caliph and to seek confirmation for his right to rule as the deputy of the Caliph. Islam being the religion of the State, it was the primary duty of the State to promote Islam. The theocratic law was supreme and the civil law was subordinate to it. The *Ulemas,* in general, interpreted the Islamic laws and thus had an influential position. The Sultan was expected to show remarkable respect to the *Shariat*, to levy taxes according to the Shariat.

In practice, however, this theory passed through some modifications. In a country like India, where non-Muslims constituted an overwhelming large majority of population, and the political and social conditions differed very widely from those contemplated by the Muslim-jurists, it was not possible to maintain the full rigidity of the Islamic law. Also the degree of modifications depended on the personality, capability and power of the ruler and the situations circumventing his freedom, initiative and judgement.

The Delhi Sultanate also combined several elements of a military state. Usually it is said that a military state does not follow religious tenets. But the Delhi Sultanate which sometimes appears to be a military state derived its inspiration from religion. In fact as against the invasions of the foreigners like the Huns, the Shakas and the Kushans, the foreign Muslim invaders invaded India primarily for the sake of spreading their religion. They therefore used their military power, defeated the Indian rulers and established their rule which by and large was based on Islamic injunctions. Military in a theocratic as well as a non-theocratic state is used for crushing internal revolts. During the period of the Sultanate the military commanders were appointed governors or 'Iqtadars' of the *'Idtas'* or provinces or territorial units. The state's major revenue was spent in maintaining the army. Accordingly state revenue policy was dictated by military expenditure. The state suppressed the internal revolts, maintained peace and defended the empire from foreign invaders on the strength of its military. The Sultan himself was the commander-in-chief of the army. The Sultan's success primarily depended upon his military skill. Balban and Alau-ud-Din paid great attention towards making effective reforms in their military organisation and successfully faced all internal and external dangers.

Nevertheless, the Sultans also took interest in public welfare programmes like construction of canals, roads, postal arrangement and currency reforms etc. Many took interest in controlling prices.

Several Sultans patronised, art, architecture, music and literature etc.

Thus we can say that the Sultanate State combined several elements.

The Delhi Sultans and the Caliphate. According to the Islamic theory, the Caliph was the spiritual and temporal head of the entire Muslim world. He was Pope and Caesar combined. A ruler of any Muslim state wherever it might be located was looked upon a Caliph's deputy. The Sultans of Delhi paid ceremonial homage to the Caliphs of Egypt (though Caliph's power had lost its earlier strength and significance) and sought formal recognition for their being his deputy. Iltutmish was the first to receive such recognition and on his coins he described himself as a deputy of the Caliph. Ala-ud-Din discontinued the practice, while his son Mubarak himself assumed the title of Caliph, brushing aside the fiction of allegiance to the Caliph. But Muhammad-bin-Tughlaq sought the recognition of the Caliph in order to recover his waning prestige. His successor Firoz had his highest regard for the Caliph and described himself as his deputy. He had his rulership twice confirmed by the Caliph. After him, no ruler sought the Caliph's confirmation. The earlier practice was in fact conventional and did not effect the Sultan's power.

Theocratic state and the Ulemas. The Muslim divines, called the *Ulemas* were the authoritative interpreters of Islamic Law. They were a highly influential body and their *fatwa* was sought on all religious questions in dispute. The Sultans consulted them not only on points of Muslim Law but also on matters of State policy. This was becoming a convention, and the *Ulemas* felt convinced that they had to be consulted on matters both sacred or secular. Few rulers had the moral courage to resist their interference or avoid consulting them. Ala-ud-Din was the first Sultan to check their pretensions and disregarded their advice. Muhammad Tughlaq also took courage and adopted a policy which was against their orthodox presumptions and sentiments. As a result he had to face the arrogance and hostility of the *Ulemas*. Firoz Tughlaq had all respect for the *Ulemas* and their views. Thus the Ulemas had a great influence over him. The Sultan was completely under their domination. And when the *Ulemas* had a free hand, their orthodoxy and narrow outlook had very harmful effects.

The Sultan as the Supreme sovereign. According to the Muslim theology sovereignty was vested in the Muslim Law. Subject to general conformity with the Law, the Sultan was the head of the state and he enjoyed unlimited powers. All legislative, executive and judicial powers were concentrated in his person. His order was the law in the state. He was the highest commander of the army. He appointed all ministers, nobles and other officers of the state. What could curb the despotism of the rulers was that they could not defy the Muslim law. But in fact, not in theory, many rulers were the supreme interpreters of the Law.

There was no law of succession to the throne. It was not necessary that the eldest son or the daughter of the Sultan should succeed. However, tradition developed that the throne belonged to the eldest son. The Sultan also had the right to nominate anyone as his successor. These were wars of succession and a lot of blood was shed for capturing the throne. However, the experiment of placing a woman (Raziya was the only example) or minor on the throne failed. In several cases 'sword' decided the issue of succession.

Another important check on the royal power was the privileged position of the nobles. At the time of Iltutmish, there was the struggle between the crown and the nobles for clutching the real power. Nobles dominated during Nasir-ud-Din Mahmud's time. Balban kept the nobles at check. Muhammad-bin-Tughlaq showed through his coins bearing the message that he was the shadow of God. During Lodhi rule nobles claimed the status of equality with the king. Everything depended on the personality of the ruler.

Q. 2. Describe the central administration of the Delhi Sultanate.
(Rajasthan University 1995)

Ans. *The Sultanate Period*

The Sultans of Delhi ruled over India from 1206 A.D. to 1526 A.D.—a period of about 320 years. Qutub-ud-Din Aibak was the first Sultan and Ibrahim Lodi, the last Sultan. With the defeat of Ibrahim Lodi at the hands of Babur in 1526, came the end of the Delhi Sultanate.

Chief Characteristics of administration of the Delhi Sultanate

The first salient feature was that it was expected to work in accordance with the Islamic jurisprudence or law. The second was that it should follow the Islamic principle of sovereignty which declares that the Muslims all over the world have only one ruler i.e. the Caliph or Khalifa of Baghdad. None else could be deemed as a sovereign ruler. The Sultan was considered as a representative of the Caliph. Most of the Sultans of Delhi regarded themselves as the Viceroys of the Khalifa in whose name they ruled. Again most of them used Khalifa's name on their coins. The first ruler to abandon this practice was Ala-ud-Din. The third feature was that the state under the Sultan rulers was an Islamic or Theocratic state. The fourth feature was that the state was a military state and the Sultan himself was the supreme commander of his forces. The fifth feature was that it was a feudal state. The sixth feature was that the Sultan was the fountain head of all authority. The seventh feature was that the *Ulemas* tried to influence administration and policy.

Central administration

1. *Sovereignty of the king and his power.* The Sultan enjoyed vast powers. He was the fountain head of all power. Some of the Sultans like Balban and Ala-ud-Din enjoyed vast powers. Ala-ud-Din used to say that his 'word was law'. Secondly the Sultan usually behaved like a despot. Thirdly he was the head of the executive, judiciary and military. Some rulers like Ala-ud-Din assumed the role of a religious head also. Fourthly, the Sultan maintained a great grandeur in his court. The court was considered as a symbol of power and glory of the Sultanate. Fifthly, the king depended mostly on the power of his army. Sixthly, in general the Sultan tried to seek the advice of the Ulemas in various types of administrative matters.

2. *The Ministers.* It is said, "The bravest of men require arms and the wisest of Kings need ministers." The Sultans tried to appoint only competent ministers who were responsible to them only. Their positions and powers were defined by law as well as by tradition. Usually there were six ministers. The *Wazir, Diwan-i-Risalt, Sadr-us-Sudur, Diwan-i-Insha, Diwan-i-Arz, Qazi-ul-Quzat.*

Sometimes, there existed a post of a *Naib* which was next only to the Sultan and he was above the *wazir.* This post became important when there were weak Sultans. The powerful Sultan either abolished the post altogether or gave it to a noble simply to honour him as was done by Ala-ud-Din Khalji. In that case the post was just 'ornamental' and the *'Naib'* enjoyed no special powers in administration.

3. *Chart showing Administrative structure at the centre*

The Sultan

Naib (The deputy to the Sultan)

1	2	3	4	5	6
Wazir (Prime Minister and Finance Minister	*Diwan-i-Risalt'* (Foreign Affairs Minister)	*Sadr-us Suddar'* (Minister of Islami Law)	*'Diwan-i-Insha* (Correspondence Minister	*Diwan-i Ariz'* (Defence or War Minister)	*'Qqzi-ul-'Quzat'* (Minister of Justice)

4. *Revenue sources.* Following were the sources of revenue

(*i*) *Ushr.* It was a tax on land which was collected from Muslim peasants. It was 10 per cent of the produce on the land watered by natural resources and 5 per cent on the land which enjoyed facilities provided by irrigation works.

(*ii*) *Kharaj.* It was a land tax charged from non-Muslims and ranged from one third to half of the produce.

(*iii*) *Khams.* It was one-fifth of the booty captured in the war. Four-fifth of it went to the army which fought war.

(*iv*) *Jizya.* It was a religious tax on Non-Muslims. According to Islam, a *Zimmi* (Non-Muslim) had no right to live in the kingdom of a Muslim Sultan. But this concession was permitted after payment of the tax called *Jizya.* Women, children, beggars, priests, Brahmans etc. and all those who had no source of income were exempted from this tax. Firoz Tughlaq levied this tax on Brahmans also.

(*v*) *Zakat.* This was a religious tax which was imposed only on rich Muslims and it was 2 1/2 per cent of their income.

(*vi*) *Trade tax.* Trade tax was charged at the rate of 2 1/2 per cent from the Muslims and 5 per cent from the Hindus.

(*vii*) *Horse tax.* There was 5 per cent tax on the sale and purchase of horses.

(*viii*) *House tax.* It was levied by Ala-ud-Din Khalji.

(*ix*) *Grazing tax.* It was also levied by Ala-ud-Din Khalji.

(*x*) *Property revenue.* All property which had no heirs passed to the state.

(*xi*) *Mines tax.* It was 1/5 of the produce of the mines.

(*xii*) *Buried treasure tax.* It was 1/5 of the buried treasure that was found.

5. *Assessment of Land and land revenue.* The land was of 4 kinds (*a*) The *Khalsa* land. This land was directly administered by the central government. The central government appointed revenue officers for the collection of revenue. (*b*) The *Walis or Muqtis.* This land was in the hands of provincial governors. The provincial governors collected land revenue from this land and after meeting the collection charges they deposited the surplus in the central treasury. (*c*) Land of the Feudary Hindu chiefs. The chiefs paid fixed annual tributes to the Sultan. (*d*) *Inam or Waqf land.* This type of land was given to the people in gift or charity and particularly to Muslim scholars and saints. It was free of tax.

Mostly the land revenue was collected in cash but sometimes in kind also.

6. *Justice.* The Sultan was the highest judicial authority He used to hold his court twice a week and decided all types of cases.

Qazi-ul-Qazat (Chief/judicial officer or the Minister for justice) heard appeals from the lower courts. There was a *'Qazi'* in every town. The *Qazis'* were appointed by the Sultan in consultation with the chief judicial officer. Usually severe punishments were awarded.

7. *Organisation of the Army.*

(1) *Royal army*
(2) *Provincial governnors' army*
(3) *Feudal lords' army*
(4) *War time army*
(5) *Holy war army*

A strong army was needed by the Sultan as his very existence depended upon it. It was needed for four purposes (*i*) For extending kingdom (*ii*) For checking rebellions (*iii*) For maintaining law and order and (*iv*) For meeting the challenge of Mongol invasions.

Royal army. It was a heterogeneous body comprising the Turks of various tribes, the Tajiks, the Persians, the Arabs, the Afghans, the Abyssinians, Indian Muslims and Hindus.

Provincial governor's army. The governors maintained their own armies. They brought their armies to the service of the Sultan when ordered.

Feudal lords or chiefs army. Feudal chiefs whether directly under the Sultan or under his suzerainty maintained armies and supplied the same when asked by the Sultan.

Wartime army. Soldiers were recruited on temporary basis.

Holy war army. There were Muslim soldiers who joined the army voluntarily to fight wars against the Hindus. They received no pay but were given the share of booty captured during war.

Q. 3. Define the *'Iqta'* system. How did it work under the Sultans of Delhi? (Delhi University 1997)

Or

Explain the meaning of the word *'Iqta'* and describe its chief characteristics and the duties of *'Iqtadars'*

Or

Describe provincial administration under the Delhi Sultanate.

Ans. *Meaning of the 'Iqta' system.*

'Iqta' is an Arabic word denoting a sort of administrative regional unit. It is usually considered equivalent to a province.

Initially the Delhi Sultans had divided their empire into several *'Iqtas'* or provinces or spheres of influence and put them under the charge of officers called *'Iqtadars'* (governors).

The number of Iqtas was not fixed. There was no uniformity in their administration.

Besides *'Iqtadar'*, other names of the heads of an *'Iqta'* were *'Naib'* Sultan, *'nazim'* might' or *'wali'*.

Each *'Iqta'* was under the charge of an experienced general who generally was the member of the royal family or a notable *'Amir'* (noble) and confidant of the Sultan.

Duties and powers of the Iqtadar

1. He was under the supervision of the Central government and carried on orders of the Sultan.

2. He enjoyed the same powers in the province as the Sultan enjoyed in the empire.

3. He maintained large armies and was required to send the same when asked by the Sultan.

4. He maintained order in the territory under his charge and protected the life and property of the people.

5. He appointed soldiers in his army.

6. He collected revenue from the people of his territory.

7. From the revenue thus collected he administered expenditure on the maintenance of his army, his pay and other administrative expenditure and deposited the rest in the state treasury.

8. He sent yearly report of his income and expenditure to the centre.

Restrictions on the Iqtadar

1. The Iqtadar did not always enjoy hereditary powers. The Sultan could take back Iqta from him whenever he pleased.

2. The Iqtadar was liable to be transferred from one place to another.

3. He could not engage himself in wars of extension without the prior approval of the Sultan.

4. He was required to send a part of the booty to the Sultan.

5. The elephants and the members of the royal family captured during wars were to be sent to the Sultan.

6. He was not allowed to hold his own court.

7. He could not use a canopy or royal emblem.

8. He could not mint coins in his name.

9. He could not read *'Khutba'* in his name.

During the rule of a weak Sultan, the *'Iqtadars'* were tempted to enjoy more powers. They even kept elephants an exclusive privilege of the Sultan.

Two categories of Iqtas. During the reign of Ala-ud-Din, the Iqtas were divided into two categories : (1) Iqtas which had been under the Delhi Sultans from the very beginning (2) The territories brought under control by Ala-ud-Din Khalji.

The *'muqtis'* or the *'walis'* i.e. the *'Iqtadars'* of the second category were given more powers so that the newly acquired territories could be brought about under more effective control.

Besides the *'Iqtadar'*, there were several other officers of the central government.

The efficient functioning of an *'Iqta'* depended on the power of the Sultan on the one hand and on the other hand on the capability of the *'Iqtadar'*.

Division of 'Iqtas' into units. In due course the *'Iqtas'* were divided into smaller units called *'shiqqs' 'parganas'* and the villages.

The head of a *'Shiqq'* was called *'Shiqqdar'*. Important officials of a *'paragana'* were the *'amil'* or *'munsif'* the treasurer and the *'quanungo'*

Local administration. The village, the smallest unit of administration was administered by local hereditary officers and the *'Panchayat'* of the village. The *'Panchayat'*. looked after education, sanitation etc. It also acted as a judicial body.

The *'Chaudhri'* the *'Patwari'*, the *'Khut'* the *'Muqaddam'* and the

'Chankidari' were the hereditary officers of the village who helped in the collection of revenue.

The Sultan or the governor or officials of the state normally did not interfere in the village administration.

Q. 4. Discuss the main characteristics of the struggle between the Sultans and the Amirs.

Or

Examine the role of the nobility in the politics of Delhi Sultanate.

(Delhi University, 1997)

Ans. *Meaning of nobility.*

The nobles normally occupied the place next to the Sultan and played a key role in the administration of the state. Nobles comprised the ruling class and belonged to different tribes and nationalities like the Turkish, Persian, Arabic, Egyptian and Indian Muslims. During the Sultanate period the number of Hindu nobles was extremely negligible.

Important functions performed by the nobles

1. They helped the Sultan in the expansion of the empire.
2. They helped the Sultan in suppressing rebellions of the Hindus.
3. They helped the Sultan in running the administration.

Nobles as kingmakers. Sometimes nobles played a crucial role in the choice of the Sultan. In the absence of any law of succession, they sided with the one or the other claimants of the throne.

Intrigues of the nobles. The nobles were very ambitious. They were usually divided into various factions and engaged themselves into conspiracies.

Nobility and the Slave Dynasty

Qutub-ud-Din Aibak. He was very skilful in maintaining a balance between the those Turkish nobles whom he had brought with him from outside India and the Non-Turkish nobles. He did not assign the important positions to one faction only.

Iltutmish. Iltutmish organised a group or Corps of Forty selected Amirs (who were originally slaves) during his reign. They were appointed on key posts in the military and civil administration. They were his 'ears and eyes'. They were his chief advisors. Iltutmish was able to obtain their unflinched loyalty and proved a successful ruler.

Powerful Nobles. After the death of Iltutmish, the Corps of Forty became very powerful. Disregarding the wish of Iltutmish, they raised Rakn-ud-Din Firoz to the throne instead of Razia. However aftersometime, they seated Razia on the throne. Razia tried to free herself from the clutches of the Turkish nobles and organised a group of non-Turkish and Indian Muslim nobles under the leadership of Yakut, an Abyssinian. They Turkish nobles resented this and organised conspiracies against Razia and ultimately were successful in murdering Razia and Yakut. The Turkish nobles made and unmade Sultans.

Balban's stern measures against the Nobles. Balban proved very powerful and he almost liquidated the Corps of Forty. He introduced stern measures against Turkish nobles and appointed Non. Turkish nobles on important posts. He followed the policy of 'blood and iron' against all those who opposed him. He himself belonged to the Corps of Forty and knew their assets and weak points. He was convinced that this group was doing a lot of destructive work and was a great danger to the stability of the Sultan and the Sultanate of Delhi. He adopted all sorts of fair and foul methods to eliminate them. He even poisoned to death some of the nobles. Balban put an end to the hereditary control of the nobles over the jagirs. He confiscated the jagirs of all those nobles who even slightly deviated from his instructions. He prescribed strict court etiquettes for the nobles.

Jal-ul-Din Khalji. He gave important posts to Khalji nobles to win over them as the Turkish nobles regarded him as the usurper of the throne.

Nobility and the Khalji Dynasty

Ala-ud-Din Khalji and the Nobility. Ala-ud-Din had realised from the very beginning that nobility was responsible for a good deal of unrest in the empire. He, therefore, took several measures to crush the power of the nobles. Broadly his measures can be categorised as under.

(*a*) *Administrative measures.* (*i*) Ala-ud-Din organised an efficient spy system to keep a strict watch on the activities of the nobles.

He prohibited the sale and use of wine and other intoxicating drinks as he felt that drinking parties among nobles provided them opportunities to intrigue.

(*b*) *Economic measures.* Ala-ud-Din was of the opinion that excess of wealth with the nobles created rebellions tendencies among them. He confiscated the jagirs of several nobles. He introduced a system of market control to check hoarding and prices.

(*c*) *Social measures.* The Sultan forebade his nobles to go to social gathering and enter into matrimonial alliance without his permission.

The nobles and the Lodis

Ibrahim Lodi. After the death of Sikandar Lodi, the Afghan Amirs placed their selfish interest above Lodi state and dynastic interests. To augment their vested influence and interest, they were successful for a while to divide the territory between two brothers namely Jalan Khan and Ibrahim. Not only this, they indulged in subversive activities. Two important noble groups were formed. The activities of the groups endangered the very existence of the Lodi dynasty. Two powerful nobles i.e. Daulat Khan Lodi and Azam Khan Lodi extended invitation to Babur to invade the Lodi state. Thus the rivalry among the nobles led to the end of the Lodi rule and the beginning of the Mughal rule in India.

8

Socio-economic Life During the Sultanate Period (Society During the Sultanate Period Economic and Technological Developments)

Q. 1. State the social life during the Sultanate period.

Or

Describe the main social divisions during the Sultanate period.

Ans. (1) *Division of Society on the Basis of Nationality.*

The most important characteristics of the society was division on the basis of nationality. Earlier such a division was very insignificant but now it had become quite distinct.

(*i*) *Foreign Muslims.* Foreign Muslims, in general, constituted the ruling class. It was the most privileged and respected section of the society. All high offices of the state were usually kept reserved for them. They received extensive jagirs in return for their services. They exercised great influence in society, politics and administration. They belonged to different nationalities such as the Persians, the Afghans, the Egyptians, the Arabs, the Turks and the Abyssinians. Such a composite group had no solidarity. The Turks claimed and maintained their superiority over all others upto the thirteenth century. Intermarriages among different sections of foreign Muslims brought them at par with each other.

(*ii*) *Indian Muslims.* The next section was that of the Indian Muslims. These belonged to two categories. Either they were converted to Islam themselves or were descendants of converted Muslims. The foreign Muslims despised Indian Muslims because most of them were converted to Islam among low-caste Hindus. Therefore, the Indian Muslims were not given equal status with foreign Muslims either in society or in administration. During the entire period of the Sultanate, only very few Indian Muslims could get high positions.

(*iii*) *Shias and Sunnis.* The Muslims—foreign as well as Indian were also divided on the basis of religious sect, education and professions. The Ulemas claimed superiority. The *Sunnis* were backed by the Sultans of Delhi and the *Shias* had entered India after the Arab conquest of Sindh and therefore were powerful in Sindh and

Multan. The *Sunnis* and the *Shias* had frequent clashes. Scholars and soldiers were divided on the basis of education and professions. Shopkeepers, artisans, peasants and the like constituted the lowest cadre among the Muslims in the society.

(*iv*) *Hindus*. The Hindus constituted the majority of the Indian society. They were treated as second rate citizens of the state. Their services were considered essential in the revenue department. They, mostly monopolised trade and agriculture. They were divided into different sects and castes.

2. *Privileged and the unprivileged class.* There was practically no middle class in the societies of those days. There were the privileged and unprivileged classes. The privileged class was small and it was made up of the members of the imperial family, the courtesans, nobles, ulemas, and other learned men in the Islamic law and theology. The rest of the people belonged to the unprivileged class.

3. *Five major social groups.* These were : (*i*) The royal class (*ii*) The aristocratic class (*iii*) The Ulemas (*iv*) Town people (*v*) Peasants and labourers and artisans.

(*i*) *The royal class.* This class included the Sultan, princes and the governors of provinces.

(*ii*) *The Aristocratic class.* This class comprised the nobles, ministers, landlords and the feudal lords.

The Sultan enjoyed a special position For stressing his special significance, several ceremonies and rituals were carried out. The Sultan held a court with a great splendour. Court etiquettes were prescribed. Balban introduced a special practice called *sajda* i.e. kneeling before the Sultan. The Sultan had a large household with many officers and servants along with slaves to work. This enabled him to live in luxury and great pomp and show.

The nobles also imitated the Sultan. They had large income from their jagirs. They lived in luxury. They also kept a large number of slaves and servants. They built palatial buildings for living in them.

(*iii*) *The Ulemas.* The priestly class and especially the *Ulemas* also occupied an important status in the society. Some of them exercised tremendous influence on the rulers. They also served as their teachers and performed religious ceremonies. They became very rich by receiving grants of land and gifts.

(*iv*) *Town people.* The nobles, merchants, and officers lived in towns. They enjoyed a decent standard of living.

(*v*) *The peasants and others.* At the lowest rung of the ladder were the peasants who lived from hand to mouth.

4. *The slave system.* Slaves were sold like any other commodity. It is understood that there were slave markets also in a few towns. The Sultans and the nobles kept slaves in large numbers. The slaves were provided education and training. They were also provided opportunities to rise in their careers. Several of them like Malik Kafur rose to eminent positions in the state.

5. *Position of women.* In general, the status of women deteriorated in the society and they suffered from many social evils. Normally monogamy was in practice but among the rich polygamy was prevalent. *'Sati'* practice in the Hindu society continued. Widow remarriage was very rare. *'Purdah'* (veil) system among Muslim women was strictly observed.

Polygamy was widely prevalent among the Muslims. The nobles and rich Muslims kept a number of wives. Very little attention was paid to the education of women.

Diet. In general, while the Hindus were vegetarian, the Muslims were non-vegetarian. Martial races among the Hindus were mostly non-vegetarian. Among the Muslims, the *'Sufis'* and the people under their influence avoided meat-eating.

'Quran' prohibits the use of liquor to the followers of Islam, yet it was consumed mostly by the wealthy class.

Relations between the Hindus and the Muslims

Historians have differed widely on the relation between the two communities i.e. the Hindus and the Muslims.

According to Dr. A.L. Srivastva, "We have unbroken tradition coming down from hundreds of years that the Turkish rule was oppressive."

In the words of Dr. R.C. Majumdar, "It is true that the Hindus occupied a large number of junior posts and towards the close of the period, occasionally a few high offices, in civil administration, and more rarely in the army. But they had no political status and lived on suffrage in the land of their birth, which was regarded as, and publicly declared to be, a Muslim state and country."

Dr. K.S. Lal is of the view that the bitterness between the two communities had its origin in political scenario. The Muslims were the conquerors and the Hindus conquered. Bitterness, therefore, was natural. However he also states that strained relations to some extent were on account of the nature of Muslim laws which were applicable to a non-Islamic country like India.

The Muslim rulers based their administrative practices on Islamic laws and did not change these in accordance with the laws of their subjects who were mostly Hindus. Barring a few Sultans, others accepted the influence of the *'Ulemas'* in state matters.

However, a small section of Bhakti saints (Hindus) and Sufi saints (Muslim saints) emphasised the spirit of harmony between the Hindus and the Muslims.

On the whole the relations between the two communities were of hostility.

Q. 2. State the economic condition during the period of the Sultanate.

Ans. *India a Rich Country*

There is no doubt that India by and large remained a rich country throughout this period. Foreign travellers who visited India during this period have observed that the people used gold, silver, diamonds, pearls and other precious stones profusely in the form of ornaments.

It was India's fabulous wealth which tempted Mahmud of Ghazni to invade India so many times.

Timur also got unimaginable wealth from only one of India's corners.

We find several prosperous cities and parts during this period.

The Sultans of Delhi, nobles, governors, merchants and elites of the society possessed vast wealth and enjoyed all comforts of material life.

Several beautiful mosques, monuments, palaces, forts and temples were built during this period.

All this indicates that there was general economic prosperity in the country.

Despite constant warfare of the Sultans of Delhi, affluent agricultural and industrial production and foreign trade had enriched India and maintained its prosperity. Achievements in various fields of Indian economy were mostly on account of private enterprise. Very little was done by the Sultans and provincial governors towards the direct development of trade and industry.

Food in general was not a problem for the common man.

The problem of shelter did not worry the people.

Prosperous agriculture. According to Ibn Batuta, a traveller who came from North Africa in India during the fourteenth century, agriculture was in a state of great progress. The soil was so fertile that it produced two crops every year; rice being sown three times a year.

Sesame, sugar-cane and cotton were grown in abundance and these formed the basis of several village industries. Rice of Sarsauti, sugar-cane of Kanauj, wheat and betel leaf of Malwa, wheat of Gwalior, ginger and spices of Malabar, grapes and pomegranates of Daultabad, betel nuts of the South India and a large variety of oranges were popular in and outside India.

Cereals, pulses, fruits and vegetables etc. were produced in almost all parts of India.

The Ganga-Yamuna Doab remained always famous for its fertility and large scale production.

Animal husbandry was in a very advanced stage.

Ordinarily there was plenty of food production. However, on account of the failure of rains, there were periods of draught.

Condition of peasants. Peasants formed the overwhelming majority of the population. They had to work hard to eke out bare subsistence. Usually they were required to pay one-third of their produce as land revenue.

Industry. Textile industry was the primary industry. Cotton, silk and woollen clothes of different varieties were produced in large quantity. The clothes were studded with gold, diamond, pearl, silver and other stones. Indian textiles were in great demand in foreign countries.

The skill of Indian craftsmen was of a high order. Indian cotton textiles were introduced in China as well where these were valued more than silk.

Bengal and Gujarat were famous for their fine quality fabrics.

Important handicrafts were such as carpet weaving, mat work and leather work.

Besides textile industry, sugar industry, paper industry, metal work, stone cutting, pearl driving out of the sea, ivory and sandal wood work were other important industries of India.

The Sultans had set up several *'Karkhanas'* (workshops).

Trade and commerce. India carried a brisk trade—both internal as well as external.

Delhi was the largest city and the most important trading centre. Other important trade centres were : Daultabad, in the south, Lahore and Multan in the north-west, Kara and Lakhnauti in the east and Anhilwara (Patan) and Cambay (Khambayat) in the west.

External trade was very profitable and it was one of the main causes of the wealth of India. India had trade relations with Iran, Arabia, European countries, Africa, China, Malaya, Afghanistan and Central Asia, etc.

The Arabs were the dominant partners in trade through Indian ocean.

The Gujarati and Tamil traders played an important part in trade.

The main items of India's exports were : cereals, cotton and silken cloth, opium, indigo, sea-pearls, sandal wood, saffron, ginger, sugar and coconuts, etc.

India imported horses, salt, rosewater, colour valvets, perfumes, wines etc. The external trade was carried on both by land and sea.

Goa, Diu, Chaula, Cochin and Quilon were the important parts on the western Sea-coast of India. There were several seaports on the eastern coast also.

India enjoyed a favourable balance of trade.

9

The North West Frontier Policy During the Sultanate Period (Mongol Invasions of India)

Q. 1. Discuss the North-West Frontier policy of the Delhi Sultans.

Or

Evaluate the measures taken by Balban and Ala-ud-Din to checkmate the Mongol invasions.

Or

What were the efforts made by Balban and Ala-ud-Din to check in the Mongolian inroads?

Ans. *Mongol Invasions on the North-West Frontier of India.*

The North-West Frontier of India always remained vulnerable to foreign attacks in ancient and medieval times. Several invaders came to India from the North-West. The rulers of India attempted to devote attention towards guarding their frontier according to their ability and competence. During those days the frontiers comprised the Hindukush mountains along with the regions of Kabul, Gazni and Gandhar.

The Mongols from Central Asia created difficult situations for several Indian Sultans. Their invasions weakened the powers of some of the rulers so much that they had to suffer humiliation and that some of the governors under them declared their independence and became independent rulers.

Mongols and the Sultans of Slave Dynasty

Iltutmish. During the beginning of the 12th century A.D., Mongols under the leadership of Changzeb Khan invaded several countries from Japan to Central Asia. Lakhs of people became victim of their atrocities. India barely escaped their fury. The Shah of Khwarizm, Jalal-ud-Din was forced by the Mongols to flee from his country. He sought refuge with Sultan Iltutmish who very diplomatically sent him back on the plea of unsuitable climate of India. The Shah was hotly being pursued by the Mongols. Fortunately for India, the Mongols had to return from the frontiers of India on account of political exigencies in Central Asia.

Baharm Shah and Nasir-ud-Din. The first Mongol invasion took place in 1241. The Mongols plundered several territories including Lahore to their heart's content. The Sultan Baharm Shah could not do anything. Another adverse effect of the Mongol invasion was that the provinces of Sind and Multan became independent of the Sultan. However, later on these two provinces were won over during Masud's time i.e. the successor of Baharm Shah.

During the next Sultan Nasir-ud-Din, the Mongols again attacked India and besieged Multan. The governor of Multan gave Rs. one lakh as war indemnity. Their attacks continued and Multan and Western Punjab came under their control.

Balban and the Mongols. The Mongol invasions increased during Balban's time but were met with great resistance. Balban knew well the strength and the savagery of the Mongols. He took the following measures to safeguard his kingdom from the invasions of the Mongols :

1. Balban decided not to leave Delhi for a long period to expand his kingdom.
2. Balban personally kept a vigilant eye over the North-West Frontier.
3. For purpose of defence, Balban divided the North-west frontier into two parts. Multan, Samanta and Dipalpur were also made as frontier provinces.
4. Balban appointed his sons and dependable relatives as the governors of those provinces. Mohammad, his eldest son and Bughra Khan were made the Governors of Samana and Dipalpur respectiveiy. Sher Shah Shangar (Sultan's cousin) was appointed the governor of Multan. After Sher Khan's death, Balban entrusted Sind, Multan and Lahore to his eldest son Muhammad.
5. Balban raised a strong army to defend the frontier itself and kept a large army at Delhi in the state of preparedness to meet the challenge of the Mongol invasions.
6. Balban built rows of strong forts at strategic points all along the frontier.
7. He posted experienced and well-trained military personnel in these forts.
8. Improved war weapons were manufactured and supplied to these forts.
9. Old forts were repaired and provided with adequate weapons and equipments.

The Mongols made their biggest invasion in 1285 in which Balban's eldest son Muhammad Khan was killed but in the end, the Mongols were defeated. Balban died the same year in the grief of his son.

The Khaljis and the Mongols

Jal-ul-Din and Mongols. During Jal-ul-Din's period, the Sultan himself defeated the Mongols near Samana. Hundreds of Mongols were killed. Many Mongols embraced Islam. The Sultan allowed several Mongols to settle down near the vicinity of Delhi. The Sultan married his daughter to one of the Mongol officers.

Mongol's and Ala-ud-Din. Alaud-Din had to face more than a dozen Mongol invasions. They trampled the frontier provinces under the hooves of their horses. On several occasions, they even reached Delhi.

Ala-ud-Din planned to fight offensively instead of defensively after some of their invasions.

The terror created by Zafar Khan, also called *Rustam-a-Hind,* one of the most prominent generals of the Sultan Ala-ud-Din, in the minds of the Mongol soldiers was so great that whenever the horses would not lower their mouths to drink water, the Mongol soldiers would mockingly shout at them whether they had seen Zafar Khan that they feared to stake their thrust.

Following were the important measures taken by Ala-ud-Din to check the Mongol invasions :

1. Old forts were repaired and seasoned officers and soldiers posted there.

2. New forts were built and experienced, well trained and well-equipped troops posted.

3. Armament manufacturing factories were set up under skilled technicians and engineers.

4. A separate and permanent army was prepared for the defence of the North-West Frontier.

5. A special governor was appointed for the North-West Frontier.

6. Strong armies were stationed at the frontier areas of Dipalpur, Samanta and Multan.

7. The most experienced generals like Zafar Khan, and Ghazni Malik were entrusted the responsibility of defending the borders.

8. A strong wall was constructed around the Capital (Siri Fort) so that the Mongols were unable to enter the capital.

9. Ala-ud-Din enforced the price control and market reform regulations in order to supply essentials commodities at reasonable rates to the army personnel.

As a result of the successful frontier policy of Ala-ud-Din, the danger from the Mongols almost disappeared. According to Barani and Ferishta, not only did the Mongols cease their aggression against India, but now they also had to defend themselves against the troops of Ala-ud-Din. Of course, in one of the Mongol invasions, the brave general Zafar Khan was killed.

Mongols and the Tughlaqs

Ghias-ud-Din. One Mongol invasion took place during his time but the Mongols were defeated.

Muhammad Tughlaq. The Mongols invaded under Tarmashirin. Historians have differed regard Muhammad Tughlaq's policy. According to one version, he defeated the Mongols and himself chased them to drive them out. However according to another version, Muhammad Tughlaq bribed the Mongols and they went back.

Firoz Tughlaq and his successors. Timur Lane's invasion proved very destructive. He massacred the population of Delhi for several days. It paved the way for Babur's invasion and the Mughal rule in India.

Effects of the Mongol Invasions

For meeting the challenge of the Mongol invasions, the Sultans of Delhi had to spend a substantial part of revenue in raising and maintaining a large army which had an adverse effect on their financial resources. Some of the Delhi Sultans like Ala-ud-Din Khalji had to increase the land revenue even to the extent of 50 per cent of the produce of the land. This had an adverse effect on agriculture and the general conditions of the peasants deteriorated.

Balban lost his dear son Muhammad in whose grief he died. Subsequently the slave dynasty fell, yielding power to the Khaljis.

Ala-ud-Din Khalji, though he was successful in driving away the Mongols, he lost one of his ablest military commanders namely Zafar Khan.

Jal-ul-Din Khalji allowed hundreds of Mongols to settle in the vicinity of Delhi and these Mongols embraced Islam. However these new Muslims created many difficulties for Ala-ud-Din Khalji.

Summing up

There is no doubt that the Mongol invasions proved very costly to all the kingdoms of the Delhi Sultanate and became one of the most important factors of its disintegration.

10

Development of Art, Architecture and Literature During the Sultanate Period

Q. 1. Give the main characteristics of the architecture during the Sultanate period. How did the Hindu architecture differ from the Muslim architecture. Describe the architecture of a few buildings constructed during the period. Write a brief note on the development of architecture during the Sultanate period. (Rajasthan University 1994)

Ans. *Three Styles of Architecture.*

Broadly speaking there were three styles of architecture during the Sultanate period in India.

1. Delhi or imperial style which primarily was confined to Delhi and Ajmer.

2. Provincial style which existed in the provinces of Multan, Jaunpur, Bengal etc.

3. Hindu architecture prevalent in Rajasthan and Vijayanagar empire.

Here we are mainly concerned with the imperial architecture.

Salient Characteristics of the Architecture During the Sultanate Period

1. *A mixture of Indian (Hindu) and Iranian (Muslim) Style.* The Sultans of Delhi wanted to construct their buildings on the pattern of Iran and Central Asia. However, their buildings could not be exact copies of these buildings. They had to employ Indian craftsmen who had their own ideas about the form and method of construction. Thus though the buildings were designed by Muslim architects to suit the requirements of their religious ideas, yet they were constructed by Hindu craftsmen who formed the finest artistry of the world. Obviously the buildings had a combination of Indo-Islamic architecture.

2. *Buildings constructed with the material of Hindu temples.* Several buildings were constructed out of the material used in the temples that were destroyed by some of the Muslim rulers. Quwat-ul-Islam Mosque in Delhi is said to have been built by Qutub-ud-Din Aibak by demolishing a Hindu temple. Likewise *'Adai-din-ka Jhopra'* a mosque in Ajmer, built in 2½ days came into being on the ruins of a Hindu building.

3. *Pointed arche in the Muslim structures.* It is noted that the Hindus used square pillars which supported their temple roofs. On the other hand

the Muslims used the arches. Besides arches, they also used domes over their buildings and minarets on sides. The use of arch and dome added charm to the Muslim buildings and also enabled them to dispense with the need of a large number of pillars to support the roof.

4. *Carvings.* The Hindus carved the figures of gods and goddesses on all sides of pillars, walls and ceilings also. They also carved various ornamental things like garlands, flowers and temple bells etc. The Muslims did not allow any representation of living things on their buildings. The Hindu workmen who were skilled in decorating the pillars and walls were allowed the use of flowers and trees in the decoration of Muslim buildings.

5. *Use of geometrical designs.* During the Sultanate period, geometrical designs began to be used for decoration purposes.

6. *Quaranic 'Ayats'.* The use of Quaranic *'Ayats'* in the buildings served two purposes i.e. religious as well as decorative.

7. *Use of stones and lime.* During the Sultanate period several types of coloured stones like red, light black, yellow and white marbles were used. A very good quality of stone was used to make the buildings strong.

Buildings of the Slave Period

Qutub-ud-Din Aibak got built the *'Quwat-ul-Islam Mosque'* at Delhi, probably on the ruins of a Hindu temple as even today one can notice the arches and pillar carvings of the Hindu design. It is said that he also started the construction of the Qutab Minar at Delhi which was completed by Iltutmish. However some historians do not accept this view and hold the view that it was built by a Hindu ruler. Still others believe that it was built by Iltutmish in the memory of a popular sufi saint Qutab-ud-Din Bakhtiar Kaki. The tower or the *'minar'* was originally 71.4 mts high. The circumference at the base is 15 mts and at the top just 3 mts. There were 5 storeys in all. At the end of each storey, there is an enclosed space for the visitors to go round it. It is constructed of red stone only. Qutab-ud-Din also built the Adai-din-ka Jhopra at Ajmer.

Iltutmish got constructed the tomb of his eldest son Nasir-ud-Din Mahmud at Sultan Garhi (Delhi). This was the first tomb built in India by the Turks. Iltutmish also got built the Dargah of Muin-ud-Din Chisti.

Balban's tomb in Delhi is in pure Islamic style.

Buildings built during the Khalji Period

Ala-ud-Din's buildings were built from perfectly Islamic view point and are regarded as few best examples of Islamic art in India. He built a new town at Delhi known as Siri, a few kilometres from the Qutab Complex. The Dargah of Hazrat-Nizam-ud-Din Aulia was also built. The *'Allai Darwaza'* a gate-way constructed near Qutab Minar has been described as "an invaluable treasure of Islamic culture." It has a beautiful combination of red sand stone and marble. The *'Ayats'* (verses) from the Quran are beautifully engraved with a unique balance in its arches. A huge tank called Hauz Khan or Hauz-i-Allai, spread over an area of more than seventy acres of land was also built near Siri. The tank was surrounded by a wall made of stone and lime mixture.

Buildings built during the Tughlaq Period. The Tughlaq Sultans were puritanical in their outlook and therefore they did not attach importance to ornamentation in their buildings. Secondly their buildings were very solid and strong. Some buildings bear mark of Hindu features.

Ghiyas-ud-Din Tughlaq built a new city of Tughlaqabad, east of Qutab area (Delhi). He also built a palace and his own tomb.

Muhammad Tughlaq built a new city of Jahanpanah near Siri (Delhi). Muhammad Tughlaq also constructed the Adalabad Fort near Tughlaqabad.

Firoz Shah is credited with the construction of several buildings and founding many towns. During his time uncarved stones were used in large quantity as a result of which buildings lacked beauty of architecture. It is also felt that the buildings of this period exhibited a vaccum of thought.

According to Ferishta, Firoz Tughlaq constructed 20 palaces, 20 cities, 30 schools, 30 mosques, 100 hospitals, 5 tombs and 150 bridges. Among his important buildings were the new city of Firozabad near the old city of Delhi, the palace fort known as Kotla Firoz Shah within it, or Madarsa (college) and his own tomb near Hauz-i-Khas.

Buildings constructed during the Lodi Dynasty. Lodi Sultans adopted a new style of constructing tombs on a raised platform. Some tombs were built within parks, e.g. Tomb of Sikandar Lodi within Lodi Gardens (New Delhi). Some tombs were octangular. Among the most important mosques was the *'Moth ki Masjid'* (New Delhi).

Q. 2. Briefly describe the development of literature during the Sultanate period.

Ans. *Growth of Literature During the Sultanate Period.*

The Sultanate period witnessed the growth of literature in different languages and in different fields. The most important aspects of the period in this respect were the following :

1. Preparation of historical texts which so far had remained neglected in India.

2. Beginning of the growth of literature in different regional languages in India.

Historical literature in Persian and Arabic This was primarily produced in Persian and Arabic by Muslim scholars. Important works are :

(1) *'Tahquiq-Hind'.* (11th century A.D.) by Al-Beruni who accompanied Mahmud Ghazni provides valuable account regarding affairs of India in the 11th century.

(2) *'Taj-ul-Maasur'* (13th century) by Hasan Nizami dealing with the events of the Slave Dynasty.

(3) *'Tarikh-Firoz Shahi'* (14th century) by Zia-ud-Barani giving information about the Tughlaq Dynasty.

(4) *'Kitab-ur-Rahlah'* (15th century) by Ibn Batuta dealing with the Lodi Dynasty.

(5) *Tarikh-i-Ferishta'* (16th century) by Ferishta.

Historical Literature in Sanskrit and Hindi

(*i*) *'Rajtarangini'* (11th century) by Kalhan dealing with the history of Kashmir.

(*ii*) *Prithvi Raj Raso* (11th century) by Chandbardoi, the court poet of Prithviraj Chauhan, describing his exploits.

Growth of regional literature. The saints of the Bhakti movement contributed richly to the development of literature in regional languages. Hindi literature owes a lot to Kabir, Surdas, Tulsidas and Mirabai.

Guru Nanak wrote in Punjabi.

Chandi Das, Vidyapati and Chaitanya composed devotional songs in Bengali.

Narsi Mehta enriched Gujarati literature.

Jnaneshwar, Namadeva, Eknath and Tukaram wrote beautiful poems in Marathi.

Amir Khusro was a prolific writer of prose, poetry and music. He was the first Muslim to write in Hindi.

The Vijayanagara rulers encouraged Tamil, Telugu and Kannada literature.

Development of Urdu. A good example of the interaction of the Hindu and Muslim cultures was the evolution of the Urdu language.

Sanskrit literature. The Hindu rulers, particularly those of Gujarat, Warrangal and Vijayanagara gave encouragement to Sanskrit literature—philosophical works, works of poetry, plays, art, astrology, music and medicine.

Q. 3. Write notes on :

(*i*) **Barani,** (*ii*) **Ibn Batuta,** (*iii*) **Ferishta.**

(*i*) *Barani.* His full name is Zia-ud-Din Barani. He hailed from Baran (present Bulandshahar) but lived in Delhi at the court of Muhammad Shah Tughlaq and Firoz Shah Tughlaq. His history *'Tarikh-i-Firoj Shahi'* is full of vivid details of the history of the Sultanate of Delhi, in the 13th and 14th centuries. Barani's accounts suffer from two defects viz. excessive exaggeration and biased attitude.

Associated with the Ulemas, he was very critical of Muhammad Tughlaq.

Although he could not get the required assistance from Firoz Tughlaq, he greatly praised his land policy.

(*ii*) *Ibn Batuta* (1304-1378). A traveller and scholar who journeyed from his home in North Africa to India. He spent about 8 years in India and described the state of affairs during the period of the Khalji and Tughlaq dynasties. The full text of his travelogue was discovered in the nineteenth century. Ibn Batuta served Muhammad Tughlaq's ambassador to China.

(*iii*) *Ferishta, Mohammad Qasim.* He is known for his historical source book entitled '*Gulshani-i-Ibrahimi*' popularly known as '*Tarikh-i-Ferishta*', written in Persian. The book has been translated into English and published under the title '*History of the Rise of the Mahomedan Power in India, till the year A.D. 1612*'.

Ferishta provides details of the affairs of the period of the Delhi Sultanate and of the Bahmani and Vijayanagara Kingdoms. He has also provided some information about the early Mughal period. Ferishta's statements are generally regarded quite accurate.

Ferishta covers the period from the 13th to the 16th century.

11

The Bhakti and Sufi Movements (Religion and Culture)

Q. 1. Explain the meaning of the Bhakti movement, What was its impact on medieval Indian society?

Or

State the main features of the Bhakti movement. What was its contribution to the establishment of a harmonious and classless society?

Or

Give a brief account of the Bhakti Movement in medieval India. (Rajasthan University 1995)

Or

Write an essay on Bhakti movement. (Rajasthan University 1994)

Ans. *Meaning of Bhakti Movement.*

Usually it is accepted that the most characteristic feature of the religious development during the medieval period was the movement which emphasised single-minded intense devotion to God. It was a complete surrender of oneself to God. The movement which emphasised primarily these ideas was the Bhakti movement—devotion to God. Bhakti to God was accepted as salvation.

Main Features of the Bhakti Movement

1. Unity of God or one God though known by different names. 2. *Bhakti,* intense love and devotion, the only way to salvation. 3. Repetition of the True Name. 4. Self-Surrender. 5. Condemnation of rituals, ceremonies and blind faith. 6. Rejection of idol worship by many saints 7. Open-mindedness about deciding religious matters. 8. No distinction of different castes, higher or low 9. Need of a *guru* for guidance advocated by some. 10. Preachings through local or regional languages and travelling from place to place for spreading the religious message.

Many doctrines of the *Bhakti* cult may be found in the *Bhagvad Gita.* The idea of the unity of God is reflected in the words, "Even those devotees who worship other gods worship Me alone." (IX 23). It is not the way of worship but the love of a selfless devotee of pure heart that matters for "Whoever offers to me with devotion, a leaf, a flower, a fruit, or water ... I accept" (IX, 26). The doctrine of self-surrender is echoed in the words of Lord Krishna, "Give up all religious paths, and take refuge in Me alone. I shall deliver thee from all sins." (XVIII 66). The idea of an open mind to decide for oneself in matters of religion may be discovered in the lines," ... you do as thou choosest" (XVIII 63). However, the real development of *Bhakti* took place in South India between the 7th and the 12th centuries through the teachings of poet saints known as *Alvars* and *Nayanar* whose hymns were collected and compiled in the 10th century.

The sufi saints of the Muslims also emphasised devotion to Allah (God).

The spiritual yearning made Kabir, Guru Nanak, Mirabai, Surdas, Tulsi Das, Chaitanya and others, the great exponents of Bhakti movement.

Impact of the Bhakti Movement on the Medieval Indian Society

With a view to understand the impact of the Bhakti movement, we have to consider the background under which the movement gained momentum.

Under the impact of the Muslim rule, the Hindus had suffered a lot materially, morally and spiritually. The Muslim rulers in general wanted to enforce the Islamic laws on the Hindus. The Muslim rule had put dread in the hearts of the Hindu masses. They wanted some solace to heal their despairing hearts. The Bhakti movement brought them hope and support and inner strength to save themselves.

During the course of time, several evil practices had crept into the Hindu society. There was a lot of caste and class distinction. Several divisions had occurred.

There was a good deal of bittermen between the two communities i.e. the Hindus and Muslims. Some healing touch was needed. Fortunately with the foreign invaders, some Sufi Muslim saints had also come to India and settled here. They were very liberal minded. They emphasised the virtues of love and devotion, brotherhood and equality etc. This helped to bring the two communities nearer. It also helped to harmonise the conflicting interests.

The saints of the Bhakti movement rejected the difference of caste and *Uati'*.

An important factor which led to the popularity of Bhakti movement was that most of the promoters of this movement attempted to reconcile the differences between the Hindus and the Muslims by stressing that Rama and Rahim were one and the same. They condemned the hatred of the fanatic Pandits and Mullas alike.

The Hindus realised that it was difficult to drive away the Muslim rulers and Muslims from India. On the other hand the Muslims also appreciated that the Hindus were in absolute majority and it was impossible to force all of them to embrace Islam. So under the impact of the new movement both sides started making efforts for coming closer to each other. For the Hindus the effort was initiated by the Hindu saints of the Bhakti movement and for the Muslims by the Sufi Saints.

The Hindu and as well as the Muslim saints emphasised religious simplicity. They stressed human qualities and moral attitudes. They stressed that a true religious man is one who is pure in thought and action.

The Bhakti saints believed in equality of man and man. According to them there was no distinction and consideration of high and low on the basis of birth. Their doors were open to all classes.

The Bhakti saints tried to generate an environment of good will between the Hindus and the Muslims.

The Bhakti saints were social reformers also. They condemned several social evils.

The Sufi Saints like Khwaja Muinuddin Chisti, Bakhyiya Kaki, Nizamudin Aulia and Nasiruddin Chirag-i-Delhi etc. attempted to restrain the fanaticism of the Muslims and tried to bring them nearer to the Hindus. Several Hindus became followers of the Sufi saints but without relinquishing their own religion.

Social impact. The most important social impact of the Bhakti movement was that the followers of the Bhakti movement rejected the caste distinction. They began to mix together on the basis of equality. They took their meals together from the common kitchen. The movement tried to loosen the bond of caste.

A spirit of harmony among different sections of society and religion received impetus.

The evil practice of *'Sati'* received some set back.

The status of women received more importance.

Religious impact. The movement aroused awakening among the Hindus and Muslims regarding the futility of ritualism and superstitions. The feeling of appreciation of the difference between the thought and practices of the two religions emerged. The movement encouraged religious toleration. Guru Granth Saheb the holiest book of the Sikhs which was complied later on included the messages of saints belonging to different sects.

This was on account of the spirit of toleration preached by the Bhakti saints.

Promotion of regional languages of the common people. In place of Sanskrit, Arabic and Persian, the Bhakti saints preached through the medium of local languages which could be understood very easily. For instance the language of Kabir was a mixture of several languages of every day use. Surdas used *'Brij'* dialect. Goswami Tulsi Das composed his works in *'Awadhi'*.

Political influence. Some of the rulers adopted liberal religious policies under the impact of the Bhakti movement.

Moral influence. The movement attempted to infuse a spirit of piety in the daily life of the people. It emphasised earning of wealth through hard work and honest means. It encouraged the value of social service to the poor and the needy. It developed a humanitarian attitude. It pointed out the virtues of contentment and self control. It drew attention to the evils of anger, greed and vanity.

Summing up

The Bhakti movement succeeded to a very small extent in realising its two-fold objective i.e. bringing about reforms in Hinduism and developing harmonious relations between the Hindus and the Muslims. It gave birth to a new sect i.e. Sikhism. It is perhaps far-fetched to say that Akbar's broad outlook was on account of the impact of the Bhakti movement. The movement further divided the Hindu society. For instance the followers of Kabir came to be known as Kabir Panthis.

Q. 2. Give the meaning of Bhakti movement. What were the causes of its rise? Do you think that it was the outcome of the Muslim influence on Hindu religion? Explain the main principles of the Bhakti movement in the light of the teachings of Sant Kabir and Guru Nanak Dev.

Ans. *Meaning of Bhakti Movement.*

The literal meaning of Bhakti is devotion. But the Bhakti movement implied the movement which emphasised intense devotion to God.

This devotion was expressed by a devotee through the repetition of the name of Almighty. The mode of expression was usually singing and dancing in the praise of God.

The saints of the Bhakti movement also emphasised that there was no distinction of class, colour, caste etc. All were equal. All had the right to salvation i.e. freedom from the cycle of births and deaths.

The saints of the Bhakti movement believed in leading a pure and simple life.

The saints emphasised that one need not go to pilgrimages to holy places for securing salvation.

Causes for the rise of the movement. The Bhakti movement was the outcome of a number of causes. The root of the movement lay deep into the soil of India. There was nothing new in the *bhakti cult,* which did not already exist in India. The elements of the cult could be traced from the Vedas onwards. Secondly the impact of the Muslim rule and Islam put dread in the heart of Hindu masses. The Hindus had suffered a lot under some of the fanatic rulers. They wanted some solace to heal their despairing hearts. The *bhakti* movement brought them hope and support and inner strength to save Hinduism. The Sufi saints of the Muslim community also inspired the movement. Some similar chords in the two evoked resonance. The Muslim society firmly believed in the unity of God, the equality and fraternity of mankind and complete surrender to God. It is a coincidence that the Hindu reformers and the mystic saints were also trying to stress these features besides others.

Kabir's (1425-1518) emphasis on Ram and Rahim: Unity of religions. Kabir's mission was to bridge the gulf between the Hindus and the Muslims and so he described himself "Kabir is the child of Allah and Ram." "Hindus and Turks were pots of the same clay. Allah and Rama were but different names." His God is the *nirguna* Supreme Being, the God of gods. He equated Rama with Rahim (the Merciful) and it went a long way to make the *bhakti* movement a unique religious experience.

Pure heart i.e. pure living. To him, the prayers, pilgrimages and fasting of the Hindus as well as of the Muslims were equally mechanical. He was against idolatory, as he said, "If by worshipping stones one can find God, I shall worship a mountain."

To him what mattered was total absorption in the devotion to the Supreme with a pure heart. He was fond of oral teachings in the shape of couplets in Hindi which were later collected in the *Bijaka* (the Seed Book). The simple fine rhythm of these couplets helped their easy remembrance and great popularity. The essence of his teachings may be found in his couplets and poems like the following :

"Mo Ko Kahan dhunro bande..."

O Servant where dost thow seek me, Lo I am beside thee.

I am neither in temple nor in mosque...

If thou art a true seeker, thou shall at once see Me..."

Kabir's teachings may be summed up as (*i*) God is one but has different names (*ii*) Devotion to God. (*iii*) Harmony between the Hindus and the Muslims. (*iv*) No caste system. (*v*) Welfare of others (*vi*) No lust for riches.

Guru Nanak Dev' teachings : Hindu Muslim Unity : glory of one God : Love and devotion

Guru Nanak Dev (1469-1539) from whose teachings, the Sikh religion was founded, was one of the foremost apostles of the *Bhakti cult*. His catholic approach aimed at bridging the gulf between the Hindus and the Muslims. The hymns of Guru Nanak have been preserved in the *Adi Granth*. In these he sang the glory of one great God, and man's duty of meditating his name with a pure heart, bereft of all desires. Guru Nanak believed that the religious acts and austerities practised by different religious sects were useless. Love and devotion to one God is the only way of obtaining his grace.

Purity of conduct. He laid emphasis on the purity of character and conduct as the first condition of approaching God.

No caste system : simple like : religious Equality. He opposed priestly ritualism, blind faith, the caste system and idol worship. His disciples were from different castes and creeds, religions and regions. He preached through his hymns, which he sang to the accompaniment of the rebele (a stringed musical instrument) played by Mardana. The following hymn closely echoes the teachings of the great saint.

Religion consisteth not in patched coat, or in a Yogi's staff,
or in ashes smeared over the body,
Religion consisteth not in earring worn or a shaven head, or in the blowing of horns.
Abide pure amidst the impurities of the world;
Thus, shalt thou find the way of religion.

Q. 3. Analyse the main features of Sufism. Discuss its influence on Indian society. Write a brief note on any Sufi saint.

Ans. *Meaning of Sufism.*

The philosophy and practices of Sufism may very aptly be stated in the words of Dr. Tara Chand, "Sufism is a religion of intense devotion; Love is its manifestation, poetry, music and dance are the instruments of its worship and attaining oneness with God is its ideal." In other words, it implies that the ideal before an individual should be to be one with God. For the attainment of this ideal, intense devotion for God is needed in the individual. Devotion is reflected in love. This love for the Almighty is expressed through three fold activities on the part of the individual i.e. poetry of love towards God, music of love towards God and dance of love towards God.

Origin of Sufism. It is generally believed that sufism is derived from two Arabic words i.e. *'Saf'* and *'Suf'*. The word *'Saf'* means a carpet. Since the Sufis meditated upon God on a carpet, sufism took its birth i.e. pure people who meditated on a carpet.

The word *'Sufi'* derives its name from another Arabic word *'Suf'* which means wool. The Muslim saints who wore garments of coarse wool began to be called sufi saints. The first epoch of sufism is said to have begun in the seventh century A.D.

Sufism entered India in the 12th century with Muslim invaders and became popular in the 13th century.

Main Features of Sufism

1. Sufism derives is inspiration from Islam. While the orthodox Muslims depend upon external conduct and blind observance of religious rituals, the sufi saints seek inner purity.

2. According to sufi saints, God is the beloved of the lover (*'Mashook'*) i.e. the devotee and the devotee is eager to meet his beloved (God).

3. The Sufis think that love and devotion are the only means of reaching God.

4. Along with Prophet Muhammad, they also attach great importance to their *'Murshid'* or *'Pir'* (Guru).

5. Devotion is more important than fast (*Roza*) or prayer (*Namaz*)

6. Sufism does not believe in caste system.

7. Sufism emphasises upon leading a simple life.

8. Sufi saints preached in Arabic, Persian and Urdu etc.

9. The Sufis were divided into 12 orders each under a mystic sufi saint. *Prominent Sufi Saints.*

Khawja Moin-ud-Din Chisti (1143-1234 A.D.) He came to India towards the close of the 12th century. Initially he stayed at Lahore. Then he moved to Delhi and finally settled at Ajmer. On account of his pious and simple life, people of different faiths looked upon him as their spiritual teacher.

He mixed freely with the lower classes of both Hindus and Muslims. He used to hold devotional musical gatherings. On account of his virtues of renunciation, meditation and selfless service, people from different parts of India came to his place at Ajmer.

His *'dargah'* (tomb) at Ajmer (Ajmer Sharif) has become a place of pilgrimage for the Muslims as well as the Hindus. His devotees believe that by offering prayer at his tomb, their wishes (*'minits'*) are fulfilled.

Baba Farid-ud-Din Ganj-i-Shakar. (13th century). His outlook was broad and humane. Some of his devotional verses are found in '*Adi-Granth*' of the Sikhs. Thousands of his devotees visit his tomb at Faridkot in the Punjab.

Nizam-ud-Din Aulia (14th century). He laid great stress on love as a means of the realization of God. He said, "O Muslims! I swear by God that he holds dear those who love Him for the sake of human beings and also those who love human beings for the sake of Him. This is the only way to love and adore Him."

During his life time he was held in great esteem by several Sultans of Delhi as well as the general public.

He also used Hindi in his teachings.

His tomb at Nizam-ud-Din in Delhi has become a place of pilgrimage for both Muslims and Hindus.

Impact of Sufism

Religions impact. The efforts of Sufi saints helped to lessen religious fanaticism in India. Hindus in larger numbers became followers of sufi saints. The tombs built after their death have continued to become places of worship for the Muslims as well as the Hindus. Their belief in unity of God helped to remove mutual differences.

Social Impact. Their stress on social welfare led to the establishment of works of charitable nature i.e. opening of orphanages and women service centres. The efforts of sufi saints helped to promote equality and lessen the evils of casteism. They also tried to infuse a spirit of piety and morality.

Political Impact. Some of the renowned sufi saints on account of their virtuous and saintly life motivated some of the Delhi Sultans to follow a liberal policy.

Cultural Impact. The sacred places built in the memory of the sufi saints clearly demonstrate the development of a new type of architecture.

The *Dargah*' of Khawaja Muin-ud-Din Chisti at Ajmer and the Tomb of Nizam-ud-Din Aulia at Delhi have a special place in architecture.

Sufi saints popularised devotional music and songs.

Several sufi saints composed literary works in vernacular languages.

Amir Khusro, a disciple of Nizam-ud-Din Aulia, was a noted '*guzzle*' writer. The poetry of Khusro was so full of sweetness that he was called '*Tutiy-i-Hind*. He is credited with more than 90 works on different subjects i.e. historical and romantic as well.

Q. 4. Write brief notes on :

(*i*) Chaitanya (*ii*) Jnanesvara (*iii*) Mirabai (*iv*) Namadeva (*v*) Narsi Mehta (*vi*) Ramananda (*vii*) Surdas (*viii*) Tulsi Das

Chaitanya (*1485-1534*). For Chaitanya, the greatest exponent of Bhakti movement in Bengal, a passionate love for Hari or Krishna was the only means of salvation. His favourite form of worship was '*Kirtan*'—a group singing and dancing accompanied by instruments like drums, cymbals etc. His emotional attachment to lord Krishna immersed him in long spells of ecstasy. He disregarded all distinctions of castes and creeds. He preached that all people should tolerate and love each other. Therefore, people of all castes were welcome in his '*Kirtan*' assembly. He disliked priestly rituals. He preached that every person, irrespective of caste or religion could engage himself in the worship of Krishna through '*Kirtan*'. Image worship was not important to him. He believed more in remembering God and singing in his praise.

Vrindavan, a holy place for the Hindus was revived as a place of pilgrimage because of the efforts of his disciples.

Jnaneswara (*1271-96*). Valuable contribution to the Bhakti movement in Maharashtra was made by *Jnaneswara*, a contemporary of Namadeva. It is said that he laid the foundation of the movement in Maharashtra. His commentary on *Bhagvad Gita*, popularly known as *Jnaneswari*, is a classic. Among the other later saints of Maharashtra associated with the movement, special mention must be made of Eknath and Tukaram (16th century) and Ramdas (17th century).

Mirabai (*1498-1546*). She was the daughter of Rana Ratan Singh of Mewar and wife of Bhoj Raj, the heir apparent of Rana Sanga of Mewar. She was God-intoxicated saint-poet who spent most of her life in *bhajan-kirtan* and in the company of saints of Mathura and Vrindavan. She was chastised and locked up as her religious ways were intolerable to the members of the royal family. The central theme of Mira's *bhajans* was Girdhar Gopal (Lord Krishna). No persuasion, no calumny and no persecution would turn her away from her exclusive devotion to Girdhar Gopal. Mira's songs are rich in devotional fervour, poetic expression and tuneful music. They portray an intense love and pangful yearning to dissolve herself in Him.

Namadeva (*1276-1350*). The ideas of the Bhakti saints from the south were transmitted to the north though slowly by scholars and saints. Among these, Maharashtra saints Namadeva and Ramananda need special mention as pioneers. It was in Maharashtra that Namadeva, a great Maratha saint made the earliest attempt to bring about harmony between Hinduism and Islam. His leadership and indomitable courage was used in abolishing class and caste distinctions. He preached the unity of God and set his face against idol worship, ritualism and scriptures. He composed poetry both in Hindi and Marathi imbued with an intense love and devotion for God. He was a tailor by caste but his devotional verses enraptured the heart of the masses. Among his disciples were Gora, the potter, Chokha, the untouchable, the Brahmans and others. Some of his verses have found a place in the Granth Saheb.

Narsi Mehta (15th century). He was a poet-saint from Saurashtra. One of his *Bhajans* was very dear to Mahatma Gandhi. It was '*Vaishnava Jana to tene kahiya je peer parayee jane re* (Him we call the man of the Lord who experiences in Himself the pain of others).

Ramananda (born in the 14th and died in 15th century). He is said to have begun the religious renaissance of medieval mysticism. Although he was brought up in the traditional school of Vaishnavism founded by Ramanuja, he gave an altogether a new turn to it. Though he was a Brahman, he championed the cause of abolishing all caste distinctions and willingly dined with the members of the low castes. Among his other reforms, mention must be made of the use of vernacular instead of Sanskrit and his disregard for all distinctions of castes and creeds. Several Muslims became his disciples.

Surdas (*1478-1583*). Blind from the birth, he set out to find by inner illumination, the glory of the Lord. In his poems he deals with the life of Lord Krishna whose childhood is described in an enchanting manner. The melody of child Krishna's defence in the poem 'I didn't eat the butter, Ma' lifts the listeners to ecstatic realms. *Sur Sagar* is the most significant work of Surdas.

Tulsi Das (*1532-1623*). He identified Lord Rama with the Absolute. *Ramcharit Manas* containing the story of the *Ramayana* is the Bible of north Indian Hindus. Its lyrical fervour and devotional sensitivity are miraculous. *Ramcharit Manas* idealises all forms of human relationships, but most impressive is Hanuman's devotion to Rama. Rama's affection for his devotees is also deep and warm. It brings out a great realization that human beings and God are indispensable to one another. The Hindus recite the couplets from *Ramcharit Manas* with great devotion and consider that by doing so they may attain salvation.

12

The Vijayanagara Kingdom and the Bahamni Kingdom (Peninsular India)

Q. 1. What is the significance of the Vijayanagara empire? What led to its rise and fall? Briefly state the achievements of Krishna Dev Raya.

Or

Write about the causes of rise and fall of Vijayanagara state.

(Rajasthan University 1997)

Ans. *Significance of the Vijayanagar Empire*

The significance of the Vijayanagara empire may be stated in the words of Dr. A.L. Srivastva, "The Vijayanagara empire served a high historical purpose by acting as a champion of Hindu religion and culture against the aggressions of the Muslims in Southern India."

Apart from above, on account of its efficient administration, prosperous economy, diplomatic polity, liberal religious policy, the Vijayanagara empire occupied a remarkable and glorious place in Indian history for more than two hundred years from 1336 A.D. to 1565 A.D.

Rise and fall of the dynasty From 1565 onwards, the empire just remained in existence only and without any worth while achievement till 1614. Its defeat at the hands of the erstwhile Bahamni rulers in 1565 gave it a crushing blow.

The 16 rulers of the empire were from 4 dynasties; the Sangma Dynasty (1336 to 1486), the Saluva Dynasty (1486 to 1509), the Taluva Dynasty (1510 to 1570) and the Arvinda Dynasty.

The Kingdom of Vijayanagara came into being as a result of the confusion that prevailed at the time of Muhammad Tughlaq. According to Dr. V.S. Smith, "There is however no doubt that the new power was the outcome of the efforts made by two brothers, sons of Sangama to stay the tide of Muslim invasion and preserve the Hindu Dharma in the peninsula". Likewise Dr. Ishwari Prasad says, "The most probable account is that which ascribes the origin of the Kingdom to the two brothers, Hari Hara and Bukka who were employed in the treasury of Pratap Rudra Deva, Kakatya of Warrangal and who fled the country when it was overrun by the Muslims in 1303."

The Kingdom comprised a substantial part of peninsular India south of the Krishna river up to Rameshwaram, including the Tamil region and that of the Cheras (Kerala). To the north was the powerful Bahamni Kingdom with whom it had constant conflicts and which ultimately led to its downfall.

Krishnadeva Raya (1509-29). Krishnadeva has been described by all the travellers who visited his empire as "an emperor of much justice." Domingos, a Portuguese traveller described Krishnadeva in these words, "He is the most feared and perfect king that could possibly be." The Mughal emperor Babur described in his '*Baburnama*', Krishnadeva "as the most powerful ruler of India."

The Vijayanagara empire reached to its zenith in peace, order, power, prosperity and learning during his reign.

Krishnadeva as a military commander. He was a brave general and bold warrior. He invaded Mysore and annexed it. He recaptured the Doab lying between the rivers Krishna and Tungbhadra from the Bahamni Sultans. The military exploits of Krishnadeva have been described in the following words, "He is one of the most distinguished and powerful kings of Vijayanagara who fought with the Muslims of the Deccan on equal terms and avenged the wrongs that had been done to his predecessors."

Religious toleration. Though his personal leanings were in favour of Vaishnavism yet he respected all the sects.

Patron of literature. Literature made a tremendous progress during his reign. He himself was a gifted scholar of Telugu and Sanskrit. He wrote a poem '*Amuktamalyada*' in Telugu. He extended his patronage to Sanskrit, Telugu, Kannad and Tamil scholars alike. The noted Telugu poet Allasani Peddana flourished in his court.

As a patron of art. He was a great builder and founded the city of Naglapur. He got several '*Gopurams*' and '*Mandapas*' built. He constructed the Krishnaswami temple and the statue of infant Krishna installed in it. He also built several ponds for irrigation.

As an administrator. He decentralised his empire into different administrative units. A province was placed under a governor who was usually a military commander.

Encouragement to trade and commerce. The ruler made special arrangements for providing trading facilities at ports.

Summing up the Achievements of Krishnadev.

Describing the achievements of Krishnadeva, Nilakanta Sastri has observed, "He was in no way less famous for his religious zeal and catholicity. He respected all sects of the Hindu religion alike, though his personal leanings were in favour of Vaishnavism... Krishnadeva's kindness to the fallen enemy, his great military prowess and above all the fabulous wealth that he conferred as endowments on temples and Brahamans, mark him out indeed as the greatest South Indian monarchs, who shed a luster on the pages of history."

Dr. Ishwari Prasad has described the qualities and achievements of Krishnadeva as, "Krishnadeva Raya was always anxious to promote the welfare of his subjects. His liberal endowments endeared him all the more to his subjects. He was polite and amiable in private society, wise and far-sighted in council, eloquent and cultured when he listened to litteratus, dignified and awe inspiring in his public duties. Krishnadeva was formidable in war and indeed a jewel among all the princes. Under him Vijayanagara attained the zenith of its greatness and prosperity." He further went on to say, "There is no ruler among the sovereigns of the Deccan, both Hindu and Muslim, worthy of Krishnadeva Raya."

Causes of the downfall of the Vijayanagara empire.

1. A despotic government.
2- Wars of succession.
3. Weak successors of Krishna Deva Raya.
4. Continuous wars with the neighbouring Bahamani Kingdom.
5. Lack of control over the provincial governors.
6. Social evils.
7. Lack of fanaticism among the Hindus as compared with the spirit of "*jehad*" among the Muslims-war against infidels.
8. Rise and fall as the law of nature.

Q. 2. Write an essay on Vijayanagara administration.

(Delhi University, 1997, Punjab University Oct. 1996 and Oct. 1997)

Ans. *A Well Organised Administrative System.*

Vijayanagara empire which lasted for more than two hundred years in the Deccan had a well-organised administrative system. It was on account of this system that there was an all round prosperity in the state. Under the leadership of its several rulers, the state made a remarkable progress in the economic, cultural, political and social fields. Many foreigner visitors like Nicolo (onti-Italian), Abdul Razaq (Persian) and Dominigos Pius (Portuguese) etc. have praised the prosperity of the state.

Kingship Krishnadeva Raya, the greatest ruler of the Kingdom of Vijayanagara explains the position of Kingship in his book '*Amuktamalyda*' that a King should gather round him people skilled in state craft and seek their advice and help in administration. He further writes, "A crowned king should always rule with an eye towards '*Dharma*".

The ruler was a benevolent despot. He was the head of the state and was regarded as the God's representative on earth.

The king was the supreme authority in civil, military and judicial matters. The king, however, was assisted and guided by a council of ministers. He was an enlightened and benevolent ruler.

Council of Ministers. The king was assisted by ministers who were nominated by the king. The ministers were appointed from the three classes i.e. The Brahmans, the Kshatriyas and the Vaishayas. The office of the minister was sometimes hereditary. The three important key posts of the state were the Prime Minister, the Chief Treasurer and the Prefect of the Police.

Rule of two rulers simultaneously. Sometimes two rulers ruled at the same time–a strange practice and perhaps the only one in history; Hari Har I and his brother Bukka Rai ruled at the same time. Likewise Vijay Rai and Dev Rai ruled at the same time.

2. *Provincial administration.* For purpose of administration, the empire was divided into 6 provinces. A province was called *Prant*, or *Rajya*. Each province was under a viceroy or *Nayak* who was either a member of the royal family or influential noble of the state. Every viceroy enjoyed civil, military and judiciary powers within the province. He was required to submit regularly account of the income and expenditure to the central government.

Decentralised administration. The rulers of Vijayanagar a adopted the principle of the decentralisation of political power. The empire was, divided into provinces *prants*, districts, '*Nadus*', '*Melagrams*' and '*grams*'. Administration of the villages was autonomous.

Local administration. The province was divided into smaller units. The village was the smallest unit. It was self-sufficient. The village assembly (Panchayat) was responsible for the administration of the village. Village accountant and the village watchman were the hereditary officers. These officers were paid either by grants of land or from a portion of the agricultural produce.

Nayankar system of administration. Under this system, the ruler assigned a land track to officials in lieu of pay *i.e.* for maintaining themselves and that of their army from the land track itself. These officials or land-lords provided military service to the ruler.

Sources of revenue. Land revenue was the chief source of income. Land was divided into four categories for purposes of assessment, wet land, dry land, orchards and woods. Usually the share was one sixth of the produce. Land revenue could be paid in cash or kind. The rates varied according to the type of the crops, soil, method of irrigation, etc. Apart from land revenue, other taxes were : irrigation tax, grazing tax and import-export duties on merchandise goods.

Administration of justice. The king was the highest authority or the supreme court of justice. His word was final. Petitions were presented to the king or the Prime Minister by all those who had a grievance and these were disposed of according to the principles of Hindu Law. Punishments were very severe. Torture was used to find out the truth from the alleged culprit. Death sentence, mutilation of the limbs of the body and confiscation of property were the deterrent punishments for the criminals. In the villages, panchayats dispensed justice for ordinary crimes.

Military organisation. The army consisted of infantry, cavalry, artillery and camels. The rulers of the Vijayanagar a empire neglected naval power.

The rulers recruited Turkish archers in the army. The military organisation was rather weak and its primary weakness was artillery.

According to Domingos Paes, a foreign traveller, Krishna Deva Raya's army included 703,000 infantry, 32600 cavalry and 551 elephants, besides an unaccounted host of camp followers. Chariots had gone out of use. The efficiency of the huge army was not proportionate to the number of force.

Splendour of the court. The court of the rulers of Vijayanagara was known for its grandeur and splendour. It was attended by nobles, priests, scholars, musicians and astrologers.

Orders of the rulers. No written orders were issued by the rulers. The royal words were carefully noted down by secretaries, whose record was the sole evidence of the commands issued.

Q. 3. Discuss the contribution of the rulers of Vijayanagara to the religious, cultural, economic, social and political history of India.

Or

What comments have been made by the foreign visitors on the prosperity, economic, political and social conditions of the Vijayanagara empire.

Describe in brief the social economic and cultural progress of the Vijayanagara empire. (Rajasthan University 1995)

Ans. *Foreign Traveller's High Praise of the Vijayanagara Empire.*

Almost all travellers who visited the Vijayanagara empire which lasted more than 200 years (1336 A.D. to 1565 A.D.) have spoken highly of the economic, cultural, political and social life of the empire. Under the leadership of some very able rulers, the Vijayanagara empire attained immense prosperity in all walks of life. The Italian traveller Nicolo and Persian traveller Abdul Razaq visited Vijayanagara empire towards the middle of the 15th century A.D. The Portuguese travellers Dominigos Pius, Barbosa and Nuniz came to India in the early part of the 16th century.

Nicolo has written specifically about the religious life of the people. He has also written about the military also.

Abdul Razaq has thrown a good deal of light about the political conditions and the administrative set-up.

Barbosa has written about the rich social life and Dominigo Pius has described the flourishing city of Vijayanagara–the capital of the Kingdom.

Prosperity of the people. Economic conditions. The Vijayanagara empire was the most prosperous state of its time in India. All commodities were available in abundance. Their prices were low and everything remained stored up properly and adequately in case of need. All the foreign travellers who visited Vijayanagara during the fifteenth and sixteenth centuries have given glowing description of the wealth and prosperity of the state and its people. The Persian ambassador Abdur Razaq, the Portuguese traveller Paes and the Italian traveller Nicolo Conti have praised the riches of the

Vijayanagara empire. They state that not only the king and the nobles were rich but even the common people enjoyed prosperity. The common people could afford to wear ornaments in their ears, necks, arms, fingers, etc.

The prosperity of the Vijayanagara empire was on account of the growth of agriculture, industries, trade and commerce. The land was very fertile, Most of the land in the countryside was under cultivation.

Trade and Commerce. Commerce was inland, coastal and overseas. The city of Vijayanagara was the most important seat of commerce in the country. It carried on trade in diamonds, rubies, pearls etc. Also Calicut was another important port on the Malabar coast. According to Abdur Razaq, "There were as many as 300 sea ports in the Vijayanagara empire. There were commercial relations with the islands in the Indian Ocean, the Malaya Archipelago, Burma, China, Arabia, Persia, South Africa, Abyssinia and Portugal. The imports were horses, elephants, pearls, copper, coral, mercury, China silk and velvet. The exports were cloth, rice, iron, salt petre, sugar and spices.

The main industries of the Vijayanagara empire were cloth, perfumes and utensils of various kinds.

The traders and those engaged in industries were organised into trade guilds to look after the interests of trade and industry.

Currency. The coins of the empire were those of copper, gold and silver. The coins carried beautiful bird 'gandabirinda'.

Glory of Vijayanagara City. Abdual Razaq has given a vivid description of the city of Vijayanagara. He wrote that it was an unprecedented city, the like of which was never seen in the whole world. This city was built in such a way that seven guarding fort gates were built within each other. In the city there was a separate market for every main occupation. The jewellers freely sold diamonds, pearls rubies etc.

The circumference of the city was sixty miles and its walls extended to the hills. About 90,000 people of the city were capable of weilding weapons.

Vijayanagara had beautiful lakes, open gardens, broad and well laid roads and splendid buildings. The Tungbhadara river had a dam which provided water for the long canal of the city. Vijayanagara city was described larger than Rome or any biggest city in the western world.

Social Conditions

Position of women. Women occupied a high position in the society. They took part in the literary, political and social life of the society. They were educated and worked at various posts in the government departments. They were trained in fine arts like music, dance and painting. They also received training in wrestling and fighting. They were employed body guards as well.

Social evils concerning women were also prevalent. These were child marriages, polygamy, dowry system and practice of 'sati'.

Women worked in different occupations. According to Nuniz, "The king of Vijayanagara has also women who wrestle, and others who are astrologers and soothsayers; and has women who write all the accounts of expenses that are incurred insides the gates of the palace and others whose duty is to write all the affairs of the kingdom and compare their books with those of writers outside; he has women also for music, who play instruments and sing. Even the wives of the kings are well-versed in music... He has judges as well as watchman who every night guard the palace, and these are women."

High position of the Brahmanas. The ruler of Vijayanagar empire gave a lot of honour and respect to the Brahmanas. Naturally therefore, the Brahmans exercised a great influence in political and religious fields. According to Nuniz the Brahmanas were honest men, very good at accounts but little fit for hard work.

Food. Brahmanas were vegetarians and all others were free to eat meat except of cows and oxen. Animal sacrifices were common.

Cultural Contribution. During the Vijayanagara empire, remarkable texts on Hindu religion, philosophy, grammar, drama, dance, music etc. were produced. The rulers encouraged Sanskrit, Tamil, Telugu and Kannada literature and languages. It is said that the reign of Krishnadeva Raya marked the dawn of a new era in the literary history of South India. He himself was a great scholar, a musician and a poet. His work in Telugu entitled *Amuktamalyada* deals with several matters including the art of government. In his court there were 8 famous poets called "*Ashta Digyajas.*'

Architecture. During the period several temples of remarkable beauty were constructed. The Hazara temple and the Vitthalaswami temples built by Krishnadeva Raya have been regarded as the finest specimens of Hindu architecture. It was evolved out of Pandyan, and Chalukyan elements of a later period. The style is ornate and magnificently exuberant. The material used was hard granite. It has got features similar to that at Tamil architecture. The pillars of *mandapas* are fully decorated and beautifully carved and their varieties are countless. The temples and monuments are situated mostly between the Kamalapuram and Hampi.

Political Conditions

Kingship. The king was considered as the representative of God. He was a benevolent ruler and worked in accordance with '*Dharmshastras*' of the Hindus.

King's orders. According to Nuniz, "No written orders are even issued, nor any charter granted for the favours he (the king) bestows or the commands he gives, but when he confers a favour on anyone it remains written in the register of the secretaries. The king however, gives to the recipient of a favour a seal impressed in wax from one of his rings which his minister keeps and these seals serve for letter patents".

Punishments. Nuniz in this connection states, "The punishments that they (kings) inflict in this kingdom are these: for a theft, whatever theft he commits, however little it be, they forthwith cut off a foot and a hand; and if this theft be a great one, he is hanged with a hook under his chin. If a man outrages a respectable woman or a virgin it was the same punishment and if he does any another such violence his punishment is of a like kind. Nobles who become traitors are sent to be impaled alive on a wooden stake thrust through the belly."

Liberal religious policy. All the rulers of the Vijayanagara empire were devout Hindus. Most of the rulers were devotees of Vaishnavism. However, they were tolerant towards all religions. The Muslims, the Christians and the Yahudis and the people of other faiths enjoyed equal freedom. According to a foreign traveller Eduardo Barbosa, "The Kings allow such freedom that every man may come and go and live according to his own creed."

Q. 4. Write short notes on the following :

(*i*) Hari Hara I (*ii*) Nayankar System of Vijayanagara Empire

Ans. (*i*) Hari Hara I (1336-1353 A.D.)

Founder of the Vijayanagara Empire. Hari Hara I, founded the Vijayanagara empire in collaboration with his brother Bukka. Earlier both of them were in the service of Pratap Rudra Deva Kakakitya of Warrangal. They fled from their place in 1323 when the Muslims captured it. They took up service with the Raja of Anagondi in the Raichur district. But soon this territory also fell in the hands of the Muslims and both the brothers were taken to Delhi. This led to a Hindu rebellion at their place and they were released. Anagondi was restored to them but they became feudatories of the ruler of Delhi. In 1335, they founded the imperial city of Vijayanagara on the banks of the river Tungbhadara. The city was named after the name of Vidyaranya, a famous sage and scholar. In 1336, a great and powerful independent Hindu kingdom named as Vijayanagara was founded by them. In 1336 itself Hari Hara accomplished his coronation ceremony according to Hindu rites and assumed the title of '*Maharajadhiraja*'.

Regarding the founding of the Vijayanagara Empire, Dr. V.S. Smith has observed, "There is however no doubt that the new power was the outcome of the efforts made by two brothers, sons of Sanghama to stay the tide of Muslim invasion and preserve the Hindu Dharma in the peninsula".

Consolidation of the empire. Before his death, Hari Hara was able to extend his kingdom in the areas along the sea coast east to west and in the north to river Krishna and river Kaveri in the south. His kingdom included the territories of Kanara, Mysore, Trichurapalli, Kanchi and Chingalpat.

Administrative reforms. Hari Hara established a sound system of administration. His system of civil administration lasted till the last days of the Vijayanagara empire.

Hari Hara encouraged agriculture and strengthened the fortification of several forts.

Nayankar System of Administration of Vijayanagara Empire

There is a great difference of opinion among historians regarding the origin and nature of the Nayankar system of administration of the Vijayanagara empire.

According to one school of thought the heads of the provinces were military commanders called '*Amarnayak*' or 'Polygar'.

According to another school of thought '*Amarnayak*' was the epithet of land lords.

The '*Amarnayaks*' were the officials whom the Vijayanagara ruler assigned a land track in lieu of pay to maintain their own expenditure and that of their army. The land track was referred to as '*Amaram*' and the assignees were called '*Amarnayak*'. After meeting the expenditure on the maintenance of the army, the '*Amarnayaks*' sent the remaining revenue realised from the land to the ruler. They were also responsible for the maintenance of law and order in the province or territory under their control and punished these who broke the law. They maintained two contact officers in the royal court.

The administration of the empire looked like military feudalism and was in some respects like the Iqta system of the Delhi Sultanate.

Usually under a Amarnayak, there was a small land track which formed a part of a province.

The Amarnayaks were relatively independent as compared with the Iqtdars of the Sultanate period.

An Amarnayak discharged military as well as financial responsibility like a military feudal chieftain.

The Amarnayaks shirking their responsibility were liable to lose their tract of land and were also punished.

In due course, the office of the Amarnayak became hereditary.

The post of an Amaranayak was rarely given to a Brahaman.

Q. 5. What were the main causes of conflict between Vijayanagara and Bahamni Kingdoms? What was the outcome of this conflict?

Or

What were the circumstances leading to the Battle of Rakshiih Tangli or Talikota? Evaluate its results.

Ans. *Main causes of conflict between the Vijayanagara and Bahamni Kingdoms.*

The two Kingdoms i.e. the Vijayanagara Kingdom (1336-1565) and the Bahamni Kingdom (1347-1527) (which was divided in due course in five states of Berar, Bijapur, Ahmednagar, Golkunda and Bidar) flourished side by side for about two hundred years. However, for all these years, they were engaged continually in conflict. Ultimately in 1565, four Muslim states barring Berar formed a confederacy, fought against Vijaynagara and gave a crushing defeat to it.

Following were the important causes of the conflict between these two kingdoms.

I. Economic reasons. These were as under :

(*i*) *Possession of Tungbhadra Doab.* The territory between the rivers Tungbhadra and Krishna known as Tungbhadra Doab was very fertile. Each kingdom wanted to possess it.

(*ii*) *Control of Krishna-Godavri Delta.* This delta had two-fold significance. One, it was very fertile. Two, it had several important ports through which profitable trade was carried with several foreign countries like Ceylon, Indonesia, Malaya and Burma, etc. Both the powers wanted to have their supremacy over this territory.

(*iii*) *Capture of Konkan or Western Coastal strip.* This was also a very fertile area and had important ports like Goa which were important outlets for foreign trade. Goa was especially important for the import of horses from Iran and Iraq. On account of these reasons, both the powers had their eyes on this area.

II. Political Conflict. Both the powers desired to extend their kingdom. Each considered the other as a danger to its existence.

III. Religious jealousy. Ever since the conquest of Deccan by Malik Kafur, the vanquished Hindu rulers had nursed a feeling of deep resentment against the Muslim oppressors. This had resulted in the emergence of a great Hindu empire of Vijayanagara in the Deccan. On the contrary, the Bahamni rulers were Muslims. So there was a religious rivalry between the two kingdoms.

IV. Possession of Diamond mines. It is held by some historians that diamond mines in the Golkunda region of the Bahamni empire tempted the rulers of Vijayanagara to establish their hold over this area.

V. Failure of diplomacy on the part of Rama Raya. Sadasiva Raya (1542-70), the ruler of Vijayanagara was a very weak ruler and he played into the hands of his powerful minister Rama Raya. For a while, Rama Raya was able to make use of the rivalry of the five Muslim powers in the Deccan and weakened their power. But ultimately this policy failed and these states unified in the name of Islam.

VI. Growing power of Vijayanagara empire. In due course, Vijayanagara had come to occupy a very important position in Southern

India. It was able to suppress the power of the three Muslim Kingdoms of Ahmedabad, Golkunda and Bidar. The growing power of the Vijaynagara empire struck terror in the minds of Muslim Sultans of Deccan and forgetting their differences, four powers as already stated formed a confederacy and launched a struggle against Vijayanagara.

Battle of Talikota (1565). The confederacy of the four states of Bijapur, Ahmednagar, Golkunda and Bidar i.e. the allied forces fought against the ruler of Vijayanagara on January 23, 1565 at Bannihathi near Talikota. According to some historians this is called the Battle of Rakshi-Tangadi – the battle site marked by these two villages.

Initially the armies of the confederation were defeated but later on Muslim artillery spelled ruin and dealt a severe blow to the army of Vijayanagara. It is also said that a few Muslim generals in the Vijayanagara army went over to their co-religionists along with their armies. Ram Rai was encircled and murdered. The victory of the allies was complete.

Results of the Talikota Battle

1. *General Slaughter.* According to Swell, the victors slaughtered the people of Vijayanagara mercilessly.

Dr. Ishwari Prasad states that about one lakh Hindus were put to death.

2. *Loot and Plunder.* Burhan-i-Malasir writes, "The victors captured jewels, ornaments, maid servants, all sorts of articles in such quantity that the whole army was enriched." Ferishta observes, "The plunder was so great that every man in the allied army became rich in gold, jewels, tents, arms, horses and slaves, the Sultans permitting every person to retain what he acquired, reserving elephants only for their own use."

3. *Ruin of temples and buildings.* According to Sewell, "Never perhaps in the history of the world so much havoc has been wrought and so suddenly on so splendid a city teaming with a wealthy and industrious population in the full plentitude of prosperity one day and next day, pillaged and reduced to ruins of savage massacre and horrors defying description... They broke down the temples and palaces."

Political significance of the battle

(*i*) *Crushing blow to the Vijayanagara empire.* The battle of Talikota is one of the most momentous and decisive battles in the history of India. It sounded the death knell of the Hindu empire in the south.

(*ii*) *Paved the way for the Mughal rule in the South.* With the weakening of the Vijaynagara empire and infighting of the Muslim Kingdoms with one another after their victory, they fell singly and severally before the Mughal invaders from the north.

Chief reason of the defeat of the Vijayanagara forces. Sewell, the author of *A Forgotten Empire* has described the reason in these words "At

Vijayanagara there was the utmost confidence. Remembering how often the Muslims had vainly attempted to injure their great capital, and how for about two centuries they have never succeeded in penetrating to the South, the inhabitants pursued their daily avocations with no shadow of dread or sense of danger". He further observed, "The king lived his profitless life in inglorious seclusion, and Rama Raya (Chief Minister) '*King de facto*', never for a moment relaxed his haughty indifference to the movement of enemies." This shows how complacent the rulers of the Vijayanagara empire were. They did not realise the seriousness of the situation and accordingly suffered a very humiliating defeat which almost wiped out the only most powerful Hindu state in the country.

Q. 6. Explain the rise and fall of the Bahamni Kingdom. Give an estimate of Hasan, the founder of the Kingdom.

Ans. *Rise of the Bahamni Kingdom.*

The emergence of Bahamni Kingdom was the outcome of the fantastic policies of Muhammad Tughalq which failed and became responsible for weakening his hold over the distant areas of his empire. Taking advantage of the weak rule of the Tughlaq empire, Hasan, an erstwhile Afghan Officer in his service founded the Bahamni dynasty in 1347 A.D. Along with Bahamni, Vijayanagara Kingdom also came into being.

Hasan's earlier name was Zafar Khan. He along with several Afghan Amirs had been deployed by Muhammad Tughlaq to exercise control in the Deccan. However in due course, the emperor had begun to suspect their royalty and they revolted and defeated the army sent by the emperor to subdue them. According to Ferishta, Hasan had served a Brahmn astrologer named Gangu and he named the dynasty Bahamni after assuming his personal name Bahamn out of gratitude for his Brahamn master. After sometimes he added the name Gangu after Hasan.

According to another version, Hasan claimed his descent from an early Persian King Bahaman Shah.

On ascending the throne, Hasan assumed the title of Ala-ud-Din Hasan Bahaman Shah.

The Bahamni empire under Hasan extended from Daultabad in the west to Bhongir in Tellinga in the east and from the Warrangal river to the north of Krishna in the South. Debhal was an important sea port.

Hasan ruled for eleven years from 1347 to 1358.

For administrative purposes, he divided his empire into four parts and appointed governor for each part.

According to Ferishta, Hasan was very generous. He followed a policy of goodwill.

Isamai has stated that he was the first Muslim ruler of India who ordered that '*Jaziya*' should not be levied on the Hindus.

Hasan allowed all agricultural produce to be imported in his Kingdom without any duties.

Fall of the Bahamni Kingdom. The Bahamni Kingdom lasted for about 180 years. Of the eighteen rulers of this kingdom, five were murdered, three were deposed, two died of excessive drinking and another two were blinded. Most of the rulers were tyrants and mostly remained busy in fighting among themselves and with the neighbouring Hindu Kingdoms particularly Vijayanagara.

The following five Kingdoms came into being after the break-up of the Bahamni Kingdom.

1. Imad Shahi Kingdom of *Berar*, founded by Ullah Imad Shah in 1488.

2. Adil Shahi Kingdom of *Bijapur*, founded by Malik Ahmad in 1489.

3. Nizam Shahi Kingdom of *Ahmednagar*, founded by Malik Ahmad in 1490.

4. Qutab Shahi Kingdom of *Golkunda*, founded by Qutab Shah in 1512.

5. Barid Shahi Kingdom of *Bidar*, founded by Kasim Barid in 1526.

These five Muslim states of South India fought against each other but their primary enemy remained the Hindu Kingdom of Vijayanagara. In 1565, the four states barring Berar formed a confederacy and fought against Vijayanagara in the battle of Talikota and gave a crushing defeat to it. Thereafter Ahmednagar conquered Berar in 1574 and Bijapur annexed Bidar in 1618-1619. The Mughal emperor Akbar occupied a part of Ahmednagar and the rest of it was occupied by Shah Jahan. The states of Bijapur and Golkunda were finally annexed by Aurangzab.

Causes of the Fall of the Bahamni Dynasty

Following were the chief causes of the downfall of the Bahamni dynasty :

1. *Civil Wars.* There were constant civil wars in the Bahamni Kingdom. Of eighteen rulers, twelve proved ineffective against their internal enemies. Royal courts were full of intrigues.

2. *Lack of any definite law of succession.* After the death of a ruler, there were several claimants to the throne. Obviously there were tussles for rulership.

3. *Two main groups.* The Bahamni Kingdom was founded by Muslim Amirs who had come from Persia and Turkey and settled in India. The original inhabitants of the Deccan who had embraced Islam wanted equal share in administration. Thus there was a clash of interest of Indian Muslims and foreign Muslims.

4. *Policy of religious fanaticism.* Some of the Muslim Sultans of the Bahamni Kingdom followed a policy of extreme hatred towards their Hindu subjects who constituted a majority of population.

5. *Defective foreign policy.* The Bahamni Sultans followed a policy of war and enmity towards all their neighbouring states like Malwa, Khandesh, Gujarat, Telingana and Vijayanagara etc.

6. *Excessive power given to provincial governors.* The provincial governors had been given the powers to collect revenue and to maintain a big army. During a weak ruler, the provincial governors started proclaiming themselves as independent.

7. *Excessive disparity in living style.* It was observed by a Russian merchant A. Nikitin who stayed in Bidar for about four years (1470-1474) that the Amirs lived a very luxurious life whereas the common man lived a life of extreme misery and hardship. The common man had to bear the major brunt of the constant warfare of the Bahamni rulers.

Q. 7. Give an estimate of the services of Mahmud Gawan to the Bahamni Kingdom. Throw light on the causes of his downfall.

Ans. *Achievements of Mahmud Gawan.*

Mahmud Gawan served with a great distinction as Prime Minister of three Bahamni Sultans for about twenty three years from 1458 to 1481 A.D. On account of his contribution to the Bahamni in making rapid progress in different fields, Ferishta described Gawan as a fruit of the royal garden and wrote an eulogy of him in about 40 lines.

'Devotion' was the world which could sum up his whole life — work, character and aim.

At the last moment of his life he said his prayer in these words, "I am old and do not mind my death but my death is bound to come because of destiny. I thank God that he gave me an opportunity to lay down my life in the cause of the dynasty."

It has been rightly remarked about him, "By virtue of his conspicuous ability, skilful diplomacy and successful military campaigns, he brought the dominion of the Bahamnis to an extent ever achieved by former sovereigns."

Military achievements. Gawan led a successful expedition against the combined armies of Orissa and Khandesh.

He occupied the fertile areas of Bidar, Daultabad and Berar.

With the help of Sultan of Gujarat, he defeated the ruler of Malwa.

He established Bahamni control over the western coast as far as Dabhol and Goa. The possession of these two ports had two-fold advantage. First, it led to increase sea trade of the Kingdom with Iran and Iraq. Internal trade also increased. Second, it weakened the power of its arch-enemy Vijayanagare Kingdom.

Diplomatic skill. Very diplomatically, Gawan secured the help of the Sultans of Jaunpur, Bengal and Gujarat to subdue the powerful ruler of Malwa. Ultimately peace was restored between Malwa and Bahamni Kingdoms.

Administrative reforms. Gawan introduced the following administrative reforms :

(*i*) The existing four provinces were divided into two each and created eight *'Tarafs'*.

(*ii*) He reduced the powers of the governors of these *'Tarafs'* (Provinces).

(*iii*) In each of these eight 'Tarafs' some areas were kept reserve for the control of the Central Government and for their administrative control, officials were appointed by the Centre.

(*iv*) Orders were issued by him for placing one fort in each province under the charge of the governor and others under the control of military commanders appointed by the Sultan.

(*v*) He put a check on the powers of the nobles.

(*vi*) He introduced a fair system of justice.

Development of agriculture. The entire agricultural land was surveyed and land revenue fixed.

He exercised strict control over local officials to ensure that they took interest in the development of agriculture and do not charge more than the fixed revenue.

Public education. He took several measures to spread education. He opened a *'Madrasa'* an institution of higher learning at Bidar. The building was of three storeys and was made beautiful with the use of lovely red titles. Several scholars for this *'Madrasa'* were invited from Iran and Iraq. Free board and lodging were provided. A library containing about 3000 books was established.

Military reforms. Service conditions of the soldiers were improved. Better discipline was enforced in the army.

Personal accomplishments. Although he was at the helm of affairs of the state, he lived a very simple life. He cooked food in earthen vessels and slept on mattress. He was a great scholar and wrote two books. He loved the company of scholars. On every Friday night, he used to visit various places of worship of the Muslims. He gave help to the poor and the needy.

Dark side. However, there was a blot on the character of this saintly person. He was very enthusiastic in the persecution of Non-Muslims. He ordered the destruction of several temples.

Sad end of Gawan. Achievements of Gawan, invited the jealousy of the Indian Muslim nobles and through a conspiracy against him they succeeded in getting death orders for him from the Sultan when he was drunk. When the Sultan came to know about the real truth, he was deeply grieved and died within a year of the murder of his faithful Prime Minister.

With the death of Gawan, all the cohesion and the power of the Bahamni Kingdom began to disappear.

Q. 8. Discuss the economic, social and cultural progress in the Bahamni empire.

Ans. *Economic Life.*

Agriculture was the main occupation of the people. Among the important industries were: Gur making, metal industry, oil production, weaving, leather works, weapon making etc. Ornaments of gold and diamonds were made in large quantity.

Golkunda and Bijapur were known for foreign trade. Cotton, woollen and silken clothes, spices, indigo etc. were exported. Important items of import were rose water, raisins, dry fruits, opium, Persian plums, horses and wine.

Trade was mostly in the hands of Muslim traders, called *'Moors'*.

The Kingdom entered into commercial treaties with the Portuguese and the Dutch.

Development of Education. Some of the Bahamni Sultans like Taj-ud-Din Firoz Shah and Ahmad Shah took several steps for the promotion of education in the Kingdom. Prime Minister Mahmud Gawan started a *'Madarsa'*, an institution of higher education. Some scholars compare this institution at Bidar with that of Nalanda of ancient India. He invited scholars from Iran and Iraq to teach in this institution. The students were given free food and clothing. Gawan also maintained a library which had 3000 books.

Literary progress. The disintegration of the Delhi Sultanate had led to the migration of several scholars from Delhi to the Bahamni Kingdom where they were greatly patronised. Some of the Bahamni Sultans invited Muslim scholars from Iran and Iraq to their Courts. Sultan Taj-ud-Din Firoz was an expert in the art of calligraphy. He was well acquainted with languages like Arabic, Persian and Turkish. Sultan Ahmad Shah used to award prizes to scholars for writing poetry. Mahmud Gawan is said to have written two books namely *'Roztul-Insha'* and *'Diwan-I-Ashar'*. Historical works were written in the regional languages as well as in Arabic and Persian.

Development in art and architecture. The Bahamni rulers built beautiful mosques, palaces and strong forts at Gulburga, Bidar and Daulatabad etc. Ala-ud-Din Hasan Bahamni built a big mosque without any open courtyard—the only mosque of this type at Gulburga. *Char Minar* in Daultabad and *Madarsa* at Bidar were built in Persian style. The styles of forts built at Bidar, Warrangal and Raichur etc. was influenced by European architecture. Muhammad Adil Shah I constructed *Gol Gumbaz* at Bijapur. This is the greatest dome in size.

Social life. Social life in the Bahamni Kingdom was greatly influenced by Arabic, Persian and Indian practices. The upper classes of Muslims were divided into two classes—one comprising the original inhabitants i.e.

converted Muslims in South India and the other coming from countries like Africa, Arab, Persia and Turkey, etc. Mutual rivalry existed between these two groups.

The life of the upper classes was very luxurious. They generally lived in beautiful palaces. They kept horses and wore lavish clothes and ornaments. The shoes of several officials belonging to upper classes were decorated with rubies, and diamonds etc.

Polygamy was the order generally among the upper classes.

Among the Muslims *purdah* was common and easy divorce practice prevailed.

13

Disintegration of the Delhi Sultanate and Rise of Independent States (Fragmentation of the Sultanate and Rise of Provincial Kingdoms)

Q. 1. Give a brief description of the independent states rising on the disintegration of the Delhi Sultanate in the 14th and 15th centuries in North India?

Ans. *Disintegration of the Sultanate Period.*

The Sultanate period covering a period of about 320 years between 1206 to 1526 A.D. had five ruling dynasties, each with an average period of about 64 years. These dynasties were : Slave Dynasty (1206 to 1290), Khalji Dynasty (1290-1320), Tughlaq Dynasty (1320-1414), Sayyid Dynasty (1415-1451) and the Lodi Dynasty (1451-1526).

The disintegration of the Sultanate had begun during the Tughlaq period. The first to break from Delhi were the Deccan States in the South, Bengal in the east and Sind and Multan in the north-west. Thereafter, the governors of Gujarat, Malwa and Jaunpur in eastern Uttar Pradesh also declared themselves independent. Various states in Rajasthan also asserted their independence.

Important independent powers were as under:

Bengal, Assam and Orissa, Gujarat, Malwa and Mewar, Sharqis of Jaunpur and Kashmir. In South India, Vijayanagara, Bahamni and Khandesh were the important powers.

BENGAL

The first Muslim invader to conquer Bengal was Ikhtiyar-ud-Din Muhammad Bin Bakhtiyar, a military commander of Muhammad Ghori. In 1204, he conquered Nadia, one of the capitals of Lakshman Sena of Bengal. During Balban's reign, Bengal broke away from the Delhi Sultanate and declared its independence. Firoz Tughlaq made two attempts to capture Bengal but failed. Bengal enjoyed freedom for about two hundred years. Several Hindu and Muslim dynasties alternatively ruled over Bengal during this period.

Sher Shah Suri annexed Bengal in his empire in 1541.

The Sultans of Bengal adorned their two capitals of Pandua and Gaur with magnificent buildings.

The rule of Sultan Ala-ud-Din Hussain (1493-1519) witnessed a peaceful period. The Sultan followed a liberal religious policy. He is said to have shown great respect to the famous saint Chaitanya. His Prime Minister was a Hindu. The chief physician, the chief of the bodyguard and the master of the mint and Sultan's private secretary were also Hindus.

Bengali literature flourished under his patronage.

GUJARAT

On account of the richness of its soil, excellence of handicrafts and its flourishing seaports, Gujarat was considered one of the richest provinces of India. Its wealth tempted Mahmud Ghazni to plunder its important places and temples. He, therefore, invaded Gujarat and plundered Somnath. In 1297, during the reign of Ala-ud-Din Khalji, it was annexed to the Sultanate of Delhi. It became one of the provinces of the kingdom of Delhi and was ruled by Muslim Governors. In 1401, Zafar Khan, the governor of the province declared himself independent.

There was a bitter rivalry between the kingdoms of Gujarat and Malwa, which weakened the two kingdoms.

After Zafar Khan, the next ruler was Ahmad Shah (1411-1422) who is considered to be the real founder of this kingdom. He fought several wars against Malwa, Khandesh and the Bahamni Kingdoms. He raised beautiful buildings and shifted his capital to the new city of Ahmedabad.

The most famous ruler of Gujarat was Mahmud Begarha who ruled for about 52 years from 1459-1511—a rare feat - (Ashoka about 40 years, Akbar 50 years and Aurangzeb 49 years). He fought many battles and supported the Bahamni Kingdom against Malwa. He fought against the Portuguese with the support of Egyptian fleet but could not check their influence on the sea and finally compromised with them.

Mahmud raised Gujarat to the status of one of the powerful states of northern India.

Gujarat made great progress under Mahmud in the field of literature and fine arts.

Mahmud, however, was not liberal in his religious outlook and he sacked Dwarka and destroyed several temples there.

Another capable ruler of Gujarat was Bahadur Shah. He conquered Malwa in 1531 and plundered Chittor, the capital of Mewar. However, he was defeated by Humayuan. Gujarat was finally conquered by the Mughal ruler Akbar in 1572 A.D.

MALWA

Malwa occupied a very strategic position from geographical as well as political point of view. Its territory included on the north-west of the Deccan plateau, between the river Narbada and Tapti. It commanded the road trunk route between Gujarat and North India and between North and South India. Its situation was such that if any of the kingdoms of the region could conquer Malwa, it would be in a very strategic and powerful position to become the master of the whole of northern India and could also play an important role in east, west and south India. As long as Malwa was strong, it acted as a barrier against any ambition of expansion by the rulers of Gujarat, Mewar and the Lodi Sultans of Delhi.

On account of its internal dissensions, Malwa became a prey to Ala-ud-Din Khalji in 1305 and remained under Delhi till 1401 when it became independent after the ransacking of Delhi at the hands of Tamer Lane.

Most of the rulers of Malwa remained intolerant towards the Hindus. Mahmud Khan Khalji (1436-69), who is considered to be the ablest and the most powerful ruler of Malwa destroyed many temples. He fought with almost all the rulers of the neighbouring states but most of his time was spent in fighting against Rana Kumba of Mewar.

MEWAR

Mewar has produced several men and women of great qualities which have made them immortal in the annals of history. Among the great figures were Rana Hamir, Rana Kumba, Rayamalla Sangram Singh, popularly known as Rana Sanga and Maharana Pratap.

Mewar is associated with bravery, chivalry, honour and respect. The Kingdom achieved so much strength and progress during the reign of Rana Hamir that according to one version, he even imprisoned Muhammad Tughlaq for some time. However, this version is not accepted by several historians.

Rana Sanga is said to have invited Babur to invade India.

Kingdom of Jaunpur

The Kingdom of Jaunpur located in eastern Uttar Pradesh was founded in 1394 A.D. by Malik Sarvar, a prominent noble of the time of Firoz Tughlaq. The dynasty had six rulers and it lasted for about 100 years.

The dynasty came into being after the chaos and confusion that followed on account of the invasion of Timur.

At the height of its glory, the Jaunpur Kingdom (also known as Sharqi Kingdom of Jaunpur after the title Sharqi assumed by its founder) extended from Aligarh in Western Uttar Pradesh to Dharbhanga in North Bihar and from the boundary of Nepal in the north to Bundelkhand in the South.

There were constant conflicts between the rulers of Delhi and Jaunpur for the expansion of the territory. Ultimately in 1505, Sikander Lodi annexed Jaunpur Kingdom.

Jaunpur, 'the Shiraz of the East'. The city of Jaunpur, situated on the river Gomati, 34 miles away from Varanasi towards the north-east, was the capital of the state of Jaunpur. On account of its being the centre of learning, art and architecture, it came to be known as 'Shiraj of the East'. Many rulers of this dynasty were great patron of culture. Ibrahim Shah who ruled from 1402 to 1436 made a special contribution. Men of letters, poets and scholars and saints used to assemble at Jaunpur and shed luste on it. Malik Muhammad Jaisi, the author of the well-known Hindi work 'Padmavat' lived at Jaunpur.

Jaunpur was beautified with magnificent buildings which included several mosques and mausoleums. The Atal Masjid is the most enduring achievement of Sharqi architecture.

KASHMIR

Till the middle of the 14th century A.D., Kashmir remained a Hindu Kingdom with the vast majority of the Hindu population. It also remained nearly unaffected from the influence of the Delhi Sultans. It became a province of the Mughal empire in 1586 under Akbar.

In 1315, Shah Mirza, a Muslim adventurer from Persia entered the service of a Hindu ruler. After the death of Udayana, the ruler of Kashmir in 1338m his wife took up the administration of the state in her hands as the sons were minors. By then Shah Mirza had become quite powerful. He imprisoned the queen and her sons and himself became the ruler of Kashmir.

Sikander Shah and Zainul Abidin were the two most important rulers of Kashmir during the medieval period. However, both of them were diametrically opposed.

Sikander Shah (1389-1413). He was a great bigot. He ordered that all Brahamans and learned Hindus should embrace Islam or leave the valley. He destroyed several temples. He got the title *'But-Shikani'* (Idol-breaker). It is said that only a few families of the Brahamans were left in Kashmir, as others were either converted to Islam or turned out of Kashmir.

Q. 2. Assess the achievements of Rana Kumha and Rana Sanga.

Ans. *Rana Kumbha* (*1438-68*).

Rana Kumbha was a very brave and talented military commander and ruler. He made his mark in the political as well as cultural field.

Military and political achievements. Rana Kumbha succeeded his father Rana Mokal in 1433 A.D. with the assistance of the Bhil chiefs. He had to meet the challenge of several intrigues. However, within a very short period of his accession, he was able to overcome all his internal troubles with great diplomacy and bravery.

Rana Kumbha conquered states like Bundi, Kota, Chatsu, Malpura, Amber, Dungerpur etc. Majority of these states accepted the suzerainty of Rana Kumbha and came under his political influence.

Rana Kumbha annexed Sambhar, Didwana, Mandore, Nagaur, Ranthambore, Sirohi, Gagran, Ajmer, Mandalgarh, Abu, Toda etc. to his empire.

Rana Kumbha defeated Sultan Mahmud Khalji of Malwa. According to inscriptions he brought Mahmud Khalji as a prisoner and after keeping him in prison for six months, sent him back to his Kingdom. According to some historians, this liberality on his part proved quite dear to him.

After making military preparations, Mahmud Khalji invaded Mewar. He destroyed the temple at Kumbhalgarh but failed to conquer Mewar. Afterwards the Rana defeated the combined armies of the Sultan Mahmud of Malwa and the ruler of Gujarat. The Rana Kumbha was able to defend his entire hereditary state and all the conquered areas as mentioned earlier.

Cultural achievements of Rana Kumbha. Rana Kumba was a great patron of art and literature. He was a great musician himself and took a keen interest in music. He was a great *Veena* player. He wrote works like *Sangit Raj, Sangit Mimansa, 'Sangit Ratnakar'* and *Sudprabandh.*

Kumbha erected a Victory Tower at Chittor as a mark of victory of his conquests. He consolidated the fortification of Chittor and constructed a road running through its seven doors.

He constructed the city of Basantpur. He built several inns, palaces, ponds, schools, and temples.

For the defence of the Kingdom, he built five forts of Kumbhalgarh, Achalgarh, Maddan, Kolana and Vairat.

Rana Kumba gave patronage to many craftsmen and sculptors.

He also patronised great scholars. Mahesh and Atri, the composers of the inscriptions of Victory Tower flourished in his court.

Sad end of Rana Kumbha. This great ruler of Mewar *i.e.* Rana Kumbha who proved a formidable ruler against his opponent rulers lost his life at the hands of his own son.

Sangram Singh Alias Rana Sanga (1509-28)

Rana Sanga, the grandson of Rana Kumbha was a ferocious brave Rajput ruler who fought several battles. He lost one eye, one arm and had about 88 scars of wounds on his body. He established his supremacy over almost all Rajput states in Rajasthan.

Rana Sanga fought successfully against the rulers of Gujarat and Malwa. He captured the ruler of Malwa who had been wounded and kept at Chittor till his wounds were healed. He also defeated the Delhi Sultan Ibrahim Lodi in 1519. It is said that he was one of the Indian rulers and nobles who invited Babur to invade India. It is not clear whether any understanding was arrived at between Babur and Rana Sanga. He lost to Babur in the battle of Khanua in 1527. Rana Sanga escaped and wanted to renew the conflict with Babur. However, he was prisoned by his own nobles who considered such a course dangerous and suicidal. Maharana Pratap also belonged to this dynasty. (See also next chapter)

Q. 3. Why is Zainul Abidin of Kashmir known as 'Akbar of Kashmir' or a great ruler?

Ans. *Zainul Abidin* (*1420-70*).

Zainul Abidin is one of the very few rulers who ruled for about 50 years and remained very popular. On account of his liberal religious policy, promotion of learning, and interest in art and architecture he can be called the fore-runner of Akbar. He also look several steps for the welfare of his subjects.

Liberal religious policy. He withdrew all the orders issued by Sikander Shah which in any manner were against the Hindus. He brought back to Kashmir all the Hindus who had left on account of the repressive policy of Sikander Shah. Those who wanted to revert to Hinduism were given freedom to do so. They were restored their grants, libraries and temples.

He abolished *'Jizya'* and forbade cow slaughter.

He appointed Hindus on high posts in administration.

He established matrimonial relations with the Hindus. Two of his queens were the daughters of a Hindu ruler of Jammu.

Economic development. Zainul paid great attention to the economic development of his state. He encouraged the development of several crafts such as gold-heating, polishing and stone-cutting etc. He also fostered the art of shawl-making, musket making and the art of manufacturing fire works. He sent two skilled persons to Samarquand to learn the art of paper making and book-binding. He took several steps to provide employment to large number of people.

Development of agriculture. He issued instructions to revenue officials to be liberal and honest in dealing with the peasants. He dug canals to provide irrigation facilities. He gave grants of grain and fodder to the people during natural calamities like famine. He got the entire land measured and kept records of all farms.

Control over market. He lessened the burden of taxation of the people and carried out currency reforms. He fixed the price of commodities and established control over the market. He made essential for the traders to sell grain at the fixed price.

Development of literature. The Sultan was well-versed in Persian, Kashmiri, Sanskrit and Tibetan. He was a great poet. He gave patronage to scholars. Several Arabic and Persian works were translated into local languages. The *Mahabharta* and *Rajtarangini* were translated into Persian

Love for music. He loved music. The ruler of Gwalior sent him two rare music books in Sanskrit.

Friendly relations with foreign rulers. He maintained cordial relations with the rulers of Mecca, Egypt and Khorasan etc. He was also on good terms with the rulers of Delhi, Gujarat and Gwalior etc.

14

Babur (1526-1530) : Beginning of the Mughal Rule

(Advent of the Mughals)

Q. 1. "The defeat of Ibrahim's army was the beginning of the task of Babur". Discuss this statement.

Or

Give a brief account of the First Battle of Panipat. Examine its significance and discuss the causes of the success of Babur.

Or

What was the political condition of India at the time of Babur's invasion? Why was Ibrahim Lodi unsuccessful against Babur?

Give an account of the First Battle of Panipat. What were the causes of Babur's success? (Punjab University April 1997, April 1998)

Ans. *Babur's Rule in India (1526-30).*

Babur (1483-1530) whose original name was Zahir-ud-Din Mohammad, came to be known by his pet name 'Babur' - a Turkish word which means a tiger. He belonged to Farghana, a small Kingdom in Central Asia. From 1519 to 1524, he led four expeditions to India but without any significant results. His fifth invasion which marked his success completely changed the political history of India. It had far-reaching consequences. The battle of Panipat made him virtually the ruler of entire India.

Vulnerable Political condition of India on the Eve of Babur's Invasion

A struggle for political supremacy among several warring powers in India was going on. Babur who had an ambition to rule India fully realised this condition and decided to try his luck. Situation is described here in brief.

Delhi. Ibrahim Lodi, the ruler of Delhi, lacked power and political diplomacy. He had created many enemies. He was not on friendly terms with several Afghan and Turk nobles. Rana Sanga of Mewar was his sworn enemy.

Punjab. Daulat Khan Lodi, the governor of Punjab distrusted Sultan Ibrahim Lodi. To settle scores with him, he invited Babur from Kabul to invade India.

Sind. The province of Sind had become independent of the rule of the Delhi Sultanate. There was a good deal of confusion and lawlessness in the state.

Kashmir. Towards the end of the fifteenth century, there began a stage of anarchy in Kashmir.

Mewar. Sangram Singh, popularly known as Rana Sanga, was the ruler of Mewar. He aspired to capture the throne of Delhi and Agra. He is said to have invited Babur to invade India. He was perhaps under the delusion that Babur like his ancestor Timur would invade, loot and go back to Kabul.

Chief reasons that led Babur to invade India.

These may be listed as under:

1. Chaotic political condition of India.
2. Temptation to acquire enormous wealth of India.
3. Legal claim on account of Timur's invasion on India — Babur a descendant of Timur.
4. Insufficient income from Kabul — Babur's earlier possessions.
5. Fear of Babur regarding Uzbek's attack on his empire of Kabul.
6. Babur's ambition of capturing territories.
7. Invitation from some Indian nobles and rulers to attack India.

First Battle of Panipat (April 21, 1526 A.D.)

After conquering Punjab, Babur proceeded towards Delhi and met the army of Ibrahim Lodi at Panipat — now a town in Haryana, 85 Kilometers north-west of Delhi.

Babur, in his *'Memoirs'* mentions that with a small army of 12000 picked horsemen he defeated Ibrahim's army of about one lakh soldiers. Whatever be the statistical details, all historians agree that Ibrahim's army was far greater in numerical strength. For about a week, both the armies faced each other and engaged in skirmishes before the real battle started on the morning of April 21, 1526 and by noon it was over. Ibrahim Lodi's army was destroyed and he died in the battle field along with his 15000 soldiers. (Estimates vary)

Pleased at his victory Babur wrote, "By the grace and mercy of Almighty God, this difficult affair was made easy to me and that mighty army, in the space of half a day was laid to dust."

Causes of Babur's Success and Ibrahim's Failure

1. *Absence of any strong power in India.* As Dr. Ishwari Prasad has put it, "In the beginning of the sixteenth century, India was a confederacy of a number of small independent states which could easily fall prey to any strong and determined invader."

2. *Babur's efficient artillery.* According to Rushbrook Williams, "If it could be possible to emphasize anyone of the factors as being the most important cause of his (Babur's) victory, one would surely have to assign the first place to his artillery".

3. *Inefficiency of Ibrahim as a military commander.* Babur himself has observed, "Ibrahim was an inexperienced youngman, careless in his movements who marched without order, halted or retired without plan and engaged in the battle without foresight".

4. *Tulghuna method of warfare-formation of the army in the battle field.* Babur took the position in the centre between the left and right wings. On the right and left extremities of the entire front line were two flying columns to wheel round on the enemy and attack them on the sides or at the rear. Along the front of the entire line, were placed the artillery on the right side and the musketeers on the left. The Afghan army came straight rapidly marching, but as they came near the Babur's frontline, they hesitated and halted, but their soldiers behind pressed on creating a little confusion. Babur did not let go this opportunity and his flying columns wheeled round, reached at the back and delivered a violent attack at the rear while the right and left wings started charging the enemies at the front. At this very time, the artillery from the right and musketeers from the left started the attack. The centre of Ibrahim's army became helpless under the attack and the rest of the army was surrounded on all sides by the rains of bullets and arrows."

5. *Babur's well-trained and disciplined army.* There is no doubt that Ibrahim's army lacked proper training and discipline. His army was a mixed crowd of soldiers.

6. *Horses versus elephants.* Babur's war horses were more swift in action as compared with the war elephants of Ibrahim.

7. *Disunity among Indian rulers.* Babur had not to face a united army of Indian rulers. He defeated them one by one and captured their kingdoms.

8. *Unpopularity of Ibrahim Lodi.* Ibrahim's treatment with his Amirs (nobles) was most discourteous and insulting and they wanted to get rid of him.

9. *Babur's personality.* Babur was determined to capture Delhi. He was indefatigable and had enormous capacity to inspire his soldiers. Babur's warm personality generated loyalty of his army.

Far-reaching effects of Babur's Victory at Panipat

1. *Foundation of a new dynasty.* The victory of Babur laid down the foundation of the Mughal dynasty that lasted for more than two hundred and fifty years in India.

2. *Fatal blow to the Afghan rule.* In the words of Stanley Lane-Poole the biographer of Babur, "The battle of Panipat became a tomb for the Afghans of Delhi. Their state was destroyed and their strength was absolutely crippled."

3. *End of the Lodi rule.* The battle of Panipat was decisive. Ibrahim Lodi was killed in the battle field along with 15000 soldiers. With his death the Lodi rule came to an end.

4. *Wide use of artillery.* After the battle of Panipat, the use of artillery became current in India.

5. *Capturing enormous wealth.* According to Lane-Poole (1899), Babur gathered such a booty as surpassed all dreams.

6. *Fulfilment of Babur's ambition.* Babur's long desire of conquering India and getting its wealth was fulfilled.

7. *Enhancing Babur's dignity.* The battle of Panipat proved that Babur was a great military commander.

8. *End of Babur's bad days.* According to Rushbrook Williams, "After being successful in this battle, the bad days of Babur came to an end. Now he had not to bother about his personal safety or throne".

Q. 2. Discuss the causes, events and consequences of the battle of Khanwa. Why did Rana Sanga lose the battle?

Ans. *Causes of the Battle of Khanwa (1527).*

1. *Ambitions of Babur and Rana Sanga.* Both had very high ambitions of name and fame. Both had an eye on the whole of India. Each wanted to become the supreme power.

2. *Charge of breach of faith.* Both accused each other of breach of faith. From records it is not clear whether any agreement was made between the two when Babur invaded India. Babur's accusation was that Rana Sanga was one of the rulers of India to invite him to attack India but he rendered no help to him in the first Battle of Panipat. Rana Sanga, on the other hand accused Babur of not accepting his claim on Kalpi, Dhaulpur and Agra.

Chief events. The armies of Babur and Rana Sanga met at Khanwa, about forty Kilometers away from Delhi. Babur arranged his army almost in the same manner as he had done at Panipat. Several important Rajput rulers and Afghan chiefs rallied to Rana Sanga. About Rana's army, Lane-Poole has observed, "Whatever the exact number might have been, a more gallant army could not be brought into the field".

The battle started at 9 A.M. on March 17, 1527 and continued for about ten hours. The Rajput began to bring havoc upon Babur's army that seemed to have been reduced almost to their last gasp. At this moment Babur made a stirring speech before his soldiers: "Noble men and soldiers, every man that comes to this world is subject to dissolution. How much better is it to die with honour than to live with infame. Let us then with one accord swear on God's holy 'Quran' that none of us will ever think of turning his face from this warfare till his soul is separated from his body." The stirring appeal had the desired result. The bloody war followed. As observed by Dr. R.P. Tripathi, "The ruthless slaughter closed the bloody episode."

The Mughals won the battle. Rana Sanga was badly wounded and taken away from the battle field. He wanted to take revenge of his defeat but his nobles did not want to take risk. He is said to have been poisoned to death by his own men.

Causes of Rana Sanga's Failure and Babur's Victory

1. *Rana Sanga not a diplomat like Babur.* Rana Sanga showed vacillation and was not a good strategist. He did not capture Agra and Delhi when Ibrahim and Babur were fighting the battle of survival. Had he done so, he would have acquired enormous treasures and resources.

2. *Rana Sanga's failure to estimate the strength of Babur.* Rana Sanga underestimated Babur's strength.

3. *Holy war (Jihad).* Babur had declared the struggle with Rana as a holy war of the Muslims against the Hindus. His stirring speech infused a new vigour among his soldiers. Everyone swore of the holy Quran.

4. *Time for formation and consolidation.* Rana Sanga did not attack when Babur was making fresh preparations. Babur was able to form the *'Tuluguma'* on protective lines.

5. *Babur as a commander.* Babur was a very capable commander. In the face of adverse situation, he exhibited rare patience and courage.

6. *Babur's artillery.* Babur's artillery wrought havoc on the Rajput army.

7. *Babur's disciplined army.* Babur's army, though small in number but it was experienced and well-disciplined. On the other hand Rana Sanga's army consisted of heterogeneous elements comprising armies of several Rajput rulers as well as Afghan rulers. It lacked unity of command.

Consequences of the Battle of Khanwa

1. *Strengthening of the Mughal rule in India.* The foundation laid at the battle of Panipat for the establishment of the Mughal empire in India was strengthened and based on firm bases.

2. *Set back to the superiority of the Rajputs.* In the words of S.R. Sharma, "Defeat of the Rajputs, at Khanwa ended the superiority of the Rajputs which they had established successfully in the last ten years and which was an eyesore to the Muslims". However, in contrast to this, A.L. Srivastva observed, "Rajput military power was no doubt crushed in the battle of Khanwa but it was not totally crushed. Within a few years they again raised their heads."

3. *Weakening of the Afghan power.* The power of the Afghans was almost crippled.

4. *Marwar and not Mewar.* According to Dr. Lunia, "After the defeat and death of Rana Sanga, Mewar lost its prestige and in its place Marwar started gaining the power."

Q. 3. Assess the achievements of Babur.

Or

State the salient features of Babur's character and personality which have assigned him an important place in the history of India.

Ans. *General Estimate of Babur's Character and Personality*

Nearly all historians have talked very high about Babur's personality and character. In the words of Lane-Poole, "Babur is perhaps the most captivating personality in oriental history". Likewise Dr. V.S. Smith observes, "He is the most brilliant Asiatic prince of his age and worth of a high place among the sovereigns of any age or country".

Founder of the Mughal empire. Babur conquered a significant part of India. He made Delhi his capital. He won three important battles in India. With his victory in the Battle of Panipat, he captured the throne of Delhi–a throne coveted by every important ruler of India. With this, he gave a severe blow to the power of the Afghans. With the victories in the battle of Khanwa and Battle of Chanderi, he destroyed the power of the Rajputs. His victory at Ghagara crushed the remaining power of the Afghans. He, thus succeeded in laying down the foundation of the Mughal empire in India that had the longest period of survival in India.

As a general. He was never discouraged by defeats. In grave crisis and heat of battle, he was calm and resourceful. He knew the art of using several tactics and strategies in war.

As a diplomat. In India, he successfully maintained a balance among his Mughal, Afghan and Indian nobles.

As a soldier. Babur was fearless in battles. He was a fine fencer, good archer and superb horseman.

As a physically strong man. He was a very stong man and could run on a rampart holding two men in his arms. He swam across several rivers in India. He could ride a horse for eighty miles without any break.

As an emotional speaker. In the Battle of Khanwa when his soldiers had lost courage, his emotional appeal to them worked wonders for them. They fought valiantly and won.

As a scholar. Babur was a scholarly king. His command over Turki language assigns him a place in the world of scholars. Babur also possessed good knowledge of Arabic and Persian. His *Tuzki-Babri* or *Baburnama* (Memoirs) ranks among the best autobiographies of the world. His collection of poems in Turki called the *Diwan* is also considered as one of the best contemporary poetic works.

As a builder. Babur constructed many buildings at Agra, Fatehpur Sikri, Bayana and Dholpur. He planted several gardens of fruits and flowers.

In his *Memoirs* Babur wrote, "Six hundred and eighty labourers used to work everyday on my buildings at Agra while 1941 stone cutters worked everyday on my buildings at Sikri, Bian, Dhaulpur, Gwalior and Kol (Aligarh)."

Affectionate in domestic relations. In his will he advised his son Humayun, "Do not fight against your brothers even though they may deserve it." Babur was an obedient son, an affectionate father, reliable friend, lovable husband and a good relative.

Overall qualities of Babur. According to Prof. Rushbrooke, Babur possessed these eight fundamental qualities: Lofty judgement, noble ambition, the art of victory, the art of government, the art of conferring prosperity upon his people, the talent of ruling mildly the people of God, ability to win the heart of his soldiers and love of justice.

Dark Side of Babur's Personality

Religious bigotry. In his battles of Khanwa and Chanderi with the Rajputs, he invoked the slogan of *Jihad* (Holy war against the non-Muslims) whereas in the Battle of Panipat with Ibrahim Lodi, he raised no such slogan.

He is said to have built a mosque at Ayodhya at the site of a temple dedicated to the birth place of Lord Rama whom Hindus worship as an *Avtar* (incarnation of God).

Non-identification with India. In his will, he desired to be buried in his native land at Kabul. This indicates that he did not identify himself with India.

Not an able administrator. According to Rush Brooke Williams, "Babur is considered as the founder of Mughal" empire not in the capacity of a ruler but rather that of a conqueror.

Personal bad habits. Babur was fond of drinking. He was a habitual opium taker.

Q. 4. What does Babur write about India? Describe briefly.

Or

Write a brief note on 'Tuzki-Babri' or Babur Nama (Babur's Memoirs)

Ans. *Memoirs of Babur.*

The book was originally written by Babur in his mother tongue Turki. It was translated into Persian during Akbar's time. In 1826, it was translated into French and English. The English translation was done by Mrs. Beveridge from the original work in Turki.

Historical significance of Babur's Memoirs. According to Beveridge, "Babur's autobiography is one of those precious gifts which are for all times and is fit to take rank with the *Confessions of St. Augustine* and Memoirs of Gibbon and Newton".

About the importance of this work, Lane-Poole has observed, "Babur and his successors have gone, his splendour and power are no more but his autobiography is still there to remind us of the greatness of the founder of the Mughal dynasty in India." This has been accepted as a meritorious book.

Contents of Babur's Memoirs. Babur has written about the climate, the people, their economic and social conditions and about the kings and political events in India. The following are some of the extracts from his memoirs :

People. Hindustan is a country of few charms. Its people have no good looks, no good manners, no genius, or capacity.

Dress. The males use mostly *languta* and the females cover their body only with one cloth.

Richness of India. Pleasant things of Hindustan are that it is a large country and has masses of gold and silver.

Season and weather. Its air and the rain is very fine. However, it creates dampness which spoils everything. The airs are excellent not only in the rains but also in the cold and hot seasons.

Artisans. It has numberless workers of every kind. There is a fixed class for every sort of work and for everything.

Political condition. The capital of India is Delhi. When I conquered that country, there were five Muslim and two Hindu rulers.

Limitations. While assessing Babur's description about India, it may be observed that he spent most of his four years in fighting battles and perhaps and he had not enough time to study the life of the people closely.

Summing up

In spite of some gaps regarding the coverage of all important events of his life, 'Babur's *Memoirs* can be considered as a great historical document. Lane-Poole is quite near the mark when he writes, "If there was a case when the testimony of a single historical document, unsupported by other evidences, should be accepted a sufficient proof, it is the case with 'Babur's *Memoirs*'.

15

Humayun (1530-40) and (1555-56)

Q. 1. "Humayun had a rich legacy of difficulties from his father which he made richer by his own mistakes". Discuss.

Or

What were the problems faced by Humayun at his accession? Discuss. (Delhi University, 1997)

Or

Give an estimate of Humayun.

Or

Give a brief description of the early life and difficulties of Humayun. How far did he enhance his problems himself?

Ans. *Humayun's early life.*

As the story goes, Humayun fell ill and his father Babur prayed for his recovery and transfer his illness to him. His prayer was granted. Humayun recovered, Babur fell ill and died soon. After the death of his father, Humayun ascended the throne of Delhi.

Nasir-ud-Din Muhammad Humayun who is popularly known as Humayun was the eldest son of Babur. Kamran, Askari and Hindal were his step brothers. He learnt Turki, Arabic and Persian. He worked as governor of a province in Kabul. He took part in the battles of Panipat and Khanwa. He looked after the administration of Hissar, Firuza and Sambhal. He was nominated by Babur as his successor.

Humayun is probably the only king in the history of India whose rule included two spells, one from 1530-40 and the other in 1555-56 after his fifteen years' exile from India. Humayun, literally meaning 'fortunate' but through most part of his life, he remained 'unfortunate'. He is again the only king who on the advice of his father treated his half-brothers in real brotherly affection but without any reciprocal response from them rather betrayal from one.

Early difficulties faced by Humayun and Babur's Legacy

The throne inherited by Humayun was full of thorns. He had to face several difficulties right from his accession. Among the major factors which contributed to his difficulties and problems were the legacy of Babur's will, the unfriendly treatment of his brothers and relatives and lastly, the hostile attitude of the Afghans and the Rajputs.

Babur had entered the country as a stranger and spoiler. He had defeated the armies and broken the power of the reigning dynasty i.e. the Lodis. The only hold which he and the Mughals had upon the people of India was military force. Babur had not created a strong administrative machinery to control such a vast empire.

1. *Division of empire according to Babur's will.* Humayun very faithfully implemented the will of his father. He treated all his young step brothers very kindly. He made Kamran the ruler of Kabul and Kandhar, Askari, the ruler of Rohilkhand and Hindal, the ruler of Mewat (comprising the modern territories of Alwar, Mathura and Gurgaon). Thus his sphere of influence and power was reduced. This division weakned the unity of the empire.

2. *Ungratefulness and incompetency of Humayun's brothers.* Kamran, after taking Kabul and Kandhar, took Punjab forcibly. Hindal too declared himself emperor. Askari lost some part of the area allotted to him. All these actions had an adverse effect on Humayun.

3. *Hostile attitude of Humayun's own relatives.* Mutual conspiracies and jealousies of Humayun's relatives created several problems for him. Muhammad Jama Mirza, a powerful noble and the husband of Humayun's sister, Muhammad Mehdi Khwaja, Babur's brother-in law, and Muhammad Sultan Mirza, Humayun's cousin were quite powerful and ambitous. They created several problems for him.

4. *Lack of suitable administrative machinery.* Babur spent almost his time in wars and could not take suitable steps to organise the administration of the territories he conquered.

5. *Want of a well-integrated and unified army.* The Mughal army was a heterogeneous body of several races—Chaghatais, Uzbeks, Mughals, Persian, Afghans and Hindustanis, etc. Such an army could be kept under control and disciplined only under the leadership of a capable, dashing and inspiring commander like Babur. Humayun was too weak for this purpose.

6. *Babur's Distribution of Jagirs.* Babur's nobles and soldiers had rendered great assistance to him in his conquests. Therefore, in order to please them Babur gave them *Jagirs* liberally, In due course these nobles became very powerful and they posed a great threat to the stability of the Mughal empire.

7. *Paucity of funds.* After getting enormous wealth from the royal treasuries of Delhi and Ajmer, Babur distributed it so lavishly among his soldiers and nobles that very little was left for Humayun to conduct the affairs of his administration.

8. *Hostility of the Afghans.* The Afghans who were ruling Delhi a few years back still had ambition to capture power again. Bahadur Shah, the ruler of Gujarat, was also an Afghan. He was also ambitious of the throne of Delhi. But the most important and powerful Afghan, who later drove away Humayun, was Sher Shah.

9. *Belied Rajput's hopes.* Though the power of the Rajputs had been weakened by Babur, yet they cherished some hopes of recovering their lost power and territories.

Humayun's own responsibility for most of his Difficulties.

As a ruler he lacked foresight and was incapable of taking a long term view of political and military problems. He was not a good judge of men and circumstances. He lacked sustained effort and after a victory he would fritter away his energy in revelry. No doubt, he inherited a rich-legacy of difficulties but he made it richer by his own blunders. His lethargy was chronic. Though beset with dangers and better enemies all around, he did not develop the 'Killer's instinct'. He was daring as a soldier but not cautious as a general. He failed to pounce upon opportunities as well as upon his enemies in time.

In the words of Lane-poole, "Humayun's greatest enemy was he himself."

1. *Weak personality.* Humayun lacked resolution and sustained energy, foresight and quick grasp of situation. "He revelled at the table when he ought to have been in the saddle". He was slow to understand men, slow to grasp golden opportunities, slow to decide, slow to win a battle. As observed by Lane-poole, "He lacked character and resolution. He was incapable of sustained efforts after a moment of triumph and would busy himself in his *'harem'* and dream away the precious hour in the opium eaters' paradise while his enemies were thundering at his gate.

2. *Underestimating Sher Shah's strength.* He failed to estimate the growing power of Sher Shah Suri. He should not have accepted the half-hearted submission of Sher Shah at chunar. In fact he should have nipped him in the bud.

3. *Negative response to Rajputs' request.* He should have given a positive response to the request of the Rajputs and attacked Bahadur Shah of Gujarat at Chittor and should have completely crushed his power.

4. *Lack of military strategies.* Humayun did not attack his strong opponents at the appropriate time. Instead of rushing to Chittor to attack Bahadur Shah, he wasted time in festivities at Mandu. Likewise, instead of punishing the rebels in Bihar, he spent several months on his way in besieging minor places. All this gave time to his adversaries to make adequate preparations and to consolidate their positions.

5. *Defensive attitude.* After his defeat at Chausa, he always remained on the defensive. He did not attempt to recapture the territory.

6. *Wrong choice of site.* In the battle of Kanauj, he made blunders in choosing a low land for encampment and for remaining inactive before the enemy for two months.

7. *Leniency to his enemies.* He pardoned again and again those who revolted against him. This he did not only in the case of Kamran but also in the case of Mohammad Zaman Mirza.

8. *Sher Shah – more capable.* It must be admitted that he was no match for Sher Khan who was in every respect superior to him in preparing and planning battles and in fighting the enemy. Sher Shah had more

experience, more knowledge of strategies, more organizing capacity. He never missed an opportunity and could use wily tricks and crafty means to conquer the enemy while Humayun could not do anything, which did not belove a king as well as gentleman, and refined person.

Success at the end. It is not doing justice to Humayun when it is said that he was a failure. True he failed against Sher Shah but after his death, he seized every opportunity to come to power. But his spirit was not subdued. Even after 15 years of exile he could recapture his throne of Delhi and restore the power and prestige of the Mughals. "He went from riches to rags and again from rags to riches."

In his personal life, Humayun was an obedient son, lovable husband, affectionate father and a good relative. He was generous and attached in temperament, cultured and fond of learning. He was the lover of humanity and the model of a gentleman.

Humayun possessed a dominant will. Dr. S. Roy has rightly commented, "With all his weaknesses and failings, Humayun has a significant place in Indian history which is not, perhaps, always duly appreciated. The well-timed restoration of the Mughal power was a real achievement which paved the way, for the splendid imperialism of Akbar."

After ruling for ten years, he was forced to spend 15 years out of India. When he was able to recover Delhi, he could hardly enjoy the fruits of his victory, as within six months, he fell down from the stairs of his library in Delhi fort and died.

Q. 2. Analyse the conflicts of Humayun with Bahadur Shah of Gujarat and Sher Shah Suri. What were the results of these conflicts?

Or

Describe the struggle of Humayun with Bahadur Shah of Gujarat and Sher Shah Suri? What were the causes for the failure of Humayun. Why did Humayun lose in these conflicts?

Ans. *Humayun's conflict with Bahadur Shah of Gujarat.*

Causes of Conflict

1. Bahadur Shah was very ambitious and he has set his eyes upon Delhi. Humayun was equally ambitious to expand his territories.

2. Bahadur Shah had given political asylum to Mahdi Khwaja, a brother-in-law of Humayun, who had claimed the throne of Delhi. He had also sheltered some of the Lodi princes who were enemies of Humayun and wanted to regain their lost territories from the Mughals.

Events

Bahadur Shah of Gujarat had started expanding his territory. He captured Malwa, Chanderi, and Ranthambore and laid siege to the fort of Chittor. The Rajputs made an appeal to Humayun for help. Humayun proceeded to Chittor but subsequently he changed his mind and did not attack Bahadur Shah. In this context it is sometimes said that Humayun changed his mind as he felt it inappropriate to attack a Muslim ruler who was fighting against infidels. Whatever be the real reason, Humayun lost a golden opportunity.

According to another version Karanwati, the '*Rajmata*' of Mewar had sent a *'rakhi'* to Humayun and sought his assistance as her brother.

According to Dr. R.P. Tripathi, Humayun desired to consolidate his army, win over those people of Malwa who were against Bahadur Shah and arrange for the stoppage of help coming to Bahadur Shah either from Mandu or Ahmedabad – both places under the control of Bahadur Shah.

Humayun reached Mandasor, 60 miles from Chittor and checked the return route of Bahadur Shah from Chittor to Gujarat. Bahadur Shah also reached Mandasor but fled away and took shelter in the fort of Mandu : Humayun pursued him. From Mandu, Bahadur Shah ran from place to place : Champner, Cambay and finally to Goa. By that time, the entire Malwa and Gujarat had come under Humayun. Humayun appointed his brother Askari as the governor of Gujarat. Askari proved incompetent. Bahadur Shah took the full advantage and captured Gujarat. Malwa was occupied by Mallu Khan in the name of Bahadur Shah.

Result of Gujarat expedition. About the loss of Gujarat and Malwa, Lane-poole has commented, "Malwa and Gujarat two provinces equal in area to the rest of Humayun's kingdom had fallen like ripe fruits into his hands. Never was conquest so easy. Never too was conquest more recklessly squandered away." Thus Humayun lost them as quickly as he had gained those two territories.

The loss of these two territories lowered the prestige of Humayun.

Humayun's Encounter with Sher Shah and his expulsion from India

Causes of the conflict. Babur had captured the throne of Delhi from the Afghans. They therefore, were quite hostile to Humayun. Sher Shah Suri was also an Afghan. While Humayun was busy in fighting against Bahadur Shah of Gujarat, Sher Shah consolidated his position in Bihar. He was in the possession of the strong fort of Chunar. Most of the Afghan nobles had gathered under his banner. He attacked Bangal twice and took huge tribute from the ruler. Humayun realised that it was necessary to subdue Sher Shah.

Events of struggle

Humayun and Sher Shah had three encounters with each offer i.e. at Chunar, Chausa and Kannauj.

Siege of Chunar. (1532). The news of Sher Shah's success in Bengal and Bihar alarmed Humayun. He hurried from Gujarat but instead of proceeding straight to Bengal where he might have secured the help of Bengal's ruler, Humayun spent about six months in besieging the fort of Chunar is Bihar which was under Sher Shah. Sher Shah, realising his weak position, made a purely perfuntory submission and Humayun raised the sieze.

Battle of Chausa (1539). There were apparently no major conflicts between Sher Shah and Humayun for about six years. During this period Sher Shah greatly strengthened his position. He reorganised his army. On the request of the ruler of Bengal, Humayun went to Bengal and spent about eight months is 1538 and 1539. During these eight months Sher Shah captured a number of places like Banaras, Sambhal etc. In the meanwhile Humayun's brother Hindal declared himself as the emperor of Delhi. Humayun decided to return to Agra from Bengal. However, Sher Shah blocked his way at Chausa, the boundary between Bihar and Uttar Pradesh. The two armies remained there facing each other for three months. In the meanwhile rainy season started. This created problems and confusion for the Mughal army which was camping in the lowland. The Mughal camp was flooded. At this juncture Sher Shah hit upon a plan. He gave out that he was preceeding against a tribal leader who had been defying him. After marching a few miles in that direction, he returned suddenly in the night and fell upon Humayun's army from three sides in the early down of June 26, 1539. Humayun lost the battle and was wounded. To save his life, he plunged his horse into a stream and was saved from drowning by a water carrier whom as the story goes, Humayun allowed to sit on the throne for two days and who struck coins of leather.

Results. It was a great victory for Sher Shah and consequently he declared himself the Sultan.

Sher Shah, thereafter captured Bengal.

Again it was a great setback to Humayun.

The Battle of Kannauj (1540). After his defeat at Chausa, Humayun reached Agra and sought help from his brothers. However, all the brothers could not unite. Humayun recruited a big army which comprised mostly new recruits and proceeded towards. Kannauj when Sher Shah had already encamped himself. Sher Shah's victory was decisive. Humayun fled and reached Agra.

Results of the conflicts

1. After his defeat at Kannauj, Humayun had to spend about fifteen years in exile from 1540 to 1554.
2. Sher Shah became the ruler of Delhi.

Causes of the defeat of Humayun and Sher Shah's success.

1. Inability of Humayun to understand the nature of Afghan power.
2. Lack of organisational ability in Humayun.
3. Unhelpful attitude of Humayun's brothers.
4. Humayun's incapability for sustained efforts.
5. Sher Shah's diplomatic submission and lifling of Chunar's sieze by Humayun.

6. Sher Shah's qualities of a military leader.
7. Humayun's revelry and wasting valuable time.
8. Humayun's war camp at low land.
9. Struggle at several fronts by Humayun. Sher Shah's sudden attack at Humayun's army in Kannauj.
10. No unity of command in Humayun's army.

Q. 3. Describe briefly how Humayun regained the throne of Delhi.

Ans. *Humayun's exile and regaining the throne of Delhi.*

After his defeat in the Battle of Kannauj, Humayun remained in exile for about 15 years from 1540 to 1555. From Agra, he went to Lahore and then to Sind.

Akbar was born at Amarkot during his exile. Humayun, not finding himself safe in India proceeded towards Persia. His brother Kamran tried to capture him but failed to do so.

Humayun reached Persia and the ruler of Persia agreed to help Humayun with money and soldiers and for doing so he put forward three conditions before Humayun. These conditions were : (*i*) Humayun to accept Shia faith (*ii*) Humayun to propagate Shia faith and (*iii*) Humayun to restore Kandhar to Persia after its conquest. Humayun accepted these conditions. Humayun ruled Afghanistan for about 10 years. He defeated Kamran and blinded him. He also defeated his other brother Askari and allowed him to go to Mecca.

In India also, conditions became favourable for Humayun after the death of Sher Shah in 1545. The unity of Sur empire came to an end written ten years of Sher Shah Suri's death. Humayun decided to try his luck to recapture his lost territory. In June 1555, a battle was fought at Sirhind between Humayun and Sikander Shah Suri, the last Suri Sultan, Humayun won and occapied Delhi in July 1555. Subsequently, he occupied Agra, Sambhal and the nearby territories.

Humayun, however, was not lucky to rule India for long. In January 1556, when he was descending from the stairs of the library at 'Din Panah in the old fort at Delhi, he slipped and died after two days.

Humayun was buried in Delhi in a beautiful tomb built by his wife Hamida Banu Begum.

16

Sher Shah Suri (1540-1545) (Second Afghan Empire)

Q. 1. Elucidate the early career and military achievements of Sher Shah Suri.

Or

Give a brief sketch of the early career of Sher Shah. Explain his military exploits. What was the impact of his military exploits?

Or

State the main events leading to Sher Shah's accession to the throne of Delhi.

Write an essay on the rise of Sher Shah.

(Rajasthan University 1996)

Or

Briefly describe the expansion of Afghan power under Sher Shah Suri. (Punjab University April 1995)

Ans. *From Humble Beginnings to the Position of Ruler of Delhi.*

Sher Shah Suri, whose original name was Farid was the founder of the Suri dynasty. Son of a petty jagirdar, neglected by his father and ill treated by his step-mother, he very successfully challenged the authority of Mughal emperor Humayun, drove him out of India and occupied the throne of Delhi. All this clearly demonstrates his extra-ordinary qualities of his hand, head and heart. Once again Sher Shah established the Afghan Empire which had been taken over by Babur.

Sher Shah's early career. The intrigues of his mother compelled the young Farid Khan to leave Sasaram (Bihar), the jagir of his father. He went to Jaunpur for studies.

In his studies, he so distinguished himself that the subedar of Jaunpur was greatly impressed. He helped him to become the administrator of his father's jagir which prospered by his efforts. His step-mother's jealousy forced him to search for another employment and he took service under Bahar Khan, the ruler of South Bihar, who gave him the title of Sher Khan for his bravery in killing a tiger single-handed. But the intrigues of his enemies compelled his to leave Bihar and join the camp of Babur in 1527. He rendered valuable help to Babur in the campaign against the Afghans in Bihar. In due course, Babur became suspicious of Sher Khan who soon slipped away. As his former master Bahar Khan, the ruler of South Bihar had died, he was made the guardian and regent of the minor son of the deceased. Slowly he started grabbing all the powers of the kingdom.

Meanwhile the ruler of Chunar died and Sher Shah married his widow. This brought him the fort of Chunar and enormous wealth.

Military achievements of Sher Shah

Military achievements of Sher Shah may be categorised under three heads namely (*i*) Encounters with Humayun (*ii*) Other encounters (*iii*) Conquests after becoming emperor of Delhi.

1. Sher Shah's encounters with Humayun.

Following were the three encounters :

(*i*) Encounter on the fort of Chunar and Sher Shah's diplomatic surrender.

(*ii*) Battle of Chausa with Humayun and Sher Shah's victory.

(*iii*) Batttle of Kannauj and Sher Shah's decisive victory over Humayun. With the victory at Kannauj, Sher Shah became the ruler of Delhi. Agra, Sambhal and Gwalior etc., also came under his sway. This victory ended the rule of the Mughal dynasty for 15 years. (For details see previous chapter)

2. Sher Shah's other conquests

(1) *Battle at Surajgarh* (1533). Sher Shah defeated the combined forces of the Lohani chiefs of Bihar and Mohamud Shah of Bengal at Surajgarh. With this victory, whole of Bihar came under Sher Shah. Dr. Qanungo has described the importance of this victory in these words, "If Sher Shah had not been victorious at Surajgarh, he would have never figured in the political sphere of India and would not have got an opportunity to compete with Humayun... for the founding of an empire."

(2) *Invasion of Bengal.* Sher Shah plundered Bengal several times and by capturing Gaur, the capital of Bengal, forced Mohammad Shah to seek refugee with Humayun.

3. Sher Shah's conquests after becoming the emperor of Delhi.

(*i*) *Conquest of Punjab* (1540-42). Sher Shah immediately, after his accession to the throne conquered Punjab from Kamran, brother of Humayun.

(*ii*) *Suppression of Khokhars* (1542). Sher Shah suppressed the turbulent Khokhars of the northern region of river Indus and Jhelum.

(*iii*) *Conquest of Malwa* (1542). The ruler of Malwa had not helped Sher Shah in his struggle with Humayun. Therefore he attacked Malwa and annexed it to his empire.

(*iv*) *Conquest of Raisin.* Sher Shah attacked Raisin - a Rajput principality and besiegect it. Rajput ruler Purnamal entered into an agreement with Sher Shah that if he surrendered, his family would not be harmed. However Sher Shah did not honour this agreement. In the words of Dr. Ishwari Prasad, "Sher Shah behaved with him very cruely."

(*v*) and (*vi*) *conquest of Multan and Sind* (1543). Sher Shah conquered and annexed these provinces into his empire.

(*viii*) *Conquest of Marwar* (1543-1545). Sher Shah brought Marwar under his control by forged letters and sowing dissensions in the army of Maldev, the ruler of Mewar.

(*ix*) *Conquest of Kalinjar* (1545). and death of Sher Shah. Sher Shah launched a fierce attack. He won but lost his life when he was grievously injured by the blast.

Impact of Sher Shah's Conquests

Sher Shah was able to bring under his control a substantial part of India. The frontiers of his empire extended on the one hand from Punjab to Malwa and on the other from Bengal to Sind. He dislodged the Mughal emperor Humayun and founded the Sur dynasty. With large areas under his control, he was able to provide a sort of uniformity to the administrative system of India.

Factors Responsible for Sher Shah's Military Achievements

1. **Service in Babur's army.** Sher Shah had worked for sometime in the army of Babur. This enabled him to familiarise with the strength and weaknesses of the Mughal army.

2. **Military organisation.** Sher Shah took the following measures to strengthen his army.

(*a*) *Strength.* Sher Shah maintained a strong standing army at the centre like Ala-ud-Din Khalji. His army included 1,50,000 cavalry, 25,000 infantry, 3000 war elephants and a part of artillery.

(*b*) *Recruitment.* He did not depend on the Jagirdars for the supply of soldiers whenever needed by the Sultan. He maintained a direct link and made them direct loyal to him and not through jagirdars.

(*c*) *Descriptive identification.* With a view to checking fraudulent practices in army in inflating the figures of soldiers and horses, Sher Shah adopted the practices of maintaining the description (*huliya*) of the soldiers and that of branding (*dag*) of the horses.

(*d*) *Payment in cash.* The soldiers were paid in cash whereas most of the officers were given the *jagirs*.

(*e*) *Mostly Afghans in the army.* He recruited mostly Afghan soldiers from every part of the country and also from Afghanistan and gave them important posts in the army.

(*f*) *Supplementary armies.* Besides the standing army under the direct command of the Sultan, provincial governors, nobles and subordinate rulers were also allowed to maintain their separate armies.

(*g*) *Discipline in the army.* In the words of Qanungo, "The severe discipline in Sher Shah's camp in one campaign was sufficient to turn a raw recruit into a seasoned veteran".

3. **Military strategies.** Sher Shah was a pastmaster in adopting successful war tactics. He believed in the maxim "Everything is fair in love and war".

He knew fully well as where to make a tactical retreat, when to strike at the enemy, how to sow dissensions in the army camp, how to make friendship with the enemy of the enemy, how to pretend to retreat. In fact he knew how to win.

Following are some of the main instances of Sher Shah's military strategy.

(*i*) Sher Shah's diplomatic surrender to Humayun at Chunar fort.

(*ii*) Sher Shah's false pretence of withdrawing but sudden attack at Humayun in the battle of Kannauj.

(*iii*) Sowing dissentions in Maldev's army by forged letters.

(*iv*) Arriving at some sort of understanding with the ruler of Gujarat and keeping Humayun engaged in conflict with him.

(*v*) Raising the cry of 'jihad' to infuse enthusiasm among his soldiers.

(*vi*) Going back from his promise with Rajput ruler Purnamal Chauhan and sudden attack by Sher Shah on him.

4. Making the best use of Humayun's weaknesses. (See the previous Chapter)

Q. 2. Briefly describe the achievements of Maldev of Mewar.

Or

Briefly discuss the relations of Sher Shah with Maldev of Mewar.

Ans. *Causes of the struggle between Sher Shah and Maldev.*

1. *Both the rulers as expansionists.* Sher Shah was an expansionist through and through. Similarly Maldev, a powerful ruler of Mewar and a contemporary of Sher Shah was an expansionist. In particular both of them wanted to occupy eastern Rajasthan because of its being a strategic military position.

2. *Maldev's dream of a United Rajasthan.* Maldev wanted to have a united Rajasthan under his control. A united Rajasthan could pose a challenge to Sher Shah.

3. *Maldev's invitation to Humayun.* It is said that Maldev had invited Humayun to his place when he was running for safety. Sher Shah had asked Maldev to imprison Humayun and hand him over to Sher Shah. However, Maldev did not do so.

4. *Maldev's policy to subdue Rajput rulers.* On account of the policy of Maldev to subdue Rajput rulers, several of them turned against him and sought Sher Shah's help. This tempted Sher Shah to attack Maldev.

Invasions and events. Sher Shah was fully aware of the strength of Maldev and therefore, he collected a vast army. The deposed Rajput ruler of Medate and a disgruntled Rajput Minister of Bikaner rendered all possible help to strengthen Sher Shah's army. About the vast army Abbas has written, "He (Sher Shah) had such a vast army that it counted not be counted at all". However, this statement seemed to be an exaggerated one. At the same time it must be admitted that Sher Shah had collected a large number. Still he was not sure of his victory against Maldev. He, therefore, resorted to a fraudulent course. He managed to sow dissensions between Maldev and some of his prominent chiefs. He prepared some forged letters and dropped them near Maldev's camp which led Maldev to suspect that a few of his chiefs had deserted to Sher Shah's side. Maldev was deeply grieved and decided to retreat. When some of the chiefs came to know about Maldev's decision not to fight and that he considered them disloyal, they separated themselves from Maldev's army. Still some of the chiefs with their armies fought very bravely. Several thousands of Afghans were killed in the battle-field. Sher Shah was able to save his own life with great difficulty. Nevertheless he won and remarked, "I had nearly lost the empire of India for a handful of 'bajra'. (produce of Mewar)

Results of the conflict. This victory proved very helpful to Sher Shah. At the same time Afghan's control over Marwar was very short-lived. Within two months of the death of Sher Shah, Maldev came back from Siwana and drove away the Afghan governor and established his control over the territory.

Q. 3. Critically review the administration of Sher Shah.

Or

"Sher Shah was the greatest ruler and administrator amongst the rulers of Medieval India". Discuss.

Or

Give an account of the administration and reforms of Sher Shah Suri. (Punjab University 1995, Oct. 1997 and Oct. 1998)

Or

Discuss the Civil, Military, Revenue and other reforms of Sher Shah.

Or

Critically examine the administrative reforms of 1996 and Sher Shah. (Rajasthan University, 1997)

Ans. *Salient Features of Sher Shah's General Administration.*

Sher Shah, by the dint of his military skill, daring acts, great courage and resourcefulness not only established a mighty empire but also by his shrewd capacity for organizing, unique foreathought and intimate knowledge of administration, made necessary arrangements for smooth and efficient administration and controlling the coveted empire.

Some of the salient features of his administration are given below.

A benevolent despot. Dr. Ishwar Prasad has rightly observed, "The Government of Sher Shah, though autocratic was enlightened and vigorous." Sher Shah himself used to say, "It behoves the great to be always active." And he himself adhered to this maxim.

According to Crooke, "He was the first Musalman ruler who studied the good of the people."

Sher Shah believed, "Tyranny is unlawful in everyone, especially in a sovereign who is the guardian of his public."

Advice of the council of Ministers. Sher Shah had a number of ministers to assist him in his administritive work. The ministers looked after their respective departments. Their appointment and dismissal was at his discretion.

Provincial administration. Historians have differed on the issue of Sher Shah's provincial administration. While Qanungo has opined that there was no administrative unit called '*Suba*' or '*Iqta*',Dr. P. Saran states that there were '*Subas*' where military officers were appointed by Sher Shah.

The entire kingdom was divided into provinces. Some provinces were very large and others small. There was no uniformity with regard to their income, size and administration. In the sensitive provinces like Lahore, Multan and Malwa, military governors looked after the administration. On the other hand, the province of Bengal was administered by a civilian.

(*a*) *Sarkars.* A province was divided into a number of *Sarkars* (Districts). In all there were 47 districts. There were two chief officers in every district. The one chief *Shiqdar* or *Shiqdar-i-Shiqdaran* was a military officer. He maintained peace and order in the district, helped in the collection of revenue and other taxes and also supervised the work of his subordinate officers called Shiqdars. The other officer was called the chief *Munsif* or *Munsif-i-Muinsfan.* He was primarily a judicial officer who looked after justice in the district. He also looked after the working of his subordinate judicial officers in the *parganas*. These two officers were helped by a number of junior officers and other subordinates in carrying out their duties.

(*b*) *Parganas.* Each *Sarkar* was divided into small units called the *parganas* and each Pargana was further subdivided into a number of villages. Like the Sarkars, there were two chief officers called a *Shiqdar* (military officer) and *Munsif* (civilian judge) who were assisted by other staff in the discharge of their duties.

(c) *Villages.* A village was the smallest self-sufficient unit, administered by village panchayats.

Sher Shah introduced the system of transferring officers of the Sarkars and the Paragans every two or three years so that they may not develop vested interest, the root cause of corruption.

Sources of income. Important sources of income were : (*i*) Land revenue (*ii*) Taxes on the transportation of raw and finished products (*iii*) The royal mint (*iv*) Confiscation of the unclaimed property (*v*) Tributes from the rajas, nawabs jagirdars, etc. (*vi*) Gifts from the foreign travellers (*vii*) Salt tax (*viii*) Jaziya on the Hindus (*ix*) One-fifth of the *Kham* (booty).

Land and revenue administration. The revenue administration of Sher Shah has been regarded as one of the best during the medieval period. Important features of the revenue administration were as under.

1. Land for the purpose of revenue was divided into three categories on the basis of production—good, average and bad.

2. Generally land revenue was one-third of the produce, but could be paid both in cash and kind.

3. The land of each cultivator was measured according to a uniform standard and its quality was ascertained.

4. Lease deeds (*pathas*) were drawn between the farmers and the government. The area, the type of the soil, and the rates of land revenue were recorded on the lease deeds which were got signed by the farmers. The deeds confirmed the rights of the farmers on the lands.

5. Land revenue was remitted on poor crops.

6. Financial assistance (*Taqavi* loans) was granted to the farmers when needed by them.

7. The Sultan had ordered that while fixing the land revenue, the peasants should be treated with generosity but once settled they were asked to pay their revenue regularly.

In the words of Qanungo, "The land revenue administration of Sher Shah was a valuable heritage for the Mughals. He tried to levy the land revenue in accordance with the income of the peasants. The British adopted this system."

Welfare of farmers. Sher Shah was very particular about the welfare of the peasants. He used to say, "If I oppress them they will abandon their villages and the country will be ruined and deserted."

Law and order. The most important contribution of Sher Shah was the reestablishment of law and order across the length and breadth of the empire. Dacoits and robbers were dealt with very sternly. It has been stated by several historians that during the reign of Sher Shah, an old woman might place a basket of golden ornaments on her head and go on a journey without any fear. No thief or robber would come near her for fear of punishment."

Local responsibility for theft. The local people or the head (*Mukhiya*) of the village was responsible for the safety of the people of the area and the travellers. It was the responsibility of the village Panchayat or the local people to produce the culprit or to pay for the stolen goods. In case the local officers of the village failed to trace the murderer, the headman was given the penalty of death. This method helped to wipe off thefts, robberies and murders.

Fair judicial administration. Sher Shah used to say and act upon it, "Justice is the most excellent of religious rites." No one could escape punishment on account of high status.

The Sultan was the highest judicial authority in the state. Sher Shah held his court every Wednesday in the evening. Next to him was the chief *Qazi* who was the head of the department of justice. There were subordinate *Qazis* in every district and in all important cities. The criminal law was severe. The offenders were punished by fines, flogging, imprisonment and even cutting of the limbs.

Efficient Espionage System. Sher Shah's efficient administrative system largely depended upon his well-organised espionage system. The king kept himself posted with the minutest happening in his kingdom. The nobles were afraid of indulging in activities not conducive to the stability of the rule of the Sultan. Even the rates prevailing in the *mandis* were made available to the king. Spies were kept at all important places and at all importantt offices.

Well organised 'dak' system. The saraits were also used as *Dak Chaukis*. Two horses were kept at every sarai so that the news-carriers could get fresh horses at short intervals to maintain speed.

Currency. The ratio of exchange between the *Dam* and rupee was fixed at 64 to 1. The same coin-rupee ratio served the basis of the currency during the Mughal and British periods. Earlier there was no fixed ratio among so many coins of various metal alloys. He abolished the old and mixed metal currency. He issued fine coins of gold, silver and copper of uniform standard.

Network of roads. Sher Shah constructed a network of roads connecting important parts of his empire within his capital. He repaired old roads. Sher Shah constructed the following four highways :

(*i*) *Sadak-e-Azam* (Grand Trunk Road) starting from Sonargaon in Eastern Bengal passing through Agra, Delhi and Lahore and terminating at Peshawar, covering a distance of about 3,000 km; (*ii*) From Agra to Jodhpur and the Chittor fort; (*iii*) From Agra to Burhanpur; (*v*) From Lahore to Multan.

Prosperous Trade and Commerce. Law and order in the kingdom, protection of traders on roads, issue of new currency and the simplication of taxes helped in the promotion of trade and commerce. Trade tax was collected only at two places. One, where the goods entered the territory of his empire and the other where the goods were sold. All other internal trade taxes were abolished.

Sarais. About 1700 *sarais* were constructed on both sides of the roads. Each *sarai* had separate rooms for the Hindus and the Muslims. Each sarai had a well and a mosque. These *sarais* also served as *dak Chaukis.* In view of the special significance of these sarais, they were called as veritable arteries of the empire."

Beautiful buildings. Sher Shah built the following buildings : (*i*) Mausoleum of Sher Shah at Sasaram in Bihar (*ii*) Fort of Rohtasgarh on the banks of the river Jhelum in the north-west. (*iii*) Purana Qila at New Delhi. (*iv*) Mosque in the Purana Qila. The Mausoleum of Sher Shah built in the midst of a lake on a lofty plinth, ranks among the most beautiful buildings in India.

Promotion of education. For the education of the Muslims, a *Maktab* was attached to every mosque for imparting elementary education and teaching Arabic and Persian. *Madrasas* were set up for higher education. Endowments and grants were given to educational institutions. Provision was also made for scholarships on the basis of merit.

Summing up

Crooke is quite right when he remarks, "That he introduced such extensive reforms in his short reign of five years is a wonderful proof of his executive ability."

Q. 4. Form an estimate of the achievements of Sher Shah.

Ans. *Estimate of the Achievements of Sher Shah.*

A safe kingdom to live. A correct estimate of the achievements of a ruler can be had on the basis of the extent of law and order maintained by him in his state. In this context the following observations made by historians about Sher Shah's reign deserve careful consideration.

According to Abbas Sarwari, "Travellers and way farers during the time of Sher Shah Suri's reign, were relieved from the trouble of keeping watch, nor did they fear to be robbed in the midst of a desert. They encamped at night at every place, desert or inhabited, without any fear." He further wrote, "An old woman might place a basket full of golden ornaments on her head and go on a journey and no thief or robber would come near her for fear of punishment which Sher Shah inflicted."

Similarly Nizam-ud-Din wrote, "A merchant could travel and sleep in the desert without any fear of being robbed of merchandise."

As a ruler. In the words of Crooke, "He, Sher Shah was the first who attempted to found an Indian empire broadly based upon the people's will."

As a conquenor. Sher Shah conquered a major part of India. He conquered Bengal, Bihar, Delhi, Punjab, Multan, Sind, a large part of Rajasthan including Chittor, Ajmer and Malwa etc.

As a military commander. He was well-versed with military strategies. He was very adept in striking at the enemy at the apporpriate time. He won victories against Humayun and the Rajput rulers with his military skill. He attacked the weak enemy like a tiger and defeated several rulers in this manner. Against a powerful ruler, he received victory by deceitful tactics of a fox. He defeated Maldev of Mewar. He adopted several military tactics to defeat Humayun. Victory by fair and foul means was his aim and he achieved this.

A brave soldier. As a soldier he had unbound bravery and patience. He knew the use of many kinds of weapons.

An enlightened administrator. In the words of Dr. Ishwari Prasad, "The government of Sher Shah though autocratic was enlightened and vigorous." Erskine wrote "Sher Shah had more of the spirit of a legislator and guardian of his people than any prince before Akbar."

His efficient spy system enabled him to carry out his reforms very successfully. He could know very easily what was needed to be done for the welfare of his subjects and accordingly he took remedial measures. His administration was welfare oriented.

Dr. Ishwari Prasad has further said, "The institution which he devised for the better governance of the country and the unremitting industry with which he looked after the business of the state had won him the admiration and esteem of friends and foes alike."

In the words of Havell, "By dint of indefatigable industry and personal attention to the smallest details of administration, he restored law and order throughout Hindustan in the short span of five years."

According to Sir Woolseley Haig, "No other ruler from Aibak to Aurangzeb, possessed such intimate knowledge of the details of administration or was able to examine and control public business so minutely and effectively as he."

As a financial expert. He did a very useful work in the matter of land reforms and promotion of trade and commerce. He was successful in increasing revenue of the state without putting any undue burden on his subjects.

As a religious man and ruler. He was a devout Sunni Muslim. His treatment with the Hindus, on the whole, can be said to be not of intoleration.

As a lover of art and literature. Sher Shah partronised learning. He took a keen intercst in the construction of buildings, roads, and bridges etc.

As a creator of law and order. Sher Shah created such a law and order that even women with heavy and precious ornaments could move about fearlessly in his kingdom.

As a just ruler. Sher Shah provided equal justice to the high or the low. In the matter of justice, he did not differentiate between his relatives and ordinary people.

As a builder of public works. Dr. Qanungo observes, "The Sarais (1700 in number) became the veritable arteries of the empire, diffusing a new life among its hitherto bebumbed limbs."

As a currency reformer. Dr. V.A. Smith has praised Sher Shah in this respect as, "Sher Shah is entitled to the honour of establishing the reformed system of currency which lasted throughout the Mughal period, was maintaimed by the East India Company upto 1825."

Dark side. Sher Shah was very calculating. He was prepared to use any foul method or craftiness to achieve his aim, as he used forged letters to capture Marwar in 1544 and broke his oath and conducted in a perfidious manner against Puran Mal.

Summing up

Although like Babur Sher Shah sat on the throne of Delhi only for five years, yet unlike Babur he left behind him the mark of a good administrator and of a benevolent ruler who was always eager to undertake numerous welfare programmes.

He was a successful warrior, enlightened administrator, expert in revenue matters, patron of art and literature and great builder.

Q. 5. Why is Sher Shah called the Fore runner of Akbar? Discuss.
(Rajasthan University 1995 and 1997)

Ans. *Sher Shah as the Fore-runner of Akbar.*

Akbar has been called "The Great" on account of his efficient administration, liberal religious policy and political insight. A close study of Akbar's policy would reveal that Akbar followed several policies of Sher Shah. Of course, he improved upon them in the new context. Akbar followed the land policy of Sher Shah. He provided equal justice to all. He engaged himself like Sher Shah for the welfare of his subjects. There is no doubt that Sher Shah was the fore-runner of Akbar.

In the words of Dr. R P Tripathi, "He paved the way for the highly enlightened policy of Akbar."

Professor Kaliranjan Qanung has observed : "His reign was short, (only five years) but importance was almost as great as Akbar's rule of half a century."

Akbar, in general, followed Sher Shah in the following fields:

1. Ideal of kingship
2. Policy of extension of empire.
3. Division of empire into viable units.
4. Advice of the council of ministers.
5. Military reforms.
6. Land revenue reforms.
7. Judicial reforms.

8. Almost similar liberal policy although Sher Shah did not dispense with *jizya.*

9. Promotion of education.

10. Promotion of art and architecture.

11. Public welfare activities.

12. Currency reforms.

'Akbar the great' but **'Sher Shah not the great'**, the observations made by Crooke deserve careful consideration, "In every aspect of administration, it is alleged, the Mughal king (Akbar) borrowed from the Afghan ruler (Sher Shah). Of course it will be unjust to say that Akbar lacked originality and that he was indebted entirely to Sher Shah for his greatness. Nevertheless it cannot be denied that the great Mughal emperor did follow Sher Shah in various fields of administration.

Sher Shah did not abolish *'Zazia'*. Sher Shah's court was not adorned by *'Navratnas'*. Akbar ruled over a far larger empire than Sher Shah. Akbar tried to reconcile the teachings of different religions. He founded a new religion which, of course, vanished during his life time. Akbar took several measures for the emotional integration of India.

Dr. Qanungo in this regard has observed, "Sher Shah had ruled for five years and five days. In the history of medieval India he had proved to be a ruler second only to Akbar in greatness." Further he has observed,"It is doubtful whether he would have done such deeds as Akbar if he had lived for fifty years more because Sher Shah had the drawbacks from which Aurangzeb suffered.

(For a thorough grasp of the topic, students are advised to go through chapter 17 entitled Akbar)

17

Akbar (1556-1605)

(Consolidation and Territorial Expansion, Growth of Composite Ruling Class)

There are only two rulers in the history of India whose names are suffixed with the two words 'the great'. These are Ashoka and Akbar. This is on account of their great contribution towards developing harmonious relations among the followers of different religions, bringing about political unity and stability, creating law order, winning the goodwill of the people, ushering in an era of peace and prosperity and patronising art and literature.

Q. 1. Briefly describe Akbar's early life and the difficulties faced by him. Also give a brief account of the territorial expansion of the Mughal empire during Akbar's reign.

Ans. *Early life of Akbar.*

Akbar whose full name was Jalal-ud-Din Mohammad Akbar was born at Amarkot in Sind when Humayun was running for shelter from place to place. He was crowned in a small town in Punjab at the age of about thirteen in 1542. As a matter of fact there was no throne or kingdom whose emperor he was declared. By dint of extra-ordinary courage, hard work and diplomacy and patience he overcame all the challenges he had to face in his early life.

Fortunately for Akbar, during his early life, he had an able tutor and guide in Bairam Khan.

Political and economic conditions when Akbar ascended the throne.

Akbar's kingdom in name only. Dr. V.S.Smith has very rightly pointed out that Akbar had only a few districts of the Pubjab under his control. At the time of the death of his father Humayun in Delhi, Akbar was in Punjab. Delhi was under the control of a Mughal governor Tardi Beg.

Rajput chiefs' growing power. The Rajputs were enjoying independent status in the states of Mewar, Jodhpur, Ranthambore, Kalanjar, Jaisalmer etc.

Power of Afghan chiefs. Malwa and Gujarat were still in the hands of Afghan chiefs.

Independent states in the West. Multan and Sind were ruled by independent kings.

Punjab. Sikander Sur, governor of Punjab wanted to gain independence.

Bihar and Bengal. Adil Shah was in control of the territory from Bihar to Chunar.

Doab and Sambhal. Ibrahim Sur, a claimant of the throne of Delhi was occupying the Doab and Sambhal.

Kabul. Kabul had declared independence.

South India. The states of Ahmednagar, Bijapur, Gol Kunda, Bidar, Berar and Khandesh were absolutely independent. However they were in continuous wars with the Hindu empire of Vijayanagara.

Growing power of Hemu. Hemu, the Prime Minister of Adil Shah of Bihar was increasing his influence. After the death of Humayun, Hemu captured Agra and Delhi. He very easily defeated the Mughal governor of Delhi and assumed the title of 'Vikramaditya' and declared himself as an independent ruler of Delhi.

Miserable financial condition. The Mughal treasury was empty. A terrible famine was raging in Delhi and Agra.

Difficulties faced by Akbar. From above it is clear that Akbar had to face very difficult and formidable challenges-both political and financial. He was a ruler in name only. Several governors had declared independence. Afghans were still struggling to regain their power and prestige. Rajput rulers had consolidated their positions. Akbar was still a minor. Financial position of the Mughals was very weak. Akbar was in Punjab when his father Humayun died at Agra.

Territorial expansion of Akbar. Akbar had inherited a very small territory when he ascended the throne. He was surrounded by enemies from all sides. But he was helped and guided by Bairam Khan for about four years i.e. 1556 to 1560 - the most difficult years for Akbar. Thereafter Akbar himself organised the state of affairs and carried out his policy of conquests and brought almost the entire country under his control.

Following were his major conquests:

1. Conquest of Delhi and Agra (1556). Battle of Panipat and defeat of Hemu.
2. Conquest of Gwalior (1558)
3. Conquest of Ajmer (1560)
4. Conquest of Jaunpur (1960)
5. Conquest of Malwa (1560)
6. Conquest of Chunar (1561)
7. Conquest of Gondwara (1564). Brave defence by Rani Durgawati. Jauhar ceremony by the Rani.
8. Conquest of Ranthambhor (1569)
9. Conquest of Kalinjar (1569)
10. Submission of Jodhpur (1570)
11. Submission of Bikaner (1572)
12. Conquest of Gujarat (1572)
13. Conquest of Bihar (1575)
14. Conquest of Bengal (1575)

15. Conquest of Mewar and the battle of Haldighatti (1576) and entire struggle (1568 to 1597)

16. Conquest of Kabul (1585)

17. Conquest of Kashmir (1588)

18. Conquest of Sind (1590)

19. Conquest of Qandhar (1595)

20. Conquest of Deccan (1595-1605)

Chand Bibi of Ahmednagar fought against the Mughals very bravely. But after her death at the hands of her own army, the mughals established their rule over Ahmednagar.

Akbar invaded Khandesh and captured its capital.

Extent of Akbar's Empire. Akbar's empire was very vast and it extended from Bengal in the east to Afghanistan in the west and from Kashmir in the north to river Godavari in the south. Akbar had divided his vast Empire into 15 provinces. Abul Fazal in his Ain-i-Akbari has given the following names of Akbar's provinces. : (1) Allahabad (2) Agra (3) Oudh (4) Ajmer (5) Ahmedabad (Gujarat) (6) Bihar (7) Bengal (8) Delhi (9) Kabul (10) Lahore (11) Multan (12) Malwa and three provinces in the South i.e. (13) Berar (14) Khandesh and (15) Ahmednagar.

Q. 2. Critically examine the Rajput policy of Akbar and state its significance.

Or

"Akbar was the first Muslim ruler who conceived clearly that there could be no permament Muslim empire without the Rajputs." Elucidate.

Or

Write about the Rajput policy of Akbar and its effects.

(Punjab University April 1996, April 1998 and Oct. 1998 Rajasthan 1995 and 1997)

Ans. *Akbar's Pragmatic Rajput Policy.*

Akbar was a great pragmatist. He was the first Muslim ruler to realise that without the help of the Rajputs, no permanent empire could be set up in India. Accordingly, he took measures to secure their cooperation. He treated them as very trustworthy friends and not mere vassals. He abandoned the old policy of repression and persecution of the Rajputs. Broadly speaking Akbar's policy was based on diplomacy and force - the two potent weapons of state craft. But he realised more on diplomacy.

Reasons for following the policy of diplomacy and force towards the Rajputs. Following were the important reasons for following the policy of reconciliation.

1. *Rajput as trustworthy race.* Akbar fully realised that the Rajputs were most trust worthy as deceit was foreign to them. They would never

betray their friend. So he could depend upon them once they were convinced that the was a friend to them.

2. *Hindus in majority.* Like a shrewd sstatesman, he was convinced that the Hindus formed the majority of the population and that the Rajputs were the great champions of Hinduism. Therefore, he needed their help for establishing a strong empire.

3. *Uzbeks not reliable.* Akbar could not depend upon the Uzbeks and the Afghans. He needed some trustworthy ally.

4. *No reliance upon his relatives.* He also fully realized that his own relatives could not always be trusted as they were too ambitious for power and jealous of him. Thus to counterbalance them, he needed the support of the Rajputs.

5. *Large hearted men of Akbar.* He was large-hearted and tolerant towards those who extended their hand of friendship.

6. *Need for best soldiers.* Rajputs were a martial race, brave and trustworthy. So he could get the best soldiers from the Rajput community. Such was his need to carry out his policy of expansion of his empire.

7. *Unstable political conditions in Rajasthan.* Akbar was an imperalist and an expansionist. He was aware of the disunity of the Rajput rulers. He therefore, utilised this disunity to exercise his control. Aggression as well as diplomacy proved very helpful.

8. *Extension of empire with minimum warfare.* It is true that Akbar wanted to expand his kingdom. But at the same time he desired not to restore to unnecessary warfare.

9. *Identification of the Mughal rule with India.* Akbar was a national ruler. He did not want to create an impression that the Mughal rule was foreign. He accordingly extended the hands of friendship towards the Rajputs.

10. *Geographical location.* Many Rajput states were very near to Delhi and there was the danger of attack by Rajput rulers. Therefore, Akbar adopted a friendly attitude towards the Rajputs.

Chief features of Akbar's Rajput policy

1. *Matrimonial alliances.* In 1562, Akbar married the daughter of Raja Bihari Mal of Amber (modern Jaipur). Akbar's son Salim who came to be known as Jahangir was born from this queen. He also married two other princesses, one of Jodhpur and other of Jaisalmer. He married his son Jahangir to the daughter of Raja Bhagwan Dass, son of Raja Bihari Mal. Khusrau, another son of Jahangir, was born to this princess.

The marriage of Akbar in the family of Jaipur is considered as of great significance. In the words of Dr. Beni Prasad." It symbolised the dawn of a new era in Indian politics, it gave the country a line of remarkable sovereigns, it secured to the four generations of Mughal emperors the services of some of the greatest captains and diplomats that medieval India produced."

2. *Appointment to high posts.* Raja Todar Mal and Raja Birbal occupied important positions. Raja Bihari Mal, his son Bhagwan Dass and grandson Man Singh were among his close confidants.

3. *Equal treatment.* Akbar accorded equal status to the Rajputs.

4. *Religious independence.* Akbar granted full religious independence to the Rajputs in respect of their religion. They could build temples, worship in them and celebrate their festivals.

5. *Religious freedom to Rajput queens.* Rajput queens were free in the observance of their faith.

6. *Full respect and honours to the defeated Rajput rulers.* All those Rajputs who submitted to Akbar after fighting against him, were given full respect and honour.

7. *Employment of Rajputs in the army.* It is said that Rajputs were holding more than 20 per cent posts in the army.

8. *Internal freedom to Rajput kingdoms.* Akbar did not interfere in the internal administration of Rajput kingdoms.

9. *Personal relations.* Akbar established personal relations with many Rajput rulers. It is said when the son-in-low of Rai singh of Bikaner died due to a fall from the palanquin, Akbar himself went there to console the family and share their grief.

10. *Reforms in Rajput Society.* Akbar attempted to remove some of the evils like the 'Sati' and child marriage from the Rajput Society. He also gave royal sanction to widow remarriage.

11. *Abolition of Jizya.* Akbar removed ***'Jizya'***, a tax which was levied by the Muslim rulers upon the Non-Muslims.

12. *Respect for cow.* He forebade the cow slaughter.

13. *Aggressive policy towards offending Rajput rulers.* Akbar, being an imperialist, never tolerated opposition. He launched military campaigns against all those Rajput rulers who did not surrender. He conquered Ranthambhor and Kalinjar - two important Rajput states. However, Akbar's campaign against Mewar was not quite successful.

Significance of the Rajput Policy of Akbar

1. *Expansion of Akbar's influence.* The policy of friendship contributed to the extension of the Mughal empire. The Rajputs had become the 'Sword and Shield' of Akbar.

2. *Military help.* The Rajput rulers provided strong military help to Akbar in waging wars and conquering several territories.

3. *Strengthening of administration.* Akbar was able to secure the services of Rajputs in the efficient running of the administration. Some of the Rajput Governors of Mughal provinces proved very helpful.

4. *Advantages to Rajputs.* The Rajput rulers got honour, high offices, big jagirs and confidential posts in the royal service. They were also free to devote their resources on welfare pursuits in place of war adventures.

5. *Cultural integration.* According to Dr. Ishwari Prasad, "A new culture - Indo-Muslim culture" was born. Akbar gave encouragement to Sanskrit, Hindi and other regional languages.

There is no doubt that the Rajputs made great contribution in the field of Akbar's expansion of empire, statecraft, administration, cultural, economic and social progress.

Q. 3. "Akbar's statemanship is no where better illustrated than in his treatment of the Hindus". Discuss.

Or

Discuss the various factors that were responsible for Akbar's policy towards the Hindus. State its impact.

Or

Discuss the factors that influenced Akbar's religious policy towards the Hindus. Give instances to show this influence.

Or

Give an account of the development of Akbar's religious views.

(Punjab University April 1995, Oct. 1996 and Oct., 1997, Rajasthan 1994)

Ans. *Akbar's Tolerant Religious Policy.*

Akbar was very broadminded. He wanted to work out a synthesis of all religions. His treatment with the Hindus was very tolerant. In fact he was so liberal in his religious outlook that he attempted to find a new religion on the basis of good points of all religions. Of course he made no effort to force his religion on his subjects.

Four pillars of Akbar's religious policy. Akbar's religious policy was based on the following four pillars:

1. Pillar of amity
2. Pillar of equity
3. Pillar of kindness
4. Pillar of tolerance

Factors influencing Akbar's Hindu Policy

1. *Influence of Bhakti movement.* The 16th century when Akbar was born, brought up and lived was marked by a new awakening of broad-mindedness. The Bhakti Saints and Sufi 'Peers' had already been stressing upon religious toleration. So it was natural for Akbar to be influenced by contemporary ideas and values.

2. *Broadmindedness by nature.* Akbar by nature was broadminded.

3. *Liberal influence of Hindu mother and tutors.* Liberal views of his mother Hamida Banu, his regent Bairam Khan, and his tutor Abdul Latif greatly influenced his mind to become broad minded.

4. *Influence of Scholars.* Three great scholars and liberal minded sufis i.e. Shaikh Mubark and his sons Faizl and Abdul Faizl exercised tremendous influence on the religious outlook of Akbar.

5. *Influence of Hindu wives.* Akbar's Hindu wives also contributed to the change of his outlook.

6. *Akbar's contact with Rajputs.* Akbar's contact with the Rajputs made him liberal.

7. *Akbar's desire to work independently.* Akbar wanted to free himself from the orthodoxy of the Muslim priestly class.

8. *Pragmatic approach. Akbar was an imperialist.* He was convinced that he could not establish a strong empire without the cooperation of the Hindus who formed the majority of his subjects.

9. *Desire to know truth.* It is said that Akbar would sit for hours together on a huge flat stone and think of the mysteries of God and religion.

10. *Akbar's desire to experiment.* Akbar experimented in all departments from religion to metallurgy. (see also next question)

Measures adopted by Akbar to establish friendly relations with the Hindus.

1. *Freedom of worship.* Akbar allowed freedom of worship to people of all religions.

2. *Abolition of Jizya.* Akbar quashed the Jizya tax on the Hindus.

3. *Matrimonial alliances with the Hindus.* He established matrimonial relations with the Hindus. Akbar married Jodha Bai, daughter of Bihari Mal of Amber. He also married Mani Bai, daughter of the Kachwaha Raja Bhan Mal. He also married a princess from Jodhpur and one from Bikaner. He married his son Jahangir to the daughter of Raja Bhagwan Dass, son of Raja Bihari Lal.

4. *High civil and military positions to Hindus.* He provided high positions to the Hindus. For example, Todar Mal was his Finance Minister. Raja Bhagwan Das and Raja Man Singh were other important ministers. Out of 12 Diwans, 8 were Hindus.

5. *No religious conversion.* He put an end to religious conversions.

6. *Abolition of pilgrim tax.* He abolished the pilgrim taxes on the Hindus.

7. *Translation of Hindu scriptures.* He got translated the Vedas, the Ramayana and the Mahabharat and the Gita from Sanskrit to Persian.

8. *Establishment of Ibadat Khana.* (House of idorship). He established Ibadat Khana (place of worship) where he used to have religious discussions.

9. *Issue of Infallibility Decree.* He issued the 'Infallibility Decree' which freed him from following the authority of the Muslim *Mullahs*.

10. *Founding a new religion.* He started a new religion called Din-i-Ilahi which included the good points of all religions.

11. *Reforms in Hindu Society.* Akbar tried to remove the evil practices like Sati prevalent in the Hindu Society.

12. *Freedom to construct temples.* Hindus were given full freedom to construct new temples and repair old ones.

13. *Land grants.* Akbar gave land grants to Hindu, Jain and Persian institutions.

14. *Consideration for Hindu sentiments.* He banned the killing of cow.

Significance of Akbar's Hindu Policy

1. *Extension and strengthening of Akbar's empire.* The cooperation of the Hindus who formed the majority of Akbar's subjects helped him in the extension and strengthening of his empire.

2. *Cultural unity.* Cultural unity between the Hindus and the Muslims was strengthened. Culturally. The Hindus and Muslims came closer.

3. *Promotion of scriptures.* Akbar established a Translation Bureau with the aim of translating Sanskrit works into Persian.

4. *Secular feelings.* Akbar's religious policy encouraged a broad religious outlook.

5. *Social reforms.* Akbar's interest in the Hindu Society led to some awakening regarding the evils of the Sati practice etc. Widow remarriage was encouraged.

Summing up

Akbar's religious policy and his treatment towards the Hindus healed strife and bitterness and produced an environment of harmony and goodwill where there had been racial and religious antagonism of a most distressing character.

Q. 4. Evaluate Akbar's religious policy with special reference to Sulehkul. (Delhi University 1997)

Or

Trace the various stages in the development of the religious views of Akbar. Do you consider the Din-i-Ilahi as a monument of Akbar's folly?

Ans. *Akbar's Religious Policy: Various stages in its Development.*

Akbar's religious policy of harmony, reconciliation, and synthesis among all the religions did not develop all of a sudden. Between 1556 and 1562, Akbar remained a staunch Sunni Muslim. He practised the tenets of Islam as a devout Muslim—prayed five times a day, kept fast in the holy month of Ramazan and honoured the Ulemas of Islam. He never hesitated to punish the opponents of Islam. However, gradually his views changed after 1562.

'Sule Kul'. According to Dr. Tara Chand, his religion was the product of the synthetic effect of the Vedanta and Sufism of the age. Akbar was deeply interested in religion and philosophy and listened very carefully not only to the arguments of the Sufi and Shia divines but also the scholars of other religions also. He watched the good men professing different creeds and 'Sule Kul' i.e. reconciliation seemed to him the only solution of developing harmony and friendship among followers of different faiths. In fact some scholars equate *'Din-i-Ilahi'* with *'Sule-Kul'*. (Please see the previous question also)

Akbar's *'Sule-Kul'* or his policy of reconciliation and liberalism in religious matters was greatly influenced by his Hindu mother, his guardian and tutor Bairam Khan and Abdul Latif respectively, his contact with philosophers and scholars like Sheikh Mubark and his sons Faizi and Abdul Fazal, his contact with Rajputs, his contact with other religions and his political ambition to expand and strengthen his empire with the cooperation of all religions. (Please see the previous question also)

Ibadat Khana (House of Worship). With the help of Shaikh Mubark and his sons Faizi and Abdul Fazal, Akbar collected a big library of books on history, religion, philosophy and sciences. These were read out and explained to him by Faizi. The result was that Akbar's views on religion became very liberal and he wanted to go deep in religious matters. For this he thought of providing a meeting ground. In 1575, Akbar established Ibadat Khana at Fatehpur Sikri for the purpose of conducting religious discussions and debates for a better understanding of deep truth in religion. Akbar himself took part in these discussions. In the beginning, *Mullahs* only participated. Akbar addressed the following words to those assembled for discussion : "My sole object, O. *Mullahs* is to ascertain truth, to find out and disclose the principles of genuine religion and to trace it to the divine origin."

In due course, exponents of Hinduism, Jainism, Buddhism, Sikhism and Christianity began to be invited. All the scholars were given due respect. However with the passage of time, Akbar found that the debates in the Ibadat Khana were not helpful in leading to better understanding between different religions, rather they created bitterness. Hence in 1582, he discontinued the debates.

Development of Akbar's religious views and measures taken (in the chronological order)

Akbar stopped the practice of converting the prisoners of war to Islam (1562)

He abolished the pilgrimage tax (1563)

He abolished *Jizya* — a tax levied on Hindus (1564)

He established the Ibadat Khana or House of Worship (1575)

He issued Infallibility Decree (1579)

He founded a new religion called *Din-i-Ilahi* (1581)

He forbade the killing of animals on certain days (1583)

Infallibility Decree (1579). Akbar was in favour of weakening the powers of the Ulemas/Mullahs. He wanted to combine in himself both political and spiritual powers. According to the Decree, Akbar became the supreme arbiter in civil and religious affairs. This declaration was signed by leading divines. Akbar himself began to read the Khutba (earlier read by the Imam of the Mosque) from the pulpit of a Fatehpuri Mosque.

'Din-i-Ilahi' or 'Tauhld-Ilahi'

After acquainted himself thoroughly with the principles and practises of different religions through listening to the debates and discussions of religious philosophers and scholars and watching their lives, Akbar founded a new religion in 1581 which included the virtues of other religions and he named it Din-i-Ilahi.

Akbar tried to emphasise the *'Sule Kul'* i.e. peace and harmony among religions.

Important principles of Din-i-Ilahi

Some of the important principles of Din-i-Ilahi were.

1. God is great. He is One.
2. Akbar is His apostle or representative.
3. Every adherent of this faith should be willing to give away property, life, religion and honour to the emperor.
4. Every member should take an oath of doing good to everybody.
5. No member should have blind faith.
6. The followers of this faith should not approve of child marriage as well as old marriage.
7. All should show respect to all religions.
8. Whenever the followers of this faith meet, one should say : Allah-hu-*Akbar* (God is great) and in reply the other should say *Jalla-Jallah - hu* (God is beautiful and merciful).
9. As far as possible, the followers of this religion should not eat meat.
10. The followers should not sleep with minor girls.
11. Every member should arrange a feast at his birth day and give charity.

Membership of the Din-i-Ilahi. The number of the followers of the Din-i-Ilahi was not large. Probably it was a few thousands only. Among the nobles, only eighteen are said to have accepted this faith. Shaikh Mubark, his two sons Faizi and Abul Fazl and Raja Birbal embraced the new faith. Akbar did not force anyone to accept Din-i-Ilahi. It was sad and unfortunate that the new faith died with Akbar's death.

Evaluation of Din-i-Ilahi

Critics of Din-i-Ilahi: Monuments of Akbar's folly.

Budauni regards the founding of Din-i-Ilahi as an un-Islamic act.

Dr. Smith writes, "The whole scheme was the outcome of ridiculous vanity, monstrous growth of unrestrained autocıacy - a monument of Akbar's folly, not of his wisdom." He further calls it "a silly invention".

Admirers of Din-i-Ilahi

According to S.R. Sharma, Din-i-Ilahi was the crowning expression of

Akbar's nationalism. Dr. Ishwari Prasad regards it very rational containing good points of all religions. Havell thinks that with the new faith Akbar won an imperishable name in Indian history.

Lane-poole has justly observed, "The broad minded sympathy which inspired such a vision of catholicity left a lasting impression upon a land of warring creeds and tribes and for a brief while created a nation where before there had been only factions". According to S.M. Zaffar, "The wisdom of Akbar's assumption of the prophetic role may be called in question but the noble ideal that prompted it deserves high praise and not condemnation. To achieve the aim of unification of India and consolidation of Mughal Empire, it was necessary first to conquer and then to command sincere devotion from all and sundry by granting them the freedom of worship and the liberty of conscience. Therefore, Akbar gave up such a religious code-in essence a political document—as would commend itself to the whole population".

The Divine Faith had far-reaching consequences. It totally changed the character of Muslim rule in India. Malleson has also felt, "Akbar's foremost aim was the union of Hindustan under one head which was difficult to achieve had he persecuted all non-Islamic religions. To accomplish such a union it was necessary, first to conquer, Secondly, to respect all consciences, and all methods of worshipping Almighty".

Q. 5. Explain the main features of Akbar's administration.

Or

Write about the central administration of Akbar.

(Punjab University 1997)

Ans. *Main features of Akbar's Administration*

Akbar was an enlightened and successful administrator. It goes to the credit of Akbar that the subsequent Mughal rulers followed in principle the administrative policy developed by him. Babur and Humayun had little time to take any initiative in formulating any administrative policy worth the name.

Important features of Akbar's administration are given below :

Akbar's ideal of Kingship. According to him, "Upon the conduct of a monarch depends the efficiency of any course of action. His gratitude to God should be shown in just government and due recognition of merit."

Concentration of all power in the King. Akbar was the centre of all powers—civil, judicial, military and religious. He was the Supreme Commander of the army. He established a centralised administration. All appointments, promotions or dismissals depended on his decision and orders. Usually he ruled according to Shariat (Islamic Law). Akbar's day started with his appearance at the *Jharokha* (balcony) of the palace. A large number of people assembled below the balcony, presented their petitions to the emperor, besides having a fortunate glimpse of their emperor. The petitions were promptly attended to on the spot or later in the open hall of public audience (*Diwan-i-am*). Special consultation with the ministers and nobles were held at the hall of Special Audience (*Diwan-i-khas*).

Council of Ministers. Akbar had a Council of Ministers to assist him in the discharge of his administrative responsibilities and state of affairs.

The Wazir. He was like the Prime Minister and advised the king in all matters. He coordinated the work of all other ministers. After the reign of Aurangzeb, the Prime Minister, then called 'Vakil' became very powerful. Likewise other Ministers became powerful.

Dewan or Finance Minister. He looked after the revenues of the state.

Mir Bakshi or Paymaster General. He was the head of the establishment department. He was also the head of the intelligence agencies of the empire.

Kham-i-Saman. He looked after the imperial house-hold. He also looked after the control of the royal body guards and etiquettes in the court.

Chief Qazi. He was the head of the judicial department.

Other important high officials who assisted the king were *Mir Atish* who supervised the artillery, *Daroga-i-Taksal*, supervisor of royal mint and *Daroga-i-Daak*, supervisor of the mail.

Mansabdari System. The *Mansab* is an Arabic word meaning rank or position or status. Thus *Mansabdari* was a system in which the rank of a government official was determined. Every civil and military official was given a *mansab* and was called a *Mansabdar*. There were two methods of making payments to the nobles. One was giving them Jagirs (land) wherefrom they got their salaries. The second was making cash payment. In the Mansabdari system no *Jagirs* were granted for the purpose of paying salaries. A *mansabdar* got his salary from the royal treasury.

Land Revenue System

Todar Mal, the revenue minister of Akbar played an important role in devising and introducing a very effective and efficient land revenue and record system. There were three systems of land revenue (1) The Zabti system (2) The Ghalla-Bakshi and (3) Nasaq or Kankat.

The Zabti system of the land revenue. This system was prevalent in the areas from Lahore to Allahabad and in Malwa and Gujarat. This covered most of the empire. Following were some of the chief features of the system.

1. *Measurement of land.* Land of each farmer was measured into 'bighas'. The land was measured by means of bamboos joined together with iron rings. This system was called Bamboo Jarib system.

2. *Four categories of land.* The land was divided into four categories according to its produce. (*i*) *Polaj* land which was regularly cultivated and yielded crops regularly. (*ii*) *Parauti* land was left uncultivated after every crop to regain its productivity (*iii*) *Chachhar* land was left uncultivated for

3 to 4 years (*iv*) Banjar land was left uncultivated for more than 4 years.

3. *Three categories of Polaj and Parauti land.* These types of lands were divided into three grades, viz., good, average and bad.

4. *Dahsala (ten year) assessment.* Under this system, the average produce of different crops as well as the average price prevailing over the last 10 years were calculated and accordingly land reveue was fixed.

5. *Land revenue in cash or kind.* The share of the state was one-third of the produce of the land. Farmers were given the option to pay the revenue in cash or kind.

6. *Loans.* Farmers could get loans easily from the state which could be paid in easy annual instalments.

7. *Remission of revenue.* In bad seasons, remissions of revenues were granted to the farmers.

8. *Records.* Farmers were issued receipts for all the payments made by them. A record of all the holdings and liabilities of every farmer was maintained.

9. *Revenue officials.* For the assessment and collection of revenue, a large number of officers like the Amil, Bitikchi, Qanungo, Muqaddam and Patwari were appointed.

The Zabti system proved very useful both to the state and the farmers. The system was for ten years. The system on the one hand determined the income of the government and on the other hand enabled the farmers to know clearly how much revenue they had to pay to the government. Now the farmers had direct link with the government and they were saved from the excesses and tyrannies of the landlords and the jagirdars. The revenue officials were instructed not to be harsh with the farmers. The farmers could deposit the land revenue direct to the treasury.

Other systems of the land revenue. According to the Batai or Ghalla-Bakshi system, the produce of the farmers was divided between the government and the farmers in the ratio settled between them. This system was in vogue in Thatta and in parts of Kabul and Kandhar.

Provincial Administration. Akbar divided his empire into fifteen provinces. These were : Agra, Ahmedabad, Ahmednagar, Ajmer, Allahabad, Awadh, Bengal, Berar, Bihar, Delhi, Kabul, Khandar, Lahore, Malwa and Multan. Each province was under the charge of Subedar (Governor). He was assisted by a 'Diwan' who looked after the revenue records. *Bakshi* looked after the needs of the army. The *Kotwal* was entrusted with the maintenance of law and order in the main cities. Qazi looked after justice. The provincial ministers and officers followed the nomenclature of the central administration and performed similar duties. Provinces were divided into Sarkars, *Sarkars* into *Parganas* and *Parganas* into villages. *Panchayats* looked after the village administration and also dispensed justice. Normally state officers did not interfere in the village affairs.

Q. 6. Write an essay on Akbar as a nation builder.

Or

How far is it correct to describe Akbar as a national ruler?

Or

How did Akbar identify himself with India?

Or

Explain how Akbar attempted to form a national state in India?

Or

Why is Akbar considered as a great emperor?

Or

Elucidate the measures taken by Akbar for the cultural and emotional integration of India.

Ans. *Akbar as the National Integrator.*

Undoubtedly Akbar was the only ruler among the rulers of medieval India who attempted to foster the national feeling in India. He did succeed to some extent. However subsequent Mughal rulers failed to catch his spirit.

The majority of historians regard Akbar as a great emperor. K.T. Shah writes, "Akbar was the greatest of the Mughals and perhaps the greatest of all Indian rulers for a thousand years, if not ever since the days of the mighty Mauryas. But without detracting in the least from the genius of the man of the inheritance of his birth, it may yet be said that Akbar was so great, because he was so thoroughly Indianised."

Akbar's claim to be a 'national king' is supported on the following basis :

1. Bringing entire India under rule of one monarch.
2. Unified system of administration.
3. Unified system of revenue administration.
4. Unified taxation policy.
5. Rajput policy of reconciliation.
6. Religious policy of synthesis and toleration.
7. Making Persian as court language.
8. Generous help in the growth of literature in all languages.
9. Developing a uniform Indian style of fine arts by bringing about synthesis of different styles.
10. Cultural harmony relating to customs and manners.
11. Welfare of his subjects belonging to different communities.

Edwardes and Gerrett wrote: "Akbar has proved his worth in different fields of action. He was an intrepid soldier, a great general, a wise administrator, a benevolent ruler, and a sound judge of character. He was a born leader of men and can rightly claim to be one of the mightiest sovereigns known to history ...During a reign of nearly fifty years, he built up a powerful Empire which could vie with the strongest and established a dynasty whose hold over India was not contested by any rival for about a century. His reign witnessed the final transformation of the Mughuls from merely military invaders into a permanent Indian dynasty."

1. *Considering India as Motherland.* Most of the Sultan rulers of India considered themselves as the representative of Caliph of Baghdad. Babur had also willed to be buried outside India and in his home country. Humayun also looked towards Kabul and Qandhar. Akbar completely identified himself with India, its people and soil etc. He worked for the prosperity of India. He had loyalty to India alone and none else.

2. *Union of Hindustan under one head.* According to Malleson, "Akbar's foremost aim was the union of Hindustan under one head which was difficult to achieve had he persecuted all Non-Islamic religions. To accomplish this, it was necessary first to conquer, secondly to respect all consciences and all methods of worshipping the Almighty." Thus Akbar's aim to expand his empire in India was to unify the scattered kingdoms under one umbrella. However according to Dr. R.P. Tripathi, the aim of Akbar was more ambitious than that of national king. Akbar in his view wanted to bring the entire world under his control as he was an expanionist.

3. *Equal treatment with all subjects.* Famous artist Ferguson has written, "There is nothing more remarkable in Akbar's character as his toleration which influenced all his activities. He had the same love and appreciation for all his Hindu subjects as he had for his co-religionists."

4. *Synthesis of all religions.* Akbar attempted to being about synthesis of all religions. '*Ibadat Khana*' was established for religious discussions.

5. *Founding of Din-i-Ilahi.* On the basis of good points of all religions, Akbar founded a new religion and such a step could he taken only by a national ruler.

6. *Appointments on merits and not on religious basis.* Merit was the basis of all appointments and this led to great efficiency in his administration. By this policy Akbar won the heart of the Hindus. Todar Mal, was appointed an Finance Minister. Bhagwan Dass, Man Singh and Birbal were among the high-ups.

7. *Akbar's 'Nav-ratnas' (Nine Jewels).* Out of nine distinguished persons of his court, four were Hindus.

8. *Removal of restrictions upon the Hindus.* Akbar abolished the pilgrim tax as well as jizya tax. He gave religious freedom to all.

9. *Matrimonial alliances with the Hindus.* Akbar entered into matrimonial alliances with several Rajput families. However it is not clear why no girl from the royal family was married into Hindu family.

10. *Cultural synthesis of Hindus and Muslims.* Akbar made vigorous efforts to bring about fusion of Hindu and Muslim art and literature.

(*a*) *Architecture.* The effects of both Persian and Indian art is clearly visible in his buildings built at Fatehpur Sikri, Agra and Delhi.

(*b*) *Painting.* It is said that not less than 13 out of 17 most important painters of his court were Hindus.

(*c*) *Literature.* Akbar established a special translation department with the objective of translating the sacred books of the Hindus from Sanskrit into Persian.

Summing up

From the accounts given above, it is clear that Akbar was a national ruler. Jawaharlal Nehru has rightly described him, "Father of Indian nationalism."

Q. 7. Write notes on :
(*a*) Bairam Khan (*b*) Hemu (*c*) Rana Pratap (*d*) Abul Fazal (*e*) Todar Mal

Ans. *(a) Bairam Khan*

Bairam Khan was a Persian Turk and Shia Muslim. He served under Babur, Humanyun and Akbar. He had also accompanied Humayun in his wanderings and gone to Persia with him. Humayun was so much pleased with his wisdom and loyalty that he regarded him as his most trustworthy follower and used to say, "There is no other so luminous a star in our family as you are."

Bairam Khan played a promiment role in Humayun's restoration of Delhi's throne. Bairam Khan's services as the guardian and tutor of Akbar are praiseworthy. He guided the affairs of the state for four years between 1556 to 1560 when Akbar was still a minor. Bairam Khan was a great commander and it was because of him that Akbar could defeat Hemu and capture the throne of Delhi and Agra. In 1560, fall of Bairam Khan began. The unbridled power made him arrogant. He showered favours on his friends and relatives. In the meanwhile, Akbar had become major. He desired to be the king not only in name but in reality also.

Akbar relieved Bairam Khan of his duties and gave him a jagir for his maintenance. Bairam Khan revolted but was defeated. Akbar pardoned him and asked him to proceed to Mecca with dignity. Unfortunately on the way, he was murdered by an Afghan.

Causes of Bairam Khan's fall

1. Unpopularity of the Bairam Khan among Muslim nobility. He was a Shia and a majority of the Mughal nobles followed Sunni faith.
2. Vanity and haughtiness of Bairam Khan.
3. Showing favours to some nobles.
4. Execution of governor Tardi Beg who had failed to defend Delhi against Hemu.
5. Akbar's own ambition to work as an independent ruler without any interference.
6. Conspiracy of royal household against Bairam Khan.
7. Bairam Khan's revolt against the emperor Akbar.

(*b*) Hemu or Hemchandra

Hemu's rise to power

It appears historians in general have ignored Hemu. Although the Battle of Panipat (1556) has been given a lot of importance yet very little is mentioned about Hemu who gave a very tough fight to the Mughal army. Hemu's defeat changed the fortune of the Mughals. Of course, Hemu's luck did not favour him. He was a conqueror of 22 battles.

Dr. R. C. Majumdar, referring to the need of rescuing from oblivion the name of Hemu or Hemchandra, a forgotten Hindu hero, states, "Historians, medieval and modern, have done scant justice to, and failed to show due appreciation of, the unique personality and greatness of a Hindu, during the heyday of Muslim rule in India who worked his way from a grocer's shop to the throne of Delhi, and but for an accident in a battle which turned victory into defeat, might have founded a Hindu ruling dynasty, instead of the Mughals in Delhi." Islam Shah ruler of Bengal recognizing his merit promoted him to the post of head of the Departments of Intelligence and Posts and trusted him with certain confidential work involving military commands. After the death of Islam Shah, emperor Adil Shah made him his Prime Minister and left all the heavy burden of administration and military affairs on his shoulders. Hemu became busy crushing rebellions and conquering 22 battles from 1553 and 1555. Humayun, a few months after re-establishing himself on the throne of Delhi died in 1556. Tardi Beg was appointed the governor of Delhi after the 13-year old Akbar was proclaimed the emperor. Hemu advanced by way of Gwalior and Agra to reach Delhi and inflicted a severe defeat on the Mughal forces. Hemu won over the Afghans by distributing the spoils of war and ascended the throne of Delhi with their concurrence. He issued coins in his name and assumed the historic name Vikramaditya as Raja Vikramajit.

Second Battle of Panipat (1556) The guardian of minor ruler Akbar met Hemu's army at the battlefield of Panipat Hemu succeeded in crushing the left and the right wings of his opponent and sought to make his victory decisive by bringing all his mountain like elephants to wipe out the centre of the enemy. The Mughal army fell into confusion and at the very moment when victory was to shake hand with Hemu, an accidental arrow pierced his eyes and lodged in the brain making him unconscious. An Indian army never could survive the loss of a leader and thus the soldiers scattered away. Thus fate deprived Hemu of victory, throne, and life. The cup of fortune just slipped as it touched the smiling lips of victory. Hemu was captured and Akbar, at the request of Bairam Khan, first struck the unconscious captive with his sword and Bairam Khan severed his head from his body. With this victory, Akbar became the ruler of Delhi.

(*c*) Rana Pratap (1540-1597)

In the history of Rajputana in particular and India in general, Rana Pratap occupies a place of prominence. It goes to his credit that Akbar, the Great Mughal emperor failed to subdue him with all the power at his command. Rana's spirit of freedom has a few parallels in Indian history.

Rana Pratap was the son of Udai Singh and grandson of Rana Sanga, the ruler of Mewar. He succeeded to the throne of his father in 1572. Chittor, the capital of Mewar had already been captured by the Mughals in 1568. Thus Rana was without a capital, without resources and his claim ecliped by reverses yet he continued the fight for the honour of Mewar. Akbar sent a series of missions to Rana Pratap to persuade him to accept Mughal suzerainty and to pay personal homage. Rana Pratap considered these conditions humiliating.

Akbar sent a strong Mughal army under the command of Raja Man Singh and Asaf Khan to attack Mewar. Rana Pratap had a very small army of 3000 horse men. A ferocious battle took place at Haldighati on June 18, 1576. The charge of Rana was so fierce that the Mughal army felt desperate. It was a hand-to-hand fight from morning till mid-day. Rana Pratap was at his best. The onslaught by the Rana's army threw the Mughal forces into disarray. In the meanwhile with the fresh Mughal reinforcements the tide of the battle turned against the Rajputs. Rana Pratap was hard pressed and encircled from all sides. Rana's life was endangered. Seeing this Bida Jhala one Rajput noble decided to save the life of his leader. He thought of a plan and snatched away the crown from Rana's head and put on his own head. The Mughal army took Jhala as Rana and encircled him. This gave an opportunity to some of Rana's followers to carry Rana to a safe place. The Rajputs were defeated.

The Battle of Haldighati did not break Rana's spirit. Far from making him give up resistance, it stiffened Rana's attitude and gave him fresh confidence. On the contrary he took an oath, "So long as I do not recover Chittor, I shall sleep on the ground, shall eat out on leaves (not in utensils) and shall not turn my moustaches." He observed the vow throughout his life.

Pratap spent nearly four years wandering about in the mountains and jungles of western Mewar and acquired intimate knowledge of every nook and corner of the territory. The brave stand of his troops against the most powerful monarch convinced him that he could continue his struggle. Thereafter he decided to change his war strategies. Henceforth he decided to adopt guerilla warfare. On the other hand Akbar also exerted relentless pressure on the Rana. The Rana was hunted from forest to forest and from valley to valley. The Rana underwent great hardships but with the support of the Bhil chiefs, he continued his fight.

For about twenty five years, struggle went on between Rana Pratap and Akbar. Before his death in 1597, Rana Pratap managed to recover practically the whole of Mewar except Chittor. He built a new capital at Chaunar near Dungarpur. Unfortunately Rana Pratap sustained some internal injury while trying to tie the string of a hard arrow and the great warrior died in 1597 at the age of 57 years.

Maharana Pratap's struggle for the independence of Mewar and his successful struggle against Akbar constitutes a glorious saga of Rajput valour and spirit of sacrifice.

(*d*) Abul Fazal (1551 to 1602)

One of the famous 'Nine jewels' of Akbar's court, Abul Fazal was an eminent historian, poet, politician and writer. His two works namely *'Akbarnama '* and *Ain-i-Akbari'* in Persian form the basic material for historical information and knowledge. These books throw valuable information on the contemporary Indian political, social, religious and economic conditions. Abul Fazal translated *'Panchatantra'* into Persian and named it *'Andheri-Sahili'*. For a considerable period he was Akbar's chief adviser and Prime Minister. His ideas were similar to Sufi saints and he was very liberal in his religious outlook. It was Abul Fazal who had inspired Akbar to start *'Din-i-Ilahi'*. Among the *'Nine Jewels'* he was the first to embrace the new faith started by Akbar. He was assassinated at the investigation of Akbar's son Salim in a conspiracy with Bir Singh Bundela, Orachha ruler. It is said that Akbar was so much grieved at this sad incident that he did not hold his court for three days. Akbar is said to have remarked that if Salim wanted the kingdom, he should have assassinated him (Akbar) but spared Fazal. Such was the regard of Akbar for Abul Fazal !

(*e*) Todar Mal

Todar Mal's name will ever remain enshrined in the history of revenue administration and system. He made a valuable contribution in strengthening the finanes of Sher Shah and Akbar through his pragmatic reforms. The system of land revenue devised by him was first used by Sher Shah. Akbar first tried this system in the province of Gujarat and thereafter in almost all territories of his kingdom. It became the basis of the *'ryotwari'* or peasant-based revenue settlement used in some parts of British India.

Todar Mal was a Punjabi Hindu and showed his administrative skills early in life. Todar Mal devised a system based on a survey and measurement of land. He classified land in four types according to its productive capacity and actual cultivation rates were accordingly fixed. The cultivators or the peasants could pay the land revenue in cash or kind. There were two important considerations in this policy. One was to increase the revenue of the state and the other was to provide security and incentive to the cultivator.

Besides being a revenue expert, Todar Mal was also a good soldier and general. He won several battles. Todar Mal was one of the *'Nine Jewels'* of Akbar's court.

18

Jahangir (1605-1627)

Q. 1. Analyse the achievements of Jahangir.

Ans. *Prominent Features of Jahangir's Rule.*

Jahangir whose original name was Salim, became the emperor of Delhi after the death of his father emperor Akbar. After his coronation, he assumed the title of Nur-ud-din Muhammad Jahangir Badshah Ghazi. Important features of his reign are as under :

First, Jahangir is perhaps the only ruler who although ruled for about 22 years but for about 16 years he was only a ruler in name only as during this period, his wife Nur Jahan was the virtual ruler.

Second, he is famous for his 'golden chain of justice'.

Third, his twelve orders issued in the early period of his reign showed his great concern for the welfare of his subjects.

Fourth, long drawn war between Mewar and the Mughals came to an end.

Fifth, relations between the Mughal rulers and the Sikhs began to deteriorate.

Sixth, two visitors namely Captain W.Cook and Sir Thomas Rao came to the court of Jahangir. The latter who was the ambassador of King James was able to get permission from Jahangir allowing the English to trade at Surat. With the passage of time, trade was followed by rule of the English over India.

Main events of the reign of Jahangir

1. *Chain of justice.* The earliest measure of Jahangir was that a golden chain having 60 bells and weighing several *'maunds'* was fastened between the Shahburj of Agra fort and a stone pillar raised on the banks of river Jamuna. People seeking justice were required to pull this chain in order to put forth their complaints or petitions to the King. This act speaks very high of Jahangir's sense of justice but to what extent it proved helpful is not clearly known.

2. *Issuance of 12 rules of conduct ('Dastur-ul-Amal').* Jahangir issued the following orders which demonstrate his concern for the welfare of the people.

(1) He abolished the *Tagma'* and *"meerwahi"* toll taxes and the taxes that the Subedars imposed on the people for their expenses.

(2) He ordered for the construction of mosques, sarais, and wells on the road-sides which reduced the dangers from the thieves and dacoits.

(3) He ordered that the property of the dead would be passed over to their legal heirs and the unclaimed property would go to the state, the income of which would be spent on public-welfare.

(4) He banned the manufacture and sale of the intoxicants although he himself was addicted to drinking.

(5) He disallowed the mutiliation of the limbs of the criminals.

(6) He ordered that the land-lords would not forcibly occupy the lands of the farmers.

(7) He ordered for the construction of government hospitals and appointed the physicians (hakims) in them.

(8) Animal slaughter was banned on two days in the week i.e. Thursday, his Coronation day, and Sunday, the day of his father and on certain other occasions in the year.

(9) Akbar held Sunday with respect because it was the day of the sun. So Jahangir did like-wise.

(10) He reinstated all the mansabdars, appointed during Akbar's reign, in their positions and promoted them on merit.

(11) The Jagirs, known as Aima and Madadgar, granted to the religious and charitable institutions were allowed to remain with them.

(12) All the convicts, serving for longer periods, were released from the jails.

Revolt of prince Khusro. In 1606, Jahangir's eldest son and an aspirant of the throne revolted but was defeated. It is said that after his arrest, he was poisoned to death.

Execution of Guru Arjun Dev (1606). Two reasons are attributed to Jahangir's conflict with the 5th Sikh Guru Arjun Dev. One, it is said that the Sikh guru helped prince Khusro against the emperor. Second, Guru Arjun Dev was becoming popular and promoting the creed of Sikhism. The execution of the Guru greatly provoked the Sikhs and they began to prepare themselves to wreak vengeance upon the Mughals, They declared their Guru a 'martyr'.

Marriage with Nur Jahan (1611). Nur Jahan's marriage with Jahangir almost eclipsed his personality. Jahangir in his biography '*Tuzuk-i-Jahangir*' himself wrote about his influence, "I have sold my kingdom to my beloved queen for a cup of wine and a dish of soup."

Treaty with Mewar (1615). Jahangir and Rana Amar Singh, son of Rana Pratap saw several ups and downs in the struggle which continued for about 10 years. In 1615 both signed a peace treaty. The treaty reflected statesmanship of Jahangir.

Following were important terms of the treaty :

1. The Rana accepted the suzerainty of the Mughal emperor.

2. The Rana was not asked to enter into matrimonial relations with the emperor and he, in place of himself, sent his son, prince Karan to the Mughul service at the court.

3. Jahangir restored all territory of Mewar including the fort of Chittor to the Rana on condition that the fort would not be repaired.

About the treaty, Dr. Ishwari has observed, "Jahangir's conduct in this affair is wholly worthy of praise. Mewar had given the Mughals no small amount of trouble but the emperor forgot the past and adopted a conciliatary policy in dealing with the Rana."

Jahangir and South India. Jahangir's repeated attempts to conquer south India were without substantial gains.

Conquest of Kangra (1619). After prolonged and terrible warfare of 14 months Kangra was conquered.

Loss of Kandhar (1621). Jahangir lost Kandhar.

Revolt of prince Khurram (1622). Prince Khurram (later on Shah Jahan) was asked by Jahangir to crush a revolt in Kandhar but he refused fearing that Nur Jahan might create difficulties for him in his absence from India. His revolt failed and he begged pardon.

Revolt of Mahabat Khan (1622). He was an able commander. He came into prominence when he suppressed the revolt of Khurram. He was, however, considered a powerful opponent by Nur Jahan who wanted to have her way. Mahabat Khan felt humiliated by her treatment. He revolted but had to seek pardon. Emperor Jahangir pardoned him keeping his past services in view.

An estimate of Jahangir

Observations made by the two historians namely, Dr. Ishwari Prasad and Dr. Beni Prasad provide us valuable information and insight about Jahangir's personality and character.

Dr. Ishwari Prasad writes, "Jahangir is one of the most interesting figures in Mughul history. The ordinary view that he was a sensual pleasure-seeker and a callous tyrant does less than justice. All accounts agree that he was intelligent, shrewd, and capable of understanding the most complex problems of the state without any difficulty...There is much in his character that deserves to be condemned, but there is a great deal that entitles him to be placed among the most fascinating personalities of Indian history." Dr. Beni Prasad says: "Jahangir's reign, on the whole, was fruitful of peace and prosperity to the empire. Under its auspices, industry and commerce progressed; architecture achieved notable triumphs; painting reached its high water mark; literature flourished as it had never done before. Tulsidas composed the Ramayan. A host of remarkable Persian and vernacular poets all over the country combined to make the period the Augustan age of medieval Indian literature. The political side of Jahangir's history is interesting enough but its virtue lies in cultural development."

(Jahangir's interest in cultural development is taken up in another chapter.)

Q. 2. "In marrying her he became her prisoner and in ruling over him she ruled over all." Critically review the effect of Nur Jahan on Jahangir's empire."

Or

Briefly discuss the career of Nur Jahan and her influence on the Mughal court.

Or

What was the role of Nur Jahan 'Junta' in Mughal politics?

(Rajasthan University 1997)

Ans. *Nur Jahan's and her "Junta's" Influence on Jahangir.*

At the outset it must be admitted that Nur Jahan emerged as the most powerful figure in contemporary history on account of her personality and influence on Jahangir. In fact probably Nur Jahan was the only queen in the entire history of medieval India who exercised such a tremendous influence on an emperor Jahangir, her husband and consequently on the affairs of the state. In Jahangir's own words, "I have sold my kingdom to my beloved queen for a cup of wine and a dish of soup."

Before we discuss in detail the nature of influence and the impact of the influence of Nur Jahan and her *'Junta'* on Jahangir and his administration, we may give her early career in brief.

Early life of Nur Jahan. Nur Jahan (1575-1645) whose original name was Mihr-un-Nisa, was the daughter of Mirza Ghiyas Beg who belonged to a noble family of Persia. Evil days fell upon him and he had to leave his native place and in search of fortune he moved towards India. When he reached Qandhar, his wife gave birth to a daughter who later on became the most beloved queen of emperor Jahangir. With the help of a friend, he was able to get some job during Akbar's time. On account of his talents, he gained importance in the court.

Marriage of Nur Jahan with Jahangir. Divergent views have been expressed regarding the marriage of Nur Jahan with Jahangir. According to one version Jahangir earlier known as prince Salim chanced to see Mihr-un-Nisa when she used to come to the palace of emperor Akbar with her mother and fell in love with her. But Akbar got her married to an Afghan chief named Sher Afghan. When Salim became the emperor of Delhi, he got Sher Afghan killed and married Mihr-un-Nisa and Nur Mahal (Light of the Palace) and later on Nur Jahan (Light of the World). However, according to the other version, there was no such romance.

Without going into details, here we quote only two historians.

Dr. Beni Prasad has rejected the story of romance between Mihr-un-Nisa and prince Salim and that Jahangir was involved in the incident of death of Sher Afghan. He writes: "An attentive study of contemporary authorities and of the well-established facts themselves knocks the bottom out of the whole romance and the character of Jahangir and Nur Jahan appear in a truer and more favourable light." Dr. R.P. Tripathi and Dr. S.R. Sharma have on the other hand also supported the contention of Dr. Beni Prasad.

Dr. Ishwari Prasad writes: "A careful persual of contemporary chronicles leaves upon oûr minds the impression that the circumstances of Sher Afghan's death are of a highly suspicious nature, although there is no conclusive evidence to prove that the Emperor was guilty of the crime."

A contemporary Dutch writer De Laet, has described the romance of prince Salim with Mihr-un-Nisa in his famous work, *Description of India and Fragment of Indian History* in these words, "as she was engaged to Sher Afghan, Akbar did not permit her marriage with Salim. But Salim never forgot his love towards her."

Character of Nur Jahan and her influence over Jahangir

Nur Jahan was a cultured educated, intelligent and dominating lady. She was fond of music, painting and poetry. She composed verses in Persian. She designed new varieties of cotton and silk fabrics. She suggested models of jewellery. Thus she set the fashions of the age.

About Nur Jahans' influence over Jahangir, Dr. Beni Prasad has observed "Nur Jahan ruled him (Jahangir) for fourteen years and during the last five years of his reign, Nur Jahan alone controlled him."

Nur Jahan's influence over Jahangir had positive as well as negative effects but the negative ones had serious effects on the running of the affairs of the state.

Positive effects

1. *Somewhat sober effect on Jahangir's Character.* Under the influence of Nur Jahan, Jahangir effected reduction in his consumption of wine.

2. *Philanthropist work.* A kind and compassionate lady, she greatly helped the poor, the orphan and the widows.

3. *Development of art and literature.* Herself a cultured lady, Nur Jahan patronised art and literature. She brought about a revolutionary change in dresses and designs of ornaments.

Negative and damaging effects

1. Undue favours to her relatives.

2. Efforts to eliminate the influence of prince Khurram (later emperor Shah Jahan) resulting in his revolt.

3. Loss of Qandhar.

4. Revolt of Mahabat Khan, a trusted officer of Jahangir.

Two phases of the influence of Nur Jahan on Jahangir

Nur Jahan's influence on Jahangir may be divided into two phases first phase (1611-1622) and the second phase (1622-1627).

First phase of Nur Jahan's influence (1611-1621). *NUR JAHAN JUNTA* SOON after her marriage with Jahangir, Nur Jahan, as highly ambitious she was, formed a group of five—herself, her mother Asmat Begum, her father Ghias beg Itama-ud-Dulla, her brother Asaf Khan and prince Khurram (son-in-law of her brother Asaf Khan). First of all, Nur Jahan gave powerful posts to this group. Her father managed to occupy the position of the Prime Minister and her brother as Finance Minister.

Nur Jahan got her name struck upon the coins of all the *'firmans'* (royal orders), her name along with Jahangir appeared. She also often appeared in the *'jharoka'* along with the emperor. She listened to the complaints of her subjects.

Nur Jahan and her *'Junta'* exercised full control over state administration. The highest nobles and dignitaries of the state presented themselves before her and listened to her dictates. All important appointments, promotions, postings, transfers and dismissals were done at her behest and consent. "She was", as Dr. V.A. Smith Says, "a power behind the throne."

Sir Thomas Roe, the ambassador of the king of England, who stayed in the Mughal court from 1615-1618 has remarked, "All power vested in the clique (*'Jinta'*) of Nur Jahan at that time. It was impossible to get any work done without the help of her brother Asaf Khan and his son-in-law Prince Khurram. Her influence had increased so much that even powerful Amirs like Mahabat Khan feared her. Jahangir himself was in pleasure day and might, resigning the entire administration to her."

Second phase of Nur Jahan's influence (1622-1627). During this period, Nur Jahan became all the more powerful. Several factors contributed to this. First, Jahangir's health deteriorated. Second, Nur Jahan's mother died in 1621 and her father in 1622. Therefore, she was deprived of the sober and beneficial influence of her parents. Thirdly, Nur Jahan's daughter Ladli Begum by her late husband Sher Afghan, was married to prince Shahryar (son of Jahangir). She, therefore desired that Shahryar and not prince Khurram (Shah Jahan) may become the emperor. So this marriage brought about a change in power-politics. Shahryar was not as capable as Khurram.

Prince Khurram's revolt. The fort of Qandhar was captured by Persia in 1622. Prince Khurram was asked to reconquer Qandhar. Khurram apprehended that his absence from the capital would be utilised by Nur Jahan to prejudice his claim to the throne and to strengthen her son-in-law Shahryar. He, therefore, refused to move. Not only this he rose in revolt.

Mahabat Khan was sent to crush the revolt. At last Khurram asked Jahangir's pardon for his mistakes. Nur Jahan who at that time wanted to check the increasing power of Mahabat Khan, got prince Khurram pardoned by Jahangir.

Revolt of Mahabat Khan (1626). Mahabat Khan was one of the most capable commanders of Jahangir. He was liked by Jahangir very much. Nur Jahan decided to break the power of Mahabat Khan. Mahabat Khan was humiliated in several ways. Ultimately he revolted.

Mahabat Khan had an upper hand in the beginning. Nur Jahan even had to surrender but very diplomatically, she sowed dissensions in the camp of Mahabat Khan and he was forced to seek pardon of Jahangir. Jahangir, keeping in view his past services, pardoned him. Thereafter, Mahabat Khan fled away to Sind.

Nur Jahan's last years. When Jahangir's sudden death took place in December 1627, Nur Jahan declared Shahryar, her son-in-law to be the emperor of Delhi but Khurram's father-in-law Asaf Khan (brother of Nur Jahan), cleverly defeated the plan of Nur Jahan. Prince Khurram who was in the Deccan, immediately came to Agra and imprisoned Nur Jahan and Shahryar. Thereafter he sanctioned sufficient pension for Nur Jahan. She spent the remaining 18 years of her life peacefully without interfering with politics. She died in 1645 and was buried at Lahore, near the tomb of Jahangir.

Q. 3. Write a short note on Guru Arjun Dev

Ans. *Guru Arjun Dev* (1563-1606) : *Period of Gurudum* (1581-1606)

Guru Arjun Dev, the fifth Guru of the Sikhs was a contemporary of emperor Akbar and Jahangir. The emperor Jahangir got him murdered at Lahore on May 30, 1606 and the Sikhs remember this sacrifice of the Guru as a 'martyrdom' in the cause of Sikh religion.

Chief events of the life of Guru Arjun Dev

1. *Establishment of the Hari Mandir/Holy Mandir/Golden Temple.* The temple is considered to be one of the most important pilgrimage centres of the Sikhs.

2. *Completion of the construction of the city of Amritsar.* On account of the efforts of the Guru, the construction of city was completed.

3. *Compilation of the Adi Granth.* The Adi Granth considered to be the pepetual Guru of the Sikhs, (Guru Gobind Singh, the 10th and the last Guru declared that after him there would be no human being as Guru of the Sikhs) was compiled in 1604 with the help of Bhai Mohan and Bhai Guru Das.

4. *Construction of several cities and ponds.* Under the inspiration of Guru Arjun Dev, many cities like Taran Taran, Kartarpur and Gobindpur

were built. Later on all the cities and ponds built during the period became sacred places of pilgrimage of the Sikh faith.

5. *Encouragement of the 'Mansad' system.* Under this system, started by the 4th Guru, Ram Das, devoted workers went to various places for the collection of money to be spent for the development of the Sikh faith. Guru Arjun Dev made it compulsory for every Sikh to devote 1/10 of his income as a sort of subscription for the promotion of the religion.

6. *Stress on a disciplined way of life.* He instructed all his followers to follow the teachings of the Guru very strictly.

7. *Martyrdom of Guru Arjun Dev.* Relations of the Guru Arjun Dev remained very cordial with emperor Akbar but during Jahangir's time, the relations turned an ugly and sad turn. Historians have greatly differed on the reasons of the conflict.

(*i*) Religious bigotry of Jahangir.

(*ii*) Help or blessings given by the Guru to prince Khusru who rose in revolt against Jahangir.

(*iii*) Compilation of *'Adi Granth'* and Jahangir's charge that it contained many things against Islam and his insistence upon including the message of Prophet Muhammad in it.

(*iv*) Conspiracies of nobles and others.

The imprisonment, torture and execution of Guru Arjun Dev by emperor Jahangir led to a great bitterness between the Sikhs and the Mughal rulers.

19

Shah Jahan (1627-1658)

Q. 1. Give a short account of the life and main events of the reign of Shah Jahan.

Ans. *Shah Jahan's Early Life and Accession to the Throne*

Earlier known as Khurram Shihab-al-Din Muhammad, Shah Jahan was the third son of Mughal Emperor Jahangir by his Rajput queen belonging to the Mewar State. He was married to Arjunmand Banu Beg (who later on came to be known as Mumtaz Mahal), daughter of the powerful noble Asaf Khan, brother of Nur Jahan (another wife of Jahangir and the most powerful queen). Prince Khurram displayed his military talents early and was given high rank by the Emperor. Nur Jahan who had married her daughter Ladli Begum (from her previous husband Sher Afghan) to Shahryar, another son of Jahangir, wanted to make Shahryar as the emperor after the death of Jahangir. Thus the conflict for succession started between Nur Jahan and prince Khurram. Prince Shahryar was no match in talents as compared with Khurram. Khurram revolted on account of the unfair treatment by Jahangir under the influence of Nur Jahan. However, his revolt failed and he felt sorry for this. Jahangir pardoned him. Of course, there was an uneasy calm.

When Emperor Jahangir died suddenly in October 1627, Nur Jahan, according to her preconceived plans declared her son-in-law Shahryar as the emperor but Khurram's father-in-law, Asaf Khan diplomatically defeated the plans of Nur Jahan. Through intrigues and counter intrigues, Khurram (Shah Jahan) was able to occupy the throne of Delhi. Nur Jahan had to spend fifteen years of her life on the pension granted to her by Shah Jahan.

Chief features of the reign of Shah Jahan

1. Cultural development and advancement especially construction of memorable buildings.
2. War of succession among his sons during his life time.
3. Famines
4. Pathetic plight of Shah Jahan during his last days.

Main events of his reign

(1) Very costly and unsucceesful military campaigns in Afghanistan and Central Asia to recover Kandhar, Balkh and Badakshan.

(2) The Deccan campaign of Shah Jahan was motivated by two factors. First, he was an imperialist. Second, he was a staunch Sunni and considered it his sacred duty to crush the Shia states of the Deccan. Shah Jahan was successful in bringing several territories under his control.

(3) Suppression of rebellions of Bundelas of Orchha.

(4) Suppression of Khan Jahan Lodi, an Afghan Chief.

(5) Famine and pestilence in the Deccan and Gujarat resulting in extreme hardships to people, besides loss of precious lives.

(6) Successful war with the Portuguese on account of their abuse of trade rights given to them by Akbar and Jahangir. Killing of about 10,000 Portuguese and imprisonment of several hundred Portuguese. Conversion of many of them to Islam to avoid torture.

(7) Golden age of architecture, magnificence of Shah Jahan's collection of jewels, display of jewels on the fifteen-foot high Peacock Throne which took seven years and 10 million rupees to construct, fine buildings—Moti Masjid of Agra, Shalimar Gardens of Lahore and Sri Nagar, entire city of Shah Jahanabad (Delhi) containing the Red Fort and Jami Masjid; the Taj Mahal of Agra etc.

(8) Intolerant religious policy; destruction of temples.

(9) War of succession during his life time among his four sons and his inability to secure Dara Shikoh's succession.

(10) Last days spent in Aurangzeb's captivity in the Agra Fort, his pathetic plight and gazing at the Taj Mahal.

Q. 2. "Shah Jahan's rule was an epoch of grandeur not unmixed with symptoms of decay." Discuss.

Or

"Shah Jahan's rule was the glorious period of Mughal history". Do you agree with this view? Give reasons in support of your answer.

Or

Is it correct to call the reign of Shah Jahan as the Golden Age of the Mughal empire? Discuss.

Or

Can the reign of Shah Jahan be referred to as the Golden Period of the Mughal empire? Comment on this statement.

Ans. *Divergent opinions in calling the Reign of Shah Jahan as the Golden period.*

Historian's have expressed divergent views on this issues. While historians like Rai Bharmal, Khafi Khan, Travernier, Bernier, Moreland, Eliphinstone, W. Hunter, Richard Barns have lavished praise on the rule of Shah Jahan, others like Dr. V.A. Smith, Edwards and Garret, and Sir William Forster put forward several points of criticism.

Dr. Yadunath Sarkar and Dr. A.L. Srivastva have given a balanced view of Shah Jahan's reign.

Before discussing the various aspects of the rule of Shah Jahan, we may list the important features of a glorious rule. These are :

1. Peace in the reign.
2. Material prosperity of the people.
3. Religious harmony.
4. Ruler and administration receptive to people's needs.
5. Equal justice.
6. Cultural development.

1. *Fatherly treatment towards his subjects.* Travernier wrote, "Shah Jahan reigned not so much as a king over his subjects, but rather as father over his family and children."

2. *Agrarian prosperity.* According to Moreland, "The reign of Shah Jahan was a period of agrarian tranquility."

Eliphinstone considered the reign of Shah Jahan, "As the most prosperous period of Indian history."

3. *Best administrative system.* Travernier wrote, "Though Akbar was a greater conqueror and an expert in formation of laws and regulations but there was no emperor equal to Shah Jahan so far as best arrangement for the administration of each part of the empire was concerned."

In the words of Khafi Khan, "Akbar was preseminent as a conqueror and law-giver, yet for the order and arrangement of his territory and finances and good administration of the state, no prince ever reigned in India that could be compared to Shah Jahan."

4. *Magnificence Period.* W.H. Hunter stated, "The Mughal empire attained its highest union of strength and magnificance under Shah Jahan."

5. *Enormous wealth of the state.* Sir Richard Barns remarked "Shah Jahan had reigned for thirteen years, during which time the empire reached the height of its glory and wealth."— Barnier has observed, "The economic condition of Bengal was very good."

Dr. Ishwari Prasad, While comparing Shah Jahan with Akbar says," The income from the Parganas had increased from Rs. 3 lakhs during Akbar's time to 13 lakhs."

6. *A benevolent rule.* Lane-Poole observed, "Shah Jahan was renowned for his kindness and benevolence which endeared him to the people."

Why is it called the golden age of the Mughal period?

7. *All round Cultural development and advancement.* In the words of K.T. Shah, "The imperial patronage was no longer the monopoly of the poet and the painter but every kind of artist was recognised and encouraged."

Percy Brown, the noted artist has praised Shah Jahan's architecture as "Shah Jahan founded the Mughal cities of sandstone and left them of marble."

The Taj Mahal of Agra has been various praised as, "Queen of architecture," "Dream in Marble" etc.

Likewise music, painting and literature made phenomenal progress (Details of Advancement of culture are given in a chapter 27).

In short the protagonists of the view of the golden period state the following reasons :

(*a*) There was peace and order.

(*b*) Trade and industry progressed.

(*c*) Peasants were well-protected.

(*d*) Corrupt officials and offenders were punished.

(*e*) Building activity was at its height.

(*f*) Several monuments were built which are still a pride for India.

(*g*) Scholars were given patronage.

(*h*) Literature flourished.

(*i*) Artists in various fields were given encouragement.

(*j*) Export trade was carried on profitably.

(*k*) Justice was available to all.

Critics of Shah Jahan's rule

Dr. V.A. Smith is the greatest critic. His observations on his personality and rule are, "Shah Jahan failed both as a man and as a ruler and that the dazzling splendour of his court and the remarkable beauty of his buildings, specially of the Taj Mahal misled the world into thinking that his reign was a golden period in Mughal history." Smith further observed, "Shah Jahan was cruel, treacherous and unscrupulous in state matters. He had no skill as a military leader and the organisation and command of his army was inefficient. Thus his administration was far from satisfactory. Besides, Shah Jahan squandered a large sum of public money which could have been used for the social and economic welfare of the people. This in due course of time led to the financial bankruptcy which proved a potent cause of the downfall of the Mughal Empire."

William Hawkins who spent some time in India calls Shah Jahan, "a talented drunkard."

Bernier states, "The Jesuits were severely punished by the Emperor."

Peter Mundy who was in Deccan when famine took place during Shah Jahan's reign, describes the disasters of famine in these words. "The highways were strewn with corpses which emitted intolerable stench. In the towns especially they drag them (dead bodies) out by the heels, stark naked of all ages and sexes, till they are out of the gates and then they are left, so that the way is half barred up".

The critics level the following charges against Shah Jahan's rule :

Barbaric penal code. About the barbarous penal code and justice, Manuchi wrote, "One official kept a basket full of venomous serpents in

Shah Jahan's court and Shah Jahan used to leave the criminals to die painfully after getting them bit by the serpents in his presence".

1. Shah Jahan's justice was very savage.

2. *Cruel towards his opponents.* Shah Jahan was very cruel and barbaric in his behaviour and action. He killed all his brothers and all probable contenders of the throne. He revolted against his own father.

3. *Extravagent expenditure.* He wasted enormous money to fulfil his personal pleasures and hobbies.

4. *Religious intolerance.* He was intolerant towards other religions. He destroyed several temples. He forced Hindu captives to accept Islam. He was very cruel to Christians.

5. *Increase in land-revenue.* He increased land revenue which created economic hardships to the peasants.

6. *Weak military leadership.* His attempts to conquer Kandhar and Central Asia failed.

7. *Corruption.* There was a good deal of corruption in his administration. He extorted money from the unwilling masses and classes.

8. *Period of disorder.* There were so many revolts during his reign. He failed to check his sons to fight among themselves during his life time.

He himself was kept in prison. In grief and sorrow, he wrote the following lines to his son Aruangzeb who had imprisoned him.

"Praised be the Hindus in all cases,
as they even offer water to their dead. And thou,
my son, art a marvellous Musalman,
As thou caused him in life to lament for lack of water."

Balanced view about Shah Jahan's rule

Dr. A.L. Srivastava has observed, "Shah Jahan's reign has been described as a golden period in the medieval history of India. This is true in one respect only and that is in the domain of art, particularly architecture." He further writes: "His religious bigotry and intolerance anticipated the reactionary reign of Aurangzeb...His love of presents accorded sanction to a pernicious custom of gilded bribery. The offering of *nazars* and presents became common not only at the royal court and camp, but also in the households of imperial nobles and officers and became responsible for a great deal of corruption in administration. His display of pomp and magnificence extorted money from the unwilling masses and classes, and his sensual tastes set a bad standard of public and private morality."

Dr. Jadunath Sarkar has stated in his book *Studies in Mughal India* that Shah Jahan was "extremely laborious, yet the seed of disintegration of the Mughal empire was sown during his reign."

While discussing pros and coins of the reign of Shah Jahan, Dr. S.R. Sharma has observed, " In spite of the early rebellions, which were soon crushed; in spite of the foreign wars of aggression beyond the frontiers, which cost enormously with no return whatsoever; in spite of the famine in the Deccan and Gujarat, which devastated a vast portion of the country; and in spite of the constant fighting in the Deccan, which, while it resulted in the subjugation of Ahmadnagar, Golkunda, and Bijapur, also involved a great drain in the resources of the empire, the age of Shah Jahan showed much that was glorious, and many an unmistakable sign of unique prosperity, to justify this period being described as the Golden Age of the Empire."

Summing up

Shah Jahan occupies a place lower than his grand father Akbar but certainly a higher place than his father Jahangir and his son Aurangzeb.

Q. 3. Discuss the causes and results of the war of succession fought during Shah Jahan's reign.

Or

Give an account of the war of succession among the sons of Shah Jahan. What were the causes of success of Aurangzeb and the failure of Dara Shikoh.

Ans. *War of Succession* (1657-1658)

Why war of succession? There was no law of succession among the Mughals. Usually the 'strength of the sword' determined the successor.

Novelty of the war of succession during Shah Jahan's reign. The war of succession which took place among the four sons of Shah Jahan had one novelty. While previously, wars were fought after the death of the emperor, this war was fought when Shah Jahan was yet alive. Besides, all sons and daughters of Shah Jahan participated in it. While the four sons Dara Shikoh, Shah Shuja, Aurangzeb and Murad Bux fought against each other, the sisters allied themselves with one or the other brother. Jahan Ara supported Dara Shikoh, Roshen Ara supported Aurangzeb and Gauhan Ara sided with Murad Bux. Likewise the nobles and army commanders sided with one or the other contestant of the throne.

Special reasons of the war of succession during Shah Jahan's reign

1. *Rumours of Shah Jahan's death.* Early in September 1657, Shah Jahan fell ill. There was practically no hope of his recovery. He failed to attend the court for a long time. The rumour spread that he was dead. The death of an emperor was always an occasion of internal disruption and disturbance of peace. The probability of his death created rival groups in the court and empire.

2. *Dara's appointment as successor.* Shah Jahan decided to appoint Dara, his eldest son as his successor. His other sons and several staunch Muslim Ulemas and nobles did not like Dara on account of his liberal religious views.

3. *Selfish interests of courtiers.* The courtiers had their selfish motives to gain power by siding with the one or the other son.

4. *Desire of each prince to succeed.* All the four princes had been trained in the art of warfare and administration. They were working as governors and had their own desires to occupy the throne. They were all working as governors in various provinces—Dara of Punjab and Northwestern Province, Shujah of Bengal and Orissa, Aurangzeb of Deccan and Murad of Gujarat. Each had vast resources at his command.

5. *'Takht'* or *'Takhta'*. There was no love lost among the four princes. Each knew that only one would get the throne and others will be killed by the victor.

6. *Kingship knows no Kinship.* This was the general attitude of the princes.

7. *Lack of definite law of succession.* Sword was the determining factor to become the emperor.

Chief events of the war of succession

(*i*) *Declaration of being the emperor.* Prince Murad declared himself independent in Gujarat, Shah Shuja in Bengal and Murad in Gujarat.

(*ii*) *Diplomacy of Aurangzeb.* Aurangzeb kept his plans secret. He won over Murad by promising to give the provinces of Punjab, Sindh, Kabul and Kashmir.

(*iii*) *Battle of Bahadarpur.* Shah Shuja reached Banaras with his army. Dara sent an army to check him. Shah Shuja was defeated and ran away towards Bengal.

(*iv*) *Battle of Dharmat.* Aurangzeb and Murad advanced towards Agra. Dara also sent an army to fight but the army faced defeat.

(*v*) *Battle of Samugarh.* Dara without waiting for his victorious troops who have defeated Shuja, advanced toward Samugarh a place at a distance of about 13 km. from Agra. Initially Dara had an upper hand but he committed a blunder. He got down from his elephant and mounted a horse. Seeing him missing, commotion and disorder ensued in his army. Dara fled from the battlefield. Battle of Samugarh proved to be decisive.

(*vi*) *Besiege of Agra.* The combined forces of Aurangzeb and Murad reached Agra and besieged the fort. The royal army opposed them. After a few days of struggle, the royal army surrendered.

(*vii*) *Imprisonment of Shah Jahan.* Shah Jahan was imprisoned and died there in a pathetic situation after six years i.e. January 1666.

(*viii*) *End of Murad and Shah Shuja.* Aurangzeb did not adhere to the agreement arrived at with Murad. He used devious methods and got him murdered in Gwalior fort.

Shah Shuja had to run away from India and died outside in obscure circumstances.

(*ix*) *Sad end of Dara and his sons.* After his defeat, Dara wandered from place in different parts of India but was hotly chased and ultimately fell into Aurangzeb's, hands. He was paraded in dirty clothes in the city and awarded death punishment. His two sons were also given death punishment. In this way the war of succession ended with the victory of Aurangzeb.

Causes of Aurangzeb's success

1. *Personal qualities of Aurangzeb.* Aurangzeb was a more able commander than his brothers.

2. *Diplomacy of Aurangzeb.* He kept his plans secret and very diplomatically made Murad as his ally and afterwards in the same manner got him murdered. Murad was called at a feast at Mathura. There he was heavily drunk and in a state of unconsciousness taken to Gwalior fort where he was killed.

3. *Lack of unity in Dara's camp.* It is said that Aurangzeb was successful in creating division among the officers of Dara's army. Even Jaswant Singh, his faithful commander did not join him in his final struggle with Aurangzeb.

4. *Superior artillery of Aurangzeb.* Aurangzeb had appointed several Europeans in his artillery division. Dara's artillery and his soldiers could not compete with the superior artillery of Aurangzeb.

5. *Weakness of Shah Jahan.* In spite of the fact that Shah Jahan had declared Dara as his successor, he remained a silent spectator. Had he taken some interest, his loyal officers and army would have worked for the success of Dara. He also did not try to stop the rumour of his death.

6. *Unlucky Dara.* Fate was against Dara. When victory was just within his reach, his getting down from the elephant and riding the horse gave a wrong signal to his army. His army thought he was missing and lost the courage to fight.

Results of the war of succession

Aurangzeb won the war of succession and with his becoming the emperor of India, a new chapter of intense religious antagonism is said to have begun. Dr. Surjit Man Singh has described the situation in these words, "Some modern historians ascribe to Aurangzeb the intention of ruling India as an Islamic country. ...Some go further in tracing the seeds of partition in 1947 to him. Far-fetched though such judgements may be, it is certain that Aurangzeb died in his own words, "forlorn and destitute" and soon after that his empire disintegrated."

Q. 4. Write a short note on Dara Shikoh.

Ans. *Dara Shikoh* (1614-1659).

Personal Characteristics Dara Shikoh was the eldest and the most favourite son of Shah Jahan. He was highly educated in mysticism and philosophy. He studied the religious books of Islam and Hinduism. He loved and respected the Sufi Saints. He possessed good moral virtues. He commissioned Persian translations of Sanskrit texts. He was greatly influenced by the philosophical thought contained in the Upanishads. He was, by nature, large-hearted and tolerant. He had liberal religious views. He was hated by the fanatic Sunni Musalmans and had invited their wrath.

War of succession

(*a*) *Shah Jahan's illness.* Dara was very obedient to his father and carried on the administration of the territories under his charge according to the advice of his father. This deprived him of initiative. Shah Jahan declared him as his successor when he was seriously ill. Dara's three brothers did not like this. Each wanted to become the emperor of Delhi. This led to the war of succession among the four brothers.

(*b*) *Battle of Bahadarpur.* Prince Shah Shuja, the governor of Bengal marched with his army against Dara in February 1658. Dara attempted to stop him and sent an army under the leadership of his son Suleman Shikoh and Raja Jai Singh of Amir. Both the armies fought at Bahadurpur near Banaras. Shah Shuja was defeated and ran away towards Bengal.

Battle of Dharmat. Aurangzeb had entered into an agreement with Murad to share the Kingdom. Their combined forces advanced towards Agra. Dara sent an army to meet the challenge. Aurangzeb won and Dara's prestige suffered.

Battle of Samugarh. On hearing the defeat of his army, Dara himself advanced as the head of the army. He did not wait for the arrival of the victorious troops of Jai Singh and his son Suleman Shikoh. A fierce battle was fought at Samugarh near Agra. Initially Dara had an upper hand but he committed a blunder as fate would have it. He got down from his elephant and mounted a horse. Seeing him missing from the elephant, commotion ensured in his army. It is also said that one of his important commanders went over to the side of Aurangzeb. Dara fled from the battle-field towards Delhi. Battle of Samugarh proved to be decisive. Aurangzeb, thereafter, captured Delhi.

Causes of the failure of Dara

1. Luck was against him. His mounting on the horse gave a wrong signal to his army.

2. Dara did not wait for the victorious army of his son and Raja Jai Singh.

3. Aurangzeb's artillery proved more effective.

4. Many Muslim officers and soldiers defected and went over to the side of Aurangzeb. It may be stated here that on account of his liberal religious views, Dara was not liked by a section of Muslims.

5. Undoubtedly Aurangzeb was a superior commander than Dara.

Sad end of Dara. Dara went from place to place to collect a large army. He, however, failed in his attempts to do so. Aurangzeb's officers were pursuing him vigorously. He sought shelter with a Balloochi chief whose life he had saved once. But the Baloochi betrayed. Dara and his son Siphir Shikoh were sent to Delhi. Aurangzeb paraded Dara in the streets of Delhi in his dirty clothes, seated on a filthy elephant. Thereafter he was beheaded and his dead body shown to the public in the streets of Delhi. Dara's two sons were also awarded death punishment. Dara was buried near the tomb of Humayun at Delhi.

20

Aurangzeb (1658-1707)

Q. 1. Briefly describe the early career and main events of the reign of Aurangzeb.

Ans. *Main Events of Reign of Aurangzeb : Early life.*

Aurangzeb who assumed the title *'Abul-Muzaffar Mohin-ud-Din Muhammad Aurangzeb Bahadur Alamgir Badshah Ghazi'* after ascending the throne was the sixth of the fourteen children of Shah Jahan. He was born at Dahod near Ujjain in 1618. He intensely studied Arabic and Persian. He also studied Qoran and Hadees—sacred books of the Muslims. He was trained in horse riding and in the art of soldiering. Soon he became a successful fighter. He was very brave and daring.

Governor of various provinces. He worked as the governor of Deccan from 1636 to 1644 and 1652 to 1658. He also worked as the governor of Gujarat, Multan and Sind from time to time. As a governor, he demonstrated his great talents as an organiser, administrator, a diplomat and general. He organised the revenue system of Gujarat in such a way that it greatly added to its prosperity.

Aurangzeb's success in the war of succession. Shah Jahan's illness in 1657 led to a bloody war of succession among his four sons—Dara Shikoh, Shuja, Aurangzeb and Murad. Aurangzeb was successful in liquidating his three brothers, putting his father in prison and becoming the emperor of Delhi, through his diplomacy and bravery.

Chief Events of his Reign

1. Early measures taken by *Aurangzeb to strengthen his position.*

(*a*) *Popularity measures.* (*i*) He enhanced the salaries of officers. (*ii*) He abolished grain trade tax. (*iii*) He declined to accept gifts. (*iv*) He gave titles to his supporters.

(*b*) *Puritan measures.* (*i*) Aurangzeb banned the celebration of *'Nauroz'* as it was an alient practice (*ii*) He banned music. (*iii*) He stopped the practice of weighing the emperor in silver and gold. (*iv*) He appointed *'Muhtasibs'* (moral preachers) for the ethical uplift of the Muslims. (*v*) He stopped the practice of *'jharokha'* (public audience) as it was termed as a blind faith.

2. *Religious disharmony.* By following anti-Hindu and anti-Shia policy, he antagonised the majority of population.

3. *Revolts on account of Aurangzeb policy.* Following revolts took place.

(*a*) *Conflict with the Jats.* There were three revolts of the Jats of Mathura against the Mughal tyranny. These revolts were primarily on account of the anti-Hindu policy of Aurangzeb. They could not tolerate the demolition of their temples. They resented the construction of a mosque at the site of the birth place of Lord Krishna at Mathura. The land revenue charged from them was very heavy. The attitude of Abdul Nalu, the Faujdar of Mathura also led to great resentment against the Mughal rule.

The conflict continued for a long time and ultimately after the death of Aurangzeb, the Jats succeeded in establishing their kingdom with its capital at Bharatpur.

(*b*) *Conflict with the Satnamis.* The Satnamis formed a Hindu religious sect in the district of Narnaul and Mewat. Most of them carried on agriculture. Generally they were pious people. However, they would not tolerate any oppression. They kept arms and weapons to protect themselves from any kind of attempt to do wrong to them. An innocent Satnami cultivator was murdered by a Mughal soldier. Being agitated they rose in rebellion and killed the local Mughal official. The Mughal army retaliated with a heavy hand. Aurangzeb himself decided to go in person to Narnaul as he apprehended a general revolt of the Hindus in the entire region. Aurangzeb attacked them with a heavy force supported by artillery. The Satnamis were massacred indiscriminately. The rebellion was crushed but the people began to hate the rule and looked forward for an opportunity to get rid of the oppressive rule of the Mughals.

(*c*) *Conflict with the Sikhs.* The conflict between the Sikhs and the Mughal rulers started during the reign of Jahangir when Guru Arjun Dev, the fifth Guru of the Sikhs was tortured to death by him. The struggle became intensive during the reign of Aurangzeb. The ninth guru Guru Teg Bahadur (1664-75) was greatly hurt and distressed at the persecution of the Hindus by Aurangzeb. He openly expressed his resentment against this policy. Aurangzeb summoned him to Delhi and asked him to embrace Islam. On his refusal to do so, he was put to death after a lot of torture. Gurudwara Sisganj at Chandni Chowk in Delhi stands at the place of his martyrdom. Conflict with the Sikhs continued during the entire period of Aurangzeb.

4. *Rajput policy of Aurangzeb and conflicts with them.* He tried to crush the Rajputs; removed them from higher offices, levied the Jizya tax on them; attempted to do away with the independence of Marwar, resulting into fateful consequences.

(1) *Conflict with Bundelkhand.* Champat Rai revolted in Bundelkhand and his son Chatrasal defeated the Mongols several times.

(2) *Conflict with Marwar.* After the death of Jaswant Singh Aurangzeb tried to secure his infant son but Durga Dass foiled his attempts. The

conflict continued for 30 years and in the end Bahadur Shah recognised Marwar as an independent kingdom.

(3) *Conflict with Mewar.* Rana Raj Singh of Mewar fought against Aurangzeb. The Rana and Durga Dass incited Akbar to rebel against his father. In 1684, he made peace with Mewar.

5. *The Deccan policy.* Aurangzeb was guided by the following reasons

(1) Aurangzeb was ambitious, (2) He wanted to conquer the Deccan, (3) The internal condition of the Shiaite kingdoms was miserable, (4) Fear of the union of the three forces, (5) Puritanism led him to do it, (6) wanted to conquer the south due to Akbar's revolt, (7) The kingdoms stopped paying the tributes.

Following were the results of his Deccan policy.

(*i*) Expansion of the empire, (*ii*) Laxity in the empire, (*iii*) Removal of the restrictions on the Marathas, (*iv*) The state treasury became empty, (*v*) Indiscipline in the north, (*vi*) Impaired the dignity of the empire; (*vii*) Slackened the development of culture.

6. *Conflict with the Marathas.* Aurangzeb's conflict with Shivaji started in 1659 and continued till Shivaji's death in 1680. In spite of the huge army and enormous resources of Aurangzeb, Shivaji was successful in establishing a strong Maratha empire.

7. *Conflict with the North-east.* In spite of best efforts Assam could not be captured.

8. *Conflict with the Afghans.* The Mughal forces suffered heavy losses in the conflict that lasted for a decade. Ultimately the united front of the Afghans was broken and slowly peace restored.

9. *Conflict with the English.* After a minor conflict, peace was restored between the parties.

10. *Conflict with sons.* Being of suspicious nature, Aurangzeb remained in conflict with his four sons. He kept three of his sons in prison for a number of years.

Aurangzeb's Character (*i*) Brave and successful general. (*ii*) Simple life. (*iii*) Scholar of merit. (*iv*) Great diplomat. (*v*) Devoted to religion. (*vi*) Firm and resolute.

Most Pathetic last days of Aurangzeb. Aurangzeb died as a frustrated and sad man. He wrote very pathetic letters to his sons. To prince Azam he wrote, "I have not done well for the country and its people." To Kam Bakh, he wrote." "Strange that I came with nothing into this world and now go away with this stupendous caravan of sins."

Q. 2. Discuss the religious policy of Aurangzeb. Also describe its effects.

Or

"By his religious policy Aurangzeb destroyed the basis of the Mughal dynasty." Discuss.

Ans. *Fanatic Religious Policy of Aurangzeb.*

The general view of historians is that Aurangzeb entirely reversed the policy of religious toleration followed by Akbar and it resulted in serious revolts among the Hindus.

In the words of Lane-Poole, "For the first time in their history, the Mughals beheld a rigid Muslim in their emperor—a Muslim as sternly repressible of himself as of his people around him, a king who was prepared to stake his throne for sake of his faith. He must have been fully conscious of the dangerous path he was pursuing, and well aware ... against every Hindu sentiment. Yet he chose this course, and adhered to this with unbending resolve through close on fifty years of unchallenged sovereignty."

Dr. S.R. Sharma, writing about the acts of religious intolerance of Aurangzeb has observed, "These were not the acts of a righteous ruler of constructive statesman, but the outbursts of blind fanaticism, unworthy of the great genius that Aurangzeb undoubtedly possessed in all other aspects."

Aims of Aurangzeb's religious policy. It is generally accepted that Aurangzeb was a fanatic Sunni Mussalman. His chief aim was to convert *Dar-ul-harb* (India : the country of *Kafirs* or infidels) to *Dar-ul-Islam* (country of Islam). He was intolerant towards other faiths, especially Hindus. He was also against Shia Muslims.

Aurangzeb's religious policy had two aspects i.e. (*i*) To promote the tenets of Islam and to ensure that the people led their lives accordingly (*ii*) To adopt anti-Hindu measures.

Anti-Hindu measures. Following were the anti-Hindu measures adopted by Aurangzeb :

1. *Demolishing temples and breaking idols.* Even as a governor of Deccan he had pulled down several temples including the important Chintamani temple of Ahmedabad which he replaced with a mosque. He followed this practice vigorously after becoming emperor of India. In the first year of his reign, he issued orders to the governor of Orissa to demolish all temples in the province. In the twelfth year of his rule, he ordered the demolition of all important and famous temples within his empire. Mosques were built at the sites of different temples.

In Mewar alone, he is said to have demolished 240 temples.

The most famous of the temples destroyed were those of Keshva (Krishan Janmabhoomi) in Mathura, Vishwanath in Varanasi and Somnath in Kathiawar.

2. *Imposition of Jaziya.* Akbar had abolished this tax on the Hindus but Aurangzeb again levied this tax.

According to Elliot, the object of reimposing the Jaziya or poll tax *"was to curb the infidels and to distinguish the land of the faithful from an infidel land."* Manucci however, holds that the object of the tax was two-fold; first to fill up his treasury which had begun to shrink on account of expenditure on his various military campaigns; secondly to force the Hindus to embrace Islam.

Aurangzeb issued very strict instructions to the officers regarding the collection of Jaziya : "You are free to grant remissions of revenue of all other kinds; but if you remit any man's Jaziya which I succeeded with great difficulty in laying on the infidels it will be an impious charge and will cause the whole system of collecting the poll tax to fall into disorder." It is alleged that when thousands of Hindus gathered to protest against this measure, the Emperor directed his elephants against the people so that many people fell trodden to death, under the feet of the elephants.

General nature of anti-Hindu policy. *Haig* draws the picture of the religious policy of Aurangzeb in the following words :

"Aurangzeb was a bigot to whom the religion of the great majority of his subjects was anathema, mischief, idolatry, which it was his duty before heaven to persecute and if possible to stamp out. His methods were iconoclasm, sacrilege, economic repression, bribery, forced conversion and restriction of worship."

3. *Discriminatory toll tax.* The Hindu traders were required to pay a toll tax of 5 per cent as against half of it paid by the Muslim traders. Later on Muslim traders were totally exempted from the payment of this tax.

4. *Removal of the Hindus from Government jobs.* Aurangzeb's predecessors, especially Akbar had appointed a large number of Hindus in the various departments, but Aurangzeb followed the policy of removal of the Hindus from these jobs. The Hindus were not allowed to occupy high administrative or executive posts. A general order prohibiting the employment of the Hindus in the revenue department was passed in 1670. But as it resulted in the complete breakdown of the efficiency, the order was slightly modified and Hindus were allowed to work on certain limited posts in the revenue department.

5. *Restrictions on Hindu educational institutions.* For destroying the culture of the Hindus, Aurangzeb destroyed their several educational institutions at Varanasi, Multan and Thatta. He placed restrictions on the starting of new pathshalas. The Hindu children were disallowed to study the fundamentals of their faith. They were not allowed to attend Muslim *Madaras* and Maqtabs.

6. *Conversion through different means.* For the Hindus the only way to escape from the payment of various taxes like pilgrim tax, trade tax, Jizya, etc. was conversion to Islam. Getting jobs after conversion also became easier. The Hindu prisoners were fieed on their conversion to Islam. All sorts of promises were made to the converted.

7. *Social restrictions.* Aurangzeb issued order that except Rajputs, no Hindu could ride an elephant, a horse and a palanquin. Holi and Diwali festivals were allowed to be celebrated with certain restrictions. The Hindus

could no longer put on fine clothes. The Hindus were not allowed to burn their dead on the banks of the river Sabarmati in Ahmedabad. Similar restrictions were placed at Delhi on the river Jamuna.

Results of the religious policy of Aurangzeb. The religious fanaticism of Aurangzeb overshadowed his virtues. His reversal of Akbar's policy of religious toleration resulted in weakening the entire structure of the Mughal empire. It led to several conflicts and wars in different parts of the country. These conflicts were (*i*) Conflict with the Jats (*ii*) Conflict with the Satnamos (*iii*) Conflict with the Sikhs (*iv*) Conflicts with the Rajputs (*v*) Conflict with the Marathas. All these rebellions destroyed the peace of the empire, disrupted its economy, weakened the administrative structure, diminished its military strength, led to the failure of Aurangzeb to make any impact. Ultimately all these contributed to the downfall of the Mughal empire.

Was Aurangzeb really anti-Hindu?

A few historians have tried to justify Aurangzeb's religious policy. They state that this policy was the outcome of his political and economic considerations. He was an imperialist and he wanted to strengthen his hold on his subjects. Since several sections of the Hindu society which formed the majority of his subjects did not want to be ruled by him, they revolted. His Deccan campaigns against the Shia Sultans were also the outcome of his expansionist policy. Regarding special taxes imposed upon the Hindus, it is argued that Aurangzeb was in need of money to carry out his policy of expansion. He therefore, imposed different kinds of taxes. Since Hindus were quite rich, they had to bear the burden of various taxes. But no argument is put forward by the protagonists of this view as why he took pains to demolish temples and break idols.

The following three letters written by him to his sons clearly establish the fact that he was a staunch Musalman and he wanted to promote his religion.

These letters also indicate that he himself considered himself a failure as a ruler.

About the letters Dr. V. Smith says that *"The sternest critic of the character and deeds of Aurangzeb can hardly refuse to recognise the pathos of these lamentations or to feel some sympathy for the old man on his lonely death-bed."*

Letter to Prince Muazzam. "My years have gone by profitless. God has been in my heart yet my darkened eyes have not recognised his light. There is no hope for me in the future. You should accept my last will. It should not happen that Musalmans be killed and the blame for their death rest upon this useless creature. I have greatly sinned and know not what torment awaits me. I commit you and your sons to the care of God and bid you farewell. May peace of God be upon you."

Letter to Prime Azam. "I know not what punishment be in store for me to suffer. Though my trust be in the mercy of goodness of God, I deplore my sins. When I have lost hope in myself, how can I hope in others? Come what will, I have launched my bark upon the waters! Farewell! Farewell!"

Letter to Kambakh. "Soul of my soul. Now I am going alone. I grieve for your helplessness. But what is the use? Every torment I have inflicted, every sin I have committed, every wrong have done, I carry the consequence with me. Strange that I came with nothing into the world and now go away with this stupendous caravan of sins! Whatever I look I see only God. You should accept my last will. It should not happen that Musalmans be killed and the reproach should fall on the head of this useless creature. I commit your and your sons to the care of God and bid you farewell. I am sourly troubled; May the peace of God be upon you."

Q. 3. Critically review the Rajput policy of Aurangzeb.

Ans. *Aurangzeb's policy of conflict with the Rajputs.*

It is generally believed by the historians that one of the major causes of the decline of the Mughal empire was the policy of conflict followed by Aurangzeb with the Rajputs. Aruangzeb completely reversed Akbar's policy.

Aurangzeb's Rajput policy led to conflict on account of the following factors :

1. Aurangzeb was an expansionist and on one or the other pretext, he wanted to annex their kingdoms.

2. Aurangzeb regarded the power and influence of the Rajputs as a stumbling block in executing his policy of religious persecution of the Hindus.

Chief events were as under :

(*i*) *Conflict with Marwar.* Raja Jaswant Singh the ruler of Marwar who was in the service of the Mughals died at Jamrud in Afghanistan. His wife, while returning from Afganistan, gave birth to a son who was named Ajit Singh. Aurangzeb wanted that if Ajit Singh was converted to Islam, he would be recognised as the ruler of Marwar. But this was not acceptable to the Rajputs. This led to the beginning of the 30-year war between the Rathors and the Mughals. Aurangzeb wanted to keep the widow of Jaswant Singh and his son Ajit Singh under his custody. Durga Das, the brave commander of the Rathors rescued the mother and the son by a stratagem, substituting the maid-servant and her child in place of the Rani and the prince. The peɔple of Marwar accepted Ajit Singh as their ruler. Annoyed at this, Aurangzeb sent his Imperial troops to subdue the Rajputs. Aurnagzeb himself camped at Ajmer. The Mughal forces captured Jodhpur, the capital of Marwar and destroyed numerous temples. Durga Das continued the struggle and the Rajputs were able to recapture many of their lost territories. After the death of Aurangzeb, his successor Bahadur Shah recognised Ajit Singh as an independent ruler of Marwar. The Rajputs still cherish the courage and bravery of Durga Das and say, "O, mother, produce a son like Durga Das." J.N. Sarkar writes of him, "Mughal gold could not subdue him. Mughal arms could not daunt that constant heart."

(*ii*) *Conflict with Mewar.* The conflict continued for about 5 years (1676-81). Raj Singh of the Sisodiya clan was the ruler of Mewar with its capital at Chittor. Aurangzeb asked him to pay the *Jaziya.* Prince Akbar (son of Aurnagzeb) deserted the Mughal army and joined hands with the Rajputs. Akbar was of liberal views and doubted the success of the policy of religious fanaticism of his father. Maharana Raj Singh and Ajit Singh assured him that if he would declare himself the emperor, the combined forces of Marwar and Mewar would support him. Prince Akbar declared himself the emperor of the Mughals. Aurangzeb had a very small force at his command at that time as he was away from the capital. So he thought of a plan of sowing dissensions among the Rajputs. He was successful in his efforts. Prince Akbar was defeated and he fled away. Aurangzeb and the new ruler of Mewar, Raja Jai Singh signed a peace treaty known as treaty of Udaipur (1681). The treaty included the following forms :

(1) The Mughals agreed to withdraw their forces from Mewar.

(2) Raja Jai Singh accepted the *Mansab* of 5,000 while his son Bhim Singh was given the title of Raja.

(3) The Chittor fort was not to be repaired.

(*iii*) *Conflict with Bundelkhand.* Akbar was not successful on account of the guerilla warfare tactics of the Bundela Rajputs. Champat Rai, Rajput ruler of Bundelkhand came into conflict with Aurnagzeb. However, he committed suicide to save himself from imprisonment. Chhatrasal, son of Champat Rai who was just 11 at the time of his father's death defied the Mughals and won several victories against them. Ultimately he was able to set up an independent state in eastern Malwa. He died in 1731 with the complete effacement of the Mughal rule in Bundelkhand. The people of Bundelkhand and Malwa hailed Chhatrasal as the "Champion of the Hindu faith and Rajput honour."

Consequences of Aurangzeb's Rajput policy. The Rajput policy proved very disastrous for the Mughals, as it made the Rajputs hostile and deprived Aurnagzeb of the loyalty of the brave Rajputs. He wasted several years in conflict with them and suffered serious setbacks. Several of his own famous generals were killed in conflict with the Rajput rulers. He failed to subdue Durga Das of Marwar. He had to enter into treaty with Mewar. Chhatrasal of Bundelkhand defied the Mughals. Prestige of the Mughal empire suffered. Aurangzeb, on account of constant conflicts could not provide good administration. No doubt, the faulty policy of Aurangzeb towards the Rajputs was one of the major causes of the disintegration of the Mughal empire.

Q. 4. Critically examine the Deccan policy of Aurangzeb. To what extent can it be held responsible for the downfall of the Mughal empire?

Or

Discuss the Deccan policy of Aurangzeb.

(Rajastan University 1993)

Or

Review the policy of Aurangzeb towards Bijapur and Golkunda. Why was it unsuccessful?

Or

How did Aurangzeb conquer Bijapur and Golkunda? What were its consequences? **(Punjab Universitv. April 1993)**

Ans. *The Deccan as the Watershed of Aurangzeb.*

Aurangzeb spent the last twenty five years (1681-1701) of his reign in his conflict with three powers of Bijapur, Golkunda and the Marathas. It is held by historians that the Deccan policy of Aurangzeb proved very disastrous for the Mughal empire.

Aurnagzeb's conflicts with the Deccan powers are given here in brief

Reasons for Aurangzeb's campaign in the South. Following were the reasons for his campaign and stay in South India.

First, Aurangzeb was highly ambitious, expansionist and imperialist and wanted the control of entire India.

Second, Aurangzeb wanted to crush the Hindu Maratha power in its infancy.

Third, two kingdoms of the South i.e. Bijapur and Golkunda were Shia Muslim Kingdoms. Aurangzeb being a fanatic Sunni Muslim could not tolerate the Shia kingdoms.

Fourth, Aurangzeb feared that if all these three Kingdoms got united, they could pose a great threat to him.

Fifth, Prince Akbar (Aurangzeb's son) had revolted against him and taken refuge with the Marathas.

Sixth, the rulers of Marwar and Mewar had established their contacts with Sambhaji (son of Shivaji).

Seventh, the rulers of the Deccan had stopped paying the annual tribute to the Mughal empire.

Eighth, the states of Bijapur and Golkunda were not on good terms and this factor could be exploited in capturing these kingdoms, one by one.

Ninth, Aurangzeb had been the governor of Deccan (which did not include Bijapur and Golkunda) for two terms, and he was very keen to complete the unfinished task.

1. *Conflict with Bijapur*

Reasons.

(*i*) Bijapur was a Shia state and Aurangzeb was a Sunni Musalman.

(*ii*) Aurangzeb was an imperialist.

(*iii*) Aurangzeb wanted the cooperation of Bijapur against the Marathas.

(*iv*) Aurangzeb wanted to recover from Bijapur the land tract of Ahmednagar which Shah Jahan had given to Bijapur.

(*v*) The ruler of Bijapur had failed to hand over the fort of Purander and one crore rupees by 1660 as decided by the treaty of Purander in 1657.

Events and result. After a fierce struggle lasting for more than twenty years, Bijapur was annexed to the Mughal empire.

2. *Conflict with Golkunda.*

Reasons

(*i*) Aurangzeb was an imperialist and he wanted to extend his empire.

(*ii*) Golkunda was a Shia State and therefore an eye-sore for Aurangzeb.

(*iii*) Aurangzeb was greatly tempted to grab the wealth and riches of Golkunda.

(*iv*) The ruler of Golkunda was helping the Marathas against the Mughals.

(*v*) The Prime Minister of Golkunda was Madana Pandit–a Hindu and he wielded a great influence.

Events and results. After conquering Bijapur, Aurangzeb laid a siege to Golkunda. The seize lasted for about eight months but without any success. Aurangzeb bribed one of the chiefs of Golkunda who opened the gates. The fort was occupied. The Sultan Abul Hasan was imprisoned and Golkunda was annexed to the Mughal empire.

3. *Conflict with the Marathas.*

The conflict with the Marathas continued for about twenty five years of the reign of Aurangzeb.

(*i*) *Conflict with Shivaji.* Aurangzeb's conflict with Shivaji started in 1659 and continued till Shivaji's death in 1680. In spite of the huge army and enormous resources of Aurangzeb, Shivaji was successful in establishing a strong Maratha empire.

(*ii*) *Conflict with Sambhaji* (1680 to 1689). In 1681, Aurangzeb's son, Akbar, came to seek the help of Sambhaji, son of Shivaji. Aurangzeb, therefore, decided to take action against him. Sambhaji was captured and tortured to death.

(*iii*) *Conflict with Raja Ram* (1689-1700). There was a great resentment among the Marathas over the execution of Sambhaji. They made Raja Ram, Shivaji's second son, their ruler and started their campaign for independence. Raja Ram died in 1700 but the Marathas continued their struggle.

(*iv*) *Conflict with Tarabai* (1700 to 1707). Raja Ram's wife Tara Devi made her four-year son Shiva II, the ruler and she acted as his guardian and fought against the Mughals. Aurangzeb and his forces became desperate and wanted some sort of settlement.

Results of the Deccan policy of Aurangzeb

Aurangzeb's Deccan policy has been condemned universally.

In the words of Dr. R.C. Majumdar, "From the conquest of the Deccan, the most disappointed and dismayed chapter of his life commenced."

J.N. Sarkar has very beautifully described the results of the Deccan policy as, "All seemed to have been gained by Aurangzeb now; but in reality all was lost. It was the beginning of the end."

According to Dr. V.A. Smith, "Deccan was the grave of Aurangzeb's reputation as well of his body."

Following were the important results of Aurangzeb's Deccan policy.

1. *Free-field for the Marathas.* The campaigns of the Deccan kingdoms kept the Mughal army so busy that restraint on the rising power of the Marathas could not be possible. Aurangzeb's failure to check the Marathas emboldened them to attack Mughal territories.

2. *Heavy Strain on financial position of the state.* The Deccan campaign led almost to financial bankruptcy of the government. As a result thereof, the army could not be paid for about three years. It led to grave demoralisation of the army.

3. *Decay of agriculture and trade.* The vast Mughal army of about 2 lakh soldiers was like a swarm of locust that destroyed the thriving agriculture.

4. *Weakening of administration.* Absence of the emperor for about twenty years from the capital led to slackness in administration. There was no effective control over government officials. Administration became corrupt as well as oppressive.

5. *Emergence of new political forces.* On account of his preoccupation with the affairs of the Deccan, several sections of population got an opportunity to consolidate their strength in North India.

6. *Adverse effect on the cultural life.* Constant wars in the North and the South during the period of Aurangzeb deprived the people of a cultured life.

7. *Loss of prestige.* The failure of Aurangzeb to deal effectively with the Marathas lowered the dignity of the Mughal empire.

Summing up the Rajput Policy of the Deccan

In the words of J.N. Sarkar, "If Spanish ulcer ruined Napoleon, Deccan ulcer also ruined Aurangzeb."

Q. 5. Write a short note on the relations of Jaswant Singh and Aurangzeb.

Ans. *Jaswant Singh's Relations with Aurangzeb*

Period of hostility Jaswant Singh, Rajput Chief of Jodhpur occupied an important place in the court of Shah Jahan. He enjoyed a *'Mansab'* of 7000 *'Zat'* and 7000 *'Sawar'*. In the war of succession during Shah Jahan's reign, in the beginning he sided with Dara and fought against Aurangzeb. After his defeat in the battle of Dharmat at the hands of Aurangzeb, he ran away to Mewar. The victory enhanced the prestige of Aurangzeb.

Period of neutrality. When Dara attempted to replenish his forces after the battle of Dharmat, he repeatedly sent letters to Jaswant Singh. However, there was no response from Jaswant Singh. Jaswant Singh thought it to be prudent to remain neutral in the war of succession.

On the Side of Aurangzeb. Rana of Udaipur was won over by Aurangzeb. Seeing this, Jaswant Singh also followed suit. Aurangzeb pardoned him, gave back his Mansab and appointed him the governor of Gujarat.

The Afghans created a lot of trouble in Afghanistan. Jaswant Singh was sent to Jamrud to suppress the Afghans. From 1671 to 1678, he was the Faujdar at Jamrud. In 1678, he died fighting there. His wife, while returning from Afghanistan, gave birth to a son who was named Ajit Singh. Aurangzeb wanted that if Ajit Singh was converted to Islam, he would be recognised as the ruler of Mewar. Aurangzeb also wanted to keep the widow of Jaswant Singh under his custody. But this was not acceptable to the Rajputs.

The treatment given to the son and widow of a faithful general indicates the low trait of Aurangzeb's personality. This led to the beginning of the 30-year war between the Rathors and the Mughals.

Q. 6. Write notes on :

(*i*) Guru Teg Bahadur (*ii*) Guru Gobind Singh

Ans. *Guru Teg Bahadur* (1621 to 1675) : (1664-1675-Period of Gurudum).

From the time of the martyrdom of Guru Arjun Dev in 1606, the Mughal-Sikh relations had been deteriorating. This deep-rooted enmity became the basic cause of Guru Teg Bahadur's martyrdom during Aurangzeb's reign.

Aurangzeb's fanaticism led to a good deal of resentment among the Hindus. The greatest victim of the fanatic activities of Aurangzeb were the Kashmiri Pandits/Brahamans. Tired of the atrocities of the emperor, they approached Guru Teg Bahadur for protection. It is said that having heard their manifold sufferings, the Guru said before his 9 year-old son Gobind Singh, "There is a need of a great sacrifice now for without this the reign of terror will never come to an end." At this moment, the son exclaimed, "What sacrifice can be more great than your own august self for such a holy and noble cause!" Greatly impressed by these words, the Guru decided to sacrifice himself. He, therefore, advised the Brahmans to approach Aurangzeb with the message that if he succeeded in converting Guru Teg Bahadur to Islam, they would all embrace Islam. Aurangzeb then called the Guru to Delhi. On his refusal to embrace Islam, the Guru was beheaded after a lot of torture.

Gurudwara Sisganj in Chandni Chowk in Delhi stands at the place of his martyrdom.

The execution of Guru Teg Bahadur is significant from religious and political points of view.

First, to die for the sake of religion was the sacred tradition of the Guru.

Second, it was responsible for Guru Gobind's resolve to wreck vengeance upon the Mughals.

Third, it led to the birth of Khalsa and made the Sikhs a martial race.

Fourth, it became a major factor which contributed to the downfall of the Mughal empire.

(Guru) Gobind Singh (1666-1708)

Early life. Gobind Singh, the tenth Guru (1675-1708) of the Sikhs and the founder of the Khalsa, whose original name was Gobind Rai, was born in Patna (Bihar). He was only nine when he had to perform cremation rites of the severed head of his father, Guru Teg Bahadur (1664-1675) who was the ninth Guru of the Sikhs. It may be recalled that the ninth Guru was executed with the approval of Aurangzeb.

For more than a decade, the young Guru lived in the foothills of western Uttar Pradesh and studied Persian and Sanskrit. He was well-versed in horse riding. He wrote devotional hymns.

Guru Gobind's return to Punjab and the founding of the Khalsa. After returning to Punjab, he settled at a place today known as Anandpur Sahib. The execution of Guru Teg Bahadur had sent a wave of resentment among the Sikhs. Guru Gobind Singh transformed the Sikh community into a strong sect. He took the following steps in this regard :

(1) He imparted military training to his followers.

(2) He built a chain of fortresses between the river Sutlej and Yamuna.

(3) He accepted offerings of arms and horses.

(4) He asked the Sikh males to add Singh (Lion) to their names and Sikh females to add *'Kaur'* (Liones or princess).

(5) He asked the Sikhs to put on a distinct dress on their person. The distinguishing characteristics of their dress are five *'Kakori'* words starting with *'Ka'* the first consonant of Nagri Varnamala. They are (*i*)—*'Kesh'* unshaven hair (*ii*) *'Kara'*—the iron bracelet worn on hand. (*iii*) *'Kachcha'*-lower undergarment (*iv*) *'Kirpan'*—sword and (*v*) *'Kangha'*—hair comb.

Guru Gobind's Singh's cultural, religious and religious contribution

(*i*) He patronised poets and scholars and sent them to Banaras to study Sanskrit and the Vedas to better interpret the teachings of the earlier Gurus.

(*ii*) He declared *Granth Sahib*, the holiest book of the Sikhs as their Guru.

(*iii*) He abolished the institution of the human Guru itself.

(*iv*) He founded the *'Khalsa Panth'* on the Baisakhi festival (April 13, 1699) amids a huge congregation from whom the Guru demanded sacrifice'. The first five men (Panj Pyaras) to offer themselves were baptised by him.

(*v*) He compiled a definitive edition of *Granth Sahib.*

(*vi*) He collected his own works in the *'Dasam Granth.*

(*vii*) He abolished all symbols of castes.

Guru Gobind's struggle with the Mughals. As already mentioned the execution (martyrdom called by the Sikhs) of Guru Teg Bahadur had sent a wave of resentment among the Sikhs. Guru Gobind Singh opposed the religious fanaticism of Aurangzeb throughout his life. He used to say, "I shall make men of all four castes lions and destroy the Mughals." He made Anandpur Sahib as his headquarters. He collected a very dedicated band of followers and imparted military training to them. He organised a force of about 80,000 men. Aurangzeb despatched many armies against Guru Gobind Singh. The local Mughal officers also constantly fought against him and besieged Anandpur five times. But the Guru maintained his spirits against all odds and fought against the Mughals. Several times, he defeated the Mughal armies but he had also to suffer heavily. The major battles of Sirsa and Chamkaur in 1705 resulted in thousands of deaths. Two of Guru's sons were killed during the course of fighting and the remaining two were captured and killed by the Faujdar of Sarhind. The Guru's death took place in 1708 at Nadir at the banks of the river Godavari. He was stabbed to death by an Afghan when he was busy in his prayers. Regarding Guru Gobind's achievements, Cunnigham has observed, "The last apostle (Guru) of the Sikhs did not live to see his end accomplished, but he effectively roused the dormant energies of a vanquished people, and filled them with a lofty, although fitful longing for social freedom and national ascendency."

Q. 7. "When judged as a sovereign, Aurangzeb must be pronounced a failure." Comment upon this statement.

Or

How far was Aurangzeb responsible for the downfall of the Mughal empire? (Punjab University, April 1997, Oct. 1997, April 1998)

Or

Give an estimate of Aurangzeb as a person and as a ruler.

Ans. *Aurangzeb's Responsibility for the Downfall of the Mughal Empire.*

Aurangzeb's failure as a man and a ruler is amply reflected in his letters which he wrote to his sons prince Muazzam Azam and Kambakh during the last days of his life.

To prince Muazzam, he wrote, "My years have gone by profitless...I have greatly sinned and know not what torment awaits me."

To prince Azam, Aurangzeb wrote, "I deplore my sins."

To prince Kambakh, he wrote, "Strange that I came with nothing into the world and now go away with this stupendous caravan of sins."

Notwithstanding his mastery over 'pen and sword', his simple habits and personal purity, and the fact that under him the Mughal empire reached its greatest extent, Aurangzeb has been considered as a failure. It is also true that some of the Muslim writers extol him as a *'Zinda pir'* (living saint) because of his pious nature and living in accordance with Islamic tenets.

The general observations of historians about Aurangzeb are that he was neither a good son, nor a good father, nor a good brother, nor a good administrator and above all not a good ruler.

After going through the events of his reign, one is forced to come to the conclusion that Aurangzeb must share the blame for the downfall of the Mughal empire.

Following are the reasons which are usually given to indicate the responsibility of Aurangzeb to the downfall of the Mughal empire.

1. *Multifarious responsibilities of Aurangzeb for the downfall of the Mughal empire.* In the words of Dr. V. Smith. "Judged as a sovereign he must be pronounced a failure. His intense suspiciousness poisoned his whole life. He never trusted anybody and consequently was ill served. His cold calculating temperament rarely permitted him to indulge in love for man or woman and few indeed were the persons who loved him. His reliance on mere cunning as the principal instrument of statecraft testified as a certain smallness of mind, and moreover, was ineffective in practice. Although he had many opportunities for winning military distinction, he failed to show ability as a general whether before or after accession. His proceedings in Deccan during the latter part of his life were simply ridiculous, as military operation. In fact nothing in the history of Aurangzeb justifies posterity in classing him as a great king. His tricky cunning was mainly directed, first to winning, and then to keeping the throne. He did nothing for literature or art. Rather it should be said that he did less than nothing, because he discouraged both."

2. *Reactionary nature of Aurangzeb.* According to J.N. Sarkar, "Obsessed by narrow ideal of duty and supremely ignorant of the real limitations of his character and not out of political cunning, as Manucci suggests, Aurangzeb practised saintly austerities and self-abasement and went regularly and even ostentatiously through all the observances of his religion. Politically, therefore Aurangzeb with all these virtues was a complete failure. But the cause of the failure of his reign lay deeper than his personal character. Though it is not true that he alone caused the fall of the Mughal empire, yet he did nothing to avert it but deliberately quickened the destructive forces always present in rigid theocratic forms of Government, because he was a reactionary by instinct and no reforming statesman."

3. *Slackness of administrative machinery.* According to Dr. V.S. Smith, "The system of administration while substantially the same as in Akbar's days, was worse in operation, because Aurangzeb failed to keep a firm hand over his subordinates, and when he grew old he was unable to make his authority respected."

4. *Religious fanaticm of Aurangzeb.* Describing acts of religious intolerance of Aurangzeb, Dr. S.R. Sharma writes: "These were not the acts of a righteous ruler or a constructive statesman, but the outbursts of blind fanaticism, unworthy of the great genius that Aurangzeb undoubtedly possessed in all other respects." The religious fanaticism of Aurangzeb set aside all his virtues. He entirely reversed the policy of religious toleration enunciated by Akbar which resulted in weakening the entire structure of the Mughal empire. It resulted in many serious revolts of the Hindus.

5. *No fear of punishment.* Khafi Khan says, "Of all the sovereigns of the House of Timur—nay, of all the sovereigns of Delhi—no one, since, Sikandar Lodhi; had ever been apparently so distinguished for devotion, austerity and justice. In courage, long-suffering, and sound judgement he was unrivalled. But from reverence for the injunction of law he did not make use of punishment, and without punishment the administration of a country cannot be maintained. Dissensions had arisen among his nobles through rivalry. He often passed his rights in vigils and devotion, and he denied himself many pleasures naturally belonging to humanity."

6. *Lack of intelligence system.* Ghulam Husain has stated, "The roads and passes being neglected everyone passed and repassed, unobserved : no intelligence report was forwarded to court of what was happening; and neither Emperor nor Minister even asked why no intelligence report of that kind ever reached their ears."

7. *Selfishment of Mughal generals.* Bernier says, "The Mughal generals conduct every operation with labour and avail themselves of any pretext for the prolongation of war which is alike the source of their emolument and dignity. It has become a proverbial saying that the Deccan is the bread and support of the soldiers of Hindustan."

8. *Laziness of Amirs.* Fryer says, "The policy of Aurangzeb was frustrated chiefly by the means of the soldiers and great Amirs (*Omrahs*), who live lazily and in pay, whereupon they term, the Deccan (Ducoan) the bread of the military men."

9. *Deccan as the graveyard.* In the words of Dr. V. Smith, "The too cunning old autocrat wasted the last twentysix years of his reign. The Deccan, from which he never returned, was the grave of his reputation as well as of his body."

10. *Luxurious army camp.* Dr. Gemelli Carei says, "On Aurangzeb's camp the enclosure of the royal tents alone measured about three miles and the whole camp, with a circumference of some thirty miles, had a population of half a million. The separate bazars or markets numbered two hundred and fifty, and every class of goods, even the most costly, was on sale."

11. *Conflicting nature of Aurangzeb : Conflicts and conflicts.* Aurangzeb's reign may be described as the reign of conflicts—Aurangzeb's conflict with his father, conflict with his brothers, conflict with his mother, conflict with his sons, conflict with the Satnamis, conflict with the Jats, conflicts with the Rajputs, conflict with the Sikhs, conflict with the Shias, conflict with the Deccan, in the South, conflict in the East, conflict with the Afghans, conflict with the English and above all conflict with himself in the last days of life.

Summing up

Sir J.N. Sarkar, a great authority on Aurangzeb has given a very objective picture of Aurangzeb's rule. He very clearly makes clear the achievements and failures of Aurangzeb.

About the achievements of Aurangzeb J.N. Sarkar states, "The history of Aurangzeb is practically the history of India for sixty years...Under him the Mughal empire reached its greatest extent, and the largest single state ever known in India from the dawn of history to the rise of British power was formed."

About the failures of Aurangzeb, J.N. Sarkar has commented, "The extension of Empire was the beginning of his end." He elaborated his statement in these words, "In Hindustan the administration rapidly deteriorated; peace, prosperity and the arts decreased and the entire Indian civilisation fell backwards. The defence of the north-western frontier was neglected, and the material resources of the empire dwindled till they ceased to suffice for its needs. The vast annexations effected by Aurangzeb in the Deccan—Bijapur, Golkunda, eastern Carnatic and Maharashtra were all illusive. Instead of adding to the strength and wealth of the empire, they brought down economic ruin upon it and destroyed its army as an instrument of power. In fact, the Mughal empire now became too large to be administered by one man or from one centre, and its disruption began which was to make the history of India in the eighteenth century one "great anarchy."

21

Mughal Administration (Mansabdari and Jagirdari : Land Revenue)

Q. 1. Explain the main elements of Mughal administration.

Or

Describe the structure of the Central Government during the Mughal period and explain how its different departments were controlled?

Ans. *Main Elements and Structure of the Mughal Administration.*

1. *Emperor as the representative of God.* Mughal emperors considered themselves as God's representatives on earth. They claimed to be the "Shadow of God". or "Visible God." or "Waqil to God" or "Khatifa of her country."

Abul Fazl, the well-known historian and scholar of Akbar's age in his preface to the *Ain-i-Akbari'* has said, "No dignity is higher in the eyes of God than royalty, and those who are wise, drink from its auspicious fountain." He further held, "Royalty is a light emanating from God as ray from the sun."

Earlier Humayun had also thought himself to be the God's representative on earth. When Askari Mirza rebelled against Humayun, he said to have exclaimed. "Am I not a king, God's representative on earth."

Babur had assumed the title of *'Padshah'* (Emperor) to denote the royal dignity. He tells in his *Memories,* "upto that date people had styled Taimur Beg's descendants as *'Mirza'*, even when they were ruling, now I ordered that people should style me *'Padshah'*."

2. *Centralised power.* The emperor was the head of administration and the state. He was the law-maker as well as dispenser of justice, the commander-in-chief and the fountain-head of all honours. He was the source of all authority.

3. *Benevolent despot.* The Mughal emperor accepted two primary duties for themselves—*'Jahan Bani'* protection of the state, and *'Jahangiri'* (*extension* of the empire). They attempted to create those conditions which were conducive to economic and cultural progress of their subjects. They devoted lot of time to look after the affairs of the state.

Akbar used to say, "Tyranny is unlawful in everyone, especially in a sovereign who is guardian of the public." He also observed, "Divine worship in monarchs consists in their justice and good administration."

According to Dr. R.P. Khosla, "The Mughal monarchy whatever its defects-and no despotism can be unalloyed blessing-was on the whole grandly conceived and well executed."

4. *Rule of Aristocracy*. Dr. Tara Chand describes the rule of the Mughal emperors as 'the rule of aristocracy'. This implies that the nobles exercised enormous influence on the administration of the state.

5. *Foreign-cum Indian system of administration*. Dr. J.N. Sarkar has observed, "The Mughal administration presented a combination of Indian and extra-Indian elements, or more correctly, it was the Perso-Arabic system in Indian setting." A compromise was affected with the older native system already in vogue and familiar to the people governed. The Mughals carried out certain modifications in it in the light of foreign experiences.

6. *Secular versus theocratic state*. The Mughal administration was not entirely based on Islamic tenets. At least important emperors like Akbar did not work under the influence of the *'Ulemas'*. Even Aurangzeb, though a fanatic Sunni never allowed the Ulemas to dictate him in administrative matters.

7. *Administration-military in origin*. The Mughal administration was a military based government from beginning to the last.

8. *Revenue administration*. Several Mughal rulers imposed taxes in accordance with Islamic laws.

9. *The administration as manufacturer*. The administration/State used to maintain several *'Karkhanas'* or factories of its own.

10. *Council of Ministers*. It was not necessary for the Mughal emperor to consult his ministers on all occasions. According to J.N. Sarkar, "The Mughal emperor had no regular Council of Ministers. The *'Wazir'* (Prime Minister) and the Diwan (Finance Minister) were the highest persons below the emperor, but the other officers were in no sense, his colleagues. They were admittedly inferior to him and deserved rather to be called secretaries than ministers. Nearly all their work was liable to revision by the *'Wazir'* and Royal orders were often transmitted to them through him."

Control of departments. Apart from the Prime Minister and the Diwan, there were several other ministers or incharges of various departments. Among the important ones were the following :

1. The Imperial Household Department under *'Khan-Saman'* or High Steward.
2. The Military Pay and Accounts Department under the Imperial Bakshi.
3. The Canon Law, both Civil and Military under the Chief *'Qazi*
4. Religious Endowments and Charity under the Chief *'Sardar*
5. Censorship of Public Morals under the *'Mahtasib'*
6. The Justice Department under. *'Qazi-ul-Quzat*

7. The Artillery Department under *'Mir Atish'* or *'Darogha-i-Topkhana'*

8. Intelligence and Postal Department under the *'Darogha-i-Dak Chauki'*

The entire structure of the administrative system of the Mughals may be stated in the words of S.R. Sharma. "Though the Mughals came to India as conquerors and foreigners, they set up traditions and conventions which were calculated to endear them to their Indian subjects. The Emperor's appearance at the *'Jharokha'* for popular *'Darshan'* daily, the opportunities they offered to the people to approach them with their petitions, their personal attention to minute details of administration, and their regular inspection tours and pageants throughout the Empire, even apart from their generally enlightened and benevolent policy in all matters, served to impart to their autocratic rule the appearance of government by consent. This character was largely the creation of Akbar's statesmanship. It was sustained during the next two reigns of Jahangir and Shah Jahan, but was progressively undermined by the reactionary policy of Aurangzeb. Nevertheless, the main framework of the administrative organisation, though in a considerably attenuated form, endured till the English East India Company stepped into the shoes of the Mughal Emperors."

Q. 2. Write a note on the provincial administration of the Mughal rulers.

Ans. *Provincial Administration of the Mughal Rulers.*

Nature of provincial administration. According to J.N. Sarkar, the administration of a province "was an exact miniature of the Central Government." Dr. Ishwari Prasad calls *'Suba'* as a "replica of the empire in every respect." The provincial administration was organised on the model of central administration. There were similar departments in the province under a governor who was appointed by the emperor. Almost all the heads of the departments were appointed by the *'Subadar'* (governor) of the provinces.

The provinces were divided into Sarkars (districts), parganas (Tehsils) and villages.

Number of provinces. Before Akbar's time, there were 12 units of administration. Akbar used the term *'Suba'* and with the conquest of some areas in the Deccan, the number of provinces rose to 15. During Jahangir's time, the number rose to 17 and Shah Jahan's time it increased to 22.

Officers in a province. Important officers of the province were : Subedar, Diwan, Bakshi, Waqa-i-Newis, Qazi and the Kotwal.

Subedar or Sipah-Salar or Nazim. Known by different names from time to time, he was the head of a suba. He was the emperor's representative. He possessed both civil and military authority. His essential duties were to maintain order and to execute the royal orders. Generally speaking Subedars were appointed from royal families.

Diwan. The Diwan was incharge of revenue administration. He was the representative of the Imperial Diwan. Although his status was not equal to that of a subedar, he reported directly to the centre.

Bakshi. He was appointed by the Central Bakshi in accordance with the advice of the emperor. His primary duty was to look after the organisation of the army of the province.

The Waqa-i-Newis. He recorded all the events of the provinces and submitted his reports to the centre. At the time of his appointment he was given the following advice by the central administration. "Report the truth, lest the Emperor should learn the facts from another source and punish you. Your work is delicate; both sides have to be served. In the words of most of the high officers, forbidden things are done. If you report them truly the officers will be disgraced. If you do not, you yourself will be undone...In every matter write the truth but avoid offending the nobles. Write after carefully verifying your statement."

Qazi. Every city had its own Qazi who administered justice to the people.

Kotwal. Every city had also a Kotwal. He was essentially a police officer who maintained peace and order in the city.

Sarkar and its administration

(*a*) *'Faujdar'* He was the executive and military head of the Sarkar. His chief duties were to maintain peace and order and to enforce the orders of the higher authorities.

(*b*) *'Amal Guzar'*. He was the finance officer of the district.

(*c*) *'Bitikchi'*. He assisted the *'Amal Guzar'* in his work.

Administration of the Pargana

'Shiqdar'-a military officer; *'Amil'* the finance officer' *'Fotadar'* the treasurer; and *'Qanugo'*, head of the village and *'Patwaris'* were the important officers in the Pargana.

Village administration. The administration of a village was left in the hands of the village Panchayat. Normally, the state officers did not interfere in the affairs of the village.

Q. 3. "Mansabdari was the pillar of the Mughal administrative system. Discuss. (Delhi University, 1997)

Or

Critically examine the Mansabdari system as established by Akbar. What changes occurred in it during the reign of Jahangir and Shah Jahan?

Ans. *Mansabdari system as Introduced by Akbar.*

Origin. *Mansabdari* was a system of army and civil services introduced by Akbar in place of the Jagirdari system. Strictly speaking Akbar was not the originator of this system. It was originally a system introduced by *'Khalifa'* Abba Saiyed and thereafter imported into India. Akbar introduced several changes in this system. This system was the pillar of the Mughal administration. By abolishing the jagirdari system, the *mansabdari* system was introduced. It proved quite effective.

Meaning of the Mansabdari System. The *'Mansab'* is an Arabic word meaning rank or position or status of a person. Thus *Mansabdari* was a system in which the rank of a government official was determined. Every civil and military officer was given a *'mansab'*. Different numbers which could be divided by ten were used for ranking officers. It was also meant for fixing the salaries and allowances of officers.

Categories of *Mansabs*. Abul Fazl has mentioned 66 grades of *mansabdars* but in practice there were not more than 33 mansabs. During the early reign of Akbar, the lowest grade was ten and the highest was 5000. Towards the end of the reign it was raised to 7000. According to Badauni it was fixed at 12,000. Higher mansabs were given to princes and Rajput rulers who accepted the suzerainty of Akbar.

Significance of a mansab. The *mansab* of a Mughal noble implied the following :

(*a*) Salary of the officer

(*b*) Status of the officer

(*c*) Number of soldiers, horses and elephants etc., maintained by an officer.

'Zat and 'Sawar'. During later years of his reign, Akbar introduced the rank of *'Zat'* and *'Sawar'* in the *Mansabdari* system. Different views have been expressed regarding these terms.

According to Blochmann, every *mansabdar* had to maintain as many soldiers as were indicated by his rank of *'Zat'* while the rank of *'sawar'* indicated the number of horsemen among them.

Irvin expressed the view that *Zat* indicated the actual number of cavalry under a *mansabdar* besides other soldiers while *sawar* was an additional honour.

According to Dr. R.P. Tripathi, the rank of *sawar* was given to *mansabdars* to fix up their additional allowances. A *mansabdar* was paid rupees two per horse. Therefore, if a *mansabdar* received the rank of 500 *sawar* he was given rupees one thousand additional allowance.

Abdul Aziz is of the opinion that while the rank of *zat* fixed the number of other soldiers under a *mansabdar,* the rank of *sawar* fixed the number of his horsemen.

Dr. A.L. Srivastava has opined that while the rank of *zat* indicated the total number of soldiers under a *mansabdar,* the rank of *sawar* indicated the number of horsemen under him. During the reign of Akbar, the *mansabdars* were asked to keep as many horsemen as were indicated by numbers of their ranks of *sawar*. But, the practice was not be maintained by other Mughal emperors.

Main Features of the *Mansabdari* System

1. The *king* himself appointed the *mansabdars*. He could enhance the mansab, lower down it or remove it.

2. A *mansabdar* could be asked to perform any civil or military service.

3. There were 33 categories of the *Mansabdars*. The lowest *mansabdar* commanded 10 soldiers and the highest 10,000 soldiers. Only the princes of the royal family and most important Rajput rulers were given a *mansab* of 10,000.

4. A *mansabdar* was paid his salary in cash.

5. The salary due to the soldiers was added to the personal salary of the *mansabdar*. Sometimes for paying the salaries to the soldier, a jagir was given to the *mansabdar*. But the revenue was realised by officers and necessary adjustments made.

6. *Mansabdari* system was not hereditary.

7. In addition to meeting his personal expenses, the *mansabdar* had to maintain out of his salary a stipulated quota of horses, elephants, camels and mules and carts.

8. A *mansabdar* holing a rank of 5000 had to maintain 340 horses, 100 elephants, 400 camels, 100 mules and 160 carts.

9. Handsome salaries were paid to a *Mansabdar*. A *mansabdar* with a rank of 5,000 got a salary of Rs. 30,000 per month; a *mansabdar* of 3,000 could get Rs. 17,000 and a *mansabdar* of 10,000 got rupees 8,200.

10. The horses were classified into six categories and the elephants into five.

11. For every ten cavalry men, the *Mansabdar* had to maintain twenty horses for horses had to be provided rest while on march and replacements were necessarily in times of war.

12. A record of the description (*'huliya'*) of each horseman under a *mansabdar* and of branding (*'dag'*) horses to prevent corruption was kept.

Changes introduced by Jahangir and Shah Jahan

1. *Difference in the highest mansab.* After Akbar, higher *mansabs* were introduced. During Jahangir and Shah Jahan's reigns, the *mansab* of a prince was raised to 40,000 and 60,000 respectively as against of 12,000 during Akbar's reign.

2. *Reduction in the number of soldiers.* Shah Jahan reduced the number of soldiers kept by a *mansabdar*. Now each *mansabdar* was required to keep one-third of the original number. Sometimes, it was even reduced to one-fourth or one-fifth.

3. *Difference in the categories of mansabdars.* During the time of Jahangir and Shah Jahan, the number of categories of *mansabdars* was reduced to 11 as against 33 mentioned by Abul Fazl in his book *Akbarnama.*

4. *Relaxation in control.* Akbar's death, the control exercised over *mansabdars* became very slack.

Merits of the *Mansabdari* System

1. *Removal of the chief defects of the jagirdari system.* The *Mansabdari* system proved very helpful in removing the defects inherent in the jagirdari system as such. Now the *mansabdars* got their salaries from the emperor, they were more loyal to him. The chances of their revolt were minimised.

2. *Increased military efficiency.* By regulating the maintenance of the horses and horsemen, the military efficiency of the army was increased.

3. *Extra revenue to the state.* Now the entire land became state land. The state officials realised the revenue. Earlier this was done by jagirdars.

4. *Merit as the basis of selection. Mansabdari* system was not hereditary. A *mansab* was given to an official on merit. It could be enhanced or lowered down.

Demerits of the *Mansabdari System*

1. The mansabdars got their salaries from the emperor and paid themselves the salaries to their troops. This made the troops more loyal to the *mansabdars* than to the king.

2. The system proved very expensive.

3. Dishonest *mansabdars* and officials used to ally together during inspection, borrowed horses from one another and showed their full quota.

4. Caste system prevailed in the *mansabdari* system.

5. Since the property of a *mansabdar* was confiscated after his death, he used to spend it lavishly during his life time.

This made the nobles luxurious and it led to their moral degradation which had an adverse effect on their efficiency.

Q. 4. Write a note on the military organisation of the Mughals.

Ans. *Military Organisation of the Mughals.*

The Mughal rulers maintained a large and efficient army till the reign of Aurangzeb. This was necessary to do so for they conquered several parts of the country and were accordingly required to maintain law and order and check revolts.

Three categories of armies

(1) *Mansabdari system.* Every military officer and chief was given a *mansab* (rank) and was expected to maintain the required number of soldiers, horsemen, horses and elephants etc. Every *mansabdar* was usually paid a salary which also included the maintenance expenditure of his army. Recruitment was made by the *Mansabdars.*

(2) *The 'Ahadi' army.* This was the army maintained by the emperor. The *'ahadi'* soldiers received higher salaries than other categories

of soldiers. Their number was not fixed. They were extremely loyal to the emperor.

(3) *'Dakhili' Soldiers.* They were recruited on behalf of the emperor but were but under the charge of *mansabdars*.

Permanent army. The permanent army of the Mughals was very large. The total army was of the order of about forty lakhs. It included all types of armies, including the armies maintained by the *mansabdars* and the feudatory chiefs.

Army units. The army was divided into the following five units.

(1) *Cavalry.* It had two types of horsemen. (*i*) *'Bargir'* were those soldiers who received horses, arms, dress etc. from the state (*ii*) *'Siledar'* were those soldiers who brought their own horses and arms.

The Mughal cavalry mostly had *'Turki'*, *'Tazi'*, *'Arabi'* and *'Parsi'* horses.

(2) *Infantry.* Infantry was organised into two units namely (*i*) *'Bandukchi'* (Riflemen) and *'Samshirbaz'* (Swordsmen)

(3) *War elephants.* The elephants were used for fighting as well as for carrying load.

(4) *Artillery.* According to Dr. R.P. Tripathi, "Excepting the Turkish artillery, Akbar's was second to none in Asia, for in Akbar's time, it had reached the high point of efficiency possible."

(5) *Navy.* The navy of the Mughals was very weak as compared with the Europeans.

Q. 5. Describe the main features of land revenue system of the Mughals.

Or

Write a short note on Zabta System of Todar Mal's land revenue system.

Ans. *Main Features of the Land Revenue System.*

1. Measurement of the entire land into *'bighas'* through a standard *'Bamboo Zarib'*

2. Classification of land according to the produce.

3. Fixing the land revenue to be paid to the Government.

4. Arrangement for paying the land revenue in cash or kind.

5. Appointment of special officers for the collection of land revenue.

(*For details, please refer to Chapter 17*)

22

Economy and Nobility During the Mughal Period

Q. 1. Discuss the main features of the economic life of the people during the Mughal period. Also trace the growth of industries.

Ans. *Main Features of the Economic Life of the People During the Mughal Period.*

Conflicting views have been expressed by the historians regarding the economic conditions of India during the Mughal period. On the one hand we hear of several famines which caused untold sufferings and on the other hand we hear of Akbar the Great and the Golden Age of Shah Jahan.

European visitors who came to India during the period of Jahangir and Shah Jahan have also given conflicting views. However, following general observations may be made about the economic conditions of the State/Government and the general conditions of the people.

1. *Rich country inhabited by the poor.* It is observed that in spite of India being a rich country, its people in general were poor.

2. *Great disparity.* While the emperors, nobles and jagirdars, mansabdars and officers had wealth in abundance, the common people had very little of it.

The economic disparity was quite evident by the standard of living, diet, dwellings, dresses and other comforts and necessities of life. The commoners which included the peasantry, artisans, and labourers used to live a poor life.

3. *Freedom to choose occupation.* People were free to choose their occupation.

4. *Agriculture as the main occupation.* A very substantial portion of India's population depended upon agriculture.

5. *Self sufficiency of villages.* The villages produced articles of daily use in such a way, that they were able to meet their requirements.

6. *Barter as well as currency system.* Barter system along with currency was also very popular in the rural areas.

7. *Low prices.* In general, it is observed that the prices of essential commodities were quite low.

Some significant views of scholars and travellers.

A large number of Europeans namely, Hawkins, Sir Thomas Roe, Bernier, Travernier and Peter Mundi visited India during the reigns of

Jahangir and Shah Jahan and left their accounts regarding the emperors, nobility and the commoners. In spite of the limitations of their accounts, they are very helpful in knowing about the life of the period.

Almost all Mughal emperors either themselves or the scholars of their court wrote about the contemporary life. Such records have great historical significance.

1. William Hawkins informs us that Jahangir possessed a huge amount of wealth and had a big treasure of jewels. The merchants also brought huge money from abroad.

2. According to Sir Thomas Roe, the condition of peasants was miserable. He has also mentioned of huge treasure of gold and diamonds of Jahangir.

3. Peter Mundy has observed that during Shah Jahan's reign, people in Deccan suffered great distress. He has further stated that the peasantry was in a miserable condition.

4. Bernier states that the artisans and labourers were not treated well. There was decline of arts and crafts during Aurangzeb's reign.

5. Ralph Fitch who came to India towards the end of the sixteenth century says that at Banaras "people go naked save a little cloth bound about their middle."

6. About the closing years of the 17th century during Aurangzeb's rule, economic condition of the country deteriorated. Sir J.N. Sarkar has observed, "There appeared a great economic impoverishment of India."

Low prices. Abul Fazl, Edward Terry and Smith are unanimous in their opinion that the prices under the Mughals were low. The *Ain-i-Akbari* written by Abul Fazl mentions the rates of several articles. Wheat was sold at that time at the rate of 12 *dams* per *man.* One dam was 1/40th part of a rupee and *Man* was equal to 55½ pounds. One rupee had 60 paise at that time. Barley was sold at 8 *dams* for *man,* gram at 16½, jawar at 10, millet at 8, ghee at 105, oil at 80, milk at 25 and white sugar at 125 dams for *man.* The price of a sheep was Rs. one and a half and of a cow Rs. 10. The prices were low and the wages were also low. A highly skilled labourer was paid 7 dams (app. 21 paise) per day.

It has been calculated that a man could feed his family on two rupees a month.

Agriculture and peasantry. The main occupation of the people was agriculture. On the whole the conditions of the peasants was not satisfactory. The peasants who did possess land of their own often belonged to the class of people known as *Kamin.* Whenever there was a famine, this class was the most sufferer and famines were frequent. Famines were often followed by epidemics.

The peasants primarily depended on rains, ponds and wells. There were canals also but not much improvement was made in man-made means of irrigation.

Wild animals used to harm cultivation as there were extensive forests.

Except during the reign of Akbar and Jahangir, land revenue was quite heavy.

The government officials often harassed the cultivators. Constant wars and rebellions adversely affected cultivation.

The rice growing areas were Assam, Bengal, Bihar, Orissa, Eastern Coast, Tamil region and Kashmir. Allahabad, Avadh, Khandesh and Gujarat also produced some rice. Wheat was mostly grown in the Punjab, Madhya Pradesh and Agra etc. Dipalpur region was known for the production of Jawar. Millets were particularly grown in Ajmer, Gujarat and Khandesh. Silk cultivation was so widespread in Bengal that there was no need to import it from China. The adoption of potato and red chillies followed during the 18th century.

'The Ain-i-Akbar'. It gives revenue rates for 16 Rabi crops and 25 Kharif crops.

Industries

(1) *Varied industrial activity.* The authors of *An Advanced History of India* have observed, "One of the most important factors in the economic history of India during the period under review was the extensive and varied industrial activity of the people, which besides supplying the needs of the local aristocracy and merchants could meet the demands of traders coming from Europe, and other parts of India."

(2) *Cotton and Silk Industry.* Important centres of cotton manufacture were found in all parts of India. Dacca attained a wide reputation for its delicate muslin. Pelsaert was of the opinion that at Chabasupur and Sonargaon "all live by the weaving industry and the produce has the highest reputation of quality. Bernier opined, "There is in Bengal such a quantity of cotton and silk, that the kingdom may be called the common store-house for these two kinds of merchandise, not of Hindustan or the Empire of the Great Mughal only, but of all neighbouring kingdoms, and even of Europe. The dyeing industry was also very popular. Printing of cloth was in vogue. Silk-weaving also arrested the notice of some persons. The imperial patronage gave it a considerable impetus." Moreland wrote that the production of silk in Bengal alone was 'about 2½ million pounds out of which one million pounds were worked up locally, ¾ million was exported raw by the Dutch and ¾ million distributed over India, most of it going to Gujarat, but some being taken by merchants from Central Asia."

Important industries and industrial centres

Cotton industry was well developed in Bengal. Sugar industry was well-developed in Bengal, Gujarat and Punjab.

Glass industry flourished at Fatehpur Sikri, Berar and Prihar.

Jaunpur and Gujarat were known for a large variety of perfumes.

Pearls were taken out of sea and it was a well-developed industry near the seacoast of South India.

Delhi, Banaras and Chunar were particularly famous for clay industry and clay toys.

Kashmir and Karnataka produced artistic pieces of wood.

Punjab and Gujarat were renowned for the production of good quality arms like swords, javelins and other traditional arms.

Delhi and Banaras were famous for brass industry. Diamonds were extracted from the mines of Golkunda and Chotta-Nagpur. India produced the world-famous *Koh-i-Nur* diamond from a mine at Golkunda.

Cannons and rifles of good quality were not produced in India. Comparatively Persia, Turkey and several European countries were far ahead of India.

Leather industry was not a well-developed industry. Similarly wine of good quality was not manufactured in India.

Trade. During the Mughal period both internal and external trade was in a healthy state. (See next question)

Q. 2. Discuss the pattern of inland trade and foreign trade during the Mughal period.

Ans. *Flourished Inland Trade.*

India's inland trade flourished during the Mughal period on account of the following reasons :

1. *Law and order.* In the words of Dr. Satish Chandra, "Perhaps the most important factor was the political integration of the country under Mughal rule and establishment of conditions of law and order over extensive areas."

2. *Use of standard currency and measures of weight.* The Mughal rulers issued standard coins and fixed weights and measures which facilitated trade and commerce.

3. *Cash payment of revenue.* The payment of land revenue in cash helped a lot in the growth of trade and commerce.

4. *Growth of new cities.* Mughal rulers founded several new cities. These cities became centres of trade and commerce.

Chief cities of the country were sufficiently presperous. Fitsch wrote, "Agra and Fatehpore are two very great cities, either of them much greater than London and very populous." Speaking of the Punjab, Terry observed, "Lahore is the chief city thereof, built very large and abounds both in people and riches, one of the principal cities for trade in India. Monserrate corroborates this account. Abul Fazl wrote of Ahmednagar as, "A noble city in a high state of prosperity for the pleasantness of its climate and display of the choicest productions of the whole globe. Burhanpur, Banaras, Patna, Burdwan, Dacca and Chittagong were the other important towns which became centres of trade.

5. *Development of industries.* Several industries flourished in India. India's products of various arts and crafts became very popular not only in India but also abroad. Naturally this led to enormous trade activity.

6. *European traders.* The arrival of the Portuguese, the Dutch and the English traders led to increased trade activities. During the reign of Jahangir, Sir Thomas Roe had secured some trade concessions.

7. *Transport facilities.* The rivers, some of which were navigable throughout the year and some through part of it, afforded excellent means for the carriage of heavy traffic.

Pattern of Trade : main features

(1) Each village had a small market.

(2) Seasonal and annual fairs attracted a large number of people and traders from the neighbouring villages and towns.

(3) There was a high degree of professionalism among the Indian traders. Some specialised in wholesale trade and others in retail trade.

(4) The wholesalers were called *'Seths'* and the *'Bohras'* and the retailers *'Beoparis'* or *'Baniks'*.

(5) In South India, *'Chettis'* formed the trading community.

(6) The *Banjaras'* specialised in varying trades. They used to move from place to place, sometimes with many oxen loaden with foodgrains, salt and ghee etc.

(7) The *Sarrofs* (money lenders) gave money on interest. They carried their money in the shape of *Hundis.*

(8) There were big traders in India who owned their own ships. Virji Vohra and Malaya Chetti were prominent traders of Surat and Coromandal coast respectively. Virji Vohra was considered to be the richest merchant in the world.

(9) Several big traders lived in important cities like Lahore, Delhi, Agra, Patna, Bhardwan and Ahmednagar.

Foreign Trade

Following were the main characteristics of the foreign trade of India.

1. *Favourable balance of trade.* On account of its extensive trade and quality of goods India exported to other countries and there was inflow of wealth in India. The *Voile* of Dhaka was supposed to be so fine that the whole packing (*'than'*) of it could be passed through two fingers or a ring. It was an item of great demand in foreign countries.

2. *Items of export.* Cotton cloth was the most important item of export. European merchants exported *'malmal'* (muslin) from Dhaka, silk from Banaras and cotton textiles from Surat, Ahmedabad and Madurai. Pepper from Malabar was eagerly sought after by foreign traders.

It is estimated that towards the end of 17th century, India had about 25 per cent of the world's market share in textile exports. Today it contributes less than 1 per cent.

3. *Main items of import.* Horses, velvet, decorative goods, guns and gun powder, scents and wine were imported. India also imported dried and fresh fruits. Carpets were imported from Persia and horses from Arabia.

4. *Countries having trade with India.* India had trade relations with France, Holland, Portugal, England, Arabia, Egypt, Central Asia, Persia, China, Japan and Nepal etc.

5. *Modes of transport.* There were a number of ports on the sea coast of Bengal, Gujarat and Deccan. Land routes were also used.

6. *Change in the pattern of trade.* Till the end of the 16th century AD, India's foreign trade to Europe was in the hands of the Portuguese. In the 17the century AD, the East India Company was formed by the English merchants. The Company set up a factory at Surat, Before the end of the 17th century AD, British settlements grew up at Madras, Bombay, Calcutta, Hooghly and many other places. The Portuguese were pushed back to Goa and the French to Pondicherry and Chander Nagar.

Q. 3. Discuss the role of Mughal nobility in polity and economy.

Ans. *Meaning of Mughal nobility.*

During the Mughal period, the nobles were counted among the ruling and upper classes. They had special privileges. Persons belonging to aristocratic families, whether they were Indian or foreigners, comprised the nobility. On the top came the princes followed by very high mansabdars, and Zamindars. Next to them were provincial rulers.

In the beginning, the bulk of the Mughal nobility was drawn from the homeland of the Mughals—Turan, Tajikistan, Khorasan, Iran etc.

Along with the Mughal nobles, were appointed from Afghan and Hindustani Muslims.

Several Rajput rulers who were appointed at various high posts by Mughal rulers also came under this category.

Later on a few Maratha officers in the Mughal court and service also formed a nobility.

In short, it may be stated that the Mughal nobility was a heterogeneous body. It comprised nobles of several religions and races like Turks, Persians, Indians, Muslims and Hindus.

Role of nobility in Politics

Nobility played an important role in the affairs of the state. The impact of their role depended on the strength of the emperor. If the ruler was strong, the influence of the nobility was very marginal. In case the ruler was weak, the role of nobility was of great magnitude. All important decisions in that case were influenced by the nobility.

The nobility indulged in intrigues and conspiracies. It played an important role even in determining the successor of a Mughal emperor after his death.

Different groups of nobility were usually at conflict with the result that sometimes they created law and order problems.

Nobility under Akbar. Akbar was a very powerful ruler. In the beginning of his reign while he was a minor, he was under the charge of his tutor and guardian Bairam Khan. Bairam was an important noble and had stood by Humayun through thick and thin. It was he who played an important part in crowning Akbar. It was he who was an instrument in winning the Second Battle of Panipat (1556) which enabled Akbar to be the real emperor. He, in due course, tried to dominate Akbar in all matters of administration. However, Akbar turned out to be very strong. When he tried to take independent decisions, Bairam Khan felt humiliated and revolted. The revolt was crushed by Akbar and Bairam Khan begged pardon which was granted to him. Thereafter Bairam Khan left for Mecca.

It can be said very safely that Akbar's rule remained free from the rebellion of the nobles.

The mansabdari system had abolished the hereditary right of nobles. Mansab was conferred on merit. This checked the power of nobility.

Mughal nobility under Jahangir. Since Jahangir proved to be a weak ruler, he worked under the influence of a clique (*'junta'*) headed by queen Nur Jahan. Nur Jahan's group in the beginning included besides she, her father, her mother, her brother and prince Khurram who later became Shah Jahan. After the marriage of her daughter from her previous husband Sher Afghan, Nur Jahan began to favour Shahryar, the husband of her daughter and another son of Jahangir from her other queen. Now Nur Jahan desired that in place of prince Khurram, her son-in-law Shahryar should succeed Jahangir. Therefore, she began to reduce the power of Prince Khurram. Prince Khurram became suspicious towards her. The conflict between the two became necessary. The nobility also joined one or the other camp.

Shah Jahan revolted against his father on account of the intrigues of Nur Jahan. His revolt was not successful but he was pardoned by Jahangir.

Mahabat Khan, a very faithful commander of Jahangir played a leading role in suppressing the revolt of Shah Jahan. This enhanced his power and influence at the court of Jahangir. Nur Jahan did not like it and she created such a situation that Mahabat Khan had to rise in revolt.

Likewise there were several minor revolts during the reign of Jahangir on account of intrigues of nobility.

Mughal nobility under Shah Jahan. In the war of succession, Mughal nobility was divided into five groups i.e. one group very close to Shah Jahan and the other four groups to four sons of Shah Jahan.

Mughal nobility under Aurangzeb. Aurangzeb proved to be too strong. Mughal nobility failed to assert itself.

Mughal nobility after Aurangzeb. After the death of Aurangzeb in 1707, eleven Mughal rulers ruled for about 150 years i.e. upto 1857. In fact after 1739, the Mughal empire was confined to Delhi and its surroundings. Mughal nobility became very powerful. The Sayyid Brothers exercised so much influence that they came to be known as 'King makers.' The governors declared their independence. Thus the Mughal empire disintegrated.

Nobility and Economy

The power and modes of life of the nobles were linked with the Mughal emperors. They were like stars round the moon and their lustre was borrowed. Like the Mughal emperors, the Mughal nobles maintained large establishments which put heavy burden on their income. Sometimes it led to heavy taxes on the people.

Although the Mughal nobles incurred heavy expenditure in leading a luxurious life, yet they contributed a lot to the development of industries and trade and commerce as detailed below :

1. Several nobles took keen interest in trade and industry. Mir Jumla owned several naval fleets. Aurangzeb's chief Qazi was the owner of many business enterprises.

2. The demand of the nobles for luxury goods led to the development of several cottage industries.

3. The nobles indulged freely in drinking wine and their taste for some foreign goods led to the development of foreign trade.

4. The nobles purchased many plots of land and laid down gardens and flower beds of different types. This increased opportunities for employment also.

5. The nobles patronised art and architecture which provided employment to many people.

6. The taste for goods of fine quality encouraged workmen to produce quality goods which also found foreign markets and contributed to the economy of the country.

23

Religious and Social Conditions During the Mughal Rule (Social Classes : Position of Women)

Q. 1. Explain the religious and social conditions of the society during the Mughal rule in India. (Delhi University 1997)

Ans. *Religious Conditions.*

Divergent views have been expressed by historians and scholars regarding the religious conditions. On the one hand there are those who state there was a lot of religious harmony among the people of different faiths and on the other hand it is stated that seeds of the partition of the country were sown by emperors like Aurangzeb and others. They point out that Hindu-Muslim discord is not the legacy of the British rule but some of the medieval narrow-minded rulers.

Division of society on the basis of religion. The majority of the Indian society consisted of the Hindus. Traditionally they were divided into four classes. Caste system had become very rigid. There were hundreds of sub-castes. The *Sudras* were in the lowest cadre of society.

The Muslims were divided into Sunnis, the Shias, the Bohras and the Khojas etc. The Sunnis were in majority and also belonged to the privileged class because the emperors were also Sunnis. The Shaikhs and Sayyids also commanded respect in the society.

The foreign Muslims like the Arabs, the Persians, the Turks, the Mongols, the Uzbeks, the Abbyssinians and the Armenians regarded themselves socially superior to converted Indian Muslims. They occupied higher position in the society.

The Sufi saints and the Bhakt Saints laid stress on religious harmony, equality in society and devotion to God.

Emperor Akbar founded a new religion of *'Din-a-Ilahi'* but it could not attract many followers and collapsed with his death.

A new faith of Sikhism among the Hindus emerged. Its followers were mostly confined to Punjab. In general, its followers and the Mughal rulers did not enjoy cordial relations.

Festivals, fairs and pilgrimages. Important festivals of the Hindus were Basant, Diwali, Dussehra, Holi, Sankranti and Shivaratri. Sankranti and Purnimah were to be considered very auspicious days and a dip in some river on that day was considered to be a pious act. People went to places of pilgrimages such as Kashi, Kurukshetra, Prayag, Puri and Pushkar. Millions of Hindus attended the *Kumbh* fair. The Hindus believed in the purity and sacredness of the water of the Ganges and that a dip in the Ganges would purify them of all their sins.

The pilgrimage to Mecca was an annual event of great importance for the Muslims. The important festivals of the Muslims were Id-ul-Juha, Id-ul-Fitr, Shab-i-Barat, Muharram and Milad-ud-Nabi.

Social divisions

Broadly speaking, Indian society was divided into four classes (1) The king and the princes (2) The nobles (3) The middle class (4) The lower class.

The king and the princely class. The king enjoyed the highest social status. He lived in great luxury. Usually he maintained a big *'harem'* (wives and concubines in the palace of the emperor). It is said that Akbar had about 500 women in his household. The princely class was quite large on account of a large number of queens the Mughal kings had. The princes followed the life style of the king.

Nobility or nobles. The noble class included descendants of the people who had come from other lands like Central Asia and Persia. It also included high mansabdars and jagirdars. Important Rajput chiefs also came under this category.

The nobles imitated the King and the princes and lived a life a extravagance. They spent lavishly. They lived in palatial buildings. They has scores of servants. They kept several women in their *'harem'*. Drinking was very common among them. Generally speaking they indulged in court intrigues and were very corrupt.

The nobles patronised art and literature. They also took interest in laying down beautiful gardens and flower beds.

(For role of nobility in economy and politics see previous chapter).

The Middle Class. It included wealthy traders and merchants, small mansabdars, jagirdars and professionals. The merchants and traders did not exhibit their wealth because of the fear that the ruler or a powerful noble might snatch it from them. In general, they enjoyed a simple life.

The Lower Class. A majority of the population belonged to this category. This class lived a life of poverty. They had a few clothes. They lived in thatched mud houses. This class comprised artisans, attendants, cultivators, labourers, peasants, small traders and shop-keepers, etc. There were slaves also.

There was a glaring inequality in the lives of other classes and the common people. The peasants lived virtually at the mercy of the mansabdars and jagirdars. They were worst hit during famines.

Position of women. Although the general condition of women was not good, there were several capable and enterprising women like Nur Jahan, Mumtaz Mahal, Jahanara, Roshanara, Rani Karnavati, Rani Durgavati, Rani Rupmati, Chand Bibi, Jijabai and Tarabai. But all these ladies belonged to the higher strata of society. In general women suffered from all sorts of handicaps. Polygamy was very common among the Muslims. *Talaq* or divorce was also very common and men could get it very easily. There was no *talaq* among the Hindus.

Sati was common among the Hindu women.

The emperors, the nobles and the rich people had reduced the position of women to articles of pleasure. They kept a large number of wives, concubines and slave girls in their harems.

The Muslim women had to observe *purdah*.

Social evils. Sati was common among the Hindus. Child marriage was also prevalent. Purda system was in vogue. Untouchability was practised on a large scale.

Dress, food habits and ornaments etc. Important changes took place in dress, food habits and ornaments etc. People of upper and middle classes both among the Hindus and Muslims wore *Qahaf* - a long coat coming down to the knees and tight trousers. The common man among the Hindus used *Dhoti* and the Muslims *Kurta* and *Pajama*. Both the Hindus and the Muslims wore turbans though their styles differed. Men, both Hindus and Muslims used *Shawls*. Hindu ladies wore *Dhoti* and Angiya and the Muslim ladies *'Pajama, Ghagra'*, *'Jacket' dupata* etc. Only rich people could afford to wear shoes or *chappals*.

While the Hindus were mostly vegetarians, the Muslims were generally non-vegetarians. Milk formed an important part of diet in the villages.

Several sections of population used wine, opium and tobacco as intoxicants.

Amusements and sports. Hunting, animal fighting, wrestling, pigeon-flying, were important sources of amusements and sports. Cock-fightings, bull-fightings and ram-fightings were also very common. Chess and chauper were also played.

Mujra. The performance of singers and dancers and Mushaira were also very popular.

Summing up

Like all societies including the present one, there were several inequalities. The majority of the people lived very poorly.

The workmen received low wages. The lofty buildings of the Mughals concealed the hardship of the workmen. They were also forced to work for higher classes without any remuneration. They lived on poor food and took one meal a day sometimes consisting of *Khichri* made of green pulse mixed with coarse rice.

In the period of the Mughals, the people of upper classes were the only beneficiaries while the common people toiled and mostly remained on mere existence level.

24

Deccan Policy of the Mughals

Q. 1. Describe in brief the political condition of the Deccan before the entry of the Mughals there. Elucidate the Deccan policy of Mughal emperors.

Or

Discuss the Deccan policy of Jahangir and Shah Jahan.

(Rajastan University 1997)

Or

Briefly describe the Deccan policies of the Mughals.

(Rajastan University Oct. 1998)

Ans. *Political condition of the Deccan before the Entry of the Mughals.* In the beginning of the sixteenth century, there were seven principal states in the Deccan namely (*i*) Khandesh (*ii*) Berar (*iii*) Ahmednagar, (*iv*) Bijapur (*v*) Golkunda, (*vi*) Bidar and (*vii*) Vijayanagar.

Of the seven states, five were the offshoots of the Bahamni Kingdom which came to an end in 1538. The kingdoms were split into five independent states as under : (*i*) The Nizam Shahi of Ahmednagar, (*ii*) The Imad Shahi of Berar (*iii*) The Adil Shahi of Bijapur (*iv*) The Badri Shahi of Bidar and (*v*) Qutb Shahi of Golkunda.

The most important characteristics of the political situation in the Deccan was that all these states were constantly at war with each other.

In 1565, four of the Muslim states namely Bijapur, Ahmednagar, Golkunda and Bidar formed a confederacy and fought against the Hindu State of Vijayanagara in the Battle of Talikota and gave a crushing defeat to Vijayanagara. Thereafter Ahmednagar conquerred Berar in 1574 and Bijapur annexed Bidar in 1618-1619.

The Marathas also emerged as great power in the Deccan.

Mughal Rulers in the Deccan

Introduction. Akbar occupied a part of Ahmednagar and the rest was occupied by Shah Jahan. Aurangzeb annexed the states of Bijapur and Golkunda.

In spite of best efforts, Aurangzeb failed to subdue Shivaji who was successful in establishing a strong empire in Maharashtra.

Babur and the Deccan

Babur's stay was very short-lived and he could not pay attention to the Deccan. He has simply mentioned the Deccan states in his *'Memoires'*.

Humayun and the Deccan

Humayun had not inherited an organised empire. He himself had to leave India and give way to Sher Shah and his successors during the period 1540 to 1555. After his exile from India, he could rule for a few months only.

Akbar and the Deccan

Akbar was the first Mughal ruler who paid his attention towards the Deccan.

Following were the reasons for his interest in the Deccan.

1. Akbar's expansionist and imperialist policy.
2. Lack of political unity among the warring Southern states.
3. Failure of the Rajputs to form any kingdom in the south.
4. Bringing about the cultural unity of the two regions of India—north and south.
5. Bringing about the political unity of India.
6. Akbar's desire to get the wealth of the Deccan.
7. Nearness of the Deccan territories to Gujarat and Malwa regions which Akbar has already annexed to his empire.
8. Settling of religious rivalries in the Muslim states of the Deccan.
9. Refusal of the Deccan states to accept the suzerainty of Akbar.

Campaigns of Akbar in Deccan

Diplomatic offensive. Akbar launched a diplomatic offensive against the Deccan States in 1593. He sent his missions to all these states asking them to accept Mughal suzerainty. Only Khandesh accepted this offer.

Strong resistance by Chand Bibi. In 1595, there was infighting in Ahmednagar over the succession issue. Akbar found this the appropriate occasion to attack this state. So Akbar sent a strong force under Khan-i-Khanan Abdul Rahim and Murad (son of Akbar) for the conquest of Ahmednagar. Chand Bibi who was acting as a regent for the young prince offered a gallant resistance. She made her name in the annals of history for her bravery and even Akbar had to accept this fact. After a close sieze of the fort of Ahmednagar for four months, the two sides came to an agreement. It was agreed to cede Berar to the Mughals in return for the recognition of the claim of the prince of Ahmednagar.

The proposal of annexation of Berar alarmed the Deccan states and they created obstruction in handing over Berar to the Mughals as they felt that the Mughals might get permanent hold in the Deccan. Soon a combined force of Bijapur, Golkunda and Ahmednagar faced the Mughal forces. Chand Bibi could not defend Ahmednagar this time on account of intrigues in her own camp. She was either killed or she committed suicide. With her death, all resistance collapsed. The fort of Ahmednagar fell to the Mughals.

The fort of Asirgarh in Khandesh was captured in 1601 after giving bribes to some nobles of Khandesh.

Results of Akbar's Deccan policy

(1) Three areas of Deccan *i.e.* Ahmednagar, Berar and fort of Asirgarh were annexed to the Mughal empire.

(2) Akbar got several important forts.

(3) The Mughals got a foothold in the Deccan.

Jahangir and The Deccan

Malik Amber's brave resistance Akbar's conquest of Ahmednagar proved to be transitory. Since Jahangir was busy in other affairs, Malik Amber, the officer at Ahmednagar declared independence. Jahangir made three attempts in 1608, 1611 and 1612 to conquer Ahmadnagar but all these failed. At last in 1617, prince Khurram (later on he became Shah Jahan) was successful in getting back all the territories. Prince Khurram received several precious presents and he was highly honoured by emperor Jahangir. The victory over Malik Amber was short-lived. He started offensive against the Mughals.

Prince Khurram was again sent to Ahmednagar to subdue Malik Amber. Malik Amber had to enter into a very humiliating treaty which again lasted for a few years only. Until his death in 1626, Malik Amber kept the Mughals at bay.

Failure of Jahangir's policy in the Deccan Jahangir failed on account of the following factors :

(*a*) Diplomacy and bravery of Malik Amber of Ahmednagar.

(*b*) Corruption in the Mughal army.

(*c*) Mutual rivalry among the Mughal nobles and military officials.

(*d*) Revolts of Jahangir's princes.

Shah Jahan's Deccan Policy

Shah Jahan's Deccan policy was prompted by political as well as religious motives. Being a staunch Sunni he wanted to crush the Shia States of Deccan which had not accepted the Mughal supremacy.

Shah Jahan, (earlier Prince Khurram) was quite familiar with the situation in the Deccan. During the reign of Jahangir, he had led two expeditions and won name and fame.

Shah Jahan secured a positive gain in the extension of his authority over the Deccan during his reign of over twenty-eight years. The Treaty of 1636 with Bijapur and Golkunda proved his skill as a statesman. The suzerainty of Mughal emperor was accepted by these states. Shah Jahan abstained from interfering in the internal affairs of these two states.

Most of the part of Ahmednagar was annexed to his empire.

The Deccan policy of Shah Jahan proved to be very successful.

Aurangzeb and his Deccan Policy

Aurangzeb spent almost second half of his reign in the protracted warfare lasting about 25 years in the Deccan. During this period he remained away from the North.

Aurangzeb's Deccan policy was prompted by the following considerations :

1. Extension of his kingdom.

2. Intolerance against the Shia kingdoms of Bijapur and Golkunda—the kingdoms which had declared independence during the war of succession.

3. Crushing the rising powers of the Marathas.

4. Acquiring the wealth of the rich kingdoms of the South.

While Aurangzeb was able to annex the kingdoms of Bijapur and Golkunda, he failed against Shivaji. Even after Shivaji's death, he failed in suppressing the Marathas completely and till the end he remained a victim of Maratha attacks.

Effects of the Deccan policy of Aurangzeb

Aurangzeb's Deccan policy has been universally denounced as baleful and blundering. According to Dr. V.S. Smith, Deccan was "the grave of Aurangzeb's reputation as well of his body." (Aurangzeb's death took place in the Deccan). In the words of Sir J.N. Sarkar, "If Spanish ulcer ruined Napoleon, the Deccan ulcer ruined Aurangzeb."

Q. 2. Write notes on (*i*) Chand Bibi (*ii*) Malik Amber.

Ans. *Chand Bibi* (16th century A.D.)

Chand Bibi, the widow of Adil Shah, the Sultan of Bijapur and the sister of Nizam Burhan of Ahmednagar was the contemporary of Mughal emperor Akbar. When Akbar sent his army in the Deccan campaign, she was acting as regent guardian of her nephew in Ahmednagar. She led the army wearing a *'Burka'*, against the Mughals. She demonstrated her bravery and courage which made her name immortal in the annals of history. After a continues struggle for a long time against the mighty Mughal forces, she was forced to sign a peace agreement with the Mughals. According to the terms of the treaty, she surrendered Berar to the Mughals and the claim of their nephew was accepted by the Mughals over the rest of the kingdom. This treaty, however, did not last long in view of the conflicting interests of the nobles of Chand Bibi. As a result Akbar again sent his army against Ahmednagar. Realising that the Ahmednagar fort was besieged constantly by the Mughals and not getting help from any source, Chand Bibi started negotiations for peace. But she was opposed by several of her nobles (Amirs), who charged her with treachery and assassinated her. It is also held by some historians that she committed suicide.

Malik Amber

From a slave to a ruler. Malik Amber, an important noble of Ahmednagar, was the contemporary of emperor Akbar and Jahangir. Very little is known about his early life. It is said he was an Abbyssinian, born in Ethiopia and his parents had sold him in the slave market in Baghdad. In course of time he was purchased by a merchant and brought to the

Deccan. Gradually he made his way to the court of Sultan of Ahmednagar and became a confidant of Nizam Shahi ruler.

Head of the civil and military affairs. Malik Amber became virtually all in all during the reign of Murtza Nizamshah II of Ahmednagar. His work embraced almost all departments of the state. He was a great financial expert also. His most important achievement was the reorganisation of the revenue system of his master's kingdom. In this he was guided by the policy followed by Todar Mal.

Malik Amber was also a great military organiser and warrior. He gathered round him a large number of Maratha troopers and trained them in guerilla warfare.

Malik Amber's encounters with the Mughals. During Akbar's time Malik Amber had to face a severe defeat. After the death of Akbar, Malik Amber strengthened his position and Jahangir's son prince Parvez had to conclude a humiliating treaty with Malik Amber.

There was peace for about two years. After that hostilities again came to the forefront. This time Amber suffered heavy losses. After about a year, Malik started counter offensive and with the assistance of other Deccan states, he gained victories over the Mughals.

Malik Amber frustrated Jahangir's attempts at consolidating the Mughal empire in the Deccan. Till his death in 1626, he kept the Mughals at bay.

25

North West and the Frontier Policy of the Mughals

Q. 1. Describe the North-Western Policy of the Mughals.
(Rajastan University 1995)

Ans. *North-Western Policy of the Mughal Emperors.*

Importance of the North-West Defence. The great mountain wall of the Himalayas protected the country from the North and acted as natural barriers against foreign invasions in the north. But the Northwestern ranges of the Himalayas, called the Sulaiman.and Hindukush, being not very high and having large number of passes as the Khurram, the Gomal, the Bolan and the Khyber did allow several horders of invaders to swarm into India. The Persian, the Greek, the Kushan, the Hun, the Turk, the Afghan and the Mughal invaders entered India through these passes. Whenever the rulers of India could strengthen their defence in the northwestern directions, they all remained protected from foreign invaders. To prevent the invaders from reaching the fertile valleys of Punjab and Sind, it was important to provide a strong defence in the northwest, and to control the area extending from Kabul, via Ghazni to Kandhar.

Babur and the North-West. Before invading India, Babur had already captured strategic points of the Hindukush range. He, therefore, did not face any serious problem from the North-West Frontier.

Humayun. Humayun was able to capture Kandhar with the assistance of Shah of Persia. He did not encounter any tribal uprising from this direction.

Akbar. Akbar followed a systematic frontier policy. He suppressed the wild tribes by sending strong forces which had to face serious challenge from the Afghan tribes, especially the Yusufzais. The tribal uprising convinced Akbar to bring the frontier provinces under his strict control. He conquered and annexed Sind, Baluchistan, Kashmir and Kandhar. He secured the empire and brought territorial gains to the Mughal empire in this direction.

Jahangir. Although the Shah of Persia professed friendship with Jahangir, he captured Kandhar.

Shah Jahan. In spite of best efforts, Shah Jahan failed to get foothold.

Aurangzeb. Aurangzeb followed a 'forward' policy on the North-West Frontier. The unruly Afghan tribes of the region created lot of trouble for the Mughals.

There were three important revolts of the Yusufzais (1667), of the Afridis (1672) and the Kataks (1674)

The Mughal Governor of Kabul took recourse to bribes to solve the problem of Afghan tribals. Aurangzeb had to pay a very high price.

Q. 2. State the main principles of the foreign policy of the Mughals. Evaluate their relations with Central Asia.

Ans. *Foreign Policy of the Mughals.*

The foreign policy of the Mughals was related to the interaction with the three great powers of the period namely the Uzbek empire of Central Asia, the Safaid empire of Persia (Iran) and the Ottoman empire of Turkey

The Mughals' original home was in Central Asia. They were driven out by the Uzbeks. The Uzbeks were Sunni Muslims.

The Safaid rulers of Persia were Shia Muslims and they considered themselves supreme and true successors of the Prophet Muhammad.

The Muslims rulers of Turkey claimed themselves to be the true representatives of the Khalifa of Baghdad. They were Sunni Muslims.

Main objectives of the foreign policy of the Mughals.

The foreign policy of the Mughals was guided by the following objectives and principles :

1. To safeguard India from foreign invasions.
2. To maintain balance of power among the Uzbeks, the Safaids and the Turks (Ottoman empire).
3. To increase trade and commerce with other countries.
4. To conquer their ancestral land in Central Asia—homeland from where Babur had been turned out.
5. To check the power of the Afghan tribes, that lived in the mountain region between Punjab and Kabul.

Relations of the Mughals with the Uzbeks in Central Asia

Before analysing the relations among the three powers, it would be desirable to understand their location.

Central Asia included Trans-Oxina. Trans-Oxina (the region in which the Amu *Darya*) earlier called Oxus river flowed, Badakhan, Balk, Bukhara, Samarqand etc.

The Uzbek empire, a land of desert land scapes was in the heart of Central Asia. It was north of Persia and Afghanistan. Its western frontier touched the Turkish empire and south-western touched the Persian empire.

Turkey is between the Black sea and the Mediterranean Sea and Persia is between Turkey and Afghanistan.

Although both the Mughals and the Uzbeks were Sunni Muslims, their political interests clashed.

Babur and the Uzbeks. Babur's homeland was Fargana. He was defeated by the Uzbeks and was deprived of Fargana and Samarqand. After leaving his homeland, Babur moved towards Kabul and he captured Kabul and Kandhar. The Uzbeks had friendly relations with Turkey. Persia's borders and the newly created kingdom of Babur were linked. Persia had been defeated by Turkey. The Uzbeks had friendly relations with Turkey. To maintain balance of power, Babur leaned towards Persia. However, Babur's efforts to capture Fargana and Samarqand failed. Babur occupied Kandhar and there was not much opposition from Persia.

Humayun. Humayun, in his wanderings took shelter with the Shah of Persia who helped him in regaining India.

Akbar. The Uzbek ruler wanted that Akbar should have no friendship with Persia. This proposition was not acceptable to Akbar and he politely declined.

Akbar and the Uzbek ruler entered into a treaty which included the following terms :

(*a*) The Mughal ruler not to take any interest in Badakshan and Balkh.

(*b*) The Uzbek ruler not to interfere in Kabul and Kandhar.

Jahangir. During the reign of Jahangir, Persia snatched Kandhar from the Mughals and Baghdad from the Turks. Then Jahangir, the Uzbeks and the Turks collaborated together to start a triangular fight against Persia. This collaboration was short-lived.

Shah Jahan. Shah Jahan sent several expeditions to conquer Bukhara from the Uzbeks but had to suffer heavy losses. In the beginning of the campaigns prince Aurangzeb had an upper hand and he had even captured Bukhara. But on his return journey, his victory was turned into a rout. The Mughal forces suffered grievous losses—in men and money. It exposed the hollowness of Shah Jahan's power.

Aurangzeb. Aurangzeb made no attempt to recapture the areas occupied by the Uzbeks. He maintained friendly relations with them. There was frequent exchange of ambassadors and gifts from both sides.

The Mughals and Persia

The relations between the Mughal rulers and Persia hanged on the superiority over Kandhar which was situated on that passage which linked India with Persia and countries of Central Asia. Each party asserted an exclusive claim over it on account of the following reasons :

1. Kandhar was very rich and had fertile land.

2. For the Mughals from the political point of view the possession of Kandhar was important as from it they could easily check the foreign invaders to India.

3. Kandhar occupied a very strategic position from the point of view of Persia also.

4. With the possession of Kandhar, it was easy to exercise check on the Afghans, the Baluchis and the hill tribes.

5. The passage of Kandhar had great significance for the pilgrims going to Mecca.

6. Economically the control over Kandhar was important as it was the starting point of traders from China and the Mediterranean sea ports.

7. The possession of Kandhar was claimed by both powers for consideration of prestige and sentiments.

Babur and Persia. Kandhar had been once ruled by Babur's cousin. In the beginning of the 16th century Kandhar was ruled by semi-independent rulers who according to their convenience sided with the Mughals or Persia. Babur conquered Kandhar before becoming the ruler of India. He pacified the ruler of Persia by addressing to him a very conciliatory letter.

Humayun and Persia. Humayun received great help from the ruler of Persia after his defeat at the hands of Sher Shah. The Shah of Persia gave him shelter and help on the condition that after his victories is Hindustan, Humayun would hand over Kandhar to him. However, Humayun after his victories did not hand over Kandhar to Persia. After the death of Humayun, Persia captured Kandhar.

Akbar and Persia. Akbar made no attempt to capture Kandhar till the Uzbeks posed a threat to it. An opportunity came when the Uzbeks attacked Kandhar. The governor of Kandhar failed to get any help from Persia. The governor of Kandhar surrendered Kandhar to Akbar after getting some concessions. Nevertheless the relations between Persia and the Mughals remained cordial.

Jahangir and Persia. Jahangir and the Persian ruler exchanged ambadassors and valuable gifts for several years. However the Mughal ruler neglected the defence of Kandhar and Persia all of sudden captured Kandhar to the great surprise of Jahangir. The ruler of Persia tried to make out that Kandhar belonged to Persia and Jahangir himself should have restored it Persia. On account of the revolt of prince Khurram, Jahangir lost Kandhar.

Shah Jahan and Persia. Shah Jahan made several efforts to conquer Kandhar but without any success. Only for a very short period he could exercise control over Kandhar. Kandhar remained in the hands of Persia. Kandhar campaigns caused a great loss to the Imperial Treasury of the Mughals.

Aurangzeb and Persia. There was no conflict worth mentioning between the Mughal ruler and the ruler of Persia. Aurangzeb made no serious attempt to take Kandhar.

26

Religious Policy and Rajput Policy of the Mughals

Introduction. This chapter recapitulates the policies of the Mughal rulers. Here only the salient features of these policies, and their consequences are summarised to avoid the repetition of the matter contained in the previous chapters.

Q. 1. Examine the religious policy of the Mughal rulers.

Ans. *Divergent views.*

Historians and thinkers have given conflicting views regarding the religious policy followed by the Mughal rulers. The matter has been made so complex, that it is not possible to sift facts. However one may try to be objective, one's vision still remains coloured according to one's prejudiced approach on account of the influence exercised by vested interests.

Religious policy of Babur

The following instances indicate that Babur was not liberal in his religious outlook.

(1) He declared the battle against Rana Sanga of Mewar as *Jihad'* and assumed the title of Ghazi after his victory at Khanwa in 1527.

(2) Babur again fought a 'holy war' against Medini Rai of Chanderi.

(3) The present Ram Janmabhoomi—Babri Masjid controversy which has done great damage to the Hindu-Muslim relations is the outcome of Babur's legacy. It is said that by the command of the emperor Babur, his governor Baqi Tashqandi built a mosque at Ayodhya by destroying an ancient temple which also marked the birth place of Rama whom the Hindus consider him as an incarnation of God.

(*a*) He discriminated against the Hindu traders when he abolished some duties for all Muslim traders.

Some of the historians think that all these acts were done on political considerations and not on religious considerations. Babur had to infuse a new spirit among his soldiers when he realised that they had to face stiff opposition from the brave Rajputs.

Religious policy of Humayun

Humayun was not a bitter persecutor of the Hindus but he never attacked

attacked a Muslim ruler when he was engaged in a fight with any Rajput ruler at the same time. Humayun wanted to crush the power of Bahadur Shah of Gujarat who had annexed Malwa also. Humayun found an opportunity to overpower Bahadur Shah when he was engaged in war with Mewar. But Humayun did not attack him as his enemy being a Muslim ruler was fighting against Non-Muslims.

Akbar's Religious Policy

Akbar is known for his liberal ideas and liberal religious policy. He adopted a policy of mutual understanding and reconciliation among followers of different faiths and equality of all religions. He tried to harmonise the relations. He founded a new religion known as *'Din-i-Ilahi'* based on the common points of all religions. Of course, in this endeavour he was not successful.

Akbar followed the policy of religious toleration on account of the following major considerations :

1. *Influence of the age over Akbar.* In the words of Dr. H.N. Sinha : "The sixteenth century is a century of religious revival in the history of the world. The grand currents of the reformation compare favourably with the staging up of a new life in India. India experienced an awakening that quickened her progress and vitualized her national life. The dominant note of this awakening was love and liberalism—love that united man to God and therefore to his brother man and liberalism, born of this love that levelled down tne barrier of caste and creed, and took its stand on the bed-rock of human existence and essence of all religions—Universal Brotherhood. With glorious ideals it inspired the Hindus and Muslim alike, and they forgot for a time the trivialities of their creed. To the Muslim as to the Hindu, it heralded the dawn of a new era, to the Muslim with the birth of the promised Mahdi, to the Hindu with the realization of the all-absorbing love of God." The Bhakti cult and the Sufis preached religious toleration

2. *Strength and prosperity of an empire depends upon unity of its people.* Dr. V.A. Smith explained the aim of his religious policy in his own words thus : "For an empire ruled by one head, it was a bad thing to have the members divided among themselves, at variance one with the other...We ought, therefore, to bring them all into one, but in such fashion that they should be one and with the great advantage of not losing what is good in any one religion, while gaining whatever is better in another. In that way honour would be rendered to God, peace would be given to the people and security to the empire."

3. Truth in every religion.

4. Influence of several personalities.

Main steps taken for religious harmony

1. Equal treatment with subjects of all faiths.

2. Abolition of *'Jazia'* and other taxes imposed on the Hindus.

3. Matrimonial alliances with Hindu families.
4. Employment of Hindus at higher posts.
5. Freedom of worship to all.
6. Founding a new religion based on the common points of all religions.

Impact of Akbar's policy

1. Empire became strong.
2. An environment of good will was developed.
3. Social reforms took place.
4. Cultural unity emerged.
5. Akbar got the credit of being a national king.

Dr. S.R. Sharma has explained the impact of his policy in these words "Among the rulers of India he occupies a very high place...among other things—his having attempted to bring Hindus and Muslims together with some success...It is worth remembering that at a time when Europe was plunged into strife of warring sects, when Roman Catholics were burning Protestants at the stake, and Protestants were executing Roman Catholics, Akbar guaranteed peace not only to 'warring sects' but to different religions. In the modern age, he was the first and almost the greatest experimentor in the field of religious toleration if the scope of his toleration, the races to which it was applied, and the contemporary conditions be taken into account."

Religious policy of Jahangir

The Hindus were not burdened with extra taxes but there are examples which point out that his treatment with the Hindus was not fair.

(*i*) Jahangir punished Hindus of Rajuri in the state of Kashmir because they used to marry Muslim girls.

(*ii*) Jahangir got a cow killed after his conquest of the Kangra fort.

(*iii*) Jahangir threw away the idol of god Varaha at Ajmer into a pond.

(*iv*) Jahangir closed Christian churches when he was at war with the Portuguese.

(*v*) The most important action of his fanaticism was that he executed the fifth Sikh Guru Arjun Dev.

(*vi*) He ordered the expulsion of all Jains from Gujarat as he suspected that they helped Khusru against Jahangir.

On the other side, he opened higher services for Non-Muslims. In the words of Dr. R.P. Tripathi, "He made practically no difference between the Hindus and the Mohammadans or the Christian subjects."

Religious policy of Shah Jahan

1. According to Khafi Khan, Shah Jahan, issued an order prohibiting employment of Hindus in services.

2. He established a separate department for securing conversion to Islam.

3. Temples in Banaras, Allahabad, Gujarat and Kashmir were broken during his reign.

4. He ordered that those Hindus who embraced Islam would get their share from the property of their father immediately.

5. The war captives were converted to Islam.

6. Culprits who accepted Islam were left free. Christians were persecuted after the capture of Hughly.

According to S.R. Sharma, "He embarked on a campaign of complete destruction of the new temples of the Hindus."

Religious policy of Aurangzeb

Aurangzeb completely reversed the religious policy of Akbar. He followed a policy of persecuting people of all faiths other than Sunnis.

1. He established a separate department for the destruction of temples. All important temples of north India including the Vishwanath Temple of Banaras, Keshav Dev Temple at Mathura etc. were destroyed during his period.

2. Mosques were raised a the sites of temples.

3. Images of Hindu gods and goddesses were broken and used for the construction of mosques.

4. Several taxes including *'Jazia'* were imposed on the Hindus.

5. Hindus in large number were turned out of services and especially of the revenue department.

6. Various kinds of temptations were offered to Hindus to embrace Islam.

7. Restrictions were imposed on the celebration of Hindu festivals and fairs.

8. The execution of the 9th Sikh Guru Teg Bahadur on his refusal to embrace Islam is the most glaring example of the bigotry of Aurangzeb.

9. During his reign, two sons of the 10th Sikh Guru Gobind Singh were buried alive.

Consequences of the religious policy of Aurangzeb. In the words of Pringle Kennedy, "What Akbar had gained...he (Aurangzeb) lost." Dr. Surjit ManSingh in *Historical Dictionary of India'* (1998) has observed, "Some modern historians ascribe to Aurangzeb the intention of ruling India as an Islamic country and depict the Maratha rebellion by Shivaji as an early stage of Hindu nationalism. Some go further in tracing the seeds of partition in 1947 to him. Far fetched though such judgements may be, it is certain that Aurangzeb died in his own words, "forlorn and destitute" and soon after that his empire disintegrated."

Q. 2. Examine the main features of the Mughal relations with the Rajputs.

Or

"Akbar built the Mughal empire by enlisting the support of the Rajputs, Aurangzeb destroyed it by alienating the Rajputs." Discuss this statement with reference to the Rajput policy of the Mughals.

Ans. *No Uniform Rajput Policy of the Mughal rulers.*

Rajput policy of the Mughals differ from ruler to ruler. On the one end was Akbar who tried to take several measures to befriend the Rajputs and on the other there was Aurangzeb who almost reversed Akbar's policy. There was no set policy of Babur, Humayun, Jahangir and Shah Jahan. They were guided by the exigency of the situation.

Babur's Rajput Policy

It is generally held by historiains that Rana Sanga, the Rajput ruler of Mewar was one of the Indian rulers who invited Babur to attack Ibrahim Lodi of Delhi. It is also presumed that some sort of understanding was reached between Babur and Rana Sanga regarding the distribution of territories in India in case Ibrahim lost.

It is held that Rana Sanga did not render any help to Babur in his fight against Ibrahim. At the same time there is no conclusive evidence that Rana Sanga had agreed to help him. He had simply invited Babur and decided not to oppose him and not to help Ibrahim.

Rana Sanga had thought that Babur like Timur Lane would loot the wealth of Delhi and return to his country. This, however, did not happen.

Since both i.e. Babur and Rana Sanga desired to increase their sphere of influence, conflict was inevitable.

Babur fought against Rana Sanga of Mewar and Medini Rai of Chanderi for the expansion of his empire. On both the occasions, he declared *'Jihad'* (Holy war) against the Rajputs who were Hindus. Thus he did not try to secure the friendship of the Rajputs. At the same time, there is no evidence that he regarded them as permanent enemies.

Humayun and Rajputs

According to a legend Rani Karnavati of Mewar sent a *'Rakhi'* to Humayun when Mewar was invaded by Bahadur Shah of Gujarat, a worn enemy of Humayun. According to some historians, Humayun marched from Agra to Gwalior to help the Rajputs but subsequently changed his mind. Perhaps the thought it not proper to invade a Muslim ruler who was fighting against a Hindu ruler. Thus Humayun lost an opportunity to befriend the Rajputs.

Likewise Humayun failed to get the support of Maldeo of Mewar against Sher Shah.

Akbar and the Rajputs

Undoubtedly Akbar pursued a planned policy of friendship in general towards Rajput rulers. He tried to befriend them but at the same time desired to bring them under his suzerainty. Akbar was very successful in his aims.

Reasons for following a policy of friendship. In brief following were the reasons :

(*i*) For establishing a permanent vast and mighty empire in India.

(*ii*) For establishing permanent peace and order.

(*iii*) For making the use of their good qualities like skill in the use of arms and faithfulness.

(*iv*) For shaking off the foreign nature of monarchy.

(*v*) For showing gratitude and affection to Rajputs as he was born under the roof of a Rajput family when Humayun was a fugitive.

For having liberal views on account of the influence of scholars who were liberal in their outlook.

Elements of his Rajput Policy. These were as under :

(*i*) Matrimonial relations with the Rajput families.

(*ii*) Important posts to Rajputs.

(*iii*) Freedom of worship to Rajputs.

(*iv*) Allowing their states with them in the events of accepting his suzerainty.

(*v*) Personal contact and close relations with Rajput rulers.

Maharana Pratap of Mewar was the only Rajput ruler who did not accept the suzerainty of Akbar.

Impact of Akbar's Rajput policy. All the Rajput states of Northern India except Mewar passed under his suzerainty. Those very Rajputs who were fighting against the Muslim rulers for more than three hundred years submitted to Akbar and participated in the expansion of the Mughal empire.

Rajput Policy of Jahangir

Jahangir, the successor of Akbar continued his policy of conciliation with the Rajputs. Jahangir's mother was a Rajput princess. He himself married princesses of many Rajput states like Jodhpur, Jaisalmer and Bikaner. He gave great honour to the rulers of all these houses.

Amar Singh, like his father Rana Pratap gave a tough fight to Jahangir. At last a treaty was signed in 1615 on the following terms :

1. The Rana accepted the suzerainty of the Mughal empires.

2. Instead of himself, he deputed his son to attend the Mughal court.

3. The Rana was not asked to enter into any matrimonial alliance with the Mughal emperor.

4. Jahangir returned to the Rana all territory of Mewar including the fort of Chittor with the condition that it would not be repaired.

Thus ended the long-drawn conflict between Mewar and the Mughals.

Shah Jahan's Rajput Policy

Shah Jahan also followed the Rajput policy of his father and grandfather. The Rajputs continued to serve the empire though they did not have the same prominent position which they enjoyed during Akbar's time.

In 1615 when Rana Jagat Singh of Mewar began to refortify Chittor in violation of the treaty of 1615, Shah Jahan sent a force against him. Ultimately the Rana was forced to tender an apology and to dismantle the new additions to the fort.

Rajput Policy of Aurangzeb

Aurangzeb, like his religious policy, reversed the Rajput policy enunciated by Akbar. He followed the policy of hostility against the Rajputs. Aurangzeb was a Sunni Musalman and he wanted to set-up an Islamic empire in India. He could not tolerate that the Rajputs under him should hold high posts and lead a life of splendour. He took all the possible steps to humiliate them. Among the most important ones were :

(1) He imposed *'jazia'* and pilgrim taxes on them.

(2) They could no longer ride a horse of good quality.

(3) Religious places of the Hindus were sacrileged.

(4) High posts were denied to them.

(5) After the death of his brave and faithful commander, Raja Jaswant Singh of Marwar, an attempt was made to imprison his two wives, his son Ajit Singh and his relatives and Aurangzeb wanted them to be converted to Islam. However he failed to do so. Rajput chief Durga Das, the Prime Minister of Rana Ajit Singh of Mewar fought bravery. Aurangzeb was not successful in subducing the Rajputs. The struggle between the Mughals and the Rajputs lasted for about 30 years. After the death of Aurangzeb, his successor Bahadur Shah recognised Rana Ajit Singh as the independent ruler of Marwar.

(6) Aurangzeb waged war against Rai Singh of Mewar (with its capital at Chittor). He sent three forces under his three sons. Prince Akbar joined the Rajputs. After the death of Rana Rai Singh in 1680, Raja Jagat Singh Signed a treaty with Aurangzeb. The Rana was recognised as the ruler. He however, agreed to part with some of his territory to Aurangzeb in lieu of payment of 'jizya'.

Aurangzeb's Rajput policy proved very disastrous for the Mughal empire.

27

Cultural Development During the Mughals and their Legacy (Progress in Architecture, Painting, Music, Literature)

Q. 1. Write a critical essay on the main features and developments of architecture during Mughal period of India.

(Rajastan University, April 1996)

Ans. *Golden Period of Architecture.*

Although all the Mughal rulers except Aurangzeb took great interest in architecture, yet Shah Jahan surpasses all in the field of architecture. There is no doubt that architecture reached the pinnacle of its glory during the period of Shah Jahan.

The period of Shah Jahan (1627-1658) witnessed a glorious outburst of activity in the development of architecture. At the same time it must also be accepted that a period of 100 years (1556-1658) covered by the reign of Akbar, Jahangir and Shah Jahan has a special significance for the promotion of architecture. Likewise there was some activity in this area in the period of Babur and Humayun. Therefore, it is said that the Mughal period was the golden period of Indian architecture.

Main features of Mughal Architecture

1. *Variety of buildings.* The Mughal rulers built magnificent gates, forts, mausoleums, mosques, palaces, public buildings and tombs etc.

2. *Synthesis of Persian and Indian style.* The specimens of architecture created under the Mughals have become the common heritage of both the Hindus and the Muslims. It is a happy blend of Hindu and Muslim architecture.

3. *Specific characteristic.* A common characteristic of the Mughal buildings is "the pronounced domes, the slender turrets at the corners, the palace hails supported on pillars and the broad/gateways."

4. *Costly decorations.* The Mughal emperors in general but Shah Jahan in particular decorated his buildings with costly articles. One of the important distinguishing features of the Mughal buildings is their ornamentation as compared with the simple buildings of the previous Muslim rulers of India.

5. *Building material.* During the Mughal period, buildings were constructed mostly of red sandstone and white marble.

Development of architecture under different Mughal rulers

Babur and architecture. Babur was not impressed by Indian architecture. At the same time he was busy in waging wars. Nevertheless he sent for the pupils of Sinan the noted Albanian architect to work with Indian craftsmen whose skills he had appreciated. But this did not materialise.

As Babur recorded in his *'Memories'*, he employed 680 workmen and 1491 stone cutters daily on his various buildings in India. He constructed several buildings but only two mosques—one at Panipat and the other at Sambhal have survived.

Humayun and architecture. Humayun's troubled reign did not allow him enough opportunity to give full play to his artistic temperament. Even then he constructed the palace of *'Din-i-Panah'* in Delhi which was probably destroyed by Sher Shah. Humayun constructed some mosques at Agra and Hissar.

Akbar and architecture. The history of Mughal architecture really starts with Akbar. Just as Akbar built up an extensive empire on the goodwill of the Hindus, in the same way he utilised local talent and took inspiration from Indian architecture.

One of the earliest buildings built is the Tomb of Humayun, in Delhi. It was built after Humayun's death by his first wife Hamida Banu Begam. This splendid tomb, designed by a Persian Architect Malik Mirza Ghiyas and executed by Indian craftsmen and masons, is a fine example of the synthesis of Indian-Persian traditions.

Important buildings built during Akbar's time include the following : (1) Red Fort at Agra. (2) City of Fatehpur Sikri (3) Lahore fort, (4) Tomb at Sikandra.

During Akbar's time, it is said that about 500 beautiful buildings were constructed in the Red Fort at Agra but only a few of them now survive.

Main features of Akbar's buildings are : (*i*) Synthesis of Hindu-Muslim art tradition (*ii*) Extensive use of red stone (*iii*) Construction of buildings for civilian purposes.

Jahangir and architecture. Jahangir had fine artistic sense but he was more fond of painting than architecture. Two important buildings were raised. One was the completion of the Tomb of Akbar at Sikandra and the other was the Tomb of Itmad-ul-Daula built by Nur Jahan over the grave of her father. The most important feature of this tomb is that it is decorated with *'pietra dura'* i.e. in-laid with semi-precious stones of different colours.

Shah Jahan and architecture. Shah Jahan's period is usually called the 'Golden Age of Mughal Architecture' and he is given the titles of 'Prince among the Builders' and 'Engineer King'. His most important and impressive buildings are the Taj Mahal, Red Fort and Jama Masjid. These buildings are extremely beautiful and soft. Shah Jahan mostly made use of marble in place of red stone. With a view to enhance the beauty and effect of the ceilings, he made full use of gold, silver, precious and coloured stones. At several places, the pictures of trees, animal scenes and other flora and fauna have been depicted. (See next question).

Aurangzeb and architecture. Aurangzeb's accession to the throne marks the end of rich harvest in building art. His puritanism gave little encouragement to the development of art. He is usually discredited with the destruction of two most important Hindu temples at Banaras and Mathura and raising mosques upon them. He built the Shahi Masjid at Lahore.

Q. 2. Discuss the main features of Mughal architecture during the period of Shah Jahan. (Delhi University, 1997)

Ans. *Shah Jahan's golden period of architecture.*

On account of the intense interest taken and vigorous efforts made in raising magnificent and spacious buildings by Shah Jahan the Mughal period in general and his period in specific came to be known as the golden period of Indian architecture. During his period architecture reached its highest water mark in India. As observed by the noted art critic Percy Brown, "As it was the proud statement of Augustus that he found Rome built of bricks and left it of marble, similarly Shah Jahan had found the Mughal cities of stones, he left them of marble".

Shah Jahan has been variously called as 'Prince among builders' and 'Engineer King' on account of his love for architecture.

Important features of Shah Jahan's buildings are :

1. Shah Jahan's buildings are unmatched in exquisite beauty of form.
2. Shah Jahan's buildings have no parallel in symmetry of design.
3. Shah Jahan's buildings are unsurpassed in grandeur.
4. Shah Jahan's buildings have great strength.
5. Shah Jahan's buildings have beautiful balance among different parts.
6. Shah Jahan's buildings have a great variety—cities, forts, gardens, mosques and palaces etc.
7. Shah Jahan's buildings are located at different places like Agra, Ahmedabad, Ajmer, Delhi, Lahore, Kabul and Kashmir etc.
8. Shah Jahan's buildings display a synthesis of Indian and foreign architectural style.
9. Shah Jahan's buildings are mostly built with white marble in place of red stone.

Taj Mahal (Agra)

Chief features. "By its perfect proportions, luminous beauty, milk-white texture assuming different tones at different times, delicacy and variety of ornamentation, flawless execution of structure and by its picturesque setting, the Taj Mahal stands as a creation of superb beauty and magnificence in Indian architecture."

Rabindranath Tagore has described the Taj as "a tear drop on the cheek of time."

Taj Mahal has been usually described as "a dream in marble, designed by fairies and finished by jewellers."

A view of the whole structure in a moonlight night (*'Chandni rat'*) and its reflection in the calm Jamuna adds the supernatural beauty to the whole structure.

This is the only magnificent monument in the world which reflects the eternal love of a king for his queen.

S.K. Saraswati has remarked : "By its stately and perfect proportions, the delicacy and purity of its lineaments, its milk-white texture assuming different hues and tones at different times and under different conditions, the flawless execution of the structure and of its varied ornaments, and, lastly, by its picturesque setting aided by the ingenuity of man, the Taj Mahal at Agra stands as a creation of superb beauty and magnificence, not only in Mughal architecture but in Indian architecture as a whole."

Why was the Taj Mahal built. The charmful Mausoleum, built in pure and white marble, was erected by the emperor Shah Jahan in the memory of his beloved wife Mumtaz Mahal. Probably it is the only memorial in the world to reflect the eternal love of a king for his queen.

Construction of the Taj Mahal. According to Travernier about 20,000 men took about 22 years to complete it and it cost about three crores of rupees.

About twenty varieties of precious stones were imported from within and outside India to decorate it.

Shah Jahan used *'pietra dura'* a method of decoration on a large scale—inlaid work of jewels.

An important feature of the building is the massive dome and the four slender minarets linking the platform to the main building.

The building stands in the midst of a formal garden.

From all available evidence it is concluded that the principal architect was Ustad Isha (Persian/Turk) who was assisted by a number of Hindu architects. There is also the possibility that for the decoration of the exterior, European artists were consulted.

Moti Masjid. Moti Masjid or Pearl Mosque at Agra is regarded as "the purest and novelist house of prayer." The mosque was built at a cost of Rs. 30 lakhs. According to one writer, "It suggests the struggle of the soul above worldly entanglements."

Jama Masjid. Jama Masjid built at Delhi was constructed with red stone for the use of the royal family. High towers and domes are its special characteristics.

Red Fort and some important buildings in it. In the fort among the important buildings are *'Diwan-Khas'*, the '*Rang Mahal*, *'Nahar Bahishit'* and *'Diwan-i-am'*.

The famous Persian poet Firdausi has said about the beauty of *'Diwan-i-khas'*.

"Gar Firdaus Barooey Zamin Ast, Hamin Asto—Hamin Asto, Hamin Asto"

(If there is heaven anywhere on the earth, it is here, it is here, and it is here,"

'Takhat-i-Tahus'. (Peacock Throne). This throne, a celebrated work of art was used for sitting in the court by Shah Jahan. The throne had an enamelled canopy supported by 12 pillars, each of which bore two peacocks inlaid with gems. A tree covered with diamonds, rubies and pearls etc. stood between the birds of each pair. It took seven years to complete at a cost of a one crore of rupees. In 1739, Nadir Shah who invaded India, carried it away with him to Persia.

Gardens. Shah Jahan was equally interested in gardens. Some of the famous gardens laid out by him are the Wazir Bagh in Kashmir, Shalimar Gardens near Lahore, the Talkatora Bagh and Shalimar Gardens at Delhi.

Summing up

Shah Jahan's buildings combine firmness and vastness with beauty and delicacy. They possess the lustre of a gem and light of the moon.

Q. 3. Write note on Fatehpur Sikri **(Delhi University 1997)**
(Rajastan University 1997)

Ans. *Fatehpur Sikri.*

The most magnificent of emperor Akbar's architectural undertakings was the new capital city of Fatehpur Sikri (city of victory) where Akbar lived for 12 years. He devoted his enormous energy to decorate this city. Several beautiful and spacious buildings could be seen here even today. Among the most famous are : the Buland Darwaza, Jama Masjid, Diwan-i-Am, Diwan-i-Khas, Panch Mahal, Jodha Bai Palace and the Dargah of Sheikh Salim Chishti.

Fatehpur Sikri is situated about 40 km away from Agra.

'Buland Darwaza'. This most striking and colossal *Buland Darwaza'* was built in 1575-76 to commensurate the conquest of Gujarat by Akbar. It is 176 feet high and is still the highest gateway in India. It is raised over a lofty stepped terrace.

Tomb of Sheikh Salim Chishti. Sheikh Salim Chishti was the saint patron of Akbar. The tomb is a marble building within the quadrangle of a mosque. Its cenotaph chamber is surrounded by a corridor with lace-work.

People of all faiths come to this tomb to offer prayer for getting the blessings of the saint for the fulfilment of their desires.

Panch Mahal. It is an unusual five storeyed structure of open pavilion, one upon the other, with pillars and roofs. It has a pyrmidal design with the biggest pavilion of 84 pillars at the base and the topmost with only four pillars as the numbers diminish with each upper storey and each pillar is of a different design.

Q. 4. Write short notes on (*i*) Mughal Painting (*ii*) Mughal Music (*iii*) Literary Activities during the Mughal Period (*iv*) Education.

Ans. *Mughal Painting.*

Main features of Mughal painting

1. *Confined to Mughal court.* Mughal painting remained confined to the Mughal court and did not reach the people.

2. *A synthesis of Indian and Persian elements.* The Mughal rulers brought Persian painters with them. At the same time they patronised Indian painters and the collaboration between these two schools of painters resulted in the synthesis.

3. *Main themes of painting.* Apart from Persian books of fables, themes from Mahabharta were also selected. Indian scenes and landscapes came into vogue.

4. *Abundant use of colours.* Golden colours considered to be the symbols of prosperity of the Mughals began to be used increasingly.

5. *Climax of Mughal painting.* Jahangir had a very discriminating eye and Mughal painting reached its climax of glory during his reign :

Mughal painting during Babur. Although a great lover of art, Babur could hardly find time to devote attention to this art as he mostly remained busy in waging war.

Mughal painting during Humayun. The foundation of Mughal painting was laid by Humayun during his exile from India in Persia and Afghanistan. Two of Persia's greatest painters Mir Sayyid Ali and Abdus Samad came with him to Delhi and helped to produce some paintings.

Mughal painting during Akbar. Under his orders *'Humayunama'* was illustrated. About 1200 paintings were drawn on lines pasted on one side of the manuscript of this book. Abul Fazal has listed 15 outstanding painters like Daswant, Basawan, Kesav and Farrukh Beg. More than 100 painters were recruited from different parts of India. Some of the finest paintings are to be found in the *'Akbarnama'*. Here we find happy blending of both Indian and Persian arts.

Mughal painting during Jahangir. It is generally stated that during Jahangir's time, the art of painting reached its climax and with him departed its soul. Jahangir was not only interested in painting, he was also its keen judge. He established a gallery of painting in his own garden.

He wrote in his biography, *Tuzuk-i-Jahangiri:* "As regards myself, my liking for painting and my practice in judging it have arrived at such a point that when any work is brought before, me, either of a deceased artist or of those of the present day, without the names being told to me, I can say at the spur of the moment that it is the work of such and such man. And if there be a picture containing many portraits, and each face be the work of a different master, I can discover which face is the work of each of them. If any person has put in the eye and eyebrow of a face, I can perceive whose work the original face is, and who has painted the eye and eyebrows." This statement of Jahangir may be regarded as an exaggeration, yet we have to accept that the emperor was not only interested in painting but also a good judge of the art. Jahangir attracted many artists at his court.

Painting became almost an industry with a fine regard for division of labour. One artist drew the outline of scenes of men and animals; the specialist in landscape drew the background; the colourist filled the colours. Sometimes four or five artists worked on a single painting.

European art also attracted Jahangir. Manohar and Basawan excelled in portrait painting, Mansaur specialised in painting rare animals and birds and Abul Hasan was expert in designing colour scheme.

Shah Jahan and painting. He was more interested in architecture and neglected painting. He reduced the number of court painters. Nevertheless *'Shahjahan name* was illustrated.

Mughal painting during Aurangzeb. Aurangzeb's lack of interest in painting reduced all the more the number of court painters. Several artists dismissed from his court found shelter in the courts of several Hindu and Muslim provincial rulers. It resulted in the development of painting in Rajasthan and the Punjab hills (Pahari Painting)

Music during the Mughal Period

Babur. Babur was keenly interested in music and poetry. He himself composed songs of a high standard. He used to spend his leisure in the company of musicians, singers and poets. Vocal and instrumental performances were a recognised feature of emperor's wine parties.

Humayun. It is said that on two days i.e. Monday and Wednesday a week, he devoted lot of time in listening to music. As the story goes when Humayun captured Mandu, he ordered a general massacre of the prisoners and when he learnt that one Baiju Bawra—a musician of fame was among the captives, he asked him to sing a song. Humayun was so much impressed by him that he enrolled him as a musician in his court.

Akbar. Akbar was a great patron of music and musician. Abul Fazal informs as that there were thirtysix musicians in his court. Apart from Akbar, several of his nobles liberally patronised the musicians. Among the famous musicians of his reign were : Tan Sen, Babu Ram Das, Baiju Bawra and Sur Das.

'Tan Sen' (1555-1610). Tan Sen was the leading singer of Akbar's court. Earlier he was a court musician of Raja Ram Chandra of Bhata. When Akbar heard of the fame of Tansen, he sent a request to the Raja to send the master musician to his court. In Akbar's court, Tan Sen became the head of the royal musician and earned wide fame and popularity. Literary sources provide fantastic anecdotes of the effects of his *'dipaka raga'*. It is claimed that through the vibrations and melody of his music, he could make the cloud rain and stream stop. Abul Fazal stated that a musician like Tan Sen had not been born in the last thousand years in India.

Jahangir. Emperor Jahangir was also a great lover of music. He himself was a great musician and composed several songs.

Shah Jahan. Shah Jahan's songs were often very thrilling. In the words of J.N. Sarkar, "Many pure-souled Sufis and holy men with hearts withdrawn from the world who attended these evening assemblies lost their sense in ecstasy produced by his singing." Lal Khan, a son-in-law of Tan Sen was the last singer of his reign. Jagannath and Janardan Bhatta were the other famous poets.

Aurangzeb. Aurangzeb was too much of a puritan to appreciate music. Paradoxically, the largest number of books on classical Indian music in Persian were written during his reign.

Literature

The Mughal period produced a vast literature. This was possible because the Mughal emperors were great patrons of literature. Apart from Persian and Hindi literature, Bengali and Punjabi literature also made strides. Some of the important source books in history were written.

Babur and literary activities. Babur whose mother-tongue was Turkish wrote his *'Tuzak-i-Baburi'* (Memories of Babur) in Turki. During the reign of Akbar, it was translated into Persian. He patronised several scholars.

Humayun and literary activities. During his time, his sister Gulabadan Begum wrote *'Humayunnama'*. Humayun also constructed a big library. In fact his death took place on account of a fall from the staircase of his library.

Akbar and literary activities. Undoubtedly, the period saw the production of a lot of literature of a very high standard. Most of his *'Navratans'* (Nine Jewels) were great literary figures. Abul Fazal was a great historian, philosopher and scholar of the period. He is famous for two important works *'Akbarnama'* and *'Ain-i-Akbari'*. Badauni, a historian of fame wrote, *'Muntakhab-ul-Tawarikh'*. An other noted historian Nizam-ud-Din wrote *'Tabaqat-i-Akbari'*. the *Arthava Veda,* the *Ramayana* and the *Mahabharat.*

Sur, Das, a blind band of Agra wrote *'Sursagar'* in Brij Bhasha.

Sant Tulsi Das produced the immortal *'Ramcharitmanas'* in Awadhi, the eastern Hindi dialect.

The period saw the production of a dictionary of Persian-Sanskrit, named *'Parsi Parkash'*.

'Guru Granth Sahib', the most sacred book of the Sikhs was compiled during this period.

Malik Muhammad Jayasi wrote the famous *'Padmavat'*.

Jahangir and literary activities. Jahangir himself wrote his autobiography *'Tuzuk-i-Jahangiri'*. Other important literary and historical works were *'Iqbalanam-i-Jahangir* and *'Masir-i-Jahangir'*.

Shah Jahan and literacy activities. Shah Jahan's courtier Abul Hamid Lahori wrote *'Padshanama'*. Prince Dara Shikoh was a great scholar of Arabic, Persian and Sanskrit. On account of his patronage, the *'Upanishadas'*, the *'Bhagvad Gita'*, the *'Yoga Vashista'* and the *'Ramayana'* were translated in Persian.

Aurangzeb and literacy activities. The most important work during the period was *'Fatwa-i-Alamgiri'*—a digest of Muslim law. Other works were *'Muntakhab-ul'*-a famous history by Khafi Khan and *'Nuskho-i-Dilkusha'* by Bhimsen.

Education

Following were the important features of the system of education during the Mughal period.

1. *Private enterprise in education. There* was no state system of education. Emperors, nobles and upper classes patronised educational institutions and scholars. Educational institutions were managed mostly by individuals.

2. *Institutions of the Hindus and the Muslims.* In general, the Hindus had their *'Pathsalas'* (schools) and *'Vidyapiths'* (Institutes of Higher learning or colleges) and the Muslims received their education in *'Maktabs'* (schools and *'Madrasas'* (Institutes of Higher Learning).

3. *Curriculum.* Emphasis was an religious education and philosophy. There was no proper arrangement for industrial, technical and vocational education.

4. *Medium of education.* Persian was the medium of education in the *'Maktab'* and *'Madrasa'*.

5. *No mass education.* There was very little provision for mass education.

6. *Women education.* **Female education did not receive due attention.** Only rich people arranged for the education of females.

7. *Role of the teacher.* The teacher was greatly respected.

8. *Examination system.* The admission and promotion of the student depended entirely on his teachers.

9. *Important centres of education.* Agra, Allahabad, Ambala, Delhi, Fatehpur Sikri, Jaunpur, Lahore, Lucknow and Sialkot were important centres of education of the Muslims.

Allahabad, Ayodya, Banaras, Mathura, Mithila, Nadia and Srinagar were important educational centres of the Hindus.

Q. 5. Describe the contribution of the Mughals in various fields.

Ans. *Contribution of the Mughals.*

The Mughal rulers made a great contribution in various fields i.e. administrative, cultural, economic, political and religious.

Administrative contribution. Several aspects of the Mughal administration were adopted not only by the Rajput and Maratha rulers but also by the British. The land revenue system introduced by Akbar exists even todays of course, with a few changes. Several rules and regulations adopted by modern administrators derive their origin to the Mughals.

Cultural contribution. See previous questions of this chapter.

Economic development. The Mughal rulers established royal *'Karkhanas'* and made a notable contribution to the development of handicrafts.

On account of industrial development the balance of trade remained in favour of India.

Political development. The Mughal rulers provided political unity to India. Several parts of the country came under one administration.

Religious development. Divergent views are expressed on this issue. Some scholars greatly highligtht the positive effect of the Sufi and Bhakti movements. There are others who are of the view that the effect of these movements was very limited.

Negative contribution

Before the partition of the country, it was believed in certain quarters that the Mughal period in general was a period of religious harmony. Whether the British were responsible or not for the great divide of the Hindus and the Muslims, the fact remains that the two-nation theory was accepted and it resulted in the partition of the country. Akbar's liberal influence was overshadowed by the fanatic influence of Aurangzeb.

Secondly, scientific and technical development was not given its due importance.

Thirdly, scientific development led to blind faith.

Fourthly, naval power was neglected.

Fifthly, female education was not given its due attention.

28

Rise of the Marathas : Shivaji (1627-1680)

Q. 1. Analyse the factors responsible for the rise of the Marathas in the Seventeenth century. (Delhi University 1997)

Ans. *Rise of the Marathas.*

The rise of the Marathas in the seventeen century is an important and fascinating event in the history of India. This rise is primarily due to Shivaji and the circumstances that shaped his character and that of his followers.

Shivaji welded the Marathas into a superbs mobile fighting force. The Marathas fought for the defence of their religion and territory against Mughal rulers. Following were the important factors responsible for the phenomenal rise of the Marathas :

1. *Inspirational influence of religious and social leaders.* Several prominent leaders in the religious and social fields of Maharashtra inspired the people to unite by preaching faith and Bhakti in one God and by condemning the caste system which had divided the society. The most famous of these reformers were : Tuka Ram, Ram Das, Vaman Pandit and Eknath. Guru Ram Das exercised a tremendous influence by underlying the philosophy of '*Karma*' (action) in his famous book '*Das Bodh*'.

2. *Love for the motherland.* Swami Ram Das's message to the Marathas was, **"Mother and mother country are dearer than heaven itself. Gods and cows, Brahmans and the faith, these are to be protected. Therefore, God has raised you up; when faith is dead, death is better than life : why live when religion has vanished? Gather ye, therefore, the Marathas together; make the dharma live again! For otherwise our forefathers will laugh at us from heaven."**

3. *Character of the Marathas.* Elphinstone has observed in this regard. "They (Marathas) are all active, laboriousy hardy and preserving. If they have none of the pride and dignity of the Rajputs, they have none of their indolence or want of worldly wisdom too. And all these traits were due to the peculiar physical features of their country." Shivaji made the best use of these characteristics of the Marathas.

4. *Ready-made and easily defensible rock forts.* The broken ranges of the hills provided natural forts and the people were inspired to regard these forts as their mother-the seats of their protection.

5. *Influence of language and literature.* Eknath taught the Marathas to take pride in their mother tongue which helped in bringing about a sense of commonness and unity among the Marathas. As remarked by J.N. Sarkar, "A remarkable community of language, creed and life was attained in Maharashtra in the 17th century even before political unity was conferred by Shivaji".

6. *The geographical conditions.* The location of Maharashtra and its physical features helped in the rise of Maratha power. The large part of Maratha land is a plateau where the Marathas had to struggle hard for their existence. This made the Marathas courageous and hard working.

7. *Economic equality.* The Marathas did not suffer much from economic inequality, as there were not many people to be accepted as rich. There was no class of economic exploiters. This gave the Marathas a spirit of self-respect and unity.

8. *Guerilla warfare.* The mountainous areas made it possible for the Marathas to adopt guerilla warfare very successfully. The scattered areas in the villages provided provision for soldiers. The invaders were prone to sudden attacks from forts located on the tops of hills. Means of communications for the large armies to move freely were not easily available. This obstructed the deployment of large armies by the outside rulers.

9. *Training in the art of administration.* Even prior to the rise of Shivaji, the Marathas had acquired experience and training in the art of administration. There were a number of Marathas employed in various departments and especially in the revenue department of the Muslim rulers of the Deccan. The Maratha Jagirdars were playing an important role in the political affairs of the states of Bijapur, Ahmednagar, Berar and Golkunda etc. Several departments were virtually controlled by Maratha statesmen and warriors.

10. *Unstable political condition of the South.* The Muslim kingdoms in the South were in the process of disintegration. The political situation was quite favourable for the rise of the Marathas.

11. *Charismatic personality of Shivaji.* J.N. Sarkar has described the influence of Shivaji in the rise of the Marathas in these words, "Before his rise, the Maratha race was scattered like atoms through many Deccani kingdoms. He welded them into a mighty nation and he achieved this in the teeth of the opposition of four mighty powers like Mughal empire, Bijapur, Portuguese India and the Abyssinians of Janjira. No other Hindu has shown such capacity in modern times. He was not only the maker of the Maratha nation, but also the greatest constructive genius of medieval India and the memory of a true hero as king like Shivaji remains imperishable historical legacy for the human race."

Q. 2. Review the life and achievements of Shivaji.

Or

Assess Shivaji as a nation builder.

Or

State the causes responsible for the success of Shivaji and briefly assess his achievements.

Or

What do you know about the early career and achievements of Shivaji?
(Rajastan University 1995 and April 1997)

Ans. *Shivaji as an empire and nation builder.*

Although several circumstances are said to be responsible for the rise of Shivaji and his building a strong nation and an empire but the fact remains that it was his charismatic personality that was responsible for his phenomenal achievement. Circumstances in fact already existed and no body tried to make use of these. It was Shivaji who took the initiative and shaped the circumstances according to his mould.

Following were the important reasons for the success of Shivaji :

1. Inspirational influence of religious and social leaders like Eknath and Guru Ram Das.
2. Love for the motherland.
3. Oppression of Mughal rulers.
4. Special characteristics of the Marathas like habits of hard work.
5. Geographical surroundings.
6. Ready-made natural forts.
7. Influence of language and literature and love for the community.
8. Economic equality on a large scale among the Marathas.
9. Guerilla warfare.
10. Training in the art of administration.
11. Diplomatic skills.
12. Unstable political situation in the south.

Early life of Shivaji. Born in 1627, in the fort of Shivnes, near Poona to Jijabai, wife of Shahji Bhonsle, an important officer in the state of Bijapur, rose to become a nation builder. He was brought up under the care and influence of his mother a pious lady, his guardian Dadaji Konddeva and religious and social reformers like Guru Ram Das.

The secluded hilly regions of the Mavals (the western valleys of Poona now Pune) offered Shivaji plenty of opportunity of or adventure.

Aims of Shivaji. (1) To protect Hinduism. (2) To organise the Marathas under him to carve out an independent kingdom in Maharashtra.

Important events and achievements of Shivaji

Shivaji was successful in achieving both the aims stated above. Important events of his reign and his achievements are given below :

1. Conquests of forts of Torna, Raigarh, Purandar and Kondana etc.
2. Killing of Afzal Khan, the general of Bijapur through his great diplomatic and military skill.

3. Shivaji's conflict with Aurangzeb.

(*i*) Defeat of Shayista Khan, a very able general of Aurangzeb. Surprise attack on him in the disguise of a marriage party.

(*ii*) Treaty of Purandhar with Aurangzeb.

(*iii*) On the persuasion of Jai Singh, a very faithful commander of Aurangzeb, Shivaji's visit to Agra in the court of Aurangzeb; Aurangzeb's ill treatment of Shivaji and his confinement; Shivaji's escape through diplomacy.

(*iv*) Shivaji's victories over the forces of Aurangzeb.

4. Attack on Surat.

5. Coronation of Shivaji in 1674.

6. Shivaji's victories in the Deccan.

Assessment of Shivaji's Achievements

1. *Creation of the Maratha empire.* From a scratch, Shivaji built a strong empire a mids the strong opposition of the mighty Mughal. Kingdom under Aurangzeb. Shivaji's kingdom included Maharashtra, Konkan and a large part of Karnataka, It comprised Ramnagar in the north to Karwar in the south. In the east, it included Baglana, half of Nasik and Poona districts, Satara and a larger part of Kolhapur district. It also included a major part of Mysore, parts of the districts of Bellary, Chittur and Arcot. He had also hold over the Kanara region as well.

He had also a large area in the Deccan under his influence from where he collected *Chauth* which yielded him substantial income.

Shivaji empire had the following four provinces according to his administrative set-up.

(*i*) *Northern provinces.* In this part were included Balaghat, Kori region, Southern Surat, Northern Konkan, Northern Bombay and Poona. It was under Peshwa Maro Trimbak Pingle.

(*ii*) *Southern provinces.* In this were included Southern Bombay, Southern Konkan, Coastal regions, Samantvari regions etc. This province was under Annaji Pant Datto.

(*iii*) *South Eastern provinces.* This province included the regions of Satara, Kolapur, Belgaon and Dharwal and Kopal. It was under the charge of Sar-Karkun Dattaji Trimbak.

(*iv*) *Far Southern province.* This province included distts from Kopal to Vellure like Zinzi, Velari Madras, Chittoore, and Arcot etc. This province was under military officials.

Shivaji's qualities

1. *An effective organiser.* Shivaji is known as one of the greatest organisers in history. By dint of his remarkable powers, he collected together the scattered Marathas and turned them into an organised formidable force.

2. *An efficient general and military strategist.* He was a successful general and knew well how to strike at the enemy. As a result of his

strategies, he was able to face the mighty armies of the Sultans of Bijapur and the Mughals.

3. *A skilful diplomat.* He never let his enemies unite against him. He got his father free from the Sultan of Bijapur on account of his diplomacy. His freedom from the detention of Aurangzeb at Agra speaks volumes of his diplomacy.

4. *Brave soldier.* He was very daring and was prepared to take calculated risks.

5. *An enlightened administrator.* Shivaji was an administrator of great ability and practical vision. He personally looked after the working of various departments. He was ruthless with those officers who indulged in corruption and oppression.

6. *Respect for others faith.* His treatment with the followers of other faiths was very fair. Even a great critic of Shivaji like Khafi Khan has observed about him that he had "made it a rule that whenever his followers went plundering, they should do no harm to the mosques, the Book of God (*Quran*) or the women of anyone."

7. *An inspiring leader.* His influence on account of his inspiring leadership grew so rapidly that his staunch enemy Aurangzeb himself had to admit "My armies have been employed against him for nineteen years and nevertheless his (Shivaji's) state has always been increasing."

8. *An obedient son.* Shivaji loved his parents greatly. He was extremely devoted to his mother Jijabai. He worshipped her like a goddess and obeyed her command.

9. *A dutiful disciple.* Shivaji had a great respect for his gurus.

10. *Regenerator of the Hindus.* Shivaji attempted to generate a new spirit of pride among the Hindus. He however, was also very particular to maintain the honour of Muslim women and the holy Quran.

11. *A benevolent ruler.* Shivaji worked for the welfare of his subjects.

12. Shivaji *as the maker of Maharashtra.* Shivaji welded the Maratha race into a mighty nation and he achieved all this in the teeth of the opposition of mighty powers like the Mughals, Bijapur and the Portuguese in India. As J.N. Sarkar, the great historian said, "He welded the Marathas into a mighty nation."

Q. 3. Discuss the treaty of Purander and its significance.

Or

Explain Shivaji's encounter with Aurangzeb. State the reason which enabled Shivaji to have an upper hand over his adverseries.

Ans. *Shivaji's Encounter's with Aurangzeb.*

A giant killer. Shivaji, the 'little great man' was a giant killer. Shivaji killed Afzal Khan, the reputed general of several successful battles he fought on behalf of the Bijapur state; defeated the famous general and governor of Shayista Khan, sent by the Mughal emperor Aurangzeb humbled Aurangzeb by escaping from his custody and by crippling his power in the Deccan. In words of Aurangzeb himself, "My armies have been employed against him for nineteen years and nevertheless his (Shivaji's) state has always been increasing." The mighty Mughal ruler Aurangzeb, ruling over a vast empire in Indian had to eat a humble pie at the hands of Shivaji.

Reasons for encounters with the Mughals. Aurangzeb was greatly alarmed at the growing power of Shivaji and his victory over Afzal Khan. He was an imperialist and he could not tolerate any challenge to his power. Moreover he was a bigot Sunni and on the other hand Shivaji wanted to protect Hinduism and enhance his power. Thus the conflict between the two was inevitable.

(1) *Defeat of Shayista Khan* (1659-63). Aurangzeb directed Shayista Khan, Governor of the Deccan to take action against Shivaji. Shayista Khan captured several forts including Poona and made it his headquarters. Shivaji was waiting for a suitable opportunity. Rainy season started.

Shivaji disguised himself in a marriage party which actually consisted of a strong and faithful troop of Maratha soldiers and made a surprise attack at Shaiyasta Khan at his palace at Poona. Shaiysta Khan lost his fingers but was successful in running away. Shivaji killed his sons and some Mughal soldiers. After some time Shivaji captured Poona.

(2) *Attack at Surat* (1664). Shivaji, emboldened by his success at Poona, launched a terrible attack on the Mughal port of Surat and got enormous wealth from this place.

(3) *Treaty of Purander* (1665). Aurangzeb deputed Raja Jai Singh, one of his ablest commanders and diplomats to take strong action against Shivaji. Jai Singh captured several forts and Shivaji was forced to sign a peace treaty in 1665. The treaty contained the following terms.

1. Shivaji surrendered twenty-three of his forts and territory yielding an annual revenue of four lakhs of *hun*.

2. Shivaji was left with only twelve forts and territory which yielded annual revenue of one lakh of *hun*.

3. Shivaji accepted the suzerainty of the Mughuls but, instead of personal attendance at the court, deputed his son, Shambhuji with 5,000 horse at the Mughul-court.

4. Shivaji agreed to support the Mughuls against Bijapur.

Another term was added to the treaty afterwards by which :

5. Shivaji agreed to pay forty lakhs of *huns* to the Mughuls in thirteen years provided the territory of Konkan which yielded annual revenue of four lakhs of *'huns'* and the territory of Balaghat which was in the possession of Bijapur and yielded an annual income of five lakhs of *'huns'* were

assigned to him.

The treaty was a great diplomatic success of Raja Jai Singh.

Shivaji personally handed over the key of Sinhgarh fort to Jai Singh's son and joined Jai Singh with his force in the war on Bijapur.

(4) *Shivaji's visit to Agra.* Jai Singh persuaded Shivaji to visit Aurangzeb's court by holding out very high hopes to him. He also took upon personal responsibility for his safety at Agra, the capital of the Mughal empire. According to some historians, Shivaji agreed to go to Agra for having personal knowledge about Aurangzeb and his sources of strength.

The Prime Minister, Asad Khan led Shivaji and his son to the emperor's presence. Both offered the customary *nazar*. Then both were taken back and asked to stand in the third row of nobles. Noticing this insult, Shivaji burst out in a sort of open defiance complaining the breach of the terms. Aurangzeb was enraged. Shivaji was sent to a new residence, more secluded where he could be killed without a public scandal.

Shivaji thought of a plan to escape. He pretended to be ill and started sending outside baskets of sweets for distribution among the Brahmans and the poor. These baskets were checked for sometime by the guards but later on watch on the sweets baskets was relaxed.

Shivaji took advantage of this and he and his son went out in two baskets. It is said that he had bribed a few Mughal officers not to check all the sweets baskets. Afterwards he disguised himself as a *Sanyasi* (hermit) and reached Maharashtra after twenty-five days. During this period he visited Mathura, Allahabad, Banaras, Gondwana and Golkunda on the way.

In 1668 peace was again restored with Aurangzeb and Shivaji.

During 1668-69, Shivaji occupied himself with the reorganisation of his internal administration.

(5) *Again struggle with the Mughals.* After a brief respite, hostilities between Shivaji and Aurangzeb again started. This time Shivaji was able to recover all the forts and territory that he had to surrender in terms of Treaty of Purandhar in 1665.

Shivaji plundered Surat again in 1670. Between 1670 and 1674, the Marathas got success everywhere. The Mughal power in the Deccan was crippled. He also snatched away several forts from Bijapur.

Coronation of Shivaji. In 1674, Shivaji held his coronation according to Vedic rites. The coronation ceremony was performed by Vishweshwar Alias Gaga Bhatt, a renowned Pandit of Banaras. He assumed the title of *Chhatrapati* and *Gau-Brahamana Prrati Palak* (Protector of Brahmans and cows). With the coronation, Shivaji became an independent ruler. Shivaji made Raigarh as his capital.

Factors responsible for the success of Shivaji against Aurangzeb

First, Shivaji received the overwhelming support of the Hindus for his proclaimed ideal of establishing an independent Hindu kingdom.

Second, some of the nobles like Raja Jai Singh and Jaswant Singh of Aurangzeb's court had a soft corner for Shivaji.

Third, when Aurangzeb imposed *Jizya* on the Hindus, Shivaji was the only Hindu ruler who protested against it and wrote a letter to Aurangzeb against Jizya. Thus the Rajput chiefs considered to be the champions of Hinduism did not show enthusiasm to fight against Shivaji, who was championing the cause of Hinduism.

Fourth, saints like Ram Das and Tukaram preached for the revival of Hinduism and their followers rendered great help to Shivaji for this cause.

Fifth, Shivaji had instructed his soldiers not to destroy any mosque or to be disrespectful to Quran or to Muslim women and children. Therefore, the Muslims were not unhappy with him.

Sixth, from time to time, Shivaji could get help from the Sultans of Deccan in his fight against the Mughals.

Seventh, Shivaji proved to be more diplomatic than the commanders of Aurangzeb and the Sultan of Bijapur.

Eighth, Shivaji's character and personality paid him dividends.

Lastly, the geographical conditions of Maharashtra made it possible for him to resort to guerilla warfare and take the enemy by surprise.

Q. 4. Give the salient features of Maratha administration under Shivaji.

Ans. *Shivajis' Administration.*

Shivaji has been called the 'father of the Maratha nation.' Besides being a great conqueror and a diplomat, he was a successful administrator. In the words of Dr. Ishwari Prasad, "His system of administration was better than the Mughal administration in several areas."

A benevolent administrator. Dr. R.C. Majumdar writes of him, "He was not merely a daring soldier and successful military conqueror but also an enlightened ruler of his people."

Shivaji was readily accessible to his all subjects. He was a popular monarch. He kept a close watch on the administrative affairs of the state. All powers were concentrated on him but he ruled with the advice of his ministers.

The common people regarded him with great devotion. They considered him as their greatest benefactor.

General features of Shivaji's administration

1. He employed members of all castes and tribes to maintain balance among them.

2. He assigned separate responsibilities to the ministers and each of them was made responsible for his work to him.

3. He made no office hereditary.

4. In general he did not assign jagirs to his civil and military officers.

5. He gave special attention towards the administration of the forts.

6. In matters of administration, he gave superior position to his civil officers as compared to military officers.

7. He established Ryotwari system in revenue administration. The state kept direct contact with the farmers.

Shivaji took special care to make his administrative system responsive to the needs of the people. In the words of Dr. Ishwari Prasad, "The institutions which he established were an improvement upon the existing order and were well adapted to the well-being of his subjects."

Central Administration. He had a council of ministers (*Asht Pradhan*) to advise him on the matters of the state but he was not bound by it. He could appoint or dismiss them. This appointment was subject to their efficiency. The *Peshwa* was the first among ministers. The word *Peshwa* stands for leader or senior one.

The Peshwa	The Amatya or Majumdar	The Mantri or Waquia Nawis	The Sachiv or Shuru-Nawis	The Sumant or Dabir —	The Senapati or San-i-Naubat	The Pandit Rao or Danadhyaksha	The Nyyaya-dhish
1. Chief Minister 2. Looked after general administration	Responsible for Finance i.e. income and expenditure	Looked after the personal safety of the king	Responsible for all correspondence	Worked as foreign minister	Commander in-chief Looked after recruitment, training and discipline etc. of the army	1. Looked after charitable work 2. worked for the moral uplift of the people	Looked after justice in the kingdom

Shivaji's *Asht Pradhan* (Council of Eight Ministers)

Excepting the *Senapati*, all other ministers were Brahmans.

All excepting the *Pandit Rao* and Nyayadish were expected to command the army whenever needed.

Provincial administration. Shivaji divided his kingdom into four provinces. Each province was under the head called *Mamlatdar* or Viceroy. Each province was divided into several districts and villages. The village was an organised institution. The chief of the village was called *Deshpande* or *Patel.* The head used to run the affairs of the village with the help of the Village Panchayat.

Like the centre, there was a committee or council of eight ministers with Sar-i-*'Karkun'* or the *'prantpati'* (Head of the province)

Fiscal system or Revenue system. Important features were :

(1) Land in every village was measured and the produce was roughly assessed. (2) On the basis of assessment, the cultivators were asked to pay 40 per cent of their produce as land revenue. (3) The Ryotwari system was introduced in which the revenue was directly collected from the farmers. (4) Wherever possible, Shivaji abolished the jagirdari system. (5) The farmers had the option to pay land revenue in cash or kind. (6) The peasants could pay the revenue in instalments. (7) The accounts of the revenue officers began to be thoroughly checked. (8) In the event of famine of natural calamity, the state offered loans to the peasants. (9) Shivaji introduced the collection of two taxes called the *Chauth* and *'Sardeshmukhi'*.

'Chauth' and *'Sardeshmukhi'*. Historians differ as to the exact nature of these two taxies levied by Shivaji. According to Ranade, *'Chauth'* was not merely a military contribution without any moral or legal obligation but a payment in lieu of protection against the invasion of a third power and he compares it with Wellesley's Subsidiary Alliance System. Sardesai holds that it was a tribute exacted from hostile or conquered territories. J.N. Sarkar is of the opinion that Chauth was only a means of buying off one robber and not a subsidiary system for the maintenance of peace and order against all enemies. Thus *'Chauth'* was a military contribution paid toward off any attack of the Marhatas. It was, in theory, ¼ of revenues of the district invaded but in practice it was sometimes much more than that.

Sardeshmukhi was an additional tax of 10% which Shivaji claimed as the hereditary Sardeshmukhi or overlord of Maharashtra.

Judicial administration. Judicial administrative system was rather simple, crude and primitive. The highest court was *'Hazar Majils'* or the court of the king. The day-to-day administration was carried on by the village Panchayats and the village *'Patel'* decided criminal cases.

Shivaji's army administration

Shivaji's army organisation was very efficient. His army was very patriotic, well trained, efficient and extremely mobile.

Shivaji introduced the following reforms in the army :

1. *Regular army.* He maintained a regular army. In the traditional military organisation, the soldiers served army for six months and thereafter, they worked in their fields. Now the soldiers were to serve around the year.
2. *Cash payment.* He paid the soldiers in cash.
3. *Patriotism.* He inspired the soldiers with patriotism.
4. *Merit.* He recruited the soldiers on merit.

5. *Branding of horses.* He introduced the system of branding the horses and keeping the identification of the soldiers.

6. *Discipline.* He enforced strict discipline.

7. *Guerilla warfare.* He trained his soldiers in the guerilla warfare.

The guerilla warfare was very suitable in the geographical location of most territories in Maharashtra. He believed in the surprise attacks on the enemy, killed or looted it and disappeared into the forest.

8. *Forts.* He paid particular attention to the maintenance of forts. Old forts were repaired and new forts built. The forts also served as military cantonments. About the sanctity of forts it is said that the "people were taught to regard them as their mother." There were about 280 forts. The inhabitants of the surrounding villages took protection in these forts.

The families of the deceased soldiers were looked after carefully.

9. *Muslim soldiers.* Shivaji had about seven hundred Muslim soldiers.

Divisions in the army. Army had six divisions namely, cavalry, infantry, camel battalions, elephant battalions, artillery and navy.

1. *The cavalry.* The cavalry formed the main part of the army. Its number was 40,000. There were two categories of horsemen :

(*i*) *Bargis.* They were paid from the state exchange.

(*ii*) *Silhadars.* They were casual soldiers and they numbered about 50,000.

Discipline in the army. Shivaji was very strict in maintaining discipline in the army. To kill or torture ladies and children, to loot the *Brahmans,* to spoil cultivation etc. were punishable offences even during the course of war. Elaborate rules for the maintenance of discipline were rigorously enforced. No soldier was allowed to take his wife in the battlefield.

Liberal Religious policy. Shivaji was a cultured and a tolerant Hindu ruler. He proclaimed to be the protector of the Hindus, the Brahmans and the cows. He showed respect to religious texts of all religions. He did not destroy a single mosque. He protected Muslim ladies and children even during the course of war. He gave financial help to Muslim scholars and saints. He employed Muslims in civil and military departments. When Aurangzeb issued a fresh order reimposing the *jizya* on all the Hindu population, it was an open challenge as much to Shivaji as to many Rajput chiefs. Shivaji wrote a strong letter of protest to Aurangzeb. He wrote "God is the Lord of all men and not of the Muhammadans only. Islam and Hinduism are only different pigments used by the Divine Painter to picture the human species." At the same time Shivaji was never actuated by a hatred of the Muslims. He respected the personal honour of a Muslim as

Short Answer Type Questions

Q. Answer the following in paragraph of about 100 words each.

(Each for five marks)

1. Effects of Muhammad Ghori's Invasions. *(Punjab Univ. April 1995)*

2. Effects of Mahmud Ghaznavi's Invasions. *(Punjab April 1996, Oct. 97 and 98)*

3. Alberuni.

4. Origin of Rajputs.

5. Military weakness of Rajputs against Invaders.

6. Chola Local Administration.

7. Chola Architecture.

8. Balban's Blood and Iron Policy *(Punjab April 97)*

9. Balban's Frontier Policy against Mongols.

10. Ala-ud-Din's Control over Markets. *(Punjab April 1995, Oct. 96 and 97)*

11. Nature of the Government of Delhi Sultans.

12. Experiments and Schemes of Muhammad Tughlaq. *(Punjab April 1997)*

13. Estimate of Firoz Tughlaq.

14. Invasion of Timur.

15. Krishnadeva Raya *(Punjab April 1998)*

16. Conflict between Vijayanagara Kingdom and Bahmni Kingdom.

17. Battle of Talikota.

18. Bhakti Movement. *(Punjab Oct. 96)*

19. Sant Kabir.

20. Guru Nanak Dev. *(Punjab April 96 and Oct. 97)*

21. Sufi Movement. *(Punjab Oct. 97 and Oct. 98)*

22. First Battle of Panipat. *(Punjab April 1995, Oct. 96 and 97)*

23. Battle of Kanwah. *(Punjab Oct. 1998)*

24. Causes of Babur's Success in India. *(Punjab April 96)*

25. Revenue Administration of Sher Shah. *(Punjab April 1997)*

26. Significance of the Second Battle of Panipat.

27. Din-i-Ilahi. *(Punjab April 96)*

28. Provincial Administration of Akbar. *(Punjab April 1995 and Oct. 96)*

29. Mansabdari System.

30. Land Revenu System of Akbar. (Punjab April 98)

31. Rana Pratap.

32. Conquest of Golkonda by Aurangzeb *(April 1995 and Oct. 96)*

33. Mughal Architecture. (*Punjab 1995, April 97 and 1998*)
34. Mughal Painting.
35. Chauth and Sardeshmukhi. (*Punjab April 97 and 98*)

Answers

1. Effects of Muhammad Ghori's Invasions

Muhammad Ghori's invasions (1179 to 1192) had far reaching consequences on the history of India. "This hero of three stupendous defeats—Andhkhud, Tarain (1191) and Anhilwara" as Professor Habib calls him "has to his credit the establishment of one of the greatest empires of the middle ages and in this he definitely rises above Mahmud of Ghazni." Muhammad fully understood the fluid and unstable political conditions of India prevailing at that time and made its best use. He gave proof of his farsightedness in dealing with different Rajputs and gave a severe blow to their power. In the words of Dr. D.C. Ganguly, "The defeat of Prithviraj in the second battle of Tarain not only destroyed the imperial power of the Chauhans but also brought disaster on the whole of Hindustan." The conquests of Ajmer and Delhi paved the way of the conquest of India by the Muslims. Besides, his other conquests demoralised the morale of other Rajput rulers to resist other Muslim invaders. His lieutenant Qutab-ud-Din Aibak consolidated his conquests. There is no doubt that Muhammad Ghori founded the Muslim rule in India.

2. Effects of Mahmud Ghaznavi's Invasions

Mahmud Ghaznavi's invasions and conquests paved the way for later conquests by other invaders. It is an irony and sad commentary on the helpless political conditions of India that Mahmud roamed about in India without facing any serious resistance. "He took from India whatever he could and destroyed the rest." He himself did not establish his empire in India. Important effects of his invasion are as under :

1. Mahmud's victories exposed the political disunity of India.
2. Victories of Mahmud exposed the military weakness of India.
3. Mahmud carried huge wealth out of India and thereby weekened the economic condition of India.
4. Mahmud, by destroying idols., temples and beautiful palaces, gave a great setback to Indian art and sculpture.
5. Mahmud paved the way for foreign invaders to invade India.
6. Mahmud provided a foothold in India for the promotion of Islam in India.

7. Mahmud's invasion which were mainly directed upon Hindu temples created a feeling of illwill among the Hindus towards the Muslims.
8. Mahmud was accompanied by a famous historian Alberuni whose accounts serve as a very useful source of information about the various aspects of life in India.

3. Alberuni (970-1039 A.D.)

Alberuni was a well known astronomer, author, historian, mathematician and philosopher of Central Asia who joined Mahmud Ghaznavi's court and accompanied him on raids in India. He studied Indian languages and civilizations, took part in learned discussions and translated some Sanskrit works on astronomy into Arabic. He wrote his accounts on India in his book. **'Tahquq-Hind'**, whose English translation *'Alberuni's India'* was published in 1888. It covers a wide range of topics—arts, literature and science and above all general conditions of India. He paid special attention to astronomy and religion and drew comparisons between Greek and Indian ideas. Alberuni's book forms a valuable source for the history of the period.

4. Origin of Rajputs

The origin of Rajputs is shrouded in mystery. Different historians hold quite different divergent views and have advanced different theories. Some of the important ones are the following :

1. *Foreign Origin Theory.* Its chief advocate is Colonel Todd, the author of *Anaals and Antiquities of Rajasthan.* In the book he has tried to show that the Rajputs are the descendants of certain foreign tribes like Kushans, Sakas, Huns and Gurjaras. These invading tribes began to marry the Indian women and were got merged in Hinduism.
2. *Theory of Descent from Kshatriya Heroes.* Some scholars hold that the Rajputs are pure Aryans. They are descendants of the *Suryavansi* and *Chandravansi* dynasties of the Kshatriyas.
3. *Theory of Descent from the original warlike Tribes of India.* Some writers are of the view that the Rajputs belonged to the indigenous tribes of Central India.
4. *Agnikund Theory.* It is a mythical theory difficult to be accepted. The legend says that when Parashurama destroyed all the Kshatriyas, the Brahmans kindled a sacred fire at Mount Abu and prayed for a warrior class to protect them. Out of the pit of fire four warriors sprang out and they founded four Rajput families.
5. *Theory of the Mixed Races.* Dr. V.A. Smith and others have come

to the conclusion that Rajputs were people of the most diverse descent. Many Rajput clans descended from the foreigners and many others descended from indigenous tribes of India. It is generally accepted as a plausible theory.

5. Military Weakness of the Rajputs against Invaders

In spite of bravery and courage, the Rajputs failed against invaders. Some of the important military causes of their defeat are given below :

1. *Lack of appropriate military organisation.* The Rajput army advanced with all the wings together—the right, the centre and the left. The Turks were not only well organised and well equipped but used a special strategy with their two units—one advanced guard and the other the reserve. The advanced guard was meant to test their strength and to find out their weak areas. The reserve was thrown into the battlefray after the Rajputs had exhausted their resources.
2. *Overdependent on elephants.* The elephants were easily struck with fright with the swiftness and the sound of the battle and as they turned to run helter-skelter they spread fear and disorder besides causing loss of life.
3. *Lack of offensive.* The Rajputs mostly fought defensive battles. This was not the way of winning a battle.
4. *Swords men versus archers.* The Muslim archers shooting arrows from their horses were more than a match for the Rajput soldiers with their swords which could become effective only if they could reach close to the enemy.
5. *Lack of military leadership.* Rajputs were very brave and chivalrous but lacked capable military leaders having the knowledge of the latest military plans, techniques and strategies and the capacity to infuse zeal in every soldier and to rouse the battle fury to do or die.

6. Chola Local Administration (Medieval Period)

The period from the 9th to 13th century under the Cholas of south India was not only remarkable for political integration in South India but also for the development of art, architecture, literature and administration etc.

Local self-government. The most important feature of the Chola administration was the working of self-government. It is generally held "No other ruling dynasty of either the North or the South had such an extensive arrangement of local self-government at different units of the administration as the Cholas."

There were 4 kinds of popular assemblies :

1. The *Natlas* assembly looked after the civic problems; 2. the *Nagarata* assembly looked after the civil and trade problems of the city; 3. the *Ur* was a gathering of the villagers; and 4. the *Mahasabha* was a powerful village assembly.

Village autonomy : a unique set up. The 'Mahasabha' or the village assembly was representative body. The number of wards in a village for the purpose of election to the 'Mahasabha' depended upon the size of the population of the village. Each ward elected one member. The meeting of the assembly was held in a temple or public hall. It had eight committees to look after eight aspects.

7. Chola Architecture (South Indian Architecture)

Temple Architecture. The Chola temples are described as the most beautiful specimens of Tamil architecture. Their best examples are the Brihadisyara Temple (also known as Rajarajaesvara temple) built by Rajaraja I in 1000 at Tanjor and another temple built by his son Rajendra I in about 1025 at Gangaikondacholapuram. Both the temples were dedicated to Shiva.

Following are the chief characteristics of South Indian temple architecture.

Firstly, in the south, a pyramidal tower rises, storey upon storey, above the chief deity room (garbhagriha). In the north, a *shikhara* (tower) rises above the chief deity room. The *shikhara* rises up and tapers to a point at the top with or without a global bulge in the middle. As the *shikhara* rises up, it displays magnificent decorative designs and sculptural art all around the face of the followers.

Secondly, the temples in the south have very lofty and majestic gateway called *'Gopurams'* which are absent in the northern temples.

Thirdly, the building material in the north consists of bricks and mortar while in the south solid rocks are used.

Fourthly, in the South, a pillared hall called mandap with elaborately carved pillars and a flat roof is generally placed in front of the sanctum.

8. Balban's Blood and Iron Policy

Balban's stern policy against several sections of nobles and the Mongols resulting in bloodshed is known as the 'Policy of Blood and Iron." For the consolidation of his kingdom Balban had to face several challenges. He had to counteract internal revolts and dissentions and foreign attacks. It was, therefore, essential for him to follow an aggressive policy.

Balban suppressed rebellions in the Doab, crushed the revolt of the

Hindus of Rohelkhand and mercilessly quelled the revolt of Tughral Khan of Bengal. Balban created a reign of terror. Barni describes the brutal scene in these words, "On either side of the principal bazar, in a street more than two miles in length, a row of stakes was set up and the followers of Tughral were impaled (put to death) upon them. None of the beholders (eye-witnesses) had ever seen a spectacle so terrible, and many swooned with terror and disgust."

With an iron hand Balban liquidated thieves and robbers by clearing out their hideouts in the forests and awarding them severe examplary punishments. He also created terror by the massacre of the Rajput Mewatis. Every Mewati caught was immediately killed.

9. Balban's Frontier Policy against Mongols

The menace of the Mongols became very grave during the reign of Balban. Balban always kept himself in readiness to meet the dangers on the frontiers. To check the Mongols invasions, Balban chalked out a detailed strategy and formulated a 'Frontier Policy' which had the following significant features :

1. Balban raised a strong army.
2. He decided not to leave Delhi for long periods in order to expand his empire in the interior parts of India.
3. For the purpose of defence, he divided the north-west frontier into two parts.
4. Special attention was paid to the administration of the frontier provinces.
5. He built rows of strong forts at strategic points all along the frontier areas.
6. Special attention was paid to post experienced and well-trained military personnel in these forts.
7. Improved war weapons and equipments were manufactured and supplied to these forts.
8. Old forts were repaired and provided with adequate weapons and equipments.
9. Balban posted his brave and trustworthy persons in the frontier provinces. The provinces of Multan, Sindh and Lahore were placed in charge of his son Prince Muhammad Khan.

All the above mentioned steps proved very helpful in repulsing Mongol invasions. The Mongols made their biggest invasion in 1285 in which Balban's eldest son Muhammad Khan was killed but in the end, the Mongols lost.

10. Alaud-Din's Control over Market

Two important considerations guided the market policy of Ala-ud-Din Khalji. The first was that he wanted to provide essential commodities to the soldiers in particular and people in general at reasonable rates and second was to raise resources for making cash payments to the soldiers.

Alu-ud-Din made the following provisions to control the market :

1. Ensuring regular supply of articles at the fixed rates.
2. Opening of shops in varying localities and supplying articles as per demand of the consumers.
3. Appointment of market inspectors and other staff to exercise check on the traders and to ensure regular supply on fixed rates.
4. Establishment of godowns for storing grain in reserve to be released in time of scarcity.
5. Registration of traders.
6. Control over weights and measures of articles.
7. Severe punishment to the breakers of laws.
8. Appointment of spies to submit their reports direct to the king.
9. Collection of revenue in cash and kind.

Prices were fixed not only of all varieties of grains, pulses, cloth, cattle and horses but also of other articles like meat, fish, dry fruits, sugarcane, vegetables, needles, colours, betel-leaves, etc.—all articles of daily use. Even prices of slaves were also fixed.

11. Nature of the Government of Delhi Sultans

The Delhi Sultanate like that of all other Muslim states of the time was a theocracy. This meant that its political and administrative institutions were, in theory, derived from the Islamic Law (*Shariat*) based upon the precepts of Quran. Islamic theocracy, in a larger sense, also meant that the entire Islamic world was united under the religious and political authority of the Caliph, the representative of the Prophet. Every Muslim State was looked upon as the Caliph's dependency and its ruler had to pay allegiance to the Caliph and to seek confirmation for his right to rule as the deputy of the Caliph. Islam being the religion of the State, it was the primary duty of the State to promote Islam. The theocratic law was supreme and the civil law was subordinate to it. The *Ulemas,* in general, interpreted the Islamic laws and thus had an influential position. The Sultan was expected to show remarkable respect to the *Shariat*, to levy taxes according to the Shariat.

12. Experiments and Schemes of Muhammad Tughlaq

Following were the experiments and wild schemes which led to his failure :

1. Heavy taxation in the Doab at a wrong time and wrong implementation policy.
2. Transfer and retransfer of capital from Delhi to Devagiri and back resulting in lot of harship to people.
3. Use of token money without any safeguards.
4. Mongol invasion and bribing them.
5. The Quarajal expedition : advance payment of one year's salary to soldiers and abandonment of expedition.
6. Defective Deccan policy.

Results. (*i*) Land remained unutilised for several months as farmers fled on account of their inability to pay heavy taxes.

(*ii*) Token currency led to fake circulation of currency.

(*iii*) Heavy drain on state treasury.

(*iv*) Transfer of capital led to Mongol invasions.

13. Estimate of Firoz Tughlaq

Dr. Ishwari Prasad evaluates the character and personality of Firoz Tughlaq in these words, "He was neither a capable general nor a stern and far-sighted administrator."

Dr. R.C. Majumdar has evaluated his rule in these words, "On the whole, in spite of peace, prosperity and contentment that prevailed during the reign of Firoz Shah, no one can possibly doubt that his policy and administrative measures contributed to a large extent to the downfall of the Delhi Sultanate."

Bright side of Firoz Shah's rule. (1) Help to the needy and the poor (2) Undertaking works of public utility (3) Reduction in taxes (4) Agricultural reforms (5) Irrigation works (6) Reforms in currency (7) Encouragement to art and architecture (8) Patronage of learning (9) Kindness to slaves (10) Reforms in providing justice (11) Construction of beautiful buildings (12) Planting of splendid gardens (13) Promotion of education.

Dark side (1) Unfair and intolerant religious policy (2) Introduction of jagirdari system again. (3) Encouragement to slave system (4) Lack of military leadership (5) Payment to soldiers by granting them lands and not payment in cash (6) No annual inspection of the cavalry.

14. Invasion of Timur (1398-99 A.D.)

Amir Timur, a Turkish chief conquered kingdom after kingdom. He iooted southern Russia and India upto Delhi. Timur's attack on India was guided by four considerations : (*i*) conquering lands. (*ii*) Plundering wealth. (*iii*) Carrying out general destruction. (*iv*) Destroying infidels Hindus.

Effects of Timur's invasion. (1) After Timur's invasion *i.e.,* Delhi was in ruins. It was almost depopulated (2) The inhabitants of Delhi had to face famine and pestilence. It was said, "For two months not a bird moved wings in Delhi, (3) Great works of art and buildings were destroyed. (4) The invasion of Timur widened the gulf between the Hindus and the Muslims. (5) Several of the provincial governors declared their independence. (6) The Tughlaq empire almost came to an end. (7) Economic conditions in India worsened because Timur had robbed of her wealth. (8) Indian agriculture suffered badly and could not revive for a pretty long period. (9) Timur's invasion cleared the wary for the future conquests of India by Babur. (10) Timur carried with him several Indian craftsmen who built several buildings in Central Asia, designed and modelled on Indian pattern.

15. Krishnadeva Raya (1509-29)

Krishnadeva Raya was the greatest ruler of Vijayanagara kingdom. The empire reached at the zenith. He was a great conqueror, tactical general, efficient ruler, a remarkable Sanskrit scholar and patron of learning. He never faced any defeat. He invaded Mysore and annexed it. Krishnadeva also defeated the combined forces of Mysore, Bidar and Golkonda. He recaptured the Doab, area between the rivers Krishna and Tungbhadra.

The Mughal emperor Babur in his autobiography *Baburnama.* Described Krishnadeva Raya "as the most powerful ruler of India" Domingos Paes a Portuguese traveller, described the ruler in the following words, "He is the most feared and perfect king that could possible be." Though his personal learnings were in favour of Vaishnavism yet he respcted all the sects.

Krishnadeva was a great builder. He founded the city of Nagallapur, built up several *Gopurams* and *Mandapas.* He also built irrigation works.

Telugu literature made tremendous progress under him. He himself was a gifted scholar of Telugu and Sanskrit. He extended his patronage to Sanskrit, Telugu, Kannada and Tamil scholars alike.

16. Conflict between Vijayanagara

Kingdom and Bahamni Kingdom

The two kingdoms *i.e.,* the Vijayanagar (1340-1565) and the Bahmani (1347-1537) flourished side by side for about two hundred years. For all these years, they were engaged continually in much conflict on account of the following reasons:

Both the kingdoms wanted to possess the three very fertile areas providing rich economic resources—the Tungbhadra Doab, Krishna-Godavari Delta and the Konkan coastal strip.

Tungbhadra Doab. The territory between the rivers Tungbhadra and the Krishna is known as the Tungbhadra Doab. This territory is very fertile and the economy of the two Kingdoms largely depended on this Doab. This very Doab has been the cause of conflict among the earlier powers *i.e.,* between the Chalukyas and the Cholas as well as between the Yadvas and the Hoysalas.

Krishna-Godavari Delta. The Krishna-Godavari delta had two-fold significance. One, it was very fertile. Two, it had several important ports through which profitable trade was carried with several countries like Ceylon, Indonesia, Malaya and Burma, etc.

Konkan or Western Coastal Strip. This was a very fertile area and had important ports such as Goa which were important outlets for foreign trade with western countries.

The conflict ended with the defeat of the Vijayanagara empire in the battle of Talikota (1565) at the hands of the Bahamni kingdom. The Vijayanagara empire consequently lost its identity.

17. Battle of Talikota (1565)

The battle was fought between the 'quadruple alliance' formed by four of the five Bahamni states namely, Bijapur, Golkonda, Ahmednagar and Bidar on the one hand and the Vijayanagara empire on the other.

In the fierce battle that raged, the allied forces won. The army of Vijayanagar was completely destroyed and so was the case with the city of Vijayanagar.

Sewell, the author of A *Forgotten Empire stated,* "The enemy slaughtered the people without mercy; broke down the temples and palaces... nothing remained but a heap of ruins." He further stated, "Never in the world history was a glorious city devastated in the manner as Vijayanagar."

According to Ferishta, "The plunder was so great that every man in the allied army became rich in gold, jewels, arms, horses and slaves, the kings (victorious) permitting every person to retain what he acquired reserving the elephants only for their own use."

According to Dr. Ishwari Prasad, "The battle of Talikota is one of the most decisive battles in Indian history. It sounded the death-knell of the Hindu empire in the south."

It is also observed that the confederacy of the four Sultans which had won the battle of Talikota did not last long.

18. Bhakti Movement

One of the most important aspects of the religious life of the people during the 13th to 16th century was the emergence of the *'Bhakti'* movement with a new emphasis on the unity of God and devotion to it. The origin of the *'Bhakti'* cult may be traced to the Veas and the Upanishads. It was developed to a large extent by the teachings of poet-saints known as *'Alvars'* and *'Nayamars'* of South India between the 7th and the 12th centuries. A.D.

Namadeva, Jnanesvara, Narsi Mehta, Kabir, Mirabai and Guru Nanak Dev were the chief *'Bhakti'* saints.

Principal teachings of the Bhakti movement are :

1. Unity of God or one God though known by different names. 2. Intense love and devotion, the only way to salvation. 3. Repetition of the True Name. 4. Self-surrender 5. Condemnation of rituals, ceremonies and blind faith 6. Rejection of idol worship by many saints 7. Open-mindedness about religious matters. 8. No distinction made of different castes, high or low 9. Need of a *guru* for guidance advocated by some. 10. Preachings through local or regional languages and travelling from place to place for spreading the religious message.

19. Sant Kabir (1425-1518)

Early life of Kabir is shrouded in mystery. All that is definitely known is that he was brought up by a Muslim weaver. His mission was to bridge the gulf between the Hindus and the Muslims and so he described himself "Kabir is the child of Allah and Ram." He equated Rama with Rahim and it went a long way to make the *bhakti* movement a unique religious experience. To him, the prayers, pilgrimages and fasting of the Hindus as well as of the Muslims were equally mechanical. He was against idolatry, as he said, "If by worshipping stones one can find God, I shall worship a mountain."

To him what mattered was total absorption in the devotion to the Supreme with a pure heart. He was fond of oral teachings in the shape of couplets in Hindi which were later collected in the *'Bijaka* (the Seed Book). The simple fine rhythm of these couplets helped their easy remembrance and great popularity. The essence of his teachings may be found in his couplets and poems like the following :

"Mo Ko Kahan dhunro bande..."

O Servant where dost thow seek me, Lo I am beside thee,

I am neither in temple nor in mosque...

If thou art a true seeker, thou shall at once see Me..."

20. Guru Nanak Dev (1469-1539)

One of the foremost apostles of the Bhakti movement, Guru Nanak is held in high reverence by several sections of the Indian people. His catholic approach aimed at bridging the gulf between the Hindus and the Muslims. The hymns of Guru Nanak have been preserved in the *Adi-Granth,* the most sacred book of the sikhs. In these he sang the glory of one great God, and man's duty of mediating His name with a pure heart, bereft of all desires. Guru Nanak believed that the religious acts and austerities practised by different religious sects were useless. Love and devotion to one God is the only way of obtaining his grace. He laid emphasis on the purity of character and conduct as the first condition of approaching God.

He opposed priestly ritualism, blind faith, the caste system and idol worship. His disciples were from different castes and creeds, religions and regions. The following hymn closely echoes the teachings of the great saint.

Religion consisteth not in patched coat, or in a Yogi's staff,

or in ashes smeared over the body,

Religion consiseth not in earning worn or a shaven head, or in the blowing of horns.

Abide pure and avoid the impurities of the world;

Thus, shalt thou find the way of religion.

21. Sufi Movement

Sufism, an offshoot of Islam started in Iran as a reform movement played an important role in the religious history of North India during the period of the Sultanate. The sufis derived their name from the garments of coarse wool (*suf*) that they wore as a mark of asceticism and self-denial. Sufis were mystics; but they did not form a single sect, nor did they have any uniform doctrines and rituals, though they had 12 orders each under a mystic. They were devout Muslims who moved within the limits of *Shariat* (Law of Islam). However, they regarded inward light as of far more importance than dogmatic formalism of the orthodox type. The orthodox Muslims depend upon external conduct and blind observance of religious rituals, while the Sufis seek inner purity and think love to be the only means of reaching God.

The Sufi saints emphasised a simple life and advocated good deeds or engaging oneself in the service of others.

Khawaja Moin-ud-Din Chisti (*1234*). Came to India towards the close of the 12th century. On account of his pious and simple life people of different faiths looked upon him as their spiritual teacher. His *dargah* (tomb) at Ajmer is a place for pilgrimage. Every year a fair is held at Ajmer where people from all faiths come to pay their homage to this great saint.

Baba Farid-ud-Din Ganj-i-shakar. (13th century) was broad minded and humane. Some of his verses are found in the *Adi-Granth* of the Sikhs. Balban held him in high esteem. He confined his activities to Hansi and Ajodhan, in Haryana and Punjab respectively. Thousands of devotees continue to visit his tomb at Faridkot in Punjab.

22. First Battle of Panipat (April 21, 1526)

Babur, a ruler from Central Asia, defeated Sultan Ibrahim Lodi at the battle field of Panipat and captured Delhi and Agra. It is widely believed that some nobles in the court of Ibrahim Lodi and Rana Sanga had assured support to him.

Babur in his *'Memoirs'* mentions that with a small army of 12000 horsemen, he defeated Ibrahim's army of about lakh soldiers. Perhaps this feat was largely due to the use of artillery by him.

Results of the First Battle of Panipat had far reaching consequences.

1. *Foundation of a new dynasty*. The victory of Babur laid down the foundation of the Mughal dynasty that lasted for more than two hundred and fifty years in India.
2. *End of the Lodi rule*. The battle of Panipat was decisive. Ibrahim Lodi was killed in the battle field along with 15000 soldiers. With his death the Lodi rule came to an end. In the words of Stanley Lane-Poole the biographer of Babur, "The battle of Panipat became a tomb for the Afghans of Delhi. Their state was destroyed and their strength was absolutely crippled."
3. *Use of artillery*. After the battle of Panipat, the use of artillery became current in India.
4. *Capturing enormous wealth*. According to Lane-Poole (1899), Babur gathered such a booty as surpassed all dreams. He had seized the royal treasuries.

23. Battle of Kanwah (March 17, 1527)

The battle of Kanwah fought between Babur after his victory at Panipat and Rana Sanga of Mewar greatly strengthened the position of Babur in India.

The battle started in the morning and continued for about ten hours, Babur started the attack with heavy artillery fire. He also made a stirring appeal to his soldiers in the name of *'Jihad'*—a holy war of the Muslims. He smashed all his drinking cups and vowed never to touch wine. The appeal had the desired effect on his soldier. They swore on the holy Quran to lay down their lives. The Rajput army was routed.

With this victory Babur became the emperor of India in reality.

24. Causes of Babur's Success in India

1. There was lack of unity among Indian rulers.
2. Ibrahim Lodi had incurred the displeasure of several Lodi chiefs.
3. Babur's formation of army into different wings took the Indian rulers by surprises. Babur was a great military strategist.

Rana Sanga, in spite of his heroism lost. One of the most important causes of his defeat was that he did not capture Agra and Delhi when Ibrahim and Babur were fighting the battle of survival. Had he done so, he would have acquired enormous treasures and resources. Second. Rana Sanga, after conquering Bayana, did not engage Babur in fighting. This allowed Babur to prepare his formation of the army. Third, Rana Sanga failed to appreciate the strength and weakness of Babur's army. Fourth, Babur's military tactics and strategies, were far superior to that of Rana Sanga's. Fifth, 'sword and shield' of the Rajput were no match for the guns of Babur's army. Lastly. Babur's appeal for 'Holy War' to his Muslim soldiers infused a new spirit among them.

25. Revenue Administration of Sher Shah

The revenue administration of Sher Shah has been regarded as one of the best during the medieval period. It became a model for several rulers. Important features of the revenue administration were as under :

1. Land for the purpose of revenue was divided into three categories on the basis of production—good, average and bad.
2. Generally land revenue was one-third of the produce, but could be paid both in cash and kind.
3. The land of each cultivator was measured according to a uniform standard and its quality was ascertained.
4. Lease deeds (*pathas*) were drawn between the farmers and the government. The area, the type of the soil, and the rates of land revenue were recorded on the lease deeds which were got signed

by the farmers. The deeds confirmed the rights of the farmers on the lands.

5. Land revenue was remitted on poor crops.
6. The Sultan had ordered that while fixing the land revenue, the peasants should be treated with generosity but once settled they were asked to pay their revenue regularly.

Sher Shah was very particular about the welfare of the peasants. He used to say, "If I oppress them they will abandon their villages and the country will be ruined and deserted."

26. Significance of the Second Battle of Panipat (November 5, 1556)

The second battle of Panipat was won by young Akbar, grandson of Babur, against Hemu, a possible contender for power in Delhi.

Results of the Second Battle of Panipat. The second Battle of Panipat again changed the course of Indian history. The last of the Hindu king of Delhi namely Hemu, was no more. The Mughals won a decisive victory over the Hindus and the Afghans. The battle proved the supremacy of the Mughals and they became the undisputed master of India.

Causes of the failure of Hemu. Hemu lost the battle on account of several reasons. But the most important reason of his defeat was "accidental" and the victory of Akbar "providential." It was the ill luck of Hemu that an arrow struck his eye and which changed the course of the battle.

Secondly, he committed the mistake of directing the movements of his troops in person in the battle field itself.

Thirdly, there was no second leader to inspire the soldiers and continue the battle till the victory was gained.

27. Din-i-Ilahi

Akbar felt that by emphasising good points of all religions an environment of harmony and unity among people could prevail. Akbar tried to promote the concept of *Sulhkul* peace and harmony among religions. All this resulted in the founding of a new faith called *Din-i-Ilahi* in 1581-82. Din-i-Ilahi aimed at achieving a synthesis of all religions.

Some of the principles of Din-i-Ilahi, were as under :

1. God is great. He is One.
2. Akbar is his apostle or representative.
3. Every adherent of this faith should be willing to give away property, life, religion and honour to the emperor.
4. Every member should take an oath of doing good to everybody.

5. No member should have blind faith.
6. The followers of this faith should not approve of child marriage as well as old marriage.
7. All should show respect to all religions.

The new religion could not become popular. Only a handful of people accepted this. It vanished with Akbar's death.

28. Provincial Administration of Akbar

Akbar divided his empire into fifteen provinces. These were : Agra, Ahmedabad, Ahmednagar, Ajmer, Allahabad, Awadh, Bengal, Berar, Bihar, Delhi, Kabul, Khandos, Lahore, Malwa and Multan. Each province was under the charge of Subedar (Governor). He was assisted by a 'Diwan' who looked after the revenue records. *Bakshi* looked after the needs of the army. The *kotwal* was entrusted with the maintenance of law and order in the main cities. Qazi looked after justice. The provincial ministers and officers followed the nomenclature of the central administration and performed similar duties. Provinces were divided into Sarkars, *Sarkars* into *Parganas* and *Parganas* into villages. *Panchayats* looked after the village administration and also dispersed justice. Normally state officers did not interfere in the village affairs.

29. Mansabdari System

The *Mansab* is an Arabic word meaning rank or position or status. Thus *Mansabdari* was a system in which the rank of a government official was determined. Every civil and military official was given a *mansab* and was called a *Mansabdar*. There were two methods of making payments to the nobles. One was giving them *Jagirs* (land) wherefrom they got their salaries. The second was making cash payment. In the Mansabdari system no *Jagirs* were granted for the purpose of paying salaries.

1. The king could enhance the mansab, lower down it or remove it.
2. There were 33 categories of the *Mansabdars*. The lowest *mansabdar* commanded 10 soldiers and the highest 10,000 soldiers. Only the princes of the royal family were given a *mansab* of 10,000.
3. A *mansabdar* was paid his salary in cash.
4. The salary due to the soldiers was added to the personal salary of the *mansabdar*.
5. Mansabdari system was not hereditary.
6. In addition to meeting his personal expenses, the *mansabdar* had to maintain out of his salary a stipulated quota of horses, elephants, camels and mules and carts.

7. A *mansabdar* holding a rank of 5000 had to maintain 340 horses, 100 elephants, 400 camels, 100 mules and 160 carts.

30. Land Revenue System of Akbar

Todar Mal, the revenue minister of Akbar played an important role in devising and introducing a very effective and efficient land revenue and record system. There were three systems of land revenue (1) The Zabti System (2) The Ghalla-Bakshi and (3) Nasaq of Kankat.

Under the Zabti system, land was divided into four categories according to produce.

Under this system, the average produce of different crops as well as the average price prevailing over the last 10 years were calculated and accordingly land revenue was fixed.

The share of the state was one-third of the produce of the land. Farmers were given the option to pay the revenue in cash or kind.

The Zabti system proved very useful both to the state and the farmers. The system was for ten years. The system on the one hand determined the income of the government and on the other hand enabled the farmers to know clearly how much revenue they had to pay to the government. Now the farmers had direct link with the government and they were saved from the excesses and tyrannies of the landlords and the jagirdars. The revenue officials were instructed not to be harsh with the farmers. The farmers could deposit the land revenue direct to the treasury. This system was in vogue from Lahore to Allahabad and Malwa and Gujarat. It covered most of his empire.

According the Batai or *Ghalla-Bakshi* system, the produce of the farmers was divided between the government and the farmers in the ratio settled between them. This system was in vogue in Thatta and in parts of Kabul and Kandhar.

31. Rana Pratap (1540-1597 A.D.)

Rana Pratap, popularly known as Maharana Pratap, the son of Uday Singh and grandson of Rana Sanga is synonymous with legendary Rajput Valour. Praises of his deeds are sung even today. Rana Pratap sustained a lonely hard and long struggle to maintain his honour and independence and also the independence of Mewar against the expanding force of the mighty Mughal emperor Akbar. Akbar sent a series of missions to Rana Pratap to persuade him to accept Mughal suzerainty and to pay personal homage. Rana Pratap did not yield to him. After his defeat by an overwhelming Mughal-Rajput force at the Battle of Haldighati in 1576, he took to the hills. In twenty-five years of guerilla warfare, before his death, he managed to recapture most of Mewar's strongholds barring Chittor.

32 Conquest of Golkonda by Aurangzeb

It is usually said that guided by his religious fanaticism, Aurangzeb wanted to extinguish the kingdom of Golkonda ruled by a Shia Sultan. Besides it was a part of his policy to capture the whole of India. A written command was sent to the Sultan to acknowledge his suzerainty, to pay tribute and to abstain from helping Shahji Bhonsle. The struggle continued for a number of years. Ultimately in 1687, the fort of Golkonda fell after a siege of about eight months when Aurangzeb bribed one of the influential chiefs of Golkonda who opened the gates of the fort. Golkonda was annexed to the Mughal empire.

33. Mughal Architecture

A period of 100 years (1556-1657) covered by the reigns of Akbar, Jahangir and Shah Jahan is usually said to be the golden period of Indian architecture. Most of Akbar's buildings were made of red stone, a very hard material but Akbar did wonders with it. One of the earliest buildings is the Tomb of Humayun in Delhi.

The most magnificent of Akbar's architectural undertakings was the new capital city of Fatehpur Sikri.

During Jahangir's time, the most important building was the Tomb of Akbar at Sikandara (near Agra). Shah Jahan's buildings are unmatched in exquisite beauty of form, in symmetry of design and in sumptuous decorations. Delhi and Agra share the best of them. The most celebrated building is the Taj Mahal. By its perfect proportion and luminous beauty, its milk-white texture assuming different tones at times, its delicacy and by its picturesque setting, the Taj stands as a creation of superb beauty in Indian architecture. Diwan-i-Am of Delhi is studded with semi precious stones.

34. Mughal Painting

The foundation of Mughal painting was laid down by Jahangir. He brought two of the Persia's greatest artists. European art also attracted him. Abul Fazal records more than 100 painters of the court recruited from different parts of India. *'Humayunama'* contains about 1200 paintings drawn on lines pasted on one side of the large sized manuscript. Some of the finest paintings are to be found in *'Akbarnama'*. They reveal a sense of realism as the portraits are life like and the details of buildings, animals, plants and landscape are real copies. The technique of shadowing and modelling was impressive.

Jahangir's paintings include colourful brush strokes of the important events of his reign such as his coronation, hunting expeditions etc.

35. Chauth and Sardeshmukhi

Chauth and Sardeshmukhi were the two important sources of revenue of the Maharashtra rulers. These were introduced by Shivaji. The realisation of these two resources depended upon the strength of the ruler.

Chauth was one fourth of the revenue not under the control of the Maratha ruler. The payment of the tax relieved the neighbouring kingdom of the attack of the Marathas. In the words of J.N. Sarkar, "The payment of this tax merely saved a place from the unwelcome presence of the Maratha soldiers but did not impose on Shivaji any correspondence obligation to guard the district from foreign invasion or any internal disorder." On the other hand Ranade is of the view that it was a payment in lieu of protection against the attack of a third party.

Sardeshmukhi was another tax realised from the neighbouring kingdom as it was asserted that the Maratha ruler was the overlord of all land. It was one-tenth of the total revenue of the kingdom.

Very Short Answer Type Questions

Q. Answer the following in not more than 25 words each.

(2 marks each)

1. Who was defeated in the first battle of Tarain? *(Punjab University April 1996)*

2. Name the autobiography of Babur and also tell the language in which he wrote. *(Punjab April 1996 and Oct. 97)*

3. Name any two sons of Shah Jahan. *(Punjab April 1996)*

4. When did Aurangzeb conquer Bijapur and Golkonda? *(Punjab April 1996 and 97)*

5. Who was Gokul? *(Punjab April 1996)*

6. What was Chauth? *(Punjab April 1996 and Oct. 97)*

7. Mention any two buildings constructed by Shah Jahan. *(Punjab April 1996)*

8. Name the first Guru of Sikhs. *(Punjab April 1996)*

9. Who was Changez Khan? *(Oct. 1996 and Oct. 1997)*

10. Write the names of two cities founded by Firoz Tughlaq. *(Punjab Oct. 1996 and April 1997)*

11. Who was defeated in the battle of Chausa by whom. *(Punjab Oct. 1996)*

12. Who was Rana Udai Singh? *(Punjab Oct. 1996)*

13. Name the wife of Shah Jahan. *(Punjab Oct. 1996)*

14. Who was Tansen? *(Punjab Oct. 1996 April 97 and Oct. 97)*

15. Write any two features of Bhakti movement. *(Punjab Oct. 1996 and April 97)*

16. Mention the names of two writers of Mahmud Ghaznai's period. *(Punjab April 1997)*

17. Write the names of two generals of Alaud-Din Khalji. *(Punjab April 97)*

18. Who was Rana Sanga? *(Punjab April 1997)*

19. Name two brothers of Aurangzeb. *(Punjab April 1997)*

20. Name the Mughal King who loved painting most. *(Punjab April 1997)*

21. Give the dates of the first and second battle of Tarain. *(Punjab Oct. 1997)*

22. Who was Krishnadeva Raya? *(Punjab Oct. 97)*

23. Who was defeated in the battle of Kanwah and by whom? *(Punjab oct. 97)*

24. Mention the name of the author of *'Akbarnama'* *(Punjab Oct. 97)*

25. When did Mahmud Ghazni invade Somnath. (*Punjab April 1998*)

26. Who was defeated by whom in the second battle of Tarain? (*Punjab April and Oct. 1996*)

27. Who was the founder of Delhi Sultanate? (*Punjab April 1998*)

28. Give the year and place of Qutub-ud-Din's death. (*Punjab April 1998*)

29. Name the two coins of Iltutmish. (*Punjab April 1998 and Oct. 1996*)

30. Who was Malik Kafur. (*Punjab April 1998*)

31. Give the period in which Muhammad Tughlaq reigned. (*Punjab April 1998*)

32. Name two dynasties which ruled Vijayanagara. (*Punjab April 1998 and 1996*)

33. When was battle of Talikota fought? (*Punjab April 1998, April 1997, Oct. 96*)

34. Give names of two sons of Babur. (*Punjab April 1998*)

35. Who was Todar Mal. (*Punjab April 1998*)

36. Who was Maldeo. (Punjab April 1998)

37. Give two features of Sher Shah's Revenue system. (*Punjab April 98*)

38. When was Din-i-Ilahi established and by whom? (*Punjab April 1998 and April 97*)

39. What was Mansabdari? (*Punjab April 1998*)

40. Name the parents of Shivaji. (*Punjab April 1998, 96 and Oct. 97*)

41. When and where Shivaji's coronation took place? (*Punjab April 1998*)

42. Who was founder of Sikhism? (*Punjab April 1998*)

43. Name the Indian State annexed by Mahmud (*Punjab Oct. 1998*)

44. Who was the founder of Slave Dynasty? (*Punjab Oct. 1998*)

45. Write the period of Iltutmish's reign. (*Punjab Oct. 1998, April 1996*)

46. Name any two reforms of Ala-ud-Din Khalji. (*Punjab Oct. 1998, Oct. 1997 and 1996*)

47. Write the second name of Devgiri.(*Punjab Oct. 1998, April 1996*)

48. Who was Ibn Batuta? (*Punjab Oct. 1998*)

49. Give the number of canals constructed by Firoz Tughlaq. (*Punjab Oct. 1998*)

50. Who founded the Vijayanagara Kingdom? (*Punjab Oct. 1998 and April 97*)

51. Write any two administrative experiments of Tughlaq.
(*Punjab Oct. 1998*)

52. Give the years of First and Second Battle of Panipat.
(*Punjab Oct. 1998, 1996*)

53. Who was Daulat Khan Lodi? (*Punjab Oct. 1998*)

54. Give the year of the Battle of Chausa. (*Punjab Oct. 1998*)

55. First name of Sher Shah Suri. (*Punjab Oct. 1998 and Oct. 97*)

56. Who was Bairam Khan? (*Punjab Oct. 1998 and Oct. 1997*)

57. Name the Mughal King who hated music.
(*Punjab Oct. 1998 and Oct., 1996*)

58. Mention the place and year of Shivaji's birth.
(*Punjab Oct. 1998 and Oct. 1996*)

Answers

(1) Muhammad Ghori (2) (*i*) *Tuzuki Babri'* or *'Baburnama'* (*ii*) Turki. (3) (*i*) Aurangzeb (*ii*) Dara Shikoh. (4) (*i*) 1686 (*ii*) 1687 (5) Jat leader of Mathura who revolted against Aurangzeb (6) A tax introduced by Shivaji. It was realised from the kingdoms not under him but that wanted to save themselves from the attack of the Marathas. It was one-fourth of the produce. (7) (*i*) Taj Mahal, Agra (*ii*) Red Fort, Delhi. (8) Guru Nanak Dev. (8) Changez Khan was the famous Mongol leader of Central Asia who overran several countries in the 13th century A.D. (10) (*i*) Fathabad (*ii*) Hissar. (11) Humayun by Sher Shah (12) Rajput ruler of Mewar and father of Rana Pratap. (13) Arjumand Banu Begum (renamed Mumtaz Mahal) (14) Renowned singer during Akbar's reign. (15) (*i*) Intense love and devotion to God. (*ii*) Purity in life. (16) (*i*) Al Beruni (*ii*) Firdausi (17) (*i*) Zafar Khan (*ii*) Malik Kafur (18) Rajput ruler of Mewar who was defeated by Babur (19) (*i*) Dara (*ii*) Murad. (20) Jahangir (21) (*i*) 1190-91 (*ii*) 1192 (22) An important ruler of Vijayanagara empire. (23) Rana Sanga by Babur. (24) Abul Fazl. (25) 1025 A.D. (26) Prithviraj by Muhammad Ghori. (27) Qutub-ud-Din Aibak. (28) Lahore in 1210 A.D. (29) (*i*) Silver *'Tanka'* (*ii*) copper *'Jital'* (30) An important commander of Ala-ud Din who subdued several rulers of South India and brought with him and imnense booty. (31) 1325 to 1351 A.D. (32) (*i*) Sangama Dynasty (*ii*) Taluva Dynasty. (33) 1565. (34) (*i*) Humayun (*ii*) Kamran. (35) An éxpert in revenue matters in the reign of Sher Shah and Akbar (36) A Rajput noble and governor of Chittor in the beginning of 14th century A.D. (37) (*i*) Measurement of land according to a uniform system (*ii*) Division of land into three categories for purpose of revenue (38) 1581-82 by Akbar (39) A system created by Akbar in the imperial service whose officers were graded and paid in cash, not in grants of land and were also required to render military service. (40) Shahji Bhonsle and Jija Bai. (41) 1674

(40) Shahji Bhonsle and Jija Bai. (41) 1674 at Raigarh (42) Guru Nanak Dev. (43) Punjab (44) Qutub-ud-Din Aibak. (45) 1211-1236 A.D. (46) (*i*) Fixation of price of essential commodities (*ii*) Supply of essential commodities at fixed rates. (47) Daultabad (48) A traveller from North Africa whose accounts of India for the history of Khalji Dynasty form an important source of history. (49) Four (50) Two brothers Harihar and Bukka (51) (*i*) Taxation of Doab (*ii*) Issue of token currency. (52) (*i*) 1526 (*ii*) 1556. (53) Governor of Punjab under Ibrahim Lodi who is said to have invited Babur to invade India. (54) 1539 A.D. (55) Farid Khan. (56) Guardian and Tutor of Akbar (57) Aurangzeb. (58) (*i*) Shivner (*ii*)1627.

Sources of Medieval Indian History

Q. 1. Write an essay on the literary sources of Medieval Indian History. **(Rajasthan University 1996)**

Or

Write a critical note on the important historical sources of the Sultanate period. **(Rajasthan University 1997)**

Ans. Sources of Medieval Indian History

As compared with ancient India, a large number of literary sources are available for the medieval period. They provide a more reliable information and insight about the life of the people of the period. These sources inform us of the administrative set up of the rulers, their theory of kingship, military achievements etc. They also reflect the state of cultural, economic, political and religious institutions.

While utilising these resources we should keep in view the following points:

(1) Absolute historical truth is elusive.

(2) Absolute impartial history is rather impossible.

(3) Every kind of prejudice, caste, faith, personal racial, regional and religious etc., possessed by the historian has exercised some influence in recording events and facts.

(4) All possible efforts need to be made to sift facts from fiction.

(5) Since most of the books were written on the command of the rulers or by them, they contain material which has to be treated with care and caution.

(6) Different sources to be used while arriving at some definite conclusion.

Two-fold division of literary sources for the medieval period

Broadly speaking, sources may be divided according to the division of the period (*i*) The Sultanate Period (*ii*) The Mughal Period.

The Sultanate Period

Following are the important sources :

(1) *'Tahqeeq-Hind'* (10th century A.D.) by Al-beruni.

(2) *'Tarikh-i-Subukitgin'* (10th century) by Baihaki.

(3) *'Shahnama'* (10th century) by Firdausi.

(4) *'Prithviraj Raso'* (12th century) by Chandbardai.

(5) *'Rajtarangani'* (11th century) by Kalhan.

(6) *'Tarikh-i-Firoz Shahi'* (13th century) by Zia-ud-Barani.

(7) *'Tuhfat-un-Nuzzar fi Gharibi-il-Ansar* by Ibn Batuta (14th century).

(8) *'Padmavati'* (14 century) by Jayasi.

(For details see chapters 1 to 6)

Sources for the Mughal Period

1. *'Tuzaki-Babri': Baburnama'* (Memoirs of Babur) by Babur.
2. *'Tazkirat-ul-Waqait'* by Jauhar about Humayun.
3. *'Humayun-Nama'* by Gulbadan Begum about Babur and Humayun.
4. *'Akbarnama'* by Abul Fazl, dealing with Akbar.
5. *'Tazuk-i-Jahangiri'* by emperor Jahangir regarding his reign.
6. *'Iqbalnamah'* by Mutamad Khan informs us about the reign of Babur, Humayun and Jahangir.
7. *'Padshah Namah'* by Abdul Hamid Lahori. Gives information on the reign of Shah Jahan.
8. *'Alamgir-Nama'* by Mirza Muhammad Khan, son of the author of *'Padshah Nama'*. It contains a history of the ten years of the reign of Aurangzeb.
9. *'Fatuhat-i-Alamgiri'* by Muhammad Masum. It relates to the events of Shah Jahan and his sons.

29

Peninsular India : Society, Economy, Religion, Education, Literature, Languages, Art and Architecture

Q. 1. Briefly describe the sources of medieval history of South India.

Ans. *Sources of medieval History of South India.*

Important sources for the medieval History of South India may be categorised broadly under the following three heads.

1. Persian chronicles
2. Indigenous works
3. Foreign traveller's accounts.

1. Persian chronicles.

Among the most significant sources, following deserve mention :–

(*i*) '*Burhan-i-Maiser*' by Syed Ali Tabatabai. It deals with the Bahmanis of Gulbarga, Bahmanis of Bidar and the Sultans of Ahmednagar.

(*ii*) '*Tuzkirat ul Mulk*' by Rafi-ud-din Ibrahim. It is primarily a chronicle of Adil Shahis of Bijapur.

(*iii*) '*Maasir-i-Qutab Shahi*' by an anonymous author. It provides a detailed account of the Bahmanis, Adil Shahis, Nizam Shahis and Qutb Shahis.

(*iv*) '*Riyaz-ul-Insha*' by Mahmud Gawan. It is a valuable source for the Bahmanis of Gulbarga.

(*v*) '*Tazkirat ul Malik*' by Rafi-ud-din Shirazi. It deals with the affairs of Adil Shahis of Bijapur.

(*vi*) '*Gulshani-i-Ibrahim*' better known as *Tarik-i-Firishta* by Muhammad Quasin Hindu Shah alias Firishta. It is considered as a monumental work on Deccan Kingdoms.

2. Indigenous Works

(*i*) *Madhura-Vijaya* by Gangadevi. The author has mostly dealt with the military exploits of her husband Prince Kampana of Vijayanagar. It is perhaps the only historical work written by a woman.

(*ii*) '*Ramappayyan Ammanai*'. It is a Tamil work which gives an account of the exploits of Ramappayyan on behalf of the rulers of Vijayanagar.

(*iii*) '*Keladinpa Vijaya*'. It is written in Kannada. It describes the foundation of Vijayanagar Kingdom.

(*iv*) '*Rayavachaka*' by Visvanatha Nayaka. Written in Telugu it throws light on the period of Krishnadevarya of Vijayanagar.

(*v*) '*Krishnaraya - Vijayam*' by Chinna Venkata. It is also in Telugu dealing with the affairs of Vijayanagar Kingdom.

(*vi*) '*Kerala Palma*'. It is a Malayalam work which describes the conquests of Devaraya-II of the Vijayanagar Kingdom.

3. Accounts of Foreign Travellers

Important accounts are given below :-

(*i*) Account given by Nicolo Conti, a Venetian merchant who spent some time in Vijayanagar in the beginning of the fifteenth century A.D.

(*ii*) Account given by Abdur Razzak (A.D. 1413-82). Abdur Razzak was an envoy from Persia. He visited Vijayanagar in 1453. He provides a graphic picture of the city of Vijayanagar with its fortification, palaces, temples and other public buildings.

(*iii*) Account given by Athanasius Nikitin, a Russian traveller who visited South India in 1470. He has left a valuable account of the Bahmani Kingdom.

(*iv*) Account given by Durate Barbosa an employee of the Portuguese Government. His account throws adequate light on the Vijaynagara kingdom during the period A.D. 1509 to A.D. 1514.

Q.2. Describe the main features of the society and economy of Peninsular India during the medieval period.

Ans. (See chapters 12 and 28)

Q.3. What were the religious and cultural conditions in India in the Peninsular India during the medieval period.

Ans. *Religious Conditions*

Hinduism was divided into two main sects in the South. These were the Shaivism and Vaishnavism. Both these sects emphasised spiritual equality of all castes, the worship of idols, pilgrimages, suppression of desires and consideration to animal life.

The rulers of Vijayanagar Kingdom patronised Hinduism, the overwhelming population of the Bahmani Kingdom comprised Hindus.

The Brahmans occupied an exhalted position in the Vijayanagar kingdom. According to traveller Linchoten, "The Brahmans are the honest and esteemed people." They occupied important posts in all spheres-administrative, military and political besides priestly positions.

All the rulers of Vijayanagar empire were devout Hindus. Most of the rulers were devotees of Vaishnavism. However, they were tolerant towards all religious. The Mulsims, the Christians, the Yahudis and the people of other faiths enjoyed equal freedom. According to a foreign traveller Eduardo

Barbosa." The kings allow such freedom that everyman may come and go and live according to his own creed."

Hindu Society : Social Conditions

The pattern of Hindu society in the South was different from that of the North. The next to Brahmans were the merchants, artisans, weavers etc. The lowest class comprised 'Jogis' and jugglers etc.

The Brahmans could not intermarry in the same '*Kula*' and '*gotra*'. There were no such restriction in other castes.

Early marriages came to be in vogue in the South primarily on account of the Muslim invasions and uncertain political conditions.

Remarriage of widows was prohibited among the upper classes but was permitted among lower classes.

Divorce was allowed on certain conditions. A wife could seek divorce on account of physical disability of the husband or his being an impotent. A husband too could seek divorce if the wife was unchaste or failed to give birth to a son.

The system of dowry was prevalent particularly among higher classes.

The custom of 'saṭi was in vogue.

Cultural Conditions

Diet. All castes excepting Brahmans, could eat all kinds of meat. Beef eating was considered as a sin. Drinking of intoxicants was common among the Kshatriyas and the Sudras. Rice was the staple food. The higher classes used rice of better quality. Various kinds of fruits and vegetables were also used. The well-to-do took '*Chappatis and puris*'. The Muslims were very fond of meat.

Dress. The usual dress of the Hindus consisted of a '*dhoti*' and piece of cloth to cover the upper part of the body. '*Chappals*' were the common foowware. Many people were barefooted. Women belonging to rich classes used '*Saris*'. The ordinary women had a piece of cloth wrapped round their waist and an upper garment.

The Muslim followed the pattern of dress of the north. It consisted of tight trousers and shirts and '*Sherwanis*' or long coats.

Women were very fond of ornaments which were either made of silver or gold.

Festivals. '*Mahanavami*' was the most important festival celebrated in Vijayanagar empire. It was held to celeberate the victory of Goddess Durga over the demons Bhandasura; Chanda and Munda. The festival lasted five days during which period the king held the court in public.

Animal sacrifices were performed to propitiate the goddess. '*Ramlila*' and '*Krishanlila*' were theatrically depicted, scenes from the Epics.

Deepavali, Karthigai and Holi were the important festivals.

Several festivals particularly connected with the Shia faith were celeberated by the Muslims. The martyrdom of Imam Husain and Prophet's birthday were the most important festivals. Drinking of wine, cutting of hair, etc. were prohibited during Muharram.

Games, Sports and Pastimes. The games, sports and pastimes of the people were similar to those in vogue in the north Cock-fighting was common. Acrobats and snake charmers entertained the people with their performances.

'*Kirtans*' among the Hindus were common. '*Urs*' among the Muslims were held on the tombs of Muslim Saints.

Houses and Furniture. The houses of the high officials and wealthy merchants were built of teakwood and had two storeys. The upper storey was used as a bedroom, for study and for any other private work.

Foreign travellers saw several houses which were 400 years old and had not suffered any damage.

The lower classes lived in thatched houses without any cellars and windows.

Q.4. Write notes on Bhakti and Sufi movements in the Deccan.

Ans. *Bhakti Movement in the Deccan*.

The Bhakti movement in the South led by Swami Shankaracharya, Nathmuni, Ramanuja and Nimbarka aimed at reforming the Hindu society. It condemned caste system, laid stress on the brotherhood of man and unity of God. It decried the observance of unnecessary rituals.

Jnaneshwar, a leading saint of the Bhakti movement played a prominent role in breaking down religious and social barriers. He brought the Maratha people together. He was instrumental in establishing closer ties among the different faiths.

Nath Sampradaya (Nath Cult) was another sect of the Bhakti cult which flourished in Karnol district. The Nathpanthis were all '*jogis*' who went from place to place to preach the main features of Bhakti. They emphasised the virtues of renunciation and leading a simple life of devotion. They did not believe in possessing material things.

The impact of Islam was quite discernible in the Lingayat Movement started in Karnataka by Basava in the 12th century A.D. It advocated devotion to one God and condemned rituals and discrimination on the basis of caste. It wanted its followers to adopt simple marriage rites.

The overwhelming population of the Bahmani Kingdom comprised Hindus. The Bhakti movement made much headway in this Kingdom.

Sufism

Sufism in India was welcomed as its teachings and philosophy were very similar to the Bhakti cult of the Hindus. Muin-ud-din Chisti who founded his '*silsilah*' at Ajmer borrowed several Hindu practices.

'*Qawalis*' were substituted for '*Bhajans*' and '*Kirtans*'. '*Khanqahas*' took the place of Hindu '*Matts*'. Chief protagonists of Sufism were Nizam-ud-din Auliya in Delhi and Khwaja Bande Nawaz Gaisu-Daraz in Gulbarga. The Khwaja had migrated to the Deccan during the reign of Firoz Shah Bahmani where he was welcomed by the Sultan. The Sultan gave him an estate where he continued his religio-socio activities. He lived in Deccan for about 24 years and died at the ripe age of about 105 years. He is said to have wirtten a number of works. His monumental work '*Isma-ul-Isvar*' is considered as an authority on Sufism. His motto of life was 'love for humanity and service of the down-trodden. He did not believe in caste system. He regarded service as the highest form of worship. He had his followers both among the Muslims and the Hindus.

Muntajab-ud-din Zarzari Zar Baksh was another well known Sufi of the Deccan.

The teachings of the Sufis led to the fusion of Hindu-Muslim culture.

Q. 5 Explain the developments of the system of education, literature and modern Indian languages in the Deccan during the medieval India.

Ans. *Education in Vijayanagar Kingdom.*

The '*pathshalas*' (primary schools) imparted elementary education and they were attached to the temples. For higher studies there were '*tols*'. Madurai became an important centre of learning during the 17th century. There were nearly 10,000 students. Several endowments were available for the maintenance of this centre of learning. There were some state-owned institutions also. Curriculum included the Vedas, astronomy, astrology and medicine etc.

Palm leaves were used for writing. Printing was introduced in this kingdom in 1577 with the publication of a book on Christian doctrines. It may be observed that the Vijayanagar rulers were very liberal and they allowed Christians to establish schools where Telugu and Tamil were taught.

Education in the Bahmani Kingdom

The main centres of Hindu learning were Nasik, Gangapur and Salotgi besides Madurai. The curriculum included '*Amar Kosh*', '*Rupavati Samskara*', '*Panchtantra*', '*Hitopadesa*' and the works of Kalidas. For those interested in advanced studies learnt grammar, logic and philosophy. The Vedic learning formed the highest stage of learning. Among the renowned scholars, names of Trivikrama Bharat, Rameshwara Bhatt, Kamalkar Bhatt, Keshva and Ganesh Daiwadnya deserve special mention.

The '*Magtahas*' (Muslim Schools) were attached to mosques. Higher learning was imparted in the '*Madrasas*'. The '*Quran*' and the '*Hadis*' (saying of the prophet) and Arabic language were taught in the schools. Calligraphy formed an important part of school curriculum.

Gulbarga, Bidar, Daultabad, and Chaul were the important centres of Muslim higher learning. Mahmud Gawan's '*Madrasa*' at Bidar became a famous centre of Muslim learning. Dar-ul-ulum at Ellichpur (Berar) was the biggest institute of higher learning and received substantial annual grant. The great Persian poet Hafiz Shiraj was invited to his court by Muhammad Shah II.

It appears there was no centre for technical education and training.

Development of Literature under the Vijayanagar Ruler's

Vijayanagar Rulers

Vijayanagar rulers were great patrons of learning and they encouraged and rewarded scholars without any distinction of caste or creed. Several Jain scholars flourished during this period. Bahubali and Madhura were great Jain scholars of the 15th century. Both of these scholars wrote on the life of Dharmanatha, the fifteenth Jain Tirthankara (path finder).

Sanskrit studies received a great impetus under the patronage of rulers of Vijayanagar. The great scholar Sayanacharya of the 15th century is still remembered for his commentaries on the Vedic text. Vyasara was another great Sanskrit scholar who flourished under the patronage of Krishnadevaraya. Vedanta Desika was another versatile Sanskrit scholar. His important works were '*yadavabhyudayam*' a long poem on the life of Lord Krishana, '*Hansa Sandesa*' '*Sankalpa Sargodaya*' and '*Subhasita Nivi*' Madhavacharya, a distinguished sanskrit scholar was a minister in the court of king Bakka I. He wrote a number of works which included '*Parasarsmriti Vyakhya*' and *Jivanmuktiviveka*. Harihara's lexicon '*Nanartharatnamala*' occupies a place of eminence among standard Sanskrit works. Gangadevi in her famous work '*Maduravijayam*' describes in '*mahakaya*' style the conquest of Madurai by her husband Kampana. King Krishnadevaraya's Sanskrit works include '*Madalsacharitra*' '*Satyavadhuprnanm*' and '*Rasmanjari*. Appayya Dikita is credited with more than 100 works.

Religious literature flowed from the manasteries of Melkote, Sringeri and Udidi.

'*Akasabhairavakalpa*' an anonymous work is a work on polity.

Works in music were also produced during the period.

Development of Modern Indian Languages and Literature in the Deccan

During the Medieval period, Tamil, Telugu and Kannada made a good deal of progress in South India.

Comparatively there was peace and prosperity which encouraged the development of modern Indian languages and literature in the south. Krishnadevaraya was a patron of Tamil scholars. The '*Bhagavata Puranam*' was translated into Tamil by Sevkaichchbuduvar. '*Irusamaya Vilakkam*' a work on Vaisnavism was authored by Annagalayyam. Jnanaprakasa Desikar wrote two works namely '*Manjarippa*' and '*Kachchi Kalambakam*'

Maraijnanasambanda, a well-known Tamil scholar wrote a number of works such as '*Patiposupasappanaval*','*Sakalagamasaran*' and '*Sankarpanirakaranam*' etc. a lexicon '*Akarathi Nikandu*' was written by Revanasiddhar. Tayumanavar was a great Tamil poet who wrote a number of works.

Telugu

It is said that the reign of Krishnadeva marked the dawn of a new era in the literary history of South India. He created a tradition of patronage of Telugu scholars which was followed by his successors. The Telugu scholars produced original literature. His work in Telugu entitled '*Amuktamalyada*' deals with several matters including the art of government. In his court there were eight famous poets called '*Ashta Diggajas*'. Nachana Somanatha was a great scholar of both Sanskrit and Telugu. He composed '*Uttara Harivamsamu* which describes the life of Lord Krishna in the closing years of his life. Pillalamarri Pina Virabhadra Kavi was the greatest poet of the era. He composed the Telugu version of Kalidasa's *Sakuntla* in verse. Tallapaka Annamacharya, a saint-poet was a pioneer in producing devotional music. Srinatha, a celeberated poet translated '*Naisadhiya-Charita*' of Sri Harsa in Telugu. It is considered as a monumental work of the Tamil literature. He wrote a large number of works in Tamil. Jakanna and Pina Virabhadra were famous poets. Sarada, a gifted poetess wrote about 18 dramas.

Kannada

During the Medieval period, a large number of works were produced in Kannada. Harihara II, the ruler of Vijayanagar (1377-1404) earned the title of '*Karnataka Vidyavilasa*' (Promoter of Karnatka Learning, for his patronage to Kannada. Devaraya II (1425-1447) gave liberal grants to scholars. Mahalingadeva wrote '*Kottara Satsthala*' and '*Satshalaviveka*' Chamarasa is credited with the authorship of '*Prabhulingabiles*'. A *Kannada* version of '*Ramayana*' was composed by Kumara Valmiki. Sridharadeva completed '*Vaidyamrta*' a work on medicine. Bhattakalam Kedeva, wrote a highly valuable grammar work entitled '*Karnatakasabda-nusasana*'.

Literature under the Bahmani Rulers

A. *Persian works*

A Sanskrit work in veterinary science was translated into Persian. It was entitled '*Tarjma-i-Salhuttad*'. Several works were produced on mysticism and '*Sufism*'. Among the major works of the famous saint Banda Nawaz, mention may be made of '*Kitab-ul-Khatima*'. '*Jawami-ul-Kalim*' and '*Amusarul Asrar*'. Mahmud Gawan, a Prime Minister of the Bahmani Kingdom wrote his works namely '*Riyaz-ul-Insha*' and '*Manazirul-Insha*', Works on history were also produced during the rule of Bahmani Sultans. Important works were :

(*i*) *Sirajut Tawarikh* by Muhammad Lari, (*ii*) '*Tuhfatus Salatin*' by Mulla Dawud (*iii*) '*Tarikha-i-Muhammad Shahi*' by Mulla Abdul Karim Hamadani.

B. *Arabic Works*

The Bahmani Sultans were great patron of Arabic literature. Several Arabic scholars flourished during their reign. Banda Nawaz wrote a number of books in Arabic. Shaikh Ala-ud-din was an other scholar who had several Arabic books to his credit.

Q. 6. Write notes on the development of art and architecture in Peninsular India.

Ans. *Development of Art and Architecture in Peninsular India*

A. Art and Architecture under the Vijayanagar Rulers

The rulers of Vijayanagar were the inheritors of the rich traditions in art and architecture of the Cholas, the Pandyas and the Hoysalas.

Nicolo Conti, an Italian traveller, Abdul Razzaq, an ambassador from Shah Rukh of Persia and Domingo Paes, a Portuguese traveller have given a vivid account of the magnificent buildings which adorned the city of Vijayanagar.

Vijayanagar has been described as large as Rome or any biggest town in the western world at that time. The city was surrounded by seven fortifications. The space in between was used for various purposes such as laying gardens and growing vegetables etc. The total area of the city was estimated at 64 square miles. There were beautiful lakes, open gardens. broad and well-laid roads and buildings. The Tungabhadra river had a dam which provided water for the 40 kilometre long canal of the city.

The palace was the most impressive building in Vijayanagar. There were halls of public and private audiences. The halls were decorated with beautiful painted pictures. Usually the walls and pillars were ornamented with sculptures made of stone or wood.

Unfortunately, most of the city of Vijayanagar is now in ruins, represented by the well-known site Hampi which is dotted with little hills of granite and where not a blade of grass grows.

Temple architecture received a new impetus and reached to new heights under the patronage of the Vijayanagar rulers. About the architecture of the period, Prof. S.K. Saraswati has observed, "The most frequent design is one in which the shaft becomes either a central core or background for a group of statuary, of substantial proportion and carved practically on the ground. Important features of Vijayanagar style of temple and architecture were : monolithic pillars, ornate brackets, decoration on exterior side of the walls, etc. A large number of temples were built during this period. Krishnadevaraya built a temple dedicated to Lord Krishna. He renovated several temples. The most important was the temple of Hazara Rama. The royal family worshipped there. Its most interesting features were the four finely polished black stone pillars which support the '*Mandapa*'. They have beautiful sculptures carved on them. The deities on the pillars represent Vishnu, Lakshminarayana, Krishna, Brahma and others. Scenes from the Epics are depicted on the outer walls of the shrine.

A number of temples were built during the medieval period in the South cities of Vellore, Kumbhakonam, Kalahsti, Srirangam, Conjeevam and Virinchipuram were dotted with magnificent temples.

The temples of Vithala and Pattabhirama also deserve mention. The most important features of the temple of Vithala are the '*Mahamandappa*' and the '*garbhagriha*'. The *Mahamandappa* has 56 pillars. The ceilings above these pillars are highly ornamented. Likewise '*garbhagriha*' is highly ornated.

A '*rath*' in stone with finely carved wheels adds beauty to Vitthalaswami temple.

'*Gopurams*'—the entrances to the courts of the temples are a unique feature of the south Indian temples, particularly built during the medieval period. These colossal gateways which lend glamour and prestige to the temples were covered by lofty pyramidal tower rising up in storeys and ultimately crowned by a lofty vault. The '*gopuram*' in the temple of Ekambaranath having ten storeys rising to the height of 188 feet is the most remarkable one.

Painting and Sculpture

Images on the outer walls and ceilings of temples were produced which greatly enhanced their beauty. The Hazara temple at Kumbakonam contains a large number of fresco paintings depicting the various scenes from the life of Lord Krishna.

The Tontada Siddhalingesvara temple at Edeyar depicts scenes from the life of Lord Shiva. Likewise the ceilings of Jain temples at Tirupparuttikkunarm and other places portray scenes from the life of Lord Mahavira.

The beautiful figures of various animals like horses, panthers and tigers decorated the houses of the nobles.

Architecture Under the Bahmani Rulers

The founders of the Bahamni rulers had come from Persia and as such they were affected by its style of architecture. The Jami Masjid at Gulbarga, Char Minar at Daultabad and Gawan's *Madrasa* at Bidar were not only planned by Persian architects but also built by their artisans. However, under the influence of Turkish military experts, who were in the service of the Bahmani rulers, the military architecture, was on the model of medieval European style.

The Jami Masjid at Gulbarga has unique structure. There is no open courtyard and the entire area is roofed to save the worshippers from rain and the sun. Another unique feature is its high dome which has been constructed on a high square clerestory over the niche of the sanctuary.

In course of time, the Deccan style of architecture developed its own individuality. It was marked by grandeur of conception and soundness of structural principles on the one hand and lavish decoration schemes on the other.

The *Madrasa* built at bidar is a unique three storeyed buildings which contains lecture halls, a library, a mosque and residential houses for teachers and students. The architecture followed the patterns of the buildings of Persian University at Samarqand.

A massive fort 180 miles in cirumference was built at Ahmadnagar during the Nizam Shahi rulers. In the fort there were a number of palaces with arches and doomed roofs with coloured and latticed walls, '*Bagh-Hasht-Bahist*' or the Eighth Paradise Garden contains a pond and two-storeyed palace with eight gates representing the eight gates of heaven.

B.A. Examination Question Papers (with answers) of Different Universities (1999 to 2001)

A. Essay Type Questions

Q.1 Examine the political condition of India on the eve of Turkish invasion. (*Allahabad, 2001*)

Or

Discuss the circumstances leading to the establishment of Turkish Rule in India. (*Allahabad, 2001*)

Ans. *Q.2 . Pages 3 to 5.*

Q.2. Compare and contrast the impact of the invasions of Mahmud of Ghazni and Mohammad Ghori on Northern India. (*Delhi, External, 2001*)

Or

Give the effects of Mahmud Ghazni and Mohammad Ghori's invasions on India. (*Punjab, April 1999 and September, 2001*)

Ans. *Q.4 Pages 15 to 17.*

Q.3. Compare the character and achievements of Mahmud Ghaznavi and Mohammad Ghori. (*Delhi, 2000*)

Ans. *Q.5 Pages 17 to 18.*

Q.4. Comment on the economic conditions of Northern India between 1000 to 1200 A.D. (*Delhi External, 2001*)

Ans. *Page 7, 8 24 and 25.*

Q.5. Discuss the political, economic and social impact of Turkish conquest of India. (*Delhi 2001*)

Ans. *Q.7 Pages 23 to 25.*

Q.6. Account for the causes of the success of Turks during 11th and 12th centuries and examine the consequences. (*Delhi, 2000*)

Ans. *Q.6. pages 19 to 25.*

Q.7. Critically examine Balban's theory of Kingship? What steps did he take to realize his objective? (*Delhi, 2000 and 2001*)

Or

Discuss the achievements of Balban with reference to his theory of Kingship.

Ans. *Q.3. Pages 34 to 35.*

Q.8. Discuss the steps taken by Balban to consolidate his empire ? (*Delhi 1999, 2000*)

Or

Discuss the measures taken by Balban for the consolidation of the Delhi Sultanate.(*Allahabad 2001, Punjab, April 1999 and Sept. 2001*)

Or

Write an essay on Balban's policy of 'Blood and Iron!' (*Lucknow 2000*)

Or

Evaluate the success of Balban as a ruler. (*Himachal 2000*)

Ans. *Q.4 Pages 36 to 39.*

Q.9. Iltutmish was undoubtedly the real founder of the so-called Slave Dynasty. (*D. Ahilya* 2000)

Or

Who was the real founder of the Delhi Sultanate? (*Lucknow 2000*)

Or

Describe briefly the achievements of Iltutmish. Why is he regarded as the real founder of the Delhi Sultatnat?

(*Punjab, April 2000, Sept. 2001*)

Ans. *Q.1 Pages 28 to 31.*

Q.10. Discuss the achievements of Qutb-ud-din Aibak.

(*Allahabad, 2000 and 2001, Ch.C. Singh 1999 Meerut*)

Ans. *Q.1 Pages 28, 29.*

Q.11. Write in detail about Razia Sultana.(*Ch. Charan Singh, Meerut 1999*)

Ans. *Page 31 and 32.*

Q.12. What led Ala-ud-din Khalji to introduce the policy of price control. Discuss its main features. (*Delhi 2000, Punjab 2001*)

Or

What were the measures adopted by Ala-ud-din to control the market. Discuss merits and demerits. (*Punjab, April 1999 and April 2001*)

Ans. *Q.5 Pages 53 to 57.*

Q.13. Discuss briefly economic and social reforms of Ala-ud-din Khalji.

(*Punjab, Sept. 2000*)

Ans. *Q.4 Pages 50 to 52.*

Q.14. Describe the Deccan policy of Ala-ud-din. What were its motives?

(*Punjab, Sept. 2000*)

Or

Critically examine the Deccan policy of Ala-ud-din.(*Allahabad, 2001*)

Or

Write about the Deccan campaign of Alauddin. What were the motives of these campaigns? (*Punjab, April 2000*)

Ans. *Q.2. P. 42 Objectives of Alauddin. P. 44. B. P. 60.*

Q.15. Point out the main features of Alauddin's administration.

(*Lucknow 2000*)

Ans. *Q.3 Pages 47 to 49.*

Q.16. Describe the Mongol policy of Alauddin. (*Delhi Ahilya, 2000*)

Ans. *Q.7 Page 59 and 60.*

Q.17. Discuss the major administrative schemes of Mohammad Tughlaq. How far did they succeed? (*Allahabad 2001*)

Or

Discuss the Character and achievements of Muhammad Tuglaq as the Sultan of Delhi. (*Allahabad 2001*)

Or

Critically examine the works of Mahammud Tughlaq.
(*Ch.C.Singh Meerut, 1999*)

Or

Discuss the Character and achievements of Muhammad Tughlaq as the Sultan of Delhi. (*Allahabad, 2001*)

Or

Describe the token currency of Mohammad Tughlaq. Why did it fail?
(*D. Ahilya 2000*)

Or

Describe the experiments of Muhammad Tughlaq.
(*Punjab 2000, April*)

Or

Discuss the projects of Muhammad Tughlaq.
(*Delhi 1999, 2000 correspondence*)

Or

Review the projects of Muhammad Tughlaq in the light of his personality. (*Delhi, 2000*)

Or

Give a brief account of the visionary plans of Muhammad Tuglaq.
(*Himachal 2000*)

Or

Discuss the various administrative experiments of Muhammad Tughlaq. Why did they fail! (*Punjab, Sept. 2001*)

Ans. *Q.1. Pages 62 to 67.*

Q.18. Evaluate Firoz Tughlaq as a ruler. (*Lucknow 2000*)

Or

Describe the reforms of Firoz Tughlaq and their effects.
(*Punjab, 1999, April 2001*)

Critically examine the achievements of Firoz Tughlaq as a reformer.
(*Allahabad 2000*)

Ans. *Q.3 PAges 69 to 74.*

Q.19. Discuss the administrative reforms of Firoz Tughlaq. How far was he responsible for the downfall of Tughlaq dynasty!
(*Allahabad 2001, Punjab Sept. 2001*)

Ans. *Q.P. 72 S.No. 2 Army organisation. P. 73, Nos. 31.7 (b) Criticism of historians. Page 73. II S.Nos. 4 to 13)*

Q.20. Discuss briefly the salient features of the administration of Delhi Sultans. (*Allahabad 2000*)

Ans. *Q.2. Pages 90 to 91 (S.Nos. 1 to 3) and Q.3. Pages 93 and 94.*

Q.21. Examine the working of the Iqta system during the period of Delhi Sultanate. (*Delhi 2000 and 2001*)

Ans. *Q.3 Pages 93 and 94.*

Q.22 Critically examine the achievements of Sikander Lodi. (*Allahabad 2000*)

Ans. Q.3 Pages 81 to 84.

Q.23 Critically examine the achievements of Bahlol Lodi. (*Allahabad 2001*)

Ans. Q.2 Pages 81 and 82.

Q.24. Discuss the causes of the failure of Ibraham Lodi in the first battle of Panipat. (*Allahabad 2001*)

Ans. Pages 85 and 86.

Q.25 Give the circumstances leading to the origin of the Bhakti movement. What were its chief features?

Or

What were the main principles of Bhakti movement? What were its effects? (*Ch. Charan Singh, Meerut, 2001and Punjab 1999, 2000*)

Ans. Pages Q.2 Page 114. Q1. Pages 111 to 114.

Q.26 Discuss the main teaching of the Bhakti Saints with reference to Kabir and Nanak.

Ans. Q.1 Page 111. Page 115.

Q.27 Discuss the impact of the Bhakti movement on medieval Indian society. (Delhi Correspondence 2000 and Delhi 2001)

Ans. Pages 112 to 114.

Q.28 Give an account of the social and economic conditions during the Sultanate period. (*Lucknow, 2000*)

Ans. Q.1 and 2 pages 97 to 101.

Q.29 Discuss the nature and consequences of Mongol invasions in the 13th century. (*Allahabad, 2000*)

Ans. Q.1 Pages 102 to 105.

Q.30 Discuss in detail the main features of the administration of the Vijayanagar Empire. (*Delhi 1999, Punjab, April 2001, Sept. 2001*)

Or

Discuss the administrative system of the Vijayanagar Kingdom (*Allahabad 2001*)

Ans. Q.2 Pages 122-123.

Q.31 Write a short note on the political and cultural achievements of the Vijaynagar Empire. (*Himachal 2000*)

Ans. Q.3 Page 124,126 and 127.

Q.32 What were the causes of the downfall of the Bahmani Kingdom ? (Allahabad 2000, Devi Ahilya 2000)

Ans. Pages 132 and 133.

Q.33 Give the main teachings of Guru Nanak Dev. (*Punjab 1999*)

Or

Write notes on Guru Nanak. (*Allahabad, 2000, Delhi, 2000*)

Ans. Pages 115 and 192.

Q.34 Evaluate the achievements and career of Babar . (*Himachal 1999*)

Ans. Q.3 pages 148 and 149.

Q.35 Give an account of the causes, events and results of first battle of Panipat. (*Himachal, 1999*)

Or

Ans. Pages 144 to 146.

Q.36 What were the difficulties of Humayun? Discuss the causes of his failure. (*Ch. Charan Singh Meerut, 1999*)

Or

"Humayun tumbled through life and tumbled through it." Examine this statement. (*Devi Ahilya 2000*)

Or

What were the difficulties of Humayun? Why did he fail as a ruler? (*Himachal 1999*)

Ans. Q.1 Pages151 tp 154.

Q.37 Why is Sher Shah Suri regarded as one of the greatest rulers of medieval India? (*Punjabi 1999*)

Or

Give an estimate of the character and achievements of Sher Shah Suri. (*Punjab, Sept. 2001*)

Ans. A.4 Pages 166 to 168.

Q.38 Critically examine the agrarian reforms of Sher Shah Suri. (*Delhi 1999*)

Ans. Page 166

Q.39 Describe the main features of the administration of Sher Shah. (Delhi 2001)

Or

Describe the administrative reforms of sher Shah Suri. (*Punjab, 1999*)

Ans. Q.3. Pages 162-165.

Q.40 Would you agree with the view that "Sher Shah Suri was an innovator in the sphere of administration"?. Give reasons. (*Delhi 2000*)

Or

"Sher Shah was the fore runner of Akbar in policy and statemanship." (Himachal , 2000)

Ans. Q.5 pages 168 and 169.

Q.41 Examine the religious policy of Akbar. (*Devi ahilya, 2000, Punjab, Sept. 2000 and September 2001*)

Ans. Q.4 Pages 177 to 180.

Q.42 Describe the various stages in the evolution of Akbar's Religious Policy. (*Punjab 1999 and Delhi 2000*)

Q.43. Examine the Rajput policy of Akbar. (Lucknow 200)

Or

Describe the Rajput Policy of Akbar. Examine its results.
(*Ch. Charan Singh, Meerut*, 1999)

Or

Give an account of Akbar's Rajput Policy. (*Himachal 1999*)

Ans. Q.2 Pages 172 to 175

Q.44 Give the salient features of central and provincial administration of Akbar. (*Punjab, April 2000 & 2001*)

Ans. Q.5 Pages 180 to 181 (Half Page) and Page 182 Bottom.

Q.45 Discuss the salient features of the Mansabdari System of Akbar. What changes were introduced in it during the reign of Jahangir and Shah Jahan. (*Delhi 2000 and Delhi External 2001*)

Ans. Q.3 Pages 227 to 230.

Q.46 Discuss Akbar's Deccan Policy. (*Punjab,1999*)

Ans. Q.1 Pages 244 to 246.

Q.47 Give a brief account of the good and bad effects of Nur Jahan on the reign of Jahangir. (*Himachal 2000*)

Ans. Q.2 Pages 192 to 194.

Q.48 Review the Central Asian Policy of Shah Jahan . (Lucknow 2000)

Ans. Q.1 Pages 248 to 252.

Q.49 Describe Aurangeb's religious policy. What were its effects ?
(*Himachal 1999*)

Ans. Q.2 Pages 209 to 213.

Q.50 Critically examine Aurangzeb's Deccan policy and indicate its results. (*Lucknow 2000, Delhi Correspondence, Delhi External 2001; Punjab, April 2001*)

Or

Examine the relations of Aurangzeb with the rulers of Deccan.
(*Delhi 2000*)

Ans. Q.4 Pages 215 to 217.

Q.51 Give an account of Aurangzeb's responsibility for the decline of the Mughal Empire. (Punjab April 2000 and Sept.)

Or

Were Aurangzeb's policy responsible for the downfall of the Mughal empire? (*Ch. Charan Singh, Meerut*)

Or

Discuss the causes of the down fall of the Mughal Empire. How far was Aurangzeb responsible for it ? (*Devi Ahilya 2000*)

Ans. Q.7 Pages 221 to 224.

Q.52 Give the main features of the Mughal Central Administrative system.
(*Himachal 1999*)

Ans. Q.1 Pages 253 to 256.

Q.53 What was the role of the nobility under the Mughals ? (*Delhi External 2001*)

Ans. Q.3 Pages 237 to 239.

Q.54 What role did religion play during the Mughal period ?(*Delhi, 1999*)

Ans. Ans. Q1 pages 253 to 256.

Q.55 Evaluate the Rajput Policy of the Mughals. (*Ch. C. Singh Meerut, 1999*)

Ans. Q.2. Pages 257 to 259.

Q.56 What changes would you notice in the architecture under the Mughals from Akbar to Shahjahan . (*Delhi 2000*)

Or

Bring out the salient features of Mughal archietecture. (*Delhi External 2001*)

Ans. Q.1 pages 260 to 262.

Q.57 Write a detailed note on the rise of Maratha power under Shivaji. (*Ch. C. Singh, Meerut, 1999*)

Ans. Q.2 pages 272 to 273.

Q.58 Discuss Shivaji's struggle against the Mughals. (*Punjab, Sept.* 2001)

Ans. Q.3 pages 274 to 277.

Q.59 Give an account of the civil administration of Shivaji. (*Punjab, Sept. 2000*)

Or

Highlight the special features of the administration of Shivaji. (*Delhi, 1999*; *Delhi external 2001*)

Or

Describe the administration of Shivaji?

What do you know about the civil and military administration of Shivaji? (*Punjab, 1999; April, 2000*)

Ans. Q.4 pages 277 to 280.

Q.60 Discuss the career and conquests of Shivaji . (*Punjab, 1999; April, 2000*)

Ans. Q.2 pages 272 to 274.

B. Important battles : dates, Places, Winners and Losers

S. No.	Battle	Date	Winner/ Loser	Effect
1.	First Battle of Tarain (Page 14)	1191 A.D.	Prithvi Raj, Muhammad Ghori	India was saved from foreign rule.
2.	Second Battle of Tarain (Page 15)	1192	Muhammad Ghori Prithvi Raj	Paved the way for Muslim rule in India during the medieval period.
3.	First Battle of Panipat (Page 144, 293)	1526	Babar, Ibrahim Lodi	Paved the way for Mughal rule in India.
4.	Battle of Kanwah (Page 146, 294-95	1527	Babar, Rana Sanga	Strengthened the position of Babar and it became easier to strengthen formation of Mughal Empire.
5.	Battle of Chausa (Page 156)	1539	Sher Shah Humayun	Mughal empire received a great set-back.
6.	Battle of Kanauj	1541	Sher Shah Humayun	Sher Shah became the ruler of Delhi
7.	Second Battle of Panipat	1556	Akbar Hemu	The Mughals under Akbar acquired the throne of Delhi
8.	Battle of Talikota (Page 130, 290) (Delhi 2000, 1998)	1565	Bahmani Kingdom Vijaynagar Kingdom	1. Passed the way for the Mughal rule in the south. 2. Death blow to Hindu empire in the south.
9.	Battle of Haldighati (Page 187)	1576	Akbar's forces under the command of Raja Man Singh and Asaf Khan Rana Pratap	After his defeat Rana Pratap adopted guerilla warfare
10.	Battle of Samugarh (Page 203)	1658	Aurnagzeb Dara	Aurangzeb became the ruler of India

C. SHORT NOTES ON IMPORTANT EVENTS AND POLICIES ETC.

Chahalgani (Delhi 1997 and 1999)

During the period of the Slave Dynasty, the Turk chiefians were known as Chahalgani. After the death of Sultan lltutmish, the Chahalgani thought of assuming power Razia Sultana became the ruler and she frustrated their ambition and plans to hold power. She even used military power to subdue them. Razia, of course, had to pay a heavy price. Several other groups conspired and which led to the liquidation of Razia Sultana.

D. Most Prominent Personalities of the Medieval Period (other than Rulers)

S. No.	Name	Page/ pages	S. No.	Name	Page/ Pages
1.	Abul Fazal (Delhi, 2001)	188	2	Alberuni (Delhi 2001)	26,283
3.	Amir Khusro/ Khusru (Delhi, 1997,99)	61	4	Bairam Khan (Delhi 2001)	185
5.	Badauni	267	6	Barani (Delhi 2001)	109
7.	Chaitanya	118	8	Farid (Baba)	117
9.	Ferishta	110	10	Firdausi	26
11.	(Guru) Arjun Dev	195	12	(Guru) Gobind Singh	219
13.	(Guru) Nanak Dev	115	14	Ibn Batuta	110
15.	Jnaseswara	118	16	(Sant) Kabir	115, 291
17.	Mahmud Gawan	133			
18.	Malik Muhammad Jaisi	267	19	Malik Kafur	60
20.	Mirabai	118	21	Khwaja Muin-u-d-din Chisti	117
22.	Namdeva	118	23	Narsi Mehta	118
24.	(Hazrat) Nizam ud-din Aulia (Delhi 1998)	117	25	Ramananda	118
26.	Surdas	118, 267	27.	Tansen	266
28.	Toder M	188	29.	Tulsi Das	118, 267

E. Very Short Answer Questions

Punjab University (April 1999)

I. Answer any ten of the following in one or two lines. (20 marks)

1. Name the famous poet in Ghazni's court. Name his famous composition.
2. Who was the founder of the SlaveDynasty?
3. Name the two coins issued by Altutmish.
4. Name the four generals of Ala-ud-din Khilji.
5. Which foreign traveller came to India during the reign of Muhammad Tughlaq ?
6. Which new department was opened by Firoz Tughlaq to help the poor?
7. Who founded the Vijaynagar Empire?
8. Name the powerful state of Rajasthan at the time of Balban's invasion?
9. When and how did Sher Shah Suri die ?
10. Name the two taxes abolished by Akbar on Hindus.
11. When did Aurangzeb conquer Bijapur and Golkanda ?
12. Name the Mughal ruler under whom Hindi literature flourished.
13. Name the two buildings constructed by Aurangzeb?
14. Who was the famous singer of Akbar's reign?
15. Mention two main sets of Sufism.
16. When was Shivaji coronated ? What title did he assume?
17. Write two effects of Bhakti Movement.
18. What was Iqta system.
19. Who was Bairam Khan ?
20. Who was Krishandeva Raya ?

Punjab (October 1999)

II. Answer any ten of the following in one or two lines.

21. Name the historian who came to India with Mahmu Ghazni. Give the name of his book.
22. When did Second Battle of Tarain take place ? Who st?
23. For how long Qutubdin ruled ?
24. Who was Razia Begum ? What was her period of reign
25. Name the four generals of Alauddin Khilji ? (Apri 999 also)
26. Give the earlier name of Muhammad Tughlaq.
27. Name the two towns founded by Firoz Tughlaq.
28. Who was the ablest ruler of the Vijaynagar empire ? To which nasty did he belong ?
29. During the Vijaynagar empire what was a district known as ?
30. Who fought the battle of Kanwah and when ?
31. Name the first battle andthe year in which Sher Shah defeat Hamayun.
32. Who was Abul Fazal. Name his two books.
33. Define Batai System.

34. Who was Todar Mal ?
35. Name the Mughal ruler who was against music.
36. Mention two buildings constructed during Shah Jahan's reign in Delhi.
37. Who headed Shivaji's Ministry ? What was it called ?
38. What were the duties of the Diwan during the Mughal Period.
39. Name two Sufi Centres in India.
40. When and where was Guru Nanak Dev born ?

Punjab University (April 2000)

III. *Answer any ten of the following.*

41. Name the Indian state annexed by Ghazni.
42. Who was the founder of the Slave Dynasty ? What was the period of his reign ?
43. Give the dates of the First and Second Battle of Tarain.
44. Who was the founder of the Slave Dynasty ? What was the period of his reign ?
45. Write any two measures taken by Ala-ud-din to control the market ?
46. Name any two towns founded by Firoz Tughlaq.
47. Name the three ruling dynasties of Vijayanagar empire.
48. Name the autobiography of Babar. In which language was it written.
49. Who was defeated by whom in the Battle of Kanwah.
50. Name two buildings built by Sher Shah Suri.
51. Name the Rajput king who did not accept the sovereignty of Akbar.
52. First of all Akbar got arrived to which Rajput ruler's daughter.
53. When did Aurangzeb conquer Bijapur and Golkanda ?
54. State two aims of Aurangzeb's Deccan policy.
55. Who was Abul fazal ? Name his two famous books.
56. When did Shivaji die ? Who was his successor ?
57. Where and when Shivaji meet Aurangzeb ?
58. Name the two saints of Bhakti movement.
59. When and where was Guru Nanak Dev born ?
60. Name the revenue expert of Sher Shah and Akbar.

Punjab University (September 2000)

IV. *Answer any ten of the following in one or two lines.*

61. For how long Qutubddin ruled ?
62. Name the two coins issued by Iltutmish. (April, 1999)
63. When was the Second Battle of Tarain fought ? Who won ?
64. Who was Malik Kafur ?
65. Name four town built by Firoz Tughlaq.
66. In place of Delhi, which new capital was founded by Muhammad Tughlaq? Give its new name.
67. The town of Vijaynagar empire was established on the bank of which river ?
68. When was the Battle of Chausa fought ? who was defeated by whom?

69. When and how did Sher Shah die ?
70. Which historian came to India along with Mahmud Ghazni ? Give the name of his historical work. (April, 1999 also)
71. Which town was founded by Akbar ?
72. Name the Rajput ruler who did not accept the subordination of Akbar. (April 2000 also)
73. Name the two buidlings constructed by Shah Jahan.
74. Give the dates of First and Second Battle of Panipat.
75. Name the Mughal ruler who loved music most and the one who hated most.
76. Name the three places where military posts were got constructed by Balban to face the Mughal invasion.
77. What was a district called in the Vijay Nagar Empire ?
78. When and where was Shivaji coronated ?
79. Name the four centres of Sufism in India.
80. Who was Bairam Khan ?

Punjab University (April, 2001)

V *Answer any ten of the following in one or two lines.*

81. Name the famous poet of Mahmud Ghazni's court. Give the name of his book. (April 1999, Sept. 2000 and April, 2001)
82. When the First and Second Battles of Tarain were fought ?
83. Who was the successor of Balban? Give the period of his reign.
84. Who was the founder of the Khalji dynasty ?
85. Which foreign traveller came to India during the period of Mohammad Tughlaq?
86. Name the founder brothers of Vijaynagar empire. Which dynasty was founded by them ?
87. Name the autobiography of Babar. In which language was it written.? (April 2000 also)
88. How and when Sher Shah was killed ? (Sept. 2000 also)
89. When and between whom Battle of Talikota was foght?
90. Who wrote Ain-i-Akbari.
91. When and why din-i-Ilahi was established ?
92. Name the two important musicians of Akbar.
93. Name two building built by Shah Jahan.
94. Name two Mughal rulers who patronised painting.
95. Name the parents of Shivaji.
96. Who was Alberuni ?
97. When and between whom First Battle of Panipat was fought ?
98. What is Iqta System ?
99. Name two rulers under whom Hindi literature flourished.
100. Write two effects of Bhakti movement.

ANSWERS

1. Firdausi. *Shahnama*
2. Qutub-ud-din Aibak
3. Silver *Tanka*, copper *jital*
4. (*i*) Ulugh Khan (*ii*) Zafar khan (*iii*) Nusrat Khan (*iv*) Alap Khan
5. Ibn Babuta.
6. Diwan-i-Khas
7. Hari Hara in collaboration with his brother Bulkka.
8. Mewar.
9. 1545, during his conquert of Kalinjar Fort when he was grievously injured by the blast.
10. (*i*) Pilgrimage tax in 1563 (*ii*) Jizya in 1564.
11. (i) 1686 (ii) 1687.
12. Akbar
13. (*i*) Shahi Masjid at Labore (*ii*) Tomb of Aurangzeb's Queen at Aurangabad.
14. Tan sen
15. (*i*) Chisti (*ii*) Qalandar
16. (*i*) 1674 (*ii*) Chattrapati
17. (*i*) Lowering of caste bonds (*ii*) Promotion of regional languages
18. A sort of administrative unit like a province under the Delhi Sultans.
19. The guardian and tutor of Akbar. He advised Akbar to face Hemu in the Second Battle of Panipat.
20. Usually regarded as the most prominent ruler of the Vijaynagar empire.
21. (*i*) Alberuni or Alberuni (*ii*) *Tahqueig-Hind*, English translation called Alberuni's India (1888).
22. (*i*) 1192 (*ii*) Prithviraj
23. Four years
24. (*i*) Ruler of Delhi during the period of Slave Dynasty (*ii*) 1236-1241
25. See answer 4 above.
26. Juna Khan Tughlaq.
27. (*i*) Firozabad (Present Kotta Firoz Shah – Delhi) (*ii*) Fatehbad
28. (*i*) Krishan deva Raya (*ii*) Tuluva Dynasty
29. Nadus
30. (*i*) Babar and Rana Sanga (*ii*) March 16, 1527.
31. Chausa in 1539.
32. (*i*) A great scholar and writer (*ii*) Akbar Nama and Ain-i-Akbari.
33. A system of giving land by the owner to the peasant for cultivation and giving some share of produce to him.
34. Todar Mal is known for devising a systematised land revenue system first used by Sher Shah and later on by emperor Akbar.
35. Aurangzeb
36. (*i*) Jama Masjid (*ii*) Red Fort
37. (*i*) Peshwa (*ii*) *Asht Pradhan*.
38. He looked after the revenues of the state.
39. (*i*) Hansi (*ii*) Ajmer
40. (*i*) 1969 (*ii*) Nankana Sahib
41. Punjab
42. Author of Shahnama on Mahmud Ghazni
43. (*i*) 1191 (*ii*) 1192
44. (*i*) Qutub-ud-din Aibak (*ii*) 1206 to 1210 AD
45. (*i*) Determination of rates of articles of daily use (*ii*) Introduction of

a sort of ration card system 46. (*i*) Hissar (*ii*) Jaunpur

47. (*i*) Sangama (*ii*) Salva (*iii*) Tuluva
48. Tuzuki-i-Baburi or Babar Nama (*ii*) Turki 49. Rana Sanga by Babar
50. (i) Mausoleum of Sher Shah at Sasaram in Bihar (*ii*) Fort of Rohtasgarh on the bank of the river Jhelum in the North-west.
51. Rana Pratap
52. Daughter of Raja Bihari Mal of Amber (Modern Jaipur)
53. (*i*) 1686 (*ii*) 1687
54. (*i*) To Subdue Shia Sultan of Deccan (*ii*) To crush the power of the Marathas.
55. (*i*) A great scholar and writer (*ii*) Author of Akbar-Nama and Ain-i-Akbari.
56. (*i*) 1680 (*ii*) Sambhaji 57. (*i*) Agra (*ii*) 1665/66
58. (*i*) Mirabai (*ii*) Sant Kabir 59. (*i*) 1969 (*ii*) Nankana Sahib
60. Todar Mal 61. 1206 to 1210 A.D.
62. (*i*) Silver tanka (*ii*) Copper jittal 63. (*i*) 1192 AD. (*ii*) Mahmud Ghazni
64. An able general of Ala-ud-din. He subdued several rulers of the south and brought huge wealth comprising jewels and diamonds etc. for Alauddin.
65. (*i*) Firozabad (Present Kotla Firoz Shah at Delhi) (*ii*) Fatehabad (*iii*) Hissar (*iv*) Jaunpur.
66. (*i*) Devagiri (*ii*) Daultabad 67. Tungbhadra river
68. (*i*) 1539 (*ii*) Humayun was defeated by Sher Shah
69. (*i*) 1545 (*ii*) At the seize of Kalinger when one of the rockets fell on the ammunication and there was an explosion.
70. (*i*) Firdausi (*ii*) Shahnama 71. Fatehpur Sikri
72. Maharana Pratap 73. (*i*) Red Fort , Delhi (*ii*) Jama Masjid, Delhi
74. (*i*) 1526 (*ii*) 1556 75. (*i*) Akbar (*ii*) Aurangzeb
76. (*i*) Sialkot (*ii*) Multan (iii) Uch 77. (*i*) Nadus
78. (*i*) 1674 (*ii*) Rajgarh 79. (*i*) Multan (*ii*) Hansi (*iii*) Ajodhan
80. The guardin, tutor and general of Akbar.
81. (*i*) Firdausi (*ii*) Shahnama 82. (*i*) 1191 (*ii*) 1192
83. In 1286, Balban before his death nominated Kai-Khushran, his grandson as his heir but the Kotwal of Delhi plotted against him and forced him to leave. He installed Kaiquabad, another grandson of Balban to the throne. He was killed in 1290.
84. Ghiyas-u-din Tughluq 85. Ibn Babuta
86. (*i*) Harihar and Bukkha (*ii*) Sangama dynasty
87. (*i*) Tuzaki-Babri or Babarnama (*ii*) Turki

88. see answer 69.

89. Between Bahmani Kingdom and Vijaynagar Kingdom.

90. Abul Fazal

91. (*i*) 1582 (*ii*) To provide a common belief by harmonising the tenets of different beliefs.

92. (*i*) Tan Sen (ii) Baz Bahadur

93. (*i*) Taj Mahal at Agra (*ii*) Red Fort in Delhi

94. (*i*) Akbar (*ii*) Jahangir

95. (*i*) Jijabai (*ii*) Shahji Bhonsle

96. Author, astronomer, mathematician, philosopher : Wrote Taliqueeq - Hind (Alberuni's India)

97. (a) 1526 (*ii*) Babar and Ibraham Lodi

98. An administrative unit equivalent to a province followed during the Sultanate period.

99. (*i*) Alauddin (*ii*) Akbar

100. (*i*) It helped in the development of regional languages
(*ii*) It inspired reforms in religion

31

B.A. Examination Question Papers (with Answers) of Different Universities (2001 to 2004)

A. Essay-Type Questions

Q.1. Analyse the achievements of Iltutmish. (*V.B.S. Purvanchal, 2001*)

Or

Give an estimate of Iltutmish as a ruler. (*Lucknow, 2001*)

Or

Give an account of various steps taken by Iltutmish to consolidate Delhi Sultanate. (*Delhi 2003, 2004*)

Ans. *Q.1. Pages 28 to 31.*

Q.2. Examine the overambitious schemes of Muhammad Tughlaq. (*Purvanchal 2001*)

Or

Describe the main projects of Muhammad Tughlaq. (*Lucknow 2001*)

Ans. *Pages 62 to 65.*

Q.3. Write an essay on the administration during the Sultanate period. (*Kanpur 2003, Agra 2003*)

Ans. *Q.2 Pages 90 to 92.*

Q.4. "Sikandar Lodi was the greatest Lodi Sultan". Discuss. (Kanpur 2004, Agra 2004)

Ans. *Q.3. Pages 81 to 84.*

Q.5. What were the causes of the defeat of the Rajputs at the hands of the Turks? What was its effect on the history of India? (*V.B.S. Purcanchal 2001*)

Or

Account for the success of Turks against the Rajputs in northern India during the 11th and 12th centuries. (Delhi 2002 and 2004)

Ans. *Q.6. Pages 19 to 23.*

Q.6. Describe the condition of India on the eve of Turkish invasion. (*V.B.S. Purvanchal, 2001*)

Or

Discuss the socio-political conditions of Northern India between 11th -12th centuries. How far were these conditions responsible for the success of the Turks? *(Delhi, 2002, 2003)*.

Ans. *Q.3 Pages 5 to 8.*

Q.7. How far was Firoz Tughlaq responsible for the decline of Delhi Sultanate ? *(Delhi 2004)*

Ans. *Q.3. Page 72. Q.4 Pages 74 to 76.*

Q.8. Write an essay on the social conditions during Sultanate period. *(Agra 2002)*

Ans. *Q.1. Pages 96 to 99.*

Q.9. Throw light on the achievements of Balban. *(V.B.S. Purvanchal 2001)*

Or

Discuss Balban's policy of consolidation. *(Lucknow, 2002)*

Ans. *Q.4. Pages 36 to 39.*

Q.10. Discuss the main features of Balban's theory of Kingship. *(Lucknow, 2001, 2002, Delhi 2004)*

Ans. *Q.3. Pages 34 and 35.*

Q.11. Evaluate the achievements of Qutab-ud-din Aibak. *(V.B.S. Purvanchal, 2001)*

Explain the difficulties before Qutab-ud-Din? How did he solve them ? *(V.B.S. Purvanchal, 2002)*

Ans. *Q.1. Pages 28-29.*

Q.12. 'Muhammad Tughlaq was a mixture of Opposites'. Examine. *(V.B.S. Purvanchal, 2001, Kanpur 2002, 2003, Agra 2003)*

Or

Estimate Muhammad Tughlaq as an administrator. *(V.B.S. Purvanchal, 2002)*

Ans. *Q.2. Pages 66 to 69.*

Q.14. Describe the reforms of Firoz Tughlaq. *(V.B.S. Purvanchal, 2001)*

Or

Give an account of reform of Firoz Tughlaq. *(Lucknow, 2002)*

Or

Throw light on the reforms of Firoz Tughlaq. *(Lucknow 2004)*

Ans. *Q.3. Pages 69 to 73.*

Q.15. Critically examine the economic policy of Ala-ud-Din with special reference to his policy of market control. *(V.B.S. 2001)*

Or

Explain the revenue policy of Ala-ud-Din. *(V.B.S. Purvanchal, 2002)*

Or

Write an essay on the market control policy of Ala-ud-Din. *(Lucknow 2001, Kanpur 2001, 2002, 2004, Agra 2004)*

Ans. *Q.4 Page 50 to 52.*

Q.16. What is your opinion about the economic policy of Ala-ud-Din? How far did it succeed in achieving its goals? (*Delhi 2002, 2004*)

Ans. *Q.5. Pages 53 to 57.*

Q.17. Describe Timur's invasion on India. What were its effects? (*V.B.S. Purvanchal 2001*)

Or

Give an account of Timur's invasion of India. (*Lucknow 2001*)

Or

Give an account of Timur's invasion of India and point out its consequences. (*Lucknow, 2002*)

Ans. *Q.5. Pages 76 to 78.*

Q.18. "Sher Shah is called the forerunner of Akbar". Examine this statement.

(*V.B.S.Purvanchal, 2001*)

Ans. *Q.5: Pages 168, 169.*

Q.19. State the main features of revenue organisation and administration of Sher Shah. (*V.B.S. Purvanchal, 2002*)

Or

Evaluate Sher Shah as an administrator. (*Lucknow, 2002*)

Or

Do you agree with the view that Sher Shah was an innovator in the sphere of administration ? (*Delhi, 2002*)

Ans. *Q.3. Pages 162 to 166.*

Q.20. Discuss the relations of Humayun with Sher Shah and Bahadur Shah. (*Kanpur 2001*)

Ans. *Q.2. Page 154 to 157.*

Q.21. Briefly describe the important aspects of the First Battle of Panipat. (*Lucknow, 2001*)

Or

Discuss the causes and consequences of Babur's invasion of India. (*Lucknow, 2002*)

Ans. *Q.1. Pages 143 to 145.*

Q.22. "The chief contribution of Bhakti movement was to establish harmonious and a casteless society." (*Delhi 2002*)

Ans. *Q.1. Pages 111 to 113.*

Q.23. Explain the impact of teachings of Kabir and Nanak on the contemporary society. (*Delhi, 2003*)

Or

Analyse the impact of Bhakti movement on Medieval Indian Society. (*Delhi, 2004*)

Ans. *Q.1. Pages 111 to 113 and 115.*

Q.24. Examine the measures of various Sultans of Delhi to safeguard the North-west Frontier from Mongol invasions. (*Delhi 2003, 2004*)

Ans. *Q.1. Pages 102 to 105.*

Q.25. Describe the salient features of Indo-Islamic architecture. Trace the construction of some important prominent monuments under the Sultans of Delhi. *(Delhi, 2003)*

Ans. *Q.1. Pages 106 to 108.*

Q.26. Examine the causes of the defeat of Humayun. *(V.B.S. Purvanchal 2001)*

Or

Throw light on the difficulties of Humayun. *(Lucknow, 2002)*

Ans. *Q.2. Page 154 to 156.*

Q.27. Discuss the causes of Humayun's early difficulties and how far was he himself responsible for them? *(Lucknow 2004)*

Ans. *Q.1. Pages 151 to 154.*

Q.28. Give an account of Akbar's conquests. *(Lucknow, 2001)*

Ans. *Q.1. Pages 170-171.*

Q.29. Examine Nur Jahan's influence on Jahangir. *(Lucknow 2002, 2003)*

Ans. *Q.2. Pages 192 to 195.*

Q.30. Explain the working of the Central Government under the Mughals. *(V.B.S. Purvanchal, 2001)*

Ans. *Q.1. page 224 to 226.*

Q.31. Write a brief note on the development of painting during Jahangir's reign. *(V.B.S. Purvanchal 2001)*

Ans. *Q.4. Pages 265-266.*

Q.32. "Shah Jahan's reign was the 'golden age' of the Mughal Empire". Comment. *(Lucknow 2004)*

Ans. *Q.2. 198 to 202.*

Q.33. What major changes do you notice in the architectural trends under the Mughals from Akbar to Aurangzeb? *(Delhi 2004)*

Ans. *Q.1. Pages 260 to 262.*

Q.34. Explain the Rajput Policy of Akbar. *(V.B.S. Purvanchal 2001, 2002)*

Or

Examine the Rajput policy of Akbar. *(Lucknow, 2004)*

Ans. *Q.2. Pages 172 to 174.*

Q.35. Explain Din-i-Illahi. *(V.B.S.Purvanchal 2001)*

Or

Analyse the evolution of Akbar's religious idea with special reference to the concept of '*Sulah-i-kul*' *(Delhi 2004)*

Or

Evaluate the various stages in the growth of Akbar's religious policy. *(Delhi 2003)*

Or

Write an essay on Akbar's religious policy. *(Lucknow 2002)*

Ans. *Q.3 and 4. Pages 175 to 180.*

Q.36. Discuss Aurangzeb's relations with the Marathas and Deccan States. Did this 'Sleepless objective' become 'an ulcer' for the Mughal empire ? *(Delhi 2003)*

Or

Discuss the relations of Aurangzeb with the states of Bijapur and Golkunda. *(Lucknow 2001)*

Or

Examine the causes and impact of Aurangzeb's relations with Deccan Kingdoms *(Delhi 2002)*

Ans. *Q.4. Pages 215 to 217.*

Q.37 Examine the Rajput Policy of Aurangzeb and point out its consequences. *(Lucknow 2004)*

Ans. *Q.3. Pages 213 to 215.*

Q.38. Give a critical assessment of working of Mansabdari System. *(Delhi 2002)*

Ans. *Q. 3 Pages 227 to 231.*

Or

Explain the War of Succession among the successors of Shah Jahan. *(V.B.S. 2001, 2002)*

Or

Throw light on the various stages of War of Succession among the sons of Shah Jahan. *(Lucknow 2001)*

Ans. *Q.3. Pages 202 to 204.*

Q.39. Explain the causes of the rise of the Maratha power. *(V.B.S. 2001)*

Ans. *Q.1. Pages 270-271.*

Q.40. Explain the rise of the Marathas under Shivaji. *(V.B.S. 2002)*

Or

Explain the achievements of Shivaji. *(V.B.S. 2001)*

Ans. *Q.2. Pages 272 to 274.*

Q.41. Describe the Deccan policy of Ala-ud-Din Khalji. *(Kanpur 2003, Agra 2003)*

Ans. *Deccan policy of Ala-ud-Din*

Objectives of Ala-ud-Din's Deccan Policy. (see page 44)

Conquests in Deccan. Ala-ud-Din conquered the following kingdoms in the South. All these kingdoms accepted the supermacy of Ala-ud-Din. However these were not annexed to his empire. Expeditions to these places were led by Malik Kafur.

1. Conquest of Devagiri (1307)
2. Conquest of Telingana (1310)
3. Conquest of Dwarsamundra (1311)
4. Pandya Kingdom (1311)

An Analysis of Deccan Policy of Ala-ud-Din

Like Samundra Gupta of the Gupta period, Ala-ud-Din did not intend to annex the territories of the rulers of South India. His primary objective was to obtain as much wealth as possible so that he could maintain a huge army. Such a huge army needed substantial amount of money. Ala-ud-Din considered the Deccan as a milch-cow. A lot of gold was available there. With this wealth, he could stabilise his position in the North. He sent Malik Kafur one of his ablest and bravest generals to South four times. Every time, Malik Kafur brought with him, huge quantities of gold, jewels, pearls and silver. He also brought with him hundreds of elephants. Following were the chief characteristics of his Deccan policy.

1. Ala-ud-Din's motive was to obtain wealth.
2. He did not resort to conversions i.e. people were not asked to change their religion.
3. He did not annex the territories to his empire.

The successful campaigns strengthened his financial position and he was able to introduce several reforms in his administration.

There is also the dark side of the picture also. Several flourishing cities were sacked. Hundreds of people were slaughtered and temples were plundred. Mosques were built to commemorate his brilliant victories.

All these measures, however, developed a feeling of discontentment in the people of the South. This ultimately led to the establishment of the Vijayanagar Empire. Thus Ala-ud-Din's Deccan policy paid short term dividends.

B. Short Answer Questions (Brief Notes)

I. Write brief notes of 100 words each on any four of the following. (*Lucknow 2001*)

(1) Nasiruddin Mahmud (*Q.2. Page 33*)

(2) Razia Sultana (*Q.2. Page 32*)

(3) Public works of Firoz Tughlaq (*Q.3. Page 71*)

(4) Battle of Khanwa (*Page 293*)

(5) Todar Mal (*Q.7. Page 188*)

(6) Fatehpur Sikri (*2001 and 2002*) (*Page 327*)

II. Write a note on Shivaji's *Ashtapradhan* (*Lucknow 2001, 2002*)

Ans. *Page 278.*

III. Write notes on : (*Lucknow, 2002*)

(1) Iltutmish (*Page 29*)

(2) Introduction of token Currency by Mohd. Tughlaq. (*Page 64*)

(3) Public works of Firoz Tughlaq (*Page 71*)

(4) Sikander Lodi (*Page 81*)

(5) Battle of Chausa (*Page 156*)
(6) Bairam Khan (*Page 185*)
(7) Second Battle of Panipat (*Page 185 and 295*)

IV. Write notes on : (*Delhi 2002*)
(1) Zia-ud-Din Barni (*Page 109*)
(2) Iqta System (*Page 93*) (*Delhi 2002, 2003*)
(3) Nur Jahan (*Page 192*)

V. Write notes on (*Delhi 2003*)
(1) Mughal Paintaings (*Page 298*)
(2) Abul Fazal (*Page 188*)

VI. Write notes on (*Delhi 2004*)
(1) Balban's Concept of Kingship (*Page 34*)
(2) Nizamuddin Auliya (*Page 117*)
(3) Krishnadeva Raya (*Page 289*)
(4) Mansabdari System (*Page 296*)

VII. Write notes on (*Delhi Correspondence 2004*)
(1) Raziya (*Page 32*)
(2) Baburnama (*Page 149*)
(3) Sulh-i-Kul (*Page 295*)
(4) Nur Jahan (*Page 192*)

Q.VIII. Attempt any five out of fifteen questions in 80 words each. (*Kanpur 2001*)

(1) What were the difficulties before Iltutmish when he ascended the throne? (*Page 30*)
(2) What Balban did to raise the prestige of crown ? (*Page 35*)
(3) What was the policy of Ala-ud-Din towards Hindus ? (*Page 45*)
(4) "Mohammad Tughlaq was a mixture of opposites." Discuss. (*Page 67*)
(5) What Firoz Tughlaq did for the development of agriculture? (*Page 70, 71*)
(6) Write a brief note on Timur's attack. (*Page 289*)
(7) What were the main causes of the downfall of the Tughlaq Dynasty ? (*Page 74*)
(8) What was the impact of Bhakti movement on society ? (*Page 112*)
(9) What were the causes of success of Babur in the Battle in the Battle of Panipat? (*Page 144*)
(10) What were the early difficulties of Humayun ? (*Page 151*)
(11) Write a brief note on Muslim education system? (*Page 72, 135*)

(12) What were the main causes of failure of Humayun against Sher Shah Suri? (*Page 156*)

(13) Write a note on Battle of Khanva. (*Pages 293-294*)

(14) What are the main principles of Sufism? (*Page 229*)

(15) What do you know about Sikandar Lodi ? (*Page 81*)

Q. IX Attempt any ten fifteen questions in 100 words each. Each question carries 2 marks. (*Kanpur 2002*)

(16) How did Iltutmish save his kingdom from the invasion of Mongols? (*Page 30-31*)

(17) What were the the difficulties of Iltutmish when he ascended the throne? (*Page 30-31*)

(18) Give a brief note on the achievements of Balban. (*Page 38*)

(19) Estimate Razia as a ruler. (*Page 33*)

(20) Do you agree that Ala-ud-Din's policy towards the South was successful? (*Page 44*)

(21) Write a brief note on military administration of Ala-ud-Din Khalji. (*Page 45*)

(22) Write a brief note on ordinances passed by Ala-ud-Din Khalj to prevent revolts. (see page 357)

(23) Write a brief note on the revenue reforms of Mohammad Tughlaq. (*Page 63*)

(24) Write a brief note on the taxation policy of Firoz Tughlaq. (*Page 70*)

(25) Write a brief note on the impact of Timur's invasion on India. (*Page 78*)

(26) Write a brief note on Bahlol Lodi. (*Page 80*)

(27) Estimate Khizr Khan as a ruler. (*Page 79*)

Q.X. Write the answer of each question in about 100 words.

(28) Throw light on Turkish conquest. (*Page 23*)

(29) Discuss the main causes of Rajput's defeat. (*Page 19*)

(30) "Iltutmish was the founder of the slave dynasty". Discuss. (*Page 29*)

(31) Write a short note on the rise and fall of Razia. (*Page 32*)

(32) Trace the causes of the decline of slave Dynastry. (*Page 40*)

(33) Critically examine the market control policy of Ala-ud-Din. (*Page 287*)

(34) Give an estimate of Jalalud-Din Khalji in brief. (*Page 40*)

(35) Why did Muhammad Tughlaq introduce token currency? (*Page 64*)

(36) Give achievements of Firoz Tughlaq in brief. (*Page 71*)

(37) Write a note on Sufi movement. (*Page 292*)

Ordinances issued by Ala-ud-Din to prevent revolts

Ala-ud-Din Khalji issued four ordinances to prevent revolts.

1. The religious endowments and free grants of lands to people were confiscated.
2. The spy system was reorganised.
3. The use of wine was prohibited.
4. Social gatherings of nobles were prohibited.

Multiple Choice Test Questions

I. Write the correct answer. (*Kanpur, 2001*)

1. Who introduced the Iqtadari System ?
   (*a*) Balban (*b*) Qutub-ud-Din Aibak
   (*c*) Iltutmish (*d*) Razia
2. Who is known as '*Lakh Baksh*' among the emperors of Delhi Sultanate ?
   (*a*) Iltutmish (*b*) Qutub-ud-din Aibak
   (*c*) Firoz Tughlaq (*d*) Balban
3. Who circulated coin '*Jital*' (*2001 and 2002*)
   (*a*) Nasir-ud-din (*b*) Qutub-ud-Din
   (*c*) Balban (*d*) Iltutmish
4. Who attempted to control prices ?
   (*a*) Firoz Tughlaq (*b*) Mohammad bin Tughlaq
   (*c*) Ala-ud-Din Khilji (*d*) Sher Shah Suri
5. The token currency was introduced ?
   (*a*) Ala-ud-Din (*b*) Mohammad Tughlaq
   (*c*) Sher Shah Suri (*d*) Firoz Tughlaq
6. Who constructed '*Adhai din Ka Jhopra*'?
   (*a*) Qutub-ud-Din Aibak (*b*) Balban
   (*c*) Ala-ud-Din Khilji (*d*) Firoz Tughlaq
7. The Battle of Khanva was fought in the year ?
   (*a*) 1528 (*b*) 1527
   (*c*) 1529 (*d*) 1526
8. During the reign of Humayun, Bahadur Shah was the ruler of
   (a) Mandu (b) Gujarat
   (c) Kalinjar (d) Kalpi
9. Who is the writer of *Tabkat-i-Nasiri* ?
   (*a*) Minhaj-us-Siraz (*b*) Firoz Tughlaq
   (*c*) Amir Khusro (*d*) Barni
10. In which year Iltutmish ascended the throne ?
    (*a*) 1209 (*b*) 1211
    (*c*) 1213 (*d*) 1215

II. Write the correct Answer (*Kanpur 2002*)

11. In which year Timur invaded India ?
    (*a*) 1398 (*b*) 1192

(*c*) 1193 (*d*) 1194

12. In which year the first battle of Tarain was fought ? (*2003 and 2004*)

(*a*) 1191 (*b*) 1192
(*c*) 1193 (*d*) 1194

13. Who was the writer of 'Fatuhat-i-Firozshah ?

(a) Yahiya-bin Ahmad (b) Ziyauddin Barni
(c) Firoz Tughlaq (d) Mir Hasan Dehalvi

14. Who constructed the '*Quwat-ul-Islam*' Mosque ?

(*a*) Qutub-ud-Din Aibak (*b*) Iltutmish
(*c*) Balban (*d*) Razia

15. Who transferred his capital from Delhi to Deogiri ?

(a) Muhammad Tughlaq (b) Firoz-Tughlaq
(c) Khizr Khan (d) Ibrahim Lodi

16. Who introduced the custom of '*Sijda*' and '*Pabosh*'?

(*a*) Razia (*b*) Balban
(*c*) Iltutmish (*d*) Ala-ud-din

III Answer the following Questions (*Kanpur 2003*)

17. Who became the ruler of Indian territories of Muhammad Ghori after his death ?

(*a*) Iltutmish (*b*) Qutub-ud-Din
(*c*) Ala-ud-Din (*d*) Bahram Shah

18. Which city was founded by Firoz Tughlaq ?

(*a*) Firozpur (*b*) Daultabad
(*c*) Firozabad (*d*) Allahabad

19. Who was the writer of *Fatwah-i-Jahandari* ?

(*a*) Barni (*b*) Hussan Nizam
(*c*) Amir Khusro (*d*) Minhaj-Siraj

20. Which was the primary education centre of Islamic learning ?

(*a*) Madarsa (*b*) Maktab
(*c*) Pathshala (*d*) Dargah

ANSWERS

1. (*c*) **2.** (*b*) **3.** (*d*) **4.** (*c*) **5.** (*b*) **6.** (*a*)
7. (*b*) **8.** (*b*) **9.** (*a*) **10.** (*b*) **11.** (*a*) **12.** (*a*)
13. (*c*) **14.** (*a*) **15.** (*a*) **16.** (*b*) **17.** (*b*) **18.** (*c*)
19. (*a*) **20.** (*b*)

Multiple Choice Test Questions

1. The Muslim Sufi who advocated the theory of 'Wahdat-ul-Shahud.
   (1) Sheikh Ahmad Sarhindi
   (2) Sheikh Salim Chishti
   (3) Maulana Abdul Hai
   (4) Hazrat Nizamuddin Auliya
2. During whose period was compiled the Adi Granth ?
   (1) Guru Arjun Dev
   (2) Guru Nanak Dev
   (3) Guru Amar Das
   (4) Guru Hargobind
3. The Mughal emperor who asked his painters to make portraits of birds, was
   (1) Shajahan
   (2) Humayun
   (3) Akbar
   (4) Jahangir
4. Name the mathematicians among the following who belonged to the Rajpur period.
   (1) Bhaskaracharya
   (2) Vagbhata
   (3) Vachaṣpati
   (4) Haradatta
5. Bhimsen's '*Nuskha-i-Dilkusha*' is a major source of information for the Mughals in
   (1) Bengal
   (2) Assam
   (3) Rajasthan
   (4) Deccan
6. Which of the following is not a work of Guru Gobind Singh?
   (1) Japji Sahib
   (2) Chandi de Var
   (3) Zafar Nama
   (4) Vachitra Natak
7. Who was the founder of the city of Agra?
   (1) Firoz Tughlaq
   (2) Khiza Khan

(3) Sikandar Lodi
(4) Bahlol Lodi

8. Name the common feature between Shivaji and Baji Rao-I that ensured their victories in battles.
(1) Support from Hindu Rajas
(2) Guerilla Warfare
(3) Hindu Padpadshahi
(4) Organised and trained army

9. Who among the following Indian rulers was a contemporary of Akbar?
(1) Ahilya Bai
(2) Rani Durgawati
(3) Martrand Varma
(4) Raja Swai Jai Singh

10. Who among the following is said to have witnessed the rule of eight Sultans of Delhi ?
(1) Amir Khusrau
(2) Minhaj-us-Siraj
(3) Shams-i-Siraj Afif
(4) Ziaud-din Barni

11. Name the Indian ruler who first organised Haj Pilgrimage at the expense of the state.
(1) Aurangzeb
(2) Akbar
(3) Ala-ud-din Khilji
(4) None of these.

12. Who among the following wrote a historical account during the Mughal period.
(1) Zebun-nissa Begam
(2) Jahanara Begam
(3) Nurjaha Begam
(4) Gulbadan Begam

13. The Mansabdari System intoduced by Akbar was borrowed from the system followed in
(1) Persia
(2) Mongolia
(3) Afghanistan
(4) Turkey

14. Fawazil in the Sultanate period meant
(1) Illegal exactions extracted from the peasants

(2) Revenue assigned in lieu of salary
(3) Extra payment made to the nobles
(4) Excess amount paid to the exchequer by the Iqtadars.

15. Chauth, the claim of the government's share of revenue amounted to
    (1) One-sixth of the revenue
    (2) One-third of the revenue
    (3) One-fourth of the revenue
    (4) One-seventh of the revenue
16. Dam was Mughal copper coin which part of a rupee was it ?
    (1) One-fourtieth part of a rupee
    (2) One-twentieth part of a rupee
    (3) One-tenth part of a rupee
    (4) Equal to a rupee
17. Ibadat Khana constructed by Akbar was a
    (1) Mosque
    (2) Temple
    (3) Meeting place of Ministers
    (4) House of worship
18. Madarasa was a place of
    (1) Islamic learning
    (2) Buddhist learning
    (3) Christian learning
    (4) None of these
19. One type of army formation is given in the figure. Name the Mughal who formed it.
    (1) Akbar
    (2) Babur
    (3) Shah Jahan
    (4) Jahangir

ANSWERS

1. **(1)**	2. **(1)**	3. **(4)**	4. **(1)**	5. **(4)**
6. **(1)**	7. **(3)**	8. **(2)**	9. **(2)**	10. **(1)**
11. **(2)**	12. **(4)**	13. **(2)**	14. **(4)**	15. **(3)**
16. **(2)**	17. **(4)**	18. **(1)**	19. **(2)**	

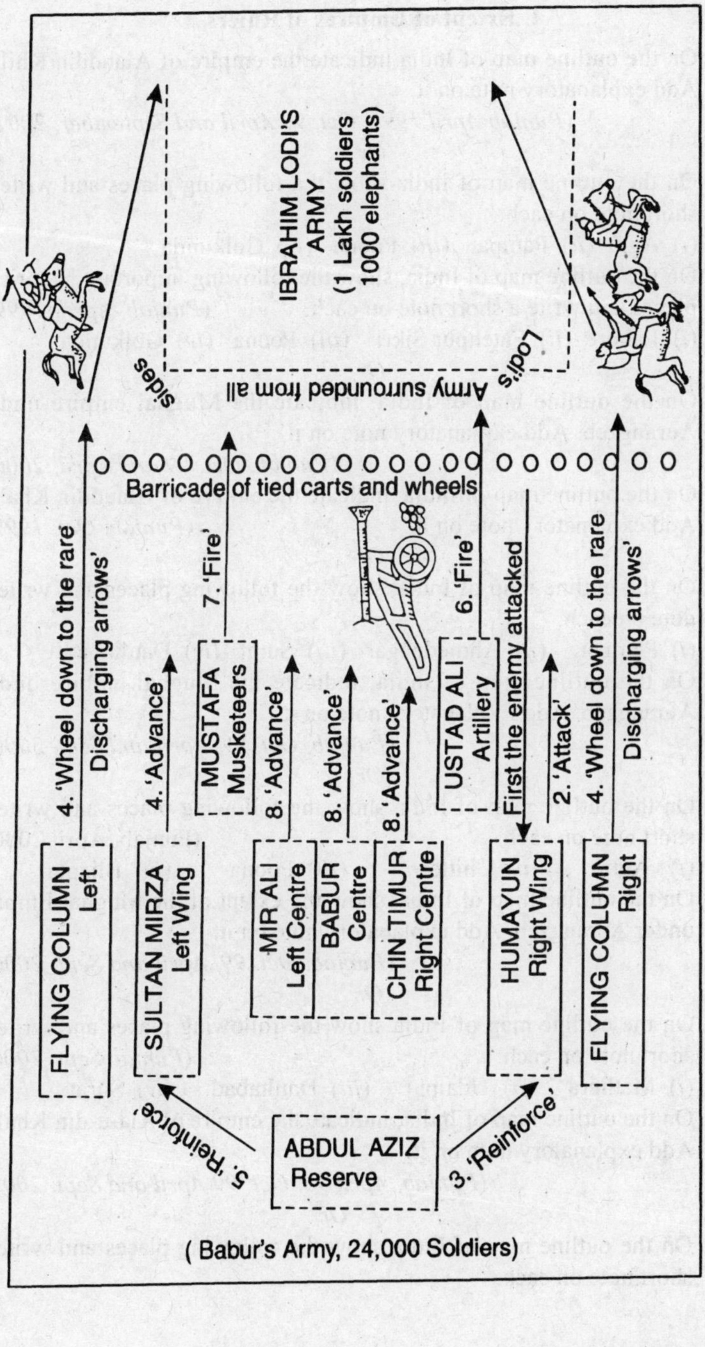

Fig. Army formation of a Mughal ruler

MAP WORK WITH EXPLANATORY NOTES

I. Extent of Empires of Rulers

Q.1. On the outline map of India indicate the empire of Alauddin Khilji. Add explanatory note on it.

(*Punjab April 1998, Oct. 99 April and September, 2001*)

Or

On the outline map of India show the following places and write a short note on each.

(*i*) Agra (*ii*) Panipat (*iii*) Poona (*iv*) Golkunda

Q.2. On the outline map of India, show the following important historical places and write a short note on each. (*Punjab, April, 1999*)

(*i*) Lahore (*ii*) Fatehpur Sikri (*iii*) Poona (*iv*) Golkunda

Or

On the outline map of India, indicate the Mughal empire under Aurangzeb. Add explanatory note on it.

(*Punjab, Oct. 99 and April, 2000*)

Q.3. On the outline map of India, indicate the empire of Alauddin Khalji. Add explanatory note on it. (*Punjab, Oct. 1999*)

Or

On the outline map of India, show the following places and write a note on each.

(*i*) Panipat (*ii*) Ahmednagar (*iii*) Surat (*iv*) Daultabad

Q.4. On the outline map of India, indicate the Mughal empire under Aurangzeb. Add Explanatory note on it.

(*Punjab, Oct. 99, April and Sept. 2000*)

Or

On the outline map of India show the following places and write a short note on each. (Punjab, April 2000)

(*i*) Agra (*ii*) Chittor (*iii*) Poona (*iv*) Bijapur

Q.5. On the outline map of India, show the extent of the Mughal Empire under Aurangzeb. Add explanatory note on it.

(*Punjab, Oct. 99, April and Sept. 2000*)

Or

On the outline map of India show the following places and write a short note on each. (*Punjab Sept. 2000*)

(*i*) Mathura (*ii*) Udaipur (*iii*) Daultabad (*iv*) Surat.

Q.6. On the outline map of India, indicate the empire pf Ala-u-din Khalji. Add explanatory note on it.

(*Punjab, April 98, Oct. 99 April and Sept. 2001*)

Or

On the outline map of India show the following places and write a short note on each.

(*i*) Panipat (*ii*) Fatehpur Sikri (*iii*) Chittor (*iv*) Bijapur
(*v*) Ahmadnagar (*vi*) Lucknow.

Q.7. On the outline map of India, indicate the empire of Ala-u-din Khalji. Add explanatory note on it.

(*Punjab, April 98, Oct. 99, April and Sept. 2001*)

Or

On the outline map of India, show the following places and write a explanatory note on each.

(*i*) Lahore (*ii*) Mathura (*iii*) Chittor (*iv*) Poona (*v*) Golkunda
(*vi*) Daultabad.

Q.8. On the outline map of India, indicate the extent of empire of Shivaji and add a explanatory note on it.

Or

On the outline map of India, indicate the following places. Write an explanatory note on each.

(*i*) Lahore (*ii*) Mathura (*iii*) Jaipur (*iv*) Poona
(v) Ahmednagar (*vi*) Surat

ANSWERS : EXPLANATORY NOTES ON MAPS

(1) **Extent of Empire of Ala-ud-din :** Ala-ud-din succeeded in establishing a vast empire in India. Towards the North-West, it extended upto the river Indus and after 1336, even Kabul and Ghazni came under his influence. Towards the East, it extended upto Avadh, Orissa, Bihar and several parts of Bengal. In the South it extended upto the Vindhyas and except the Pandayas in the far south, all other rulers accepted his suzerainty. Kashmir in the North and Hassan in the East were not included in his empire. Ala-ud-din regarded the South as 'milch cow for the gold' and he required this to strengthen his position. He sent Malik Kafur four times to South not to conquer it but to get gold, silver, pearls, diamonds etc. and he got what he wanted.

(2) **Extent of Empire of Aurangzeb :** Aurangzeb achieved the greatest expansion of the Mughal empire. His empire extended from Afghanistan to Assam and from Himalayas to the river Kaveri in the south. It excluded the Maratha territory. Aurangzeb had enemies on all sides. He could defeat them but could not crush them. The Deccan ulcer ruined the Mughal empire.

Several European countries had established their factories. These trading centres ultimately proved in the coming century as the spring boards for the British to capture and rule over India.

(3) **Extent of Empire of Shivaji :** Shivaji's empire included some parts of Maharashtra, Konkan and a large part of Karnataka and Mysore. His Kingdom extended roughly from Ramnagar (Surat) to Karwar in the south. It comprised the Western Karnataka including Kopal, Bellary, Sira, Kolar, Vellore, Arni, Ginji together with a share in his brother's estate at Tanjore.

II Important Places of Historical Interest

Q.1. On an outline map of India show the following places and write a short note on each. (*Punjab, Sept. 2000*)
(*i*) Lahore (*ii*) Mathura (*iii*) Chittor (*iv*) Poona (*v*) Golkunda (*vi*) Daultabad

Q.2. On the outline map of India, show the following places, and write a short note on each. (*Punjab, April 2001*)
(*i*) Panipat (*ii*) Fatehpur Sikri (*iii*) Chittor (*iv*) Bijapur (*v*) Ahmednagar (*vi*) Lucknow

Q.3. On an outline map of India, show the following places and write a short note on each. (*Punjab, Sept. 2000*)
(*i*) Mathura (*ii*) Udaipur (*iii*) Daultabad (*iv*) Surat (*v*) Golkunda (*vi*) Daultabad

Q.4. On the outline map of India, show the following places and write a short note on each. (*Punjab,April 2000*)
(*i*) Agra (*ii*) Chittor (*iii*) Poona (*iv*) Bijapur

Q.5. On the outline map of India, show the following places and write an explanatory note on each. (*Punjab, Oct. 1999*)
(*i*) Panipat (*ii*) Ahmednagar (*iii*) Surat (*iv*) Daultabad

ANSWERS

Agra . Probably founded by the Rajputs in the medieval period, Sikander Lodi made it as the capital of his kindgom in 1505. During the time of the Mughals in the 16th and 17th centuries, it remained the capital of India. Both Babar and Humayun made some buildings here. Agra reached its heights of magnificance during the reign of Akbar who built the Agra Fort. But Shah Jahan's name is inevitably connected with Agra on account of the important buildings like Jami Masjid and several palaces in the Fort. Of course, the Jaj Mahal erected by Shah Jahan, in memory of his beloved queen Mumtaz Mahal is the most amazing, graceful and magnificent monument.

Ahmednagar. Ahmednagar in Maharashtra has a colourful history. It was here that the Emperor Aurangzeb died in 1707 at the age of 97. Jawaharlal Nehru was imprisoned here by the British. The town's imposing fort was built in 1550. Ahmednagar was one of the important states in the Deccan in the 16th century A.D. It is associated with queen Chand Bibi. After her death, Ahmednagar was captured by Emperor Akbar.

Bijapur (Karnataka). Sometimes called 'the Agra' of the south, Bijapur is full of ruined and still intact gems of 15th to 17th century architecture – mosques, mausoleums, palaces and fortifications and like Agra, it has its world-famous Golgumbaz mausoleum. It was built during the reign of Mohammad Adil Shah (1626-1656 A.D.) and was the capital of the Adil Shah king (1459-1686). Earlier it was a provincial capital of the Chaulkaya dynasty. Bijapur formed part of the Bahmani Kingdom in the 14th century. It declared its independence in 1489. In 1686, Aurangzeb annxed it.

Chittor or **Chittorgarh** (Rajasthan). About 12 kilometers in circumference, the hill top fort of Chittorgarh reminds us of the ideal of Rajput chivalry. It was the capital of the Sisodia Clan of Rajputs who ruled Mewar. Bapa Rawal, the founder of this dynasty made Chittor his capital. Rana Pratap the son of Udai Singh and grandson of Rana Sanga was the ruler of Mewar. When he succeeded the throne in 1572, Chittor had already been captured by the Mughals in 1568. Rana Pratap recovered several territories when he realigned his forces, after his defeat at the Battle of halidghati but failed to fulfil his dream of getting back Chittor. Chittor was sacked three times in history; by Alauddin Khalji in 1303, Bahadur Shah of Gujarat in 1534 and by the Mughal Emperor Akbar in 1588 after which it was abandoned. It is noted for the **Jauhar**. The popular legend of Rani Padamini is associated with Chittor.

Daultabad-Devagiri (Maharashtra). The magnificent fort of Daultabad is situated between Aurangabad and Ellora Caves. The Fort is surrounded by five kilometer of sturdy wall. In the 14th century, Muhammad Tughlaq, conceived the idea of making Daultabad his capital as he considered it a central place in his kingdon. Secondly, he considered it safe from the Mongol invasions. He named Devagiri (Hill of gods' as Daultabad 'city of fortune'. It is said that he ordered the entire population of Delhi, his capital to the new place. a magnificent tower of victory; the Chand Minar built in 1435 soars 60 meters high. The last king of Golconda was imprisoned for 13 years until his death. Aurangzeb's name is engraved on the 6-meter canon in the fort.

Delhi : The traditional and present day capital of India has been built and rebuilt several times. It includes capital cities of Indraprastha, Yoginikpura, Delhi, Lal Kot, Siri, Kilokheri Chirag, Jahanpanah, Tughlaqabad, Firozabad, Quila Froze Shah, Mubarakabad, Din Panah, Shajahanabad and of course New Delhi, has been a coveted prize for all conqueors , especially those from time immemorial. Tradition places Indraprastha of **Mahabharta** at or near Delhi Prithvi Raj Chauhan was the last Rajput ruler of Delhi, Delhi or Shillika. Though Delhi has not always been the capital of India but it has played an important role since the Mahabharta. Under the emperor Chandragupta and Ashoka, over 2000 years ago, Patliputra, modern Patna was the capital. It became an important city towards the end of 11th century A.D. Delhi was plundered by Timur-lane in the 14th century and in 1739, the Persian Emperor Nadir Shah sacked the city and took away the

Kohinoor Diamond and the famour Peacock throne to Iran. Aurangzeb shifted the capital from Agra to Delhi. The British captured it in 1803 and it became a centre of 1857 Events. The British shifted the capital from Calcutta to Delhi (New Delhi) in 1911. Important old monuments are : Red Fort, Jami Masjid, Iron Pillar, Qutab Minar-to name a few.

Fatehpur Sikri (City of Victory) : The most magnificent building erected by Emperor Akbar was the new capital city of Fatehpur Sikri. It remained the capital of the Mughal Empire during 1570and 1586. It is located nearly 40 km west of Agra and is an attraction. No visitor to Agra normally misses it. According to the legend, Akbar was without a male heir and he made a pilgrimage to this spot at Sikri to see the Saint Shaikh Salim Chisti. The saint foretold the birth of Akbar's son. In gratitude, Akbar named his son Salim, (Emperor Jahangir). Akbar transferred his capital to Sikri and built a new and spendid city. Fatehpur Sikri was abandoned as dramatically as it had been built. Probably water supply in the town led to its abandonment. Important buildings at Fatehpur Sikri are: Jamia Masjid, Shahi Darwaja, Dargah or Tomb of Shaikh Salim Chisti, Palace of Jodh Bai, Birbal Bhavan, Panch Mahal etc. Fatehpur Sikri's mosque is said to be a copy of the mosque at Mecca.

Golkunda or Golconda (Andhra Pradesh). The city of Golconda remained the capital of the Qutab Shahi Kings (16th and 17th centuries). Of course, the history of Golconda fort is traced back to the earlier Hindu period of the Yadvas and later, the Kakatiyas. In 1512 A.D. Quli Qutab Shah the governor of Telanganga under the Bahmani rulers declared independence and made Golconda his capital. Golconda was captured by Aurangzeb in 1687 after a fierce struggle and through treacherous means. Following Aurangzeb's death, the viceroys whom he had installed to look after Mughal interests became independent and came to be known as Nizams. They chose Hyderabad as their capital and abandoned Golconda. Important monuments of this place are : the Fort and Tombs of Qutab Shahi Kings.

Jaipur. The present day capital of the State of Rajasthan, Jaipur takes its name from Maharaja Jai Singh II (1699-1799). The city was founded by him when he shifted his capital from the fort of Amber in 1727. The city was planned according to Shilpa–Shastraa a Hindu treatise on architecture to accommodate ten times more than its 25,000 inhabitants at that time. The city is popularly known as the 'pink city' from the pick-coloured sandstone with which the buildings in the old walled city are constructed. The erstwhile ruling dynasty of Jaipur belonged to the Kachwaha clan of Rajputs.

Jaipur was the first Rajput ruling family to sign a matrimonial alliance with the Mughal Emperor Akbar. Important places of historical interest at Jaipur are : Jantar Mantar Observatory, the Hawa-Mahal, City Palace and Central Museum.

Lahore (Now in Pakistan): Lahore has always occupied an important place in the political history of India. It was the capital of undivided Punjab and now it is the second largest city of Pakistan. It was raided in 1615 by Mahmud Ghaznavi. After his raids, he appointed a governor at Lahore. Punjab with Lahore as its capital remained a part of the Ghaznavi empire till 1186, when it came under the control of Muhammad Ghori. After Muhammad Ghori's death his able general and confidant Qutub-ud-din Aibak took the reigns of government at Lahore in 1208. His death took place at Lahore in 1210. Later on Lahore became an important province of Delhi rulers. It was the capital of Aibak. Iltutmish made Delhi as his capital. With this, political importance of Lahore somewhat declined. During the reign of Sultan Nasir-ud-din, Lahore passed into the hands of Mongols for sometime but soon it again came under the rule of the Sultan. Humayun spent some time at Lahore when he lost to Sher Shah Suri. Lahore Fort built by Akbar is an important monument of medieval India. Aurangzeb erected here the Shahi Masjid. It was the capital of the Sikhs before the British took over it in 1849. In 1947, after the Partition of the country, Lahore was made the capital of West Punjab.

The goal of 'Complete Independence' (Puran Swaraj) of the country was declared by the Indian National Congress at its Lahore Session in 1929.

Lucknow (Uttar Pradesh). Presently capital of Uttar Pradesh, Lucknow came into prominence as the capital of the Nawabs of Oudh or Awadh. After the decline of Mughal power in the beginning of the 18th century, the Nawabs controlled a fertile region around Ayodhya in the middle of Ganges Valley, west of Banaras. In ancient times, the region was known as Kosali. Lucknow became central place of Shia Muslims. During the period of Nawabs, Lucknow became well-known for its refined way of life, known as 'Lucknow culture' or 'Lucknavi culture' and magnificent architecture. It was annexed in 1856 by Lord Dalhousi. This place became an important centre of the events of 1857. Important places of historical interest are : Great Imambara, Runi Darwaza , Clock Tower, and Jami Masjid.

Mathura (Uttar Pradesh). On the Delhi-Agra road, nearly 60 km north of Agra, Mathura is a city of ancient times. According to popular Hindu belief, it is the birth place of Lord Krishna. Mahmud Ghaznavi, Sikandar Lodi and Aurangzeb did a good deal of damage to this temple town. Aurangzeb demolished the sacred Kesava Deo Temple considered to be the birth place of Lord Krishna and built a mosque in its place. The modern Kesava Temple has been rebuilt. Important places are : Jami Masjid, Sati Burji, Kans Quila, Dwarkadeesh Temple and the standing Buddha image in the Mathura Museum.

Panipat (Haryana). An ancient town 85 kilometers northwest of Delhi on the river Yamuna, Panipat is the place of three historically decisive battles which changed the course of Indian history. It is close to Kurukshetra, the battle field of Mahabharta. Sometimes Panipat is called the Northern Gatway of India's for whose-ever won in the battle field of Panipat. could rule India. Babar's victory over Sultan Ibraham Lodi in 1556 led to the establishment of the Mughal Empire in India. Akbar's victory over Hemu, in the Second Battle of Panipat in 1556 enabled him to consolidate Mughal Empire in India. In fact, it restored the power to the Mughals which Humayun had lost to Sher Shah and after Sher Shah's death, Hemu had assumed power at Delhi. In the Third Battle of Panipat in 1761, the Marathas who had become very powerful and the Mughal Emperor was at their mercy, lost to Ahmad Shah Abdali, an invader from Kabul. The defeat of the Marathas shattered their dream of becoming a super power in India. Abdali plundered Delhi and went back. This power vaccum in India paved the way for the East India Company to establish the British rule in India.

Poona-Pune (Maharashtra). The city located at the Influence of the Mula and Mutha rivers in the Deccan, it finds mention in a copper plate inscription of the Rastrakutta King Krishna I (8th century A.D.). Shivaji, the great Maratha lender spent his childhood at this place and rebuilt it after his coronation in 1674. Later it became the capital of the Peshwas and an important centre of culture and learning under them. Leading social reformers and freedom fighters like Mahadev Govind Ranade, Bal Gangadhar Tilak and Gopal Krishna Gokhale spent most of their lives in Poona.

Surat (Gujarat). Situated at the mouth of the Tapti river on the Gulf of Cambay, Surat has been a major port on the west coast of India throughout historical times. It was the main port of export for goods destined to the West-Arabia, Egypt, Iran and Turkey etc. Under the Mughals, prosperity of Surat reached its height. European trading companies sought Mughal permission in the 16th 17th and early 18th centuries to set up their factories at Surat. Shivaji attacked Surat several times and got immense wealth. The British took control of Surat in 1759. As Bombay (Mumbai) grew, Surat lost its important for some time. The port was revived after independence and regained prosperity in the wake of India's flourishing trade.

Udaipur (Rajasthan). Udaipur, also known as the 'city of sunrise' and the 'city of lakes' was founded in 1567 by Maharana Udai Singh, son of Rana Sanga and father of Maharana Pratap, after the sack of Chittor by Bahadur Shah of Gujarat. It is an Oasis in the dry heart of Rajasthan.

Atop the Pearl Hill overlooking Fateh Sagar is Pratap Samark–a statue of Rajput hero, Maharana Pratap, riding his charger Chetak. Other historical places at Udaipur are : the Lake Palau, Pichola Lake, City Palace and Lake Fateh Sagar and Jagdish Temple.

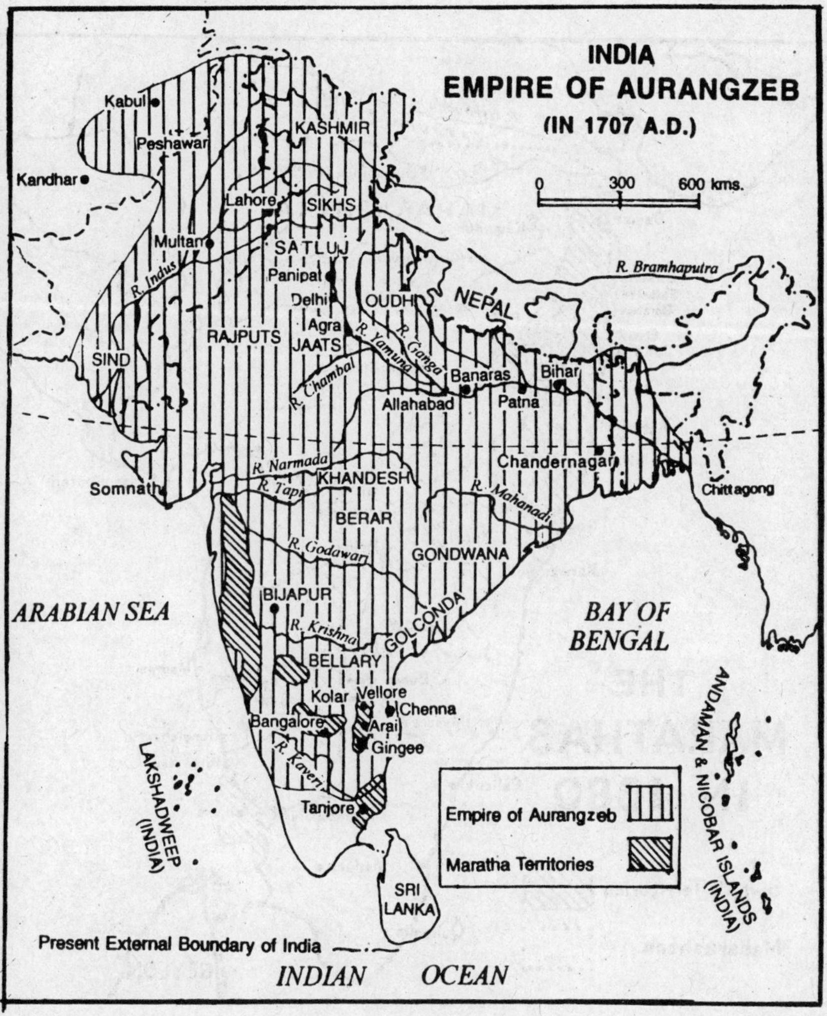
INDIA
EMPIRE OF AURANGZEB
(IN 1707 A.D.)
0 300 600 kms.
Kabul
Peshawar
Kandhar
KASHMIR
Lahore
SIKHS
Multan
SATLUJ
R. Indus
Panipat
Delhi
OUDH
NEPAL
R. Bramhaputra
Agra
R. Yamuna
R. Ganga
RAJPUTS
JAATS
SIND
R. Chambal
Banaras
Bihar
Allahabad
Patna
R. Narmada
Chandernagar
KHANDESH
R. Tapi
Somnath
Chittagong
R. Mahanadi
BERAR
R. Godawari
GONDWANA
BIJAPUR
ARABIAN SEA
BAY OF BENGAL
R. Krishna
GOLCONDA
BELLARY
Kolar
Vellore
Chenna
Bangalore
Arai
Gingee
R. Kaveri
Tanjore
LAKSHADWEEP (INDIA)
ANDAMAN & NICOBAR ISLANDS (INDIA)
Empire of Aurangzeb
Maratha Territories
SRI LANKA
Present External Boundary of India
INDIAN OCEAN

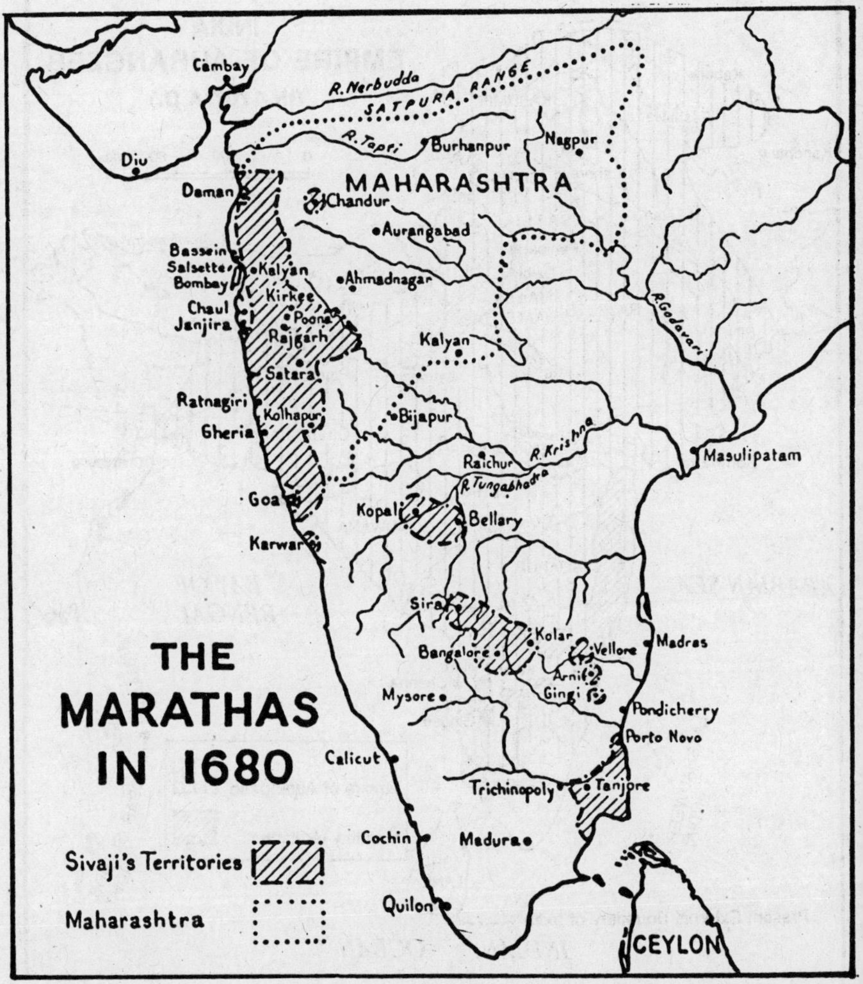
THE MARATHAS IN 1680
Sivaji's Territories
Maharashtra
Cambay
Diu
Daman
R. Nerbudda
SATPURA RANGE
R. Tapti
Burhanpur
Nagpur
MAHARASHTRA
Chandur
Aurangabad
Bassein
Salsette
Bombay
Kalyan
Ahmadnagar
Kirkee
Poona
Chaul
Janjira
Rajgarh
Kalyan
Satara
R. Godavari
Ratnagiri
Kolhapur
Bijapur
Gheria
Raichur
R. Krishna
R. Tungabhadra
Masulipatam
Goa
Kopal
Bellary
Karwar
Sira
Kolar
Vellore
Madras
Bangalore
Arni
Gingi
Mysore
Pondicherry
Porto Novo
Calicut
Trichinopoly
Tanjore
Cochin
Madura
Quilon
CEYLON

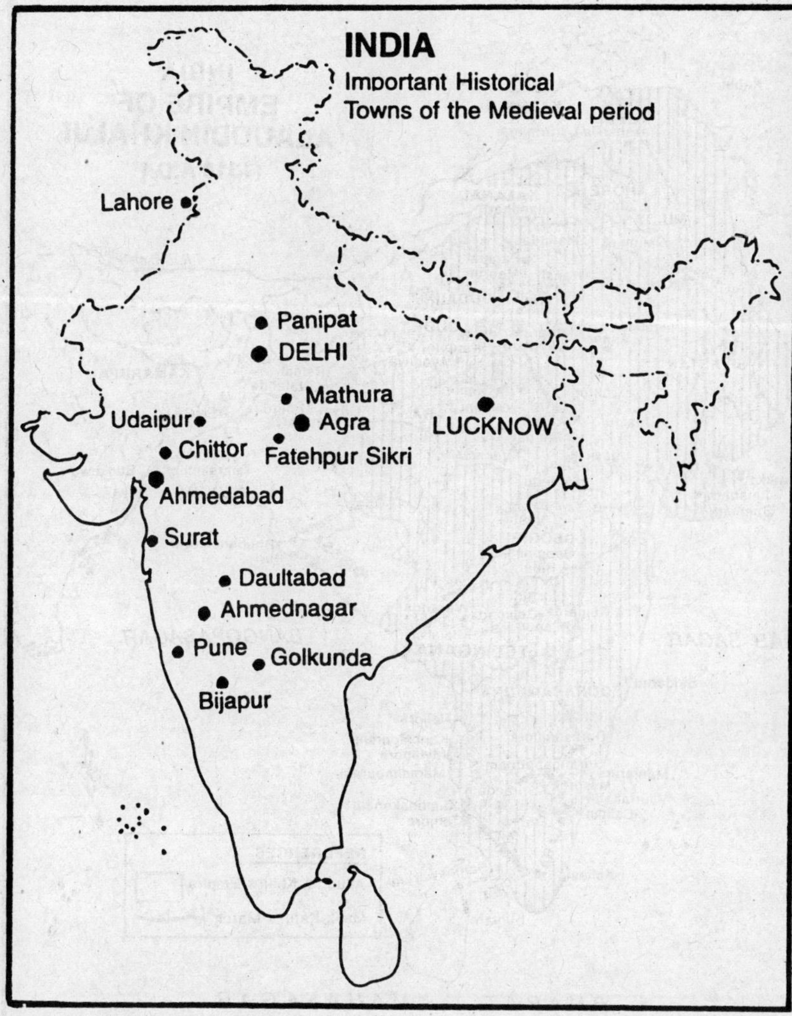
INDIA
Important Historical
Towns of the Medieval period
Lahore
Panipat
DELHI
Mathura
Udaipur
Agra
LUCKNOW
Chittor
Fatehpur Sikri
Ahmedabad
Surat
Daultabad
Ahmednagar
Pune
Golkunda
Bijapur

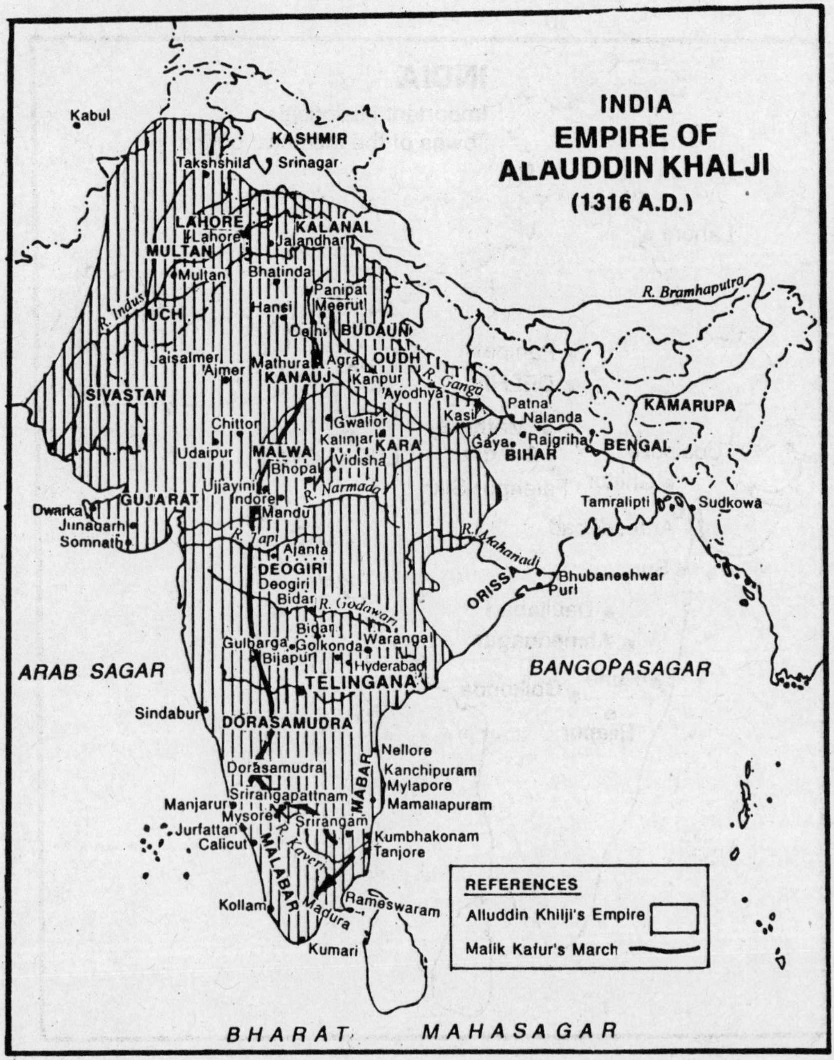
INDIA
EMPIRE OF
ALAUDDIN KHALJI
(1316 A.D.)
Kabul
KASHMIR
Takshshila
Srinagar
LAHORE
Lahore
KALANAL
Jalandhar
MULTAN
Multan
Bhatinda
R. Indus
UCH
Panipat
Meerut
Hansi
Delhi
BUDAUN
R. Bramhaputra
Jaisalmer
Ajmer
Mathura
Agra
OUDH
KANAUJ
Kanpur
R. Ganga
Ayodhya
SIVASTAN
Kasi
Patna
Nalanda
KAMARUPA
Chittor
Gwalior
Kalinjar
KARA
Gaya
Rajgriha
BENGAL
BIHAR
Udaipur
MALWA
Vidisha
Bhopal
Ujjayini
R. Narmada
GUJARAT
Indore
Tamralipti
Sudkowa
Dwarka
Mandu
Junagarh
Somnath
R. Tapi
R. Mahanadi
Ajanta
DEOGIRI
Deogiri
ORISSA
Bhubaneshwar
Puri
Bidar
R. Godawari
Bidar
Warangal
Gulbarga
Golkonda
Bijapur
Hyderabad
ARAB SAGAR
TELINGANA
BANGOPASAGAR
Sindabur
DORASAMUDRA
Nellore
MABAR
Dorasamudra
Kanchipuram
Mylapore
Srirangapattnam
Manjarur
Mamallapuram
Mysore
Srirangam
Jurfattan
Calicut
R. Kaveri
Kumbhakonam
MALABAR
Tanjore
REFERENCES
Alluddin Khilji's Empire
Malik Kafur's March
Rameswaram
Kollam
Madura
Kumari
BHARAT MAHASAGAR